Praise for *Working With Adoptive Parents: Research, Theory, and Therapeutic Interventions*

"With adoption, including those that across international boundaries, on the rise, the salutary impact of human kindness as well the tragic potential for developmental complications has greatly increased. Brabender and Fallon, the editors of this well-organized volume, are keenly aware of this. They have cast their net wide and brought together the perspectives of attachment theory, empirical research, and clinical experiences to deepen our understanding of the challenges faced by adoptive parents. Conceptually rich and yet unabashedly pragmatic, their book addresses the issues of parent-child bonding, the subjective dilemmas of adoptive mothers, the role of adoptive fathers, and parenting children with special health care needs. Attention is also given to the specific tasks involving the adoption of very young children as well as to the resurgence of difficulties during adopted children's adolescence. This wide-ranging discourse consistently maintains a tone of respect, concern, and shared humanity of all of us. A most impressive contribution to the adoption literature indeed!"

Salman Akhtar, MD,
Professor of Psychiatry,
Jefferson Medical College,
Training and Supervising Analyst,
Psychoanalytic Center of Philadelphia

"This book is a tour de force, a must read for all involved in the world of adoption. A comprehensive history of adoption, including current controversies, sets the stage. Every chapter is a gem, but contributions on research to inform best practices, the role of the adoptive father, diversity, and adoption of children with special health care needs, help fill significant gaps in the adoption literature. Rich clinical material and the practical points summarized throughout, demonstrate the wisdom of seasoned practitioners."

Jennifer Bonovitz, PhD,
Supervising and Training Analyst,
Psychoanalytic Center of Philadelphia

"This volume is a major contribution to our understanding of adoptive parenting. The book is thorough, full of helpful insights, case studies, and perspectives on the complicated dance involved for adoptive parents and their children. The portrait of adoptive parenting is both hopeful and realistic, and is framed with thoughtful attention to what we actually know from careful research. This book should be a helpful guide and resource for both mental health professionals and adoptive parents."

Sam Osherson, PhD,
Professor of Psychology,
Fielding Graduate University, Cambridge, MA

WORKING WITH ADOPTIVE PARENTS

Research, Theory, and Therapeutic Interventions

EDITED BY

Virginia M. Brabender
April E. Fallon

WILEY

Library of Congress Cataloging-in-Publication Data:

    Working with adoptive parents : research, theory, and therapeutic interventions / edited by Virginia M. Brabender, April E. Fallon.
       1 online resource.
    Includes bibliographical references and index.
    Description based on print version record and CIP data provided by publisher; resource not viewed.
    ISBN 978-1-118-41891-8 (ebook) — ISBN 978-1-118-41615-0 (ebook)
    ISBN 978-1-118-61169-2 (ebook) — ISBN 978-1-118-10912-0 (pbk. : alk. paper)
    1. Adoptive parents. 2. Parenting. 3. Parent and child. I. Brabender, Virginia II. Fallon, April.
    HV875
    362.734—dc23

                                              2013000371

Printed in the United States of America

10 9 8 7 6 5 4 3 2 1

*Virginia dedicates the book to two of her favorite
adoptive parents, John and Rebecca Brabender,
and to a very loving foster mother, Dona Aida Barrientos.*

*April dedicates the book to Hafeez and Theo Shaikh,
whose generosity were instrumental in our adoptive process.*

Contents

Foreword ————————————————————————

Adoption, a gift to humanity, is the rescuing of humans, most commonly very young ones, who would otherwise be destined to a state of being unwanted or at risk in their environment unable to provide the basics needed for health and self-fulfillment. The complexity of adoption, its challenges, its rewards, and its heartbreaks, needs more attention than mental health has given to it to date. Those among us who have been drawn to adoption must record our findings, thereby opening them to further exploration, study, and dissemination among mental health professionals. In addition, and perhaps of greater importance, putting forward what we mental health professionals learn about the subject is a service that for many can and may be enormously helpful—for both other professionals who deal with the issue of adoption (such as pediatricians or those in the legal system) and the public at large, with its many adoptive parents, and I would add its adopted no-longer kids, as well as those who willingly or not give up their child for adoption. This book makes a significant contribution to both a greater understanding of adoption and its complex dynamic constellations as well as to serving those who are or come across adoption families, many of whom count on us adoption-informed mental health professionals to clarify and facilitate the challenges they face.

Multiple real-life characters play their part: the family of adoption, including especially the adoptive parent(s), the adopted child, and the birth parents, and the surround of each of these real-life characters.

The need to progressively learn as much as our clinical experiences with adoption constellations afford us has become increasingly recognized as we see the specific dynamics that adoption produces and as more and more adoptions seem to be taking place. Foremost, an unhappy percentage of women are unable to conceive; their experience of it is laden with pain—and more. Then, more teenagers than we like to think conceive due to compelling intrapsychic and external pressures, carelessness, or even against their will; for them, being pregnant causes them painful embarrassment, and giving up their infant can cause them great distress, both tending to lead to much uncertainty about what they should do, much self-doubt and internal conflict that may last a lifetime. In addition, as our world has evolved, lengthy education, the women's liberation movement, and the march toward human rights progresses, given the added years needed by many to achieve yearned for goals of self-development and life-work, resulting in increasing numbers of women delaying their procreation plans. As mental health professionals have witnessed in and outside of the clinical situation, some among us believe that such delay has often led to failure in the ability to conceive among many an accomplished woman, now a professional who decides the time has come to have a child. Such failure to conceive, like with those who have tried and failed to conceive in their twenties, brings with it reactions ranging from anxiety and depression to distress and heartbreak. But like their young cohorts, for the now-professionals, whatever their field, commonly after years of trying, the self-disappointment, the shame, and the guilt experienced by many, the self-blame experienced by the failure to conceive gets slowly worked through and after debates between many a couple for or against the question, adoption is considered. The idea of adoption is met with a wide range of reactivities from trepidation and uncertainty to dedicated pursuit and hopefulness.

The decision to adopt brings with it a number of questions: How to proceed? What options do we have? Which channels to follow? From where? What age? A child in what kind of circumstance: A teenage mother's newborn? A child in physical distress? A traumatized, abused child? Often, all this without, except in general terms, knowing critical characteristics and conditions of the circumstances of the birth mother and her environment.

And that is only the beginning of their labors.

This thoughtfully conceived and illuminating volume takes us into some of the many areas of concern and factors at play once the adoption is set in motion. It is fortunate that, as is the case with most innovations, research, and study, we come to issues that interest us vigorously, determined in large measure by our own formative experiences. What we experience gives us direct insight. We gather our own reactions and meanings of it, we find the key factors in the experience that make us feel as we do, and when we add formal study, research, and thought-laden consideration to the entire experience, we come away with experience-based plus acquired knowledge that qualifies us with down-to-earth expertise. This then we can offer to others similarly impacted by life. Driven by their own experience as adoptive parents and their clinical work with adoption constellations, the editors and contributors to this volume have produced a volume with real-life value: They have put down what they have learned and conceptualized, and have molded it to make it available to the many who treat real-life adoption characters, as well as those living with adoption in the hope that they can be better informed and that the challenges they face can be made more clear and their efforts at coping with the experience optimized.

It is especially important for those among us who work with adoption constellations as well as for adoptive parents to know that adoptive parents can truly rescue a child (not just a young one) not only from continuing trauma and/or neglect, but also that they can in good measure bring about the lessening of the effects of their adopted child's past trauma, indeed foster healing from it, and prevent adverse consequences that can otherwise burden them for a lifetime.

HENRI PARENS, MD
Professor of Psychiatry, Thomas Jefferson University;
Training and Supervising Analyst, Psychoanalytic Center of Philadelphia

Preface

Adoption touches many lives. Most obviously, it profoundly influences the adopted child. According to some estimates, 2% of children are adopted within the United States each year, and 2% to 4% of all families have an adopted child (Child Welfare League of America [CWLA], 2005). Yet, these statistics apply only to formal adoptions. Informal adoptions exist in the absence of any legal process or in absence of recognition by any regulatory group, and are by no means uncommon. Adoption engages the parents, birth parents, and adoptive parents, as well as siblings and extended family members. Participants in the adoption situation are a range of human service professionals: social workers, psychologists, and psychiatrists who both evaluate prospective adoptive parents and monitor the family postadoptively; teachers who may witness the adoptive child's efforts to master particular elements of the adoptive experience; therapists who provide assistance to different members of the adoptive family; and physicians who treat any special medical problems of the adoptive child. Hence, any strides made to understand more fully, or help more completely, any member of the adoptive family is likely to have positive reverberations far beyond the initial targets of such efforts.

OUR OWN JOURNEY

We became interested in adoption in the context of our own experiences as adoptive parents. Virginia and her husband adopted a baby girl from Honduras (now almost 18 years old), and April and her husband adopted a 4-year-old girl from Pakistan (now 14 years old). Prospective adoptive parents tend to consult the adoption literature, even the professional literature, on what to expect and we were no exception. For both of our families, the wait until a child was assigned to us was painfully long. In Virginia's case, it took 3 years, and for April, 2. We struggled with a great variety of uncertainties, such as for example, having the host country close its doors to adoption. During this period, we found our immersion in the literature to be helpful in enabling us to summon patience. The literature ranged from professional books on attachment theory to our adoption agencies' newsletters featuring stories of adoptive families to adoption blog posts. This material enabled us to form accurate anticipations about what we were likely to encounter and experience once our child entered our family. Our grade-school-aged sons, both nonadopted children, did not have the advantage of that resource, but relied on us and our spouses—both human service professionals—to contain their yearnings to get to know their new sisters.

During this period of waiting, each of us realized that over our years of practice as therapists, we had treated a number of adoptive parents and adults who had been adopted. It hit us like that proverbial ton of bricks that had we taken advantage of this literature at the time we were seeing patients or supervising our students' treatment of patients, our work would have been deeper and richer. Since we have been acquainted with this literature, we have found that the valuable insights we derived have played a key role in informing the treatment of adoptive parents. Furthermore, we now had our own direct experience on which to draw in understanding our clients. A kind of synergy developed among the three elements: our clinical experiences, our reading, and our personal involvement in adoption.

At the same time that in our personal lives we were becoming interested in adoption, in our professional lives we were writing a book on the therapist's pregnancy (Fallon & Brabender, *Awaiting the Therapist's Baby: A Guide for Expectant Parent-Practitioners*, 2003). As part of that book, we interviewed a small group of individuals who were therapists and adoptive parents. From that sample, we learned a great about the experiences of being an adoptive parent. For example, we learned firsthand that adoptive parents are often unsupported by the systems in which they function. Our interviewees told us that their families questioned them about the decision to adopt far more than they would ever have felt entitled to do in regard to the decision to have a biological child ("Why would you want to have someone else's baby?"). To learn more about adoptive families, but in particular, adoptive parents, we organized a group of mental health professionals and students from our two doctoral programs. Over the past 8 years, this group has collected data on adoptive and foster families, some of which is cited in the chapters of this book.

THE IMPORTANCE OF THE SUBJECT MATTER

Our work in this area has led us to believe that to achieve a complete understanding of adoption, the perspectives of all of the members of the kinship network but particularly the adoptive triad—the birth parents, the adoptive parents, and the child—must be taken into account. The adoption literature has addressed some aspects of the adoption situation intensively, such as the comparisons of the outcomes of adopted versus nonadopted children (Palacios & Sanchez-Sandoval, 2005). Yet, much remains to be done in achieving a comprehensive understanding of the viewpoints and psychologies of each of the major stakeholders. In many textbooks on adoption, often a chapter will be devoted to each of the members of the adoptive triad. A single chapter can provide the big picture, but it cannot offer an in-depth treatment of the distinctive needs, thoughts, feelings, impulses, fantasies, and conflicts that each of these triad members experiences through the stages of adoption and beyond. We believe that each member of the triad merits his or her own concentrated focus, but never to the neglect of a consideration of the other members. This volume seeks to contribute to the construction of a comprehensive picture of the adoption triad through a thoroughgoing exploration of the experiences and developmental processes of the adoptive parent.

The Influence of the Parent on the Child

An effort to illumine the behavior and internal life of the adoptive parent is important for three broad reasons. First, the parent has a crucial influence on the development of his or her child. Although this view may seem self-evident, it cannot be legitimately and fully accepted without empirical support. Furthermore, in some instances early trauma may be so great that the question of whether the best subsequent parenting could make a difference to the child is a reasonable one. In the past decade or so, researchers have demonstrated the importance of the quality of adoptive parenting in the well-being of the child.

For example, Simmel (2007) examined pre-adoptive risk factors and postadoption factors in the behavioral outcomes of adopted children in the child welfare system. In all, 293 families were studied. Simmel found that the parents' self-perceived readiness was a more powerful factor in mediating short-term and long-term outcomes than most of the pre-adoption risk factors such as prenatal drug or nicotine exposure. In another study of children who were adopted at an older age, children's adjustment levels were more affected by parental perceptions (for example, the capacity to see strengths in the child that others might ignore) than by child pre-adoptive behaviors (Clark, Thigpen, & Yates, 2006). Similarly, Smith-McKeever (2005) in a study of 83 African American adoptive families found that the child's adjustment is more affected by the facets of the parent-child relationship (for example, how often the parent thinks of the child when separated) than pre-adoptive aspects of either the parent or the child. This trio of studies represents a small sample of the research showing the importance of the adoptive parent in the life of the adopted child. Kriebel and Wentzel (2011) found that highly responsive parenting can counter significant factors such as a pre-adoptive history of maltreatment in predicting adjustment in adopted children.

The Adoptive Parent's Relational Context

The adoptive parent affects other individuals besides his or her child. Certainly, the adoptive parents' happiness or misery influences the psychological status of all those close to him or her—spouses, other children, parents. What might be less obvious is that the well-being of the adoptive parents can also can bear on the quality of the other important member of the adoption triad, the birth parent. A variety of factors shape the adoptive parent's stance toward the birth parent. One factor is the adoptive parent's sense of security in his or her parental role. To the extent that the parent feels insecure or vulnerable or lacks a sense of entitlement to embrace fully the parental role, he or she is likely to view any interest in or contact between the adoptive child and his or her birth parent as a threat rather than a potentially enriching tie for all parties.

The Well-Being of the Adoptive Parent

A third reason is that the adoptive parent is a human being with his or her own psychological needs, a person entitled to the achievement and sustenance of a sense of well-being. Although adoptive parents are likely to have the range of problems that afflict all human beings, related to adoption are a particular set of problems. In contemporary society, many couples pursue adoption as an alternate means of building a family subsequent to difficulties with fertility. For some, a definitive diagnosis of infertility precedes their embarking on a course toward adoption. Fertility challenges and infertility are states known to induce a range of painful reactions and even psychological problems (Fassino, Pierò, Boggio, Piccioni, & Garzaro, 2002). Individuals may struggle with the psychological effects of infertility at the same time that they are considering adoption as a possible route to creating a family. In fact, for many, reactions associated with the loss of the dream of having a biological child continue to occur during the various stages of adoption and beyond (Bonovitz, 2006). As the adopted child develops, problems arise that evoke a range of internal reactions and behaviors in the adoptive parent. These reactions are often intensified by a social context that continues to see blood relations as pre-eminent, thereby attaching stigma to adoption (Carp, 2002). All of the aforementioned factors can affect the adjustment and life satisfaction of the adoptive parent.

Although in this book we talk about some of the challenges adoptive parents face, several points must be made in this regard. First, despite whatever difficulties surface, the pleasures and gratifications of adopting a child are enormous. Speaking as adoptive parents, we can say that having made the decision to bring a child into our families via adoption has been among the best in our lives. We simply cannot imagine our lives without our cherished daughters. From our professional and personal travels, we know that most other adoptive parents feel as positively as we do. Second, in describing the issues faced by adoptive families, we are not assuming that somehow such issues are greater in number or severity than other types of families. We do believe that within adoptive families, common challenges exist so that a family currently struggling with a problem may use strategies others have developed. Third, in identifying adoptive parents as having particular difficulties, we are not viewing the problems as residing within the adoptive parent. Rather, like many other writers in this area, we hold that the circumstances faced by the adoptive parent are inherently challenging. The adoptive parent's particular psychological issues may intensify problems that erupt in the parenting of any child. Yet, the evidence suggests that adoptive parents are no more likely to have psychological difficulties than parents in other family structures. Moreover, adoptive parents appear to have a host of strengths that they bring to caregiving, and some of these we discuss in the first chapter.

INTENDED AUDIENCE OF THIS BOOK

Relative to the population at large, adoptive parents tend to use mental health resources when problems arise. The inclination to use available supports is one of the strengths adoptive parents have. Yet, do they get the help that they need? The answer to this question is a qualified "only sometimes." As Pertman (2011) noted, at some point every adoptive family needs postadoption counseling. Only within the child welfare system are postadoption services consistently supported and even there, coverage falls far short of needs. In pre-adoption counseling, which also is undersupported, prospective parents are often not given the necessary education on what might signal the need for treatment. Hence, even though adoptive parents do seek treatment, they may not always know when treatment or consultation for one or more members of the family might be helpful.

Another significant obstacle to adoptive parents' obtaining effective assistance is the serious lack of professionals who can competently address adoption issues. Certainly, an adoption specialist, a professional whose training and experience emphasize adoption, could treat such problems effectively (Child Welfare Information Gateway, 2006). Yet, for many reasons, adoptive parents may not seek the services of an adoption specialist in pursuing solutions to problems. The number of adoption specialists simply is not large enough to accommodate the needs of adoptive parents. In particular geographic areas, few or no adoption specialists may be present. Adoptive parents may pursue help for a problem that they believe is not related to adoption, but actually is. Adoptive parents may have an existing relationship with a mental health professional, and feel comfortable seeking help from that person. For example, a woman may have begun treatment with a therapist at the point when she was trying to cope with possible infertility. Now that she is experiencing some concerns in the context of parenting her adoptive child, her first instinct is to return to that trusted therapist.

The problem that we see is the lack of knowledge that the general mental health practitioner is likely to have in relation to adoption. Few graduate programs provide training in adoption, even as part of an elective curriculum. Furthermore, in the absence of training, this practitioner is likely to be vulnerable to some of the biases of the culture in relation to adoption. These biases are many, and this book identifies a good number of them. One bias is that adoption is a second-best way of building a family. Another bias is that adopted children have irremediable problems. Still another bias, which logically conflicts with the prior one, is that when adoptive children are having difficulties, it's the fault of the parents. Those therapists who take any of these unrecognized prejudices into their work with the client may not merely fail to help him or her, but may exacerbate that individual's difficulties. In Chapter 1, we illustrate how these therapist/societal prejudices may play out in treatment.

Our primary intended audience, then, is the generalist mental health practitioner. We believe that by a greater exposure to the array of issues with which adoptive parents grapple, the practitioner will be able to work with those parents more fruitfully. Part of competence involves recognizing its limits. An immersion in this material can help the generalist mental health practitioner to recognize that in some instances, securing the services of an adoption specialist is crucial. Finally, we would also like to believe that the book would stimulate interest in adoption and inspire the reader to delve into writings concerning the other members of the triad. We also expect that adoption specialists and child welfare workers will derive benefit from this book. We have synthesized fairly new research in the area of the adoptive parent (ours and others) and we believe that it is useful for professionals working in this area.

A secondary audience is adoptive parents themselves whom we know through our own research to be a highly literate group and who make frequent forays into the professional literature. For example, adoptive parents frequently read books on attachment written for a professional audience. We believe that prospective adoptive parents could be assisted in forming accurate expectations about their likely experiences, and that by doing so, their ability to adjust to the changing circumstances of adoption will be enhanced. One repeated finding in the literature is that correct parental anticipations contribute to the adjustment of all members of the adoptive family.

ORGANIZATION OF THE BOOK

In organizing the chapters of this book, we as editors work from the premise that no professional can make a helpful intervention in the absence of understanding. In consonance with this view, our next five chapters offer the reader the knowledge base to understand the adoptive parent fully. Chapter 1 looks at the literature to synthesize what we know about adoptive parents. It also offers a thumbnail history of adoption with an emphasis on societal changes in perceptions of the adoptive parent and his or her rights and responsibilities. The history leads to the current situation, which is defined by a set of controversies, the resolution of which will have great importance for many specific aspects of adoption such as who can adopt and access to information by members of the adoptive triad (adoptive parents, birth parents, and adopted child).

Chapters 2 and 3 respectively cover the theory and research related to adoption and the relationship between parent and child. We hope to convince our reader that each of the psychoanalytic theories covered provides a kind prism through which new facets of adoption can be illuminated. Although research is being done on many fronts, we home in most especially on the research in the area of attachment because it has such relevance for parent-child adjustment. Chapter 4 introduces the reader to the adoptive mother and her changing psychological states as she moves through the stages of preparenting and parenting. Chapter 5 focuses on the adoptive father, a topic far less covered in the literature. Both of these chapters feature some of our qualitative work.

The next seven chapters provide a more practical focus. Chapter 6 focuses on the amazing variability among and within adoptive families, particularly on those dimensions that reflect core elements of individuals' identities. We attempt to give parents assistance in responding not merely constructively, but joyfully, to the differences within the family, such as differences in race between parent and child. Chapter 7 provides critically important information to the many families of adoptive children who have special needs, and their therapists. Readers within these families will, we believe, identify with the case material presented. They will also see that fostering connections with the broader special needs community—adoptive and nonadoptive—may be helpful.

The next two chapters form a couplet: Together, they cover the years of active parenting. Two contributors who have spent their professional lives working with families within the child welfare system wrote Chapter 8 on parenting the young child. They talk about the different stages of development and how these require a different pattern of response from the adoptive parent. They assist the therapist in seeing the kinds of supports parents need as they react to their child's changing experiences and behaviors. For example, at some points the parent may feel that the child is rejecting him or her and be inclined to recoil. Our authors talk about the obstacle this parental behavior creates in the parent's goal for an attachment to be formed between child and parent. Chapter 9 finds the adoptive child in adolescence and offers the adoptive parent wise counsel on how to assist the teenager through the developmental struggles of identity formation and separation, tasks that are somewhat different for the adoptive child.

Chapter 10 provides a framework for therapists to conceptualize their work with adoptive parents and recognizes that while many of the developmental tasks faced by both child and adult are universal, in adoptive families these tasks have unique facets. Chapter 11 recognizes that adoptive parents are called on to serve a range of roles on behalf of their own adopted child, and all adopted children. The chapter discusses the common situations that signal the need for the parent to engage in advocacy on the part of his or her child, and discusses some of the obstacles that the parent may have in successfully filling that role. This chapter is relevant to therapists in that it helps therapists to see that what may appear to the therapist as sensitivity is often a response justified by subtle biases in others, reflecting societal values, that parents discern.

Chapter 12 highlights some of the broad themes in the book. One section of this chapter looks at practice through a developmental lens by following an adoptive couple through the phase of contemplating adoption to that of having grown adopted children. This section shows the range of modalities and types of interventions that can assist the adoptive parent in achieving well-being and a high level of parental functioning. Another section addresses education. It recognizes that no one book—even ours—can do it all, and identifies the areas that therapists may wish to pursue to deepen their knowledge in this area. We encourage our readers to advocate for more adequate graduate and postgraduate training in the area of adoption. Finally, because we believe that some of the readers of our book are likely to be researchers as well as clinicians, important research directions vis-à-vis the adoptive parent are identified. Research on adoptive families is important not only to provide information that will help adoptive families but also to add to our understanding of such important processes as attachment and identity construction.

Acknowledgments

We have many people to thank. Our daughters add immeasurably to our lives and our gratitude to them is boundless for the continual inspiration they provide. We thank our spouses for being such wonderful fathers to our daughters and for sharing our view of the importance of the topic of this book. We recognize our sons who enthusiastically reached beyond their normal adolescent egocentrism to embrace the complexities and inconveniences that the adoptive process brought to family life. We thank the publishing staff at John Wiley & Sons, particularly Rachel Livsey, for her confidence in us and for her expert assistance throughout all of the stages of this project. We also want to express our gratitude to Amanda Orenstein for keeping us organized and on-task with such competence and good humor, and to Thomas Caruso for his expert management of the manuscript in the later phase of development. We also would like to thank the following colleagues who either reviewed the proposal or first draft of this book and provided valuable feedback: Naomi Chedd, licensed mental health counselor and educational consultant, Lexington, MA; Juliet Fortino, licensed professional counselor and registered play therapist, Tucson, Arizona; and Lawrence C. Rubin, PhD, professor, St. Thomas University. We acknowledge with appreciation the grant from Widener University that funded parts of this project. We are also appreciative of Henri Parens, who agreed to write the foreword for this volume. We are grateful for the research assistance of Jennette Von Bargen, Meredith Carter, Robert Eberwein, and Antoneal Swaby, and the secretarial assistance of Matthew Summerford. Above all, we thank the many adoptive parents who have been willing to share their stories with us, and have allowed us to share these stories with you, the reader.

About the Editors

Virginia M. Brabender, PhD, ABPP (Cl) is a professor at Widener University's Institute for Graduate Clinical Psychology, where she served as director for 13 years. She has authored six books, including *Introduction to Group Therapy*. Five books are co-authored with April Fallon (see below). Virginia Brabender is a fellow of Divisions 12 and 49 of the American Psychological Association. Dr. Brabender is co-founder of the Widener-Fielding Universities Adoption Research Collective. Dr. Brabender has authored many articles including those concerning the development of the mental health professional. She serves on various editorial boards. She is a mother of two children, one of whom was adopted 17 years ago from Honduras.

April E. Fallon, PhD received her degrees at Allegheny College and the University of Pennsylvania. She is professor at Fielding Graduate University and associate clinical professor at Drexel College of Medicine. Dr. Fallon is co-founder of the Widener-Fielding Universities Adoption Research Collective. She has received numerous awards for her teaching of psychiatric medical residents and was most recently awarded the Psychiatric Educator 2012 from Philadelphia Psychiatric Society. She has researched and written on the development of emotion in both children and adults and bonding and adoption. She is the mother of two children, one of whom was adopted 10 years ago.

Other texts co-authored by Brabender and Fallon include: *Models of Inpatient Group Psychotherapy*; *Awaiting the Therapist's Baby: A Guide for Expectant Parent-Practitioners*; *Essentials of Group Therapy*, and *Group Development in Practice: Guidance for Clinicians and Researchers on Stages and Dynamics of Change*.

Contributors

Bret A. Boyer, PhD
Institute for Graduate Clinical Psychology, Widener University

Virginia M. Brabender, PhD
Institute for Graduate Clinical Psychology, Widener University

Meridith C. Carter, MA
Institute for Graduate Clinical Psychology, Widener University

April E. Fallon, PhD
Fielding Graduate University
Drexel College of Medicine

Theodore J. Fallon Jr., MD, MPH
Chair, Child Psychoanalytic Program, Psychoanalytic Center of Philadelphia
Drexel College of Medicine

Elaine Frank, MSW
Co-Director of Parenting Services for Families & After Adoption, Philadelphia

Rama Rao Gogineni, MD
Cooper Medical School at Rowan University

Barbara L. Goldsmith, PsyD
Institute for Graduate Clinical Psychology, Widener University

S. Ileana Lindstrom, MDiv, MA
School of Psychology
Fielding Graduate University

Sanjay R. Nath, PhD
Institute for Graduate Clinical Psychology, Widener University

Alicia Padovano-Janik, PsyD, MEd
Prince William Family Counseling, Virginia

Henri Parens, MD
Professor of Psychiatry (Volunteer Faculty), Thomas Jefferson University Training and Supervising Analyst (Adult and Child), Psychoanalytic Center of Philadelphia; Director of Parenting for Emotional Growth.

Patricia G. Ramsey, EdD
Professor of Psychology and Education, Mount Holyoke College

Denise Rowe, BA
Co-Director of Parenting Services for Families & After Adoption, Philadelphia

Philip A. Rutter, PhD, LP
Human Sexuality Studies, Widener University

Hal S. Shorey, PhD
Institute for Graduate Clinical Psychology, Widener University

Amanda B. Swartz, PsyD
Counseling, Testing and Mental Health Center, Texas Christian University

Sonia Voynow, LCSW
Private Practice, Narberth, PA
Founder of Surviving and Thriving

Joseph D. White, PhD, LP
Private Practice, Austin, Texas

Antoinette Whitmore, AB, MEd
Consultant, Boston, MA

Mary E. Winzinger, PhD, LPC
Private Practice, Hackettstown, New Jersey

Chapter 1

SETTING THE STAGE
The Adoptive Parent in Context
Virginia M. Brabender and April E. Fallon

We begin our odyssey into the psychological life of adoptive parents by telling the tale of three couples.

> Raina and Liam, parents of a 3-year-old daughter, had been trying for 2 years to conceive their second child. They had gone through some fertility testing and treatment. However, when further testing revealed that Raina's husband had physical issues that made additional fertility intervention unlikely to be successful, the couple began to contemplate adoption. From their meetings with a counselor at an adoption agency, they formed a plan to adopt internationally. After an 18-month wait, they adopted a daughter from Ecuador, Lily, who entered their home when she was 13 months old.
>
> Soledad and Roger, who had 7-year-old twin sons, had been foster parents for 4 years. The children who previously had been placed with them were preteens and teens who had stayed in the home 1 to 2 years. However, when baby Rose was placed with the couple, they discovered an ever-increasing desire for her to join their family permanently. When it became clear that the child would be unable to return to the home of the birth mother, they began to discuss with one another the potential of adoption.
>
> Doris and Basil had spent 5 years trying to conceive a child. They had been told that the likelihood of pregnancy occurring was low. They decided to attempt domestic adoption because they desired both a newborn and a relationship with the birth mother. Doris herself had been adopted and after months of a protracted search in her early adulthood, achieved contact with her birth mother. After 8 months of having spoken with different birth mothers, a match was made and Doris and Basil were present at the birth of their baby boy.

These stories capture only some of the variability among adoptive parents and the circumstances of adoption. In these three cases, we see variation in how the child was identified, the conditions preceding the adoption, the amount of contact with the child and birth mother before the adoption. These differences create varied psychological experiences among parents. The longer waiting period for Raina and Liam may have been associated with a higher anxiety level. Soledad and Roger's intimate knowledge of Rose may have reduced particular fears about their future child's psychological and physical health. Doris and Basil's waiting experience may have been laced with the fear that no birth mother would find them good enough for her child.

Yet, were these couples to convene as a group, many commonalities might they find. For example, despite the variation in their circumstances, they might identify some common ground in their motivations for adoption. They may share a worry that the child's initial experience of loss may affect self-esteem, identity, and capacity for attachment. They might discover that all of them experienced concern about how their children would negotiate the interpersonal dynamics at school when peers, teachers, or both assumed that all children come from a traditional family. All six may have curiosity about aspects of their child's background, although each type of parent may have access to a different fund of information. In the international adoption, the parents may have had no information about the child's birth parents or early life, except perhaps to know that the child came from a particular orphanage. The foster parents may know the birth parents and a great deal about the child's years prior to entering his or her home. In the domestic adoption, the adoptive parents may have been with the birth mother at the time of the birth and may have personal acquaintance with many of their child's blood relatives such as the birth grandparents.

Both the commonalities and the differences among adoptive parents are critical for the therapist or other human service professional working with the family to grasp. Through sensitivity to differences and the unique characteristics of any adoptive family's situation, the therapist can achieve a high level of empathy for what that family is experiencing. Without a conveyance of accurate empathy, nothing else that the therapist does is likely to hit the mark. The awareness of commonalities is also crucial because it enables the therapist to anticipate what the family is likely to need. For example, all of these couples will require a great deal of information about many aspects of the adoption prior to bringing the child into the family. This need is served by pre-adoption counseling. Once the child enters the family, and as the child moves through the developmental stages, myriad challenges will arise, some large and some small. To ensure that the challenges are met in a way that supports the psychological and physical health of all family members, postadoption counseling is also critical. Mental health professionals working with members of the adoption family, if not able to provide such postadoption counseling themselves, need to know how to help families access it. This book is intended to help the mental health professional work effectively with adoptive parents. We help therapists understand the adoptive parent, and from this understanding, advise and treat him or her. This book also may be of interest to adoptive parents themselves. Finally, we hope that students who may in the future work with adoptive parents read it.

The importance of knowing the adoptive parent well to provide competent service to him or her necessitates that we take a closer look at the characteristics of adoptive parents in relation to one another—the similarities and differences among them and the population at large.

CHARACTERISTICS OF ADOPTIVE PARENTS

To appreciate the diversity among adoptive parents and their circumstances, one must recognize the different types of adoptions that have informed their family's lives. According to the 2007 National Survey of Adoptive Parents, inter-country adoptions account for approximately 25% of all adoptions; domestic, private adoptions 38%; and foster care adoptions, 37% (Vandivere, Malm, & Radel, 2009). Among domestic private adoptions, about 40% are by stepfathers, stepmothers,[1] or other relatives. A domestic adoption by a biological relative is a kinship adoption and it can be formal or informal. The biological parent may even live in the home but not function in a parental capacity (Pierce, 1999c). This type of adoption has been increasing as the number of non-relative adoptions decline. Foster children are most commonly adopted by foster parents (U.S. Department of Health and Human Services, 2009). A relatively new form of adoption is the adoption of an embryo, and the literature base (e.g., Finger et al., 2012; MacCallum, Golombok, & Brinsden, 2007) for these families is only recently emerging. As later chapters reveal, each type of adoption has its own benefits and difficulties. In this respect, adoptive parents are similar to other types of nontraditional families. Although adoptive families predominantly consist of a mother and father, single parent adoptions are becoming increasingly coming (Haslanger & Witt, 2005), a trend reflective of the increasing societal separation of marriage and parenthood (Smock & Greenland, 2010).

Psychological Characteristics

Adoption is a lifelong process that can bring immeasurable joy to parents. Yet, the precursor to adoption is often loss. That is, adoptive parents frequently embark on adoption following a long and unsuccessful effort to have a biological child. The road to consummating an adoption can be perilous. Long waits, reversals of decisions by birth parents, and political upheavals in countries in which adoption applications are made are just a few examples of potential frustrations. Many adoptive children entering the adoptive family have a range of physical and psychological problems that become evident over time and affect the child's adjustment at different developmental stages. Even in the absence of such problems, adoptive parents face the challenge of helping their children build healthy self-esteem, a task that can be more difficult in a society that values biological ties, and an identity that is inclusive of all aspects of the child's background and denying of none. Those parents who embrace openness with birth parents, while reaping potential rewards for their child and themselves, take on an added layer of complexity. Some parents adopt children with special needs—children who have particular physical problems, autism, learning disabilities, or trauma—and their special needs require great parental sensitivity and responsiveness.

Despite this list of potential stressors, according to a recent survey, 86% of adopted parents reported that their relationship with their children exceeded or met their expectations (U.S. Department of Health and Human Services, 2011). Malm and Welti (2010) found that parents who adopted because of infertility reported finding happiness in adoption. Adoptive parents as a group have considerable resources for coping with whatever problems and challenges the adoption of their child might present. These resources are important for the mental health professional working with the parents to recognize so that he or she can mobilize them. Adoptive couples tend to show a high level of relational stability (Rijk, Hoksbergen, ter Laak, van Dijkum, & Robbroeckx, 2006). Although married couples tend to report a decrease in marital satisfaction on the entrance of a child into the family, the decrease is less for adoptive than biological parents (Ceballo, Lansford, Abbey, & Stewart, 2004). In general, adoptive parents show a high level of marital satisfaction (Leve, Scaramella, & Fagot, 2001). One study found that adoptive parents reported more positive expectations and experienced greater satisfaction on becoming parents than biological parents (Levy-Shiff, Goldschmidt, & Har-Even, 1991). Adoptive parents appear to have a lower level of psychopathology than the general population. They have lower scores on measures of anxiety and depression and higher on measures of positive affect than married women without children or biological mothers (Gjerdingen & Froberg, 1991). Adoptive mothers report significantly fewer physical problems than these same two comparison groups (Gjerdingen & Froberg, 1991). As parents, adoptive mothers report fewer parenting doubts than nonadoptive mothers (Cohen, Coyne, & Duvall, 1996).

Part of the reason may be that adoptive parents tend to be older than biological parents and thereby have more experience in coping with a range of stressors. They also tend to be better educated and more affluent. As one manifestation of the latter, relative to biological parents, adoptive parents are more likely to own their own homes (Teachman & Tedrow, 2008). A word of caution about these findings is in order. Studies to date are limited by small samples, lack of racial/cultural diversity among parents, and a focus on the mother only (McKay, Ross, & Goldberg, 2010). Also, the type of adoption has a bearing on parental characteristics. The subgroups outlined at the beginning of this chapter (foster, intercountry, private domestic) vary in terms of education and income. For example, those who adopt from foster care tend to have lower incomes than parents adopting privately, whether that adoption is domestic or international. Often, parents who adopted from foster care are more similar to birth parents than those who adopt privately (Gailey, 2010).

Motivation for Adopting

Parents' motivations to adopt a child are varied, but, particularly in private adoptions, compensation for the inability to have a biological child is primary (Goldberg, Downing, & Richardson, 2009). Within the public system, altruism is the primary motive for foster care and adoption from foster care, and the desire to expand the family is second (Cole, 2005; Office of the Assistant Secretary for Planning and Evaluation [ASPE], 2011). Coping with infertility among individuals who adopt their foster children is only a tertiary reason (ASPE, 2011). Yet, to acknowledge fully the different driving forces in a parent's decision to adopt, one must go back to the motives that any human being has in wanting to have a child (Langridge, Sheeran, & Connolly, 2005). These include, but are by no means limited to, wanting to be in the parental role, to create a family, to experience the pleasure of being with children, and to enjoy relational comforts in old age. Specific subpopulations of adoptive parents have these motives and others that reflect the values and emphases of that group. For example, first-time adoptive gay males identified their cardinal motive as being that of raising tolerant human beings (Goldberg, Downing, & Moyer, 2012). Parents in a kinship adoption are motivated often by the desire to keep a child within his or her broader biological family or out of the child welfare system (Child Welfare League of America, 2007). However, like other subgroups of adoptive parents, sometimes parents adopting their kin are motivated to do so because of infertility problems.

According to Malm and Welti (2010), adoptive parents generally select their particular type of adoption after investigating various options. Prospective parents select international adoption because they see domestic adoption as too difficult. Adoption within the foster care system is often chosen because it is a more affordable option. Zhang and Lee (2010) observed that parents adopting internationally see children adopted from other countries as presenting interesting challenges. Children available for adoption nationally are seen as merely having problems. Their study underscores the social construction element of adoption, that is, the shaping of behavior based on how a phenomenon is framed. By helping prospective parents to recognize the diversity of narratives available, therapists can facilitate them to make the best possible decision for their particular circumstance in the type of adoption they pursue.

Use of Treatment

One noteworthy finding is that adoptive parents seek psychological interventions for their children much more often than their biological parent counterparts (Howard, Smith, & Ryan, 2004). They seem to do so both because adopted children are more likely to present psychological difficulties but also because adopted parents seem to have a greater receptivity to psychological interventions. That is, they tend to be more comfortable with the idea of therapy and other mental health services. The unfortunate reality is that often the therapists whom they see are not familiar with issues related to adoption and how parents and children in this group may have differences from those biologically intact families. As we noted in our introduction, frequently parents when trying to obtain services for themselves (or their child) see multiple mental health service providers before they find someone who has the necessary knowledge base and skills to be truly helpful. In fact, it is precisely for this reason that the current text was written—to raise the level of knowledge of the mental health practitioner who provides psychological services to adoptive parents. In the next section, we see some of the problems adoptive parents may encounter as they pursue services through therapists lacking a background in adoption.

SERVING THE NEEDS OF ADOPTIVE PARENTS

Best practices in all mental health services demand that practitioners have mastered the accumulated knowledge from research and clinical practice for whatever problem or issue the client is seeking services. When mental health professionals are not adoption-knowledgeable, and yet provide services to adoptive parents, problems arise such as the following:

> A prospective mother went to a psychologist for personality testing in conjunction with her adoption application. The assessor proceeded through the evaluation, at the end of which she asked the prospective mother her reasons for wanting to adopt. The mother explained that although she had three biological children, she wanted to adopt a child from a particular country for humanitarian reasons. Also, she indicated that she would love to have a fourth child. The assessor expressed the view that the mother could be taking on a great deal of trouble and should seriously consider the toll on other family members. She ended her comments saying that from her knowledge of adopted children "things didn't tend to turn out well."

This vignette calls to mind the truism "a little bit of knowledge can be a dangerous thing." This psychologist's comments designed to discourage the woman from adopting, were half-true, but half-false. Yes, adopted children do exhibit more problems than nonadopted children and these differences are due to the early history of the adopted child. However, what the assessor did not appear to know is that with the proper supports, and sometimes even in their absence, if particular protective factors are present, then parents and children do very well. This psychologist may have been competent to do an assessment, but she was not competent to do pre-adoption counseling. She went beyond the parameters of her role.

A second example concerns an issue of contact with the birth mother:

An adoptive mother, a single woman, had been seeing a therapist, a clinical social worker with a psychodynamic orientation, off and on for many years, even long before she contemplated adoption. The therapy covered a range of concerns including the mother's relationship with her own mother, and the dissolution of her marriage. This adoptive mother's daughter, Jill, was now 12 years old. The issue she was currently discussing in the therapy was the fact that the biological mother was lessening her contact with Jill, and it was painful to both adoptive mother and Jill. Jill had invited her to a number of school performances and the birth mother declined.

The therapist revealed that she had always been puzzled by the daughter's capacity to have relationships with both biological and adoptive mothers, and she felt it could well be confusing to Jill. She said she believed that this development was positive despite the misery it caused because it would create greater clarity for Jill on who the authority figure is in her life. The mother was somewhat perplexed by the therapist's comment because she did not believe that Jill was in any way confused about her adoptive mother's distinctive role. The mother felt that the therapist failed to grasp that the lessened attention was a loss for both her and her daughter.

In this situation, the therapist uses her theoretical orientation as a guide to intervention without a full understanding of the phenomena at hand. She fails to appreciate the value that knowledge of and contact with birth parents can have in the lives of many adoptive children such as Jill, although certainly for some, contact is not indicated. In the absence of specific information about adoption, therapists naturally fall back on what they already know, cultural values or what theory dictates. Inevitably, circumstances will arise—such as those in the vignette—that demand more particular, adoption-related knowledge for an appropriate response.

Often clients will have developed a therapeutic relationship prior to their adoption of a child. Given the great importance of the therapeutic alliance, it is most reasonable that once a client forges a successful relationship with a therapist, he or she would want to continue with that therapist. We are not recommending that adoptive parents in a knee-jerk fashion abandon therapeutic relationships they already have formed. Rather we are encouraging that those therapists whose clients experience that life-altering event of adoption take the necessary steps to educate themselves about adoption. In some situations, however, the problems that are tied to adoption may be so complex and severe that they may necessitate calling on someone who specializes in adoption.

A third example concerns a circumstance in couple therapy:

A couple, a pair of adoptive parents, saw a couple therapist about conflicts they were experiencing about raising their three adopted sons, a sibling group from Haiti. The wife felt that the sons had no playmates who were adopted or who looked anything like them. The mother felt that as the children advanced in age, it was imperative that they had access to children whom they could perceive as like themselves. She suggested moving, or sending the children to a school that would provide a more diverse social landscape. Her husband thought that such changes were excessive. He pointed out that overall, the boys had done quite well: They earned good grades in school and had many friends. The mother argued that having friends who looked like them was vital to their development of a healthy sense of identity. The therapist attempted to assist the husband and wife in finding middle ground, for example, sending the boys to a camp that would accomplish the mother's goals. Yet, the mother felt that the therapist had not heard her at all and was minimizing the issue she was raising.

The issue of identity construction becomes more important as children move into the years of early adolescence. In interracial adoptions, the matter is especially tricky in that the task of the child is to recognize and integrate all parts of him- or herself. These parts include the child's own race, the parents' race(s), his or her own ethnic/ cultural background, and that of the parents. The couple therapist was understand-ably conceptualizing the problem as a relationship issue and was working on the skill of compromise. However, from the perspective of the adopted children, the issue was developmental: What would be optimal to help these boys develop healthy self-esteem and an inclusive identity?

The therapists in our vignettes are proceeding in the way an ordinarily competent therapist might if he or she lacked a background in adoption. In all likelihood, none of these therapists had had the advantage of graduate training in adoption because the presence of adoption topics in graduate curriculums in mental health disciplines is exceedingly rare, almost nonexistent. Some might argue that graduate programs cannot cover everything. As true as this point is, it is worthwhile to consider Hen-derson's (2007) observation that most graduate programs provide coverage of the topic of schizophrenia, and clinicians are far more likely to come into contact with members of the adoptive triad than persons with a schizophrenic diagnosis. Although continuing education opportunities do exist, to take advantage of them therapists need a recognition that adoption is a life-transforming experience that continues to unfold over the lives of adoptive parents, birth parents, adopted children, and other members of the *adoptive kinship network* (that is, the constellation of biological and adoptive family members, and other important individuals in the family's life). Apart from the silence from graduate training programs in this area, another reason that therapists are inclined to disattune themselves to adoption issues is because they are reflecting the prevailing view of society about adoption. Adoption is broadly regarded as an event that occurs in a moment of time. Once a child is adopted, the family's situation is regarded as identical to that of other families. This view exists alongside a sense that adoptive parenting is something less than biological parenting. To a large extent, denial that adoption is not single event but a lifetime process exists as a camouflage of societal notions that biology trumps other types of connections. The consequence of this posture is significant: Although much has been done by govern-mental entities to help children find permanent families, little has been offered to assist families once a child enters his or her forever home (Smith, 2010). Support is especially lacking outside of the child welfare system. This circumstance leads families to seek private service from generalist practitioners.

General practitioners themselves attest to their lack of preparation for addressing the issues of adoptive families. A survey (Sass & Henderson, 1999) of 221 psychologists revealed that only 22% saw themselves as "well prepared" or "very well-prepared" to treat adoptive parents. Adoptive families also experience this lack of effectiveness on the part of many clinicians. Porch (2007) reported that members of the adoption triad report that they must travel from therapist to therapist before they find one who understands their special concerns.

For the generalist therapist who wishes to treat adoptive families, we recommend an immersion in the adoption literature, involving reading books such as this one and other books focused on other members of the triad and various online newsletters that provide a wealth of information on adoption. We also see as enormously helpful attending adoption conferences where participants have an opportunity to hear from all members of the triad, and other members of the kinship network. These training experiences should be used to enhance reflection on clinical work with members of the adoption triad. From pursuing these directions, the generalist mental health practitioner, although not being an adoption specialist, will achieve adoption competence and a level of knowledge uncommon for a generalist practitioner. As such, it can serve as a springboard for further work with this population. This background will also give the general mental health practitioner recognition of the circumstances in which a referral to an adoption specialist is essential.

HISTORY OF ADOPTION

Many fine sources provide a history of adoption, both within the United States (Esposito & Biafora, 2007) and beyond (Askeland, 2006); in fact, entire texts (Carp, 2002; Herman, 2008) are devoted to this topic. This chapter looks at the historical aspects of adoption from the vantage of the adoptive parent. We believe that those mental health professionals who treat adoptive parents should know something about the history of adoption. Among the many reasons for therapists treating adoptive parents to have some familiarity with the broad lines of this history, two are particularly salient. By seeing how adoption and adoptive parents have been regarded over time, the mental health professional can more easily recognize the distinctive aspects of the current adoption landscape. Some notions that can seem self-evident—such as the idea that the well-being of the adoptive child would be paramount in the eyes of the adoptive parent—have been inconstant over the history of adoption. Second, certain tensions within adoption practices—such as balancing the rights of different stakeholders—have been recurrent over the history of adoption. The identification of these tensions and recognition of their longevity enable researchers, ethicists, practitioners, and others in the adoption community to see where resources should be brought to bear to solve inherently difficult problems. This brief history will provide a context for examining the multidimensional characteristics of contemporary adoptive parents.

European History

From ancient cultures through the industrial revolution, many important developments in adoption took place in Europe, particularly Western Europe. These changes concerned the definition of adoption and the societal and personal needs it was envisioned to fulfill.

Ancient Cultures

When the Pharaoh's daughter found Moses (Exodus 2:10), his adoption was not characteristic of the times. In fact, it was not typical of ancient civilizations as a whole. Jochebed, Moses' mother, placed the baby Moses in a basket in the reeds on the bank of the Nile. She trusted that the kindness of strangers would protect her child from the Pharaoh's intent to kill all Jewish newborns. On encountering the helpless child, the Pharaoh's daughter responded as Jochebed had intended—she took the baby Moses under her care. Although this story has facets for each member of the adoptive triad (for example, it was a first example of a birth parent actively placing a child), in this case it would seem that the adoptive mother, the Pharaoh's daughter, was motivated primarily by concern for the child's well-being. It would be many centuries later that the desire to respond to a child's need was the driving force behind an individual's seeking to adopt a child.

The Hammurabi Law Code, the first known code that regulated the practice of adoption, was written in Babylonia in 1780 BCE. Its laws ensured that if the parent provided sustained care for a child, the adoption would have permanency. It specified that under particular circumstances, the adoption could be terminated, but the adoptive parent was seen as having obligations to provide for the child once the adoption is established. This law also spoke to what might have been in Babylonia a motive for adoption—the failure of a couple to produce their own biological offspring. In the 21st century this same motive remains predominant as we saw in our third example at the beginning of the chapter (Doris and Basil).

In ancient Rome, either or both of two motives drove the common practice of adoption (Colón & Colón, 2001). First, men adopted sons for the purpose of having an heir, a motivation demonstrating the lesser emphasis placed within that culture on genetic ties, relative to that of the present day. Second, adoptions occurred to forge an alliance between typically aristocratic families. As this latter motive might require, once the adoption was established, an active relationship often existed between birth and adoptive families, and the adopted child was not impeded from maintaining ties with his biological mother and father. As in contemporary society, both formal and informal adoption existed. The *familia*, as distinct from the nuclear family, might include alumnae or permanent foster children whose needs and well-being may or may not be served by their circumstance (Rawson, 1986). In ancient Rome, only men adopted because it was the male's lineage whose continuation was sought. Yet, toward the end of the Roman Empire, Christian emperors allowed women to adopt (Lindsay, 2009; Shaw & Saller, 1984). One reason this expansion was important was that it signaled that society was broadening the range of human needs for which adoption was seen as a solution.

Middle Ages

The Roman Catholic Church was the dominant influence on adoption during this era. Adoption was firmly established within the writings of St. Paul who saw the relationship between God, the father, and Christians as an adoption. In the late Middle Ages, the renowned Italian philosopher St. Thomas Aquinas (1274) developed the parallel between God and God's children, and adoptive parents and their children. Early Catholic canon law was rooted in the conception of adoption within the Roman Empire (Pollack, Bleich, Reid, & Fadel, 2004). However, as the Middle Ages progressed, social disorganization occurred as tribes invading the Holy Roman Empire dismantled social structures, which gave greater importance to adoptions to remedy the plight of abandoned or dispossessed children (Pollack et al., 2004). Yet, adoption was not the only means of caring for such children. *Oblation* refers to the practice of giving a child to a convent or monastery for the purposes of religious life. The novel *Pillars of the Earth* by Ken Follett (1989), set in the middle of the 12th century, features a character, Jonathan, who is abandoned by his destitute father on the death of Jonathan's mother. Jonathan is taken in by an order of monks who planned for him a religious profession. Even when the father rediscovers his son, he allows him to be raised by the monks who adopt the boy in an informal way. Such arrangements were not unusual.

The Renaissance and Adoption

During the Renaissance, the many children who lost parents found themselves facing deplorable conditions, as they remained largely unprotected by society. Yet, during this period we see the glimmerings of a slowly awakening social conscience that would ultimately offer some of these children the structures that would safeguard their well being. Because of the scourge of plagues, and poverty, many children found themselves alone. Terpstra (2005) draws a picture of the fate these children suffered. He notes that they either cared for themselves on the street or were cared for by others in diverse ways. Older siblings cared for some children. Others sought refuge in orphanages, where the administrators came to see themselves as paternal and maternal figures. Still other children would apprentice with artisans, and, as Terpstra notes, this relationship constituted a kind of informal adoption. In general, formal adoption was fairly unusual during the Renaissance.

The European Industrial Age

During the Industrial Age when societies turned to machines to make labor more efficient, children were seen as a resource given their ability to operate these machines as well as adults (Hackett, 1992). As in Medieval and Renaissance periods, many children without parents found themselves working as indentured servants but others were adopted to provide families with labor resources (Groza & Rosenberg, 2001). The abuse of children was captured in literary works of the time, perhaps most memorably Charles Dickens' *Oliver Twist* (1837). In Oliver's odyssey, we see many of the conditions that befell children of that era. Oliver begins as an orphan after his mother dies of illness and his father mysteriously disappears. At the age of 9, he is consigned to a workhouse, but when he asks for a second helping of food, a task assigned to him by less ingenuous boys, he is perceived by the management as a diminutive reprobate and reassigned to work as an apprentice. When intolerable conditions within his new environment compel Oliver to escape, he travels to the city where the Artful Dodger ensnares him, and, ultimately, Fagin, who becomes a kind of malevolent father figure, indoctrinates Oliver to the world of crime. Many further plot developments consummate in Oliver being extricated from Fagin and reunited with his family, in particular, his mother's sister. His ultimate destiny was a kind of kinship adoption. *Oliver Twist* and other novels and articles appearing in the popular press performed a service in nurturing public outrage and empathy for the plight of children.[2]

Adoption in America

The history of adoption in America was no less dynamic than that in Europe.

Adoption in America in the 20th Century

Many of the conditions of poverty, disease, and overcrowding documented in Europe also affected large Eastern cities in the United States, particularly New York and Boston. These cities were often the destination for the many immigrants who came to the United States from Europe. Child relinquishment was a common problem because many parents simply did not have the funds to provide for their children. Impoverished parents would attempt to secure a safe harbor for their progeny with the hope and expectation that when circumstances were more favorable, they would be reunited.

Prominent among the efforts to create a safe harbor was the program established by Charles Loring Brace, founder of the New York Children's Aid Society (CAS). Beginning in 1854, children who were of an age to be able to work were sent by train[3] to parts of the country where labor was needed. Based on Brace's notion that children are better served by abiding within families rather than institutions, groups of children were transported to other parts of the country in the hope that they would be chosen by a family who would care for that child (O'Connor, 2001). Esposito and Biafora (2007) note that the program, though involving a work element, was envisioned to abet these children in meeting their physical, emotional, and educational needs.[4] In fact, work and the well-being of children were viewed as compatible elements in that, from the vantage of the Protestant work ethic, work improves character. Some receiving families were motivated by the opportunity to obtain subsidized labor (O'Connor, 2001). Others, driven by their concern for the suffering of children, their longing to build their families, or an admixture of both motives, reared these children as they would have their biological children. As time went on, the transported children were younger and younger in large part in response to the interest in adopting these children rather than treating them as indentured servants.

In placing children, CAS did not strive to make a match between the receiving family and the family of origin. For example, Irish Catholic children were placed in Protestant homes and were indoctrinated in the Protestant faith. In response to this development, representatives of the Catholic and Jewish faiths founded their own organizations to enable children to be in a context consonant with their religious backgrounds (Esposito & Biafora, 2007). Both the CAS program and the response to its breadth of application raised the issue that has been a perennial one in the adoption field—the extent to which the placement of a child in a family should be predicated on the degree of similarity between the two parties along certain dimensions.

In 1851, the first state law, "An act to provide for the adoption of children," was passed in Massachusetts; it required that for an adoption to proceed, the consent of the biological parents must be obtained (Mabry & Kelly, 2006). This statute was groundbreaking in that it required a judicial review for individuals to be granted the status of adoptive parents; a judge had to be convinced that this legal action was in the best interest of the child. Initially, this statute received very little attention in the other states (Adamec & Miller, 2007), but by 1925 all 48 states had enacted some type of adoption legislation (Wegar, 1997).

In the beginning of the 20th century, a very gradual shift in the notion of childhood occurred (Briggs & Marre, 2009). Less commonly was the child perceived as a diminutive adult, capable of being deployed for adult purposes, and more commonly was he or she regarded as a human being in a distinct period of life. The societal recognition burgeoned that the responsiveness of adults shaped the child's capacity to develop.

In the 1930s, major developments occurred in the application of the "best interests of the child" principle (Freundlich, 2007). First, states increasingly required that the agencies involved in the placement of children be licensed. Second, standards for adoptive parenting were raised as the statutory requirement of home visits of prospective adoptive parents was established. Third, permanent record keeping of adoptions became a mandated component of the process (Freundlich, 2007).

The flourishing and formalization of adoption were part of the progressive aspect of U.S. culture and the growth of the middle class (Melosh, 2002). Middle-class individuals perceived themselves as actively choosing the families they wanted. Individuals chose their spouses based not on the need to satisfy family obligations or preserve wealth, but to establish romantic love as the foundation of marriage. The role of choice in creating families was underscored by the availability and burgeoning use of contraceptives. Melosh writes that consistent with the zeitgeist of the times, the perception was that "those denied parenthood by nature might in turn defy the sentence of infertility through adoption" (p. 16).

During World War II, European countries provided for imperiled, abandoned children by engaging in intra- and intercountry adoption. Within the United States, this practice was not broadly embraced until after the Korean War when children, often racially mixed, immigrated from South Korea and were adopted by American families (Briggs & Marre, 2009; Selman, 2009).[5]

Postwar Developments

Amidst many developments during the years from 1945 to 1970, a particularly significant movement for all members of the adoptive triad was the sealing of adoption records. Although some states had sealed adoption records much earlier, many more took this step in the 1940s and 1950s. The sensibility driving policy about adoption was a protraditional family, pronatalist view that saw the purpose of marriage as giving birth to and raising children (Samuels, 2001). Hence, the childlessness of a married couple is a situation in need of remedy, and if that couple cannot have its own biological children, then adoption becomes a viable alternative. Reciprocally, children—so the view held—are best served by being raised by a married mother and father. Another situation in need of remedy is the unmarried pregnant woman; again, adoption is a solution. Just as sealed records were a reflection of an attitude about family, so, too, was this mandated secrecy a causal force in its own right, shaping adoptive attitudes toward the other members of the triad. As Lifton (1994) noted, it created a kind of oppositional dynamic between birth and adoptive parents. It also conveyed implicitly that were greater openness to occur, some negative, possibly catastrophic, consequences would ensue. For example, adoptive parents may have felt a sense that the adoption would be undone by the child's reconnection with the birth parents. Psychoanalytic theory may have inadvertently supported this notion as well. Healthy development was seen as predicated on children resolving their oedipal struggles, which used as a template one mother and one father. Evidence exists that these kinds of worries continue today (Zhang & Lee, 2011), particularly when families do not obtain adequate support before and after the adoption.

1970s Through the 1990s

The past three decades of the 20th century saw a more considered response to issues pertaining to adoption. Key issues in relation to adoption have crystallized over the past several decades. Different constituencies achieved a clearer and stronger voice by recognizing that uniting with one another increases their power. Hence, the conversation about adoption is not merely among individuals, but groups of individuals. The consequence of these conversations is the forming of complex adoption policies that take into account the needs of multiple stakeholders, especially but not exclusively the child, the adoptive parent, and the birth parent. These policies have been informed not only by the voices of the triad members and other groups but also by the accretion of information about adoption phenomena. For example, Biafora and Esposito (2007) write about the importance of local, state, and national population surveys in recognizing adoption patterns. The systematic collection of data and maintenance of national databases—especially for international adoptions—and the tracking of cases have enabled a clearer identification of problems necessitating solution.

Recognizing the Adoption Triad

One example of such a problem was the large variability that existed among statutory requirements for all aspects of adoption. This variability invited confusion and abuses. As Freundlich (2007) points out, one type of abuse was states' attempts to relieve themselves of caring for needy children by placing them in foster homes in other states. The *Interstate Compact on the Placement of Children*, developed in 1974, was enacted to protect children by establishing a uniform set of procedures for the movement of foster and adoptive children across jurisdictions in the 50 states, the District of Columbia, and the Virgin Islands. Among the protections it offers is the requirement for both sending and receiving parents to provide written consent before a child is moved. It also mandates that children who have been placed receive monitoring to ensure that their well-being is being served. The Compact is continually being examined for potential revisions to bring the ways in which states implement the code in greater conformity with one another.

The members of the adoption triad were finding their voices in diverse ways. Birth parents became increasingly active in challenging the abrogation of their rights. A number of key federal court decisions (for example *Stanley v. Illinois* [405 U.S. at 645] in which Stanley successfully appealed that he had never been shown to be an unfit father despite being unwed) occurred that gave birth fathers the power to give or withhold consent in whether their offspring would be adopted. The practice of sealing adoption records was challenged by search activists (e.g., Lifton, 1976), many of whom were adopted children, who saw access to information about biological parents as a basic human right. Feminists argued that the sealing of adoption records was a punitive practice in relation to birth mothers, many of whom do not freely relinquish parental rights (DeSimone, 1996). As is discussed in the next section, this issue is very present today.

Permanent Homes for Foster Children

For many years, a situation existed in which foster children would languish in a foster home for many years or be moved from one foster home to another. These children were deprived of the right to permanent and predictable attachments.[6] African American and Hispanic children were shown to have longer tenures in foster homes than Caucasian children. In part, this trend was a response to advocacy efforts by the National Association of Black Social Workers and others in the 1970s: they held that to develop a strong sense of racial identity, African American children needed to be adopted by parents of their own race (Brooks, Simmel, Wind, & Barth, 2005). Research (for example, McRoy, Zurcher, Lauderdale, & Anderson, 1984; Silverman & Fiegelman, 1981) demonstrated that in many respects, those children who grew up in a transracial family demonstrated outcomes comparable to those whose family members shared their race.

An effort to address this problem occurred in 1997 when President Clinton signed into law the Adoption and Safe Families Act (ASFA, Pub.L. 105–189), which established timetables for a child's foster care status and offered financial incentives to states for completed adoptions. The number of adoptions from foster care did increase although some argue that this trend was underway prior to the legislation. A diminution in the number of children in foster care waiting to be adopted has also occurred. For example, in 2002, almost 134,000 foster children were waiting to be adopted, whereas in 2009, this number had dropped to 114,500 (U.S. Department of Health and Human Services, 2010). This act has been quite controversial; those who perceive it as encroaching upon the rights of biological parents or who see it as insufficiently effective in promoting permanency have attacked it (see Gendell's discussion, 2001). Related to this change is another trend: Whereas prior to 1985, foster parents were encouraged to embrace exclusively this role, subsequently they were invited to be open to the possibility of adopting those children they foster.

Whatever benefit is derived from the implementation of this law, by no means is it sufficient to address the problem of the many children in foster care. One need is for individuals other than foster parents to adopt. In a recent survey of attitudes toward adoption conducted by the Dave Thomas Foundation for Adoption in cooperation with the Evan B. Donaldson Institute (Evan B. Donaldson Adoption Institute, 2002), it was found that out of 10 Americans, four had considered adopting a child at some time. This statistic may speak to an untapped pool of adoptive parents. Yet, the study also shows that Americans harbor worries and concerns about foster children and adoptive children. For example, 82% of all Americans believe that a significant risk exists that the birth parent would attempt to reclaim the child following adoption although such events are rare. Educational programs to address those misconceptions that discourage individuals from adopting a child, despite an interest in doing so, may be part of the solution to helping the 114,500 children currently in foster care to find permanent homes.

Beyond legal and attitudinal changes, we need good scientific information about the foster-to-adoption transition. Goldberg, Moyer, Kinkler, and Richardson (2012) identified a variety of special challenges faced by foster parents as they move toward adoption. These include legal difficulties, issues related birth parents, and problems in interactions with social service agencies. The creation of mechanisms to alleviate these sources of stress for foster/prospective adoptive parents is likely to enhance their ability to respond optimally to their child.

The 21st Century

Adoption practices are integrally connected with developments in the sociocultural landscape, and these changes—particularly over the past 50 years—have been significant. As many (e.g., Grotevant & McRoy, 1998) have pointed out, the sexual revolution of the 1960s lessened the stigma associated with being a single mother, a stigma that had motivated many women to develop for their birth children an adoption plan. Particularly within the United States but also within Western European countries, women who are pregnant and unmarried are far more likely to parent their children than they once were. The consequence of this shift is the radically decreased availability of domestic children. The one exception is the availability of older foster children. However, many couples desire an infant. To satisfy the wish for a child, many couples now look to international adoption. This circumstance not only exists within United States but also within many developed countries. According to a United Nations (2009) report, out of 27 receiving countries, international adoptions account for over 50% of all adoptions in 20 of them. In the United States, it currently accounts for approximately 15% of all adoptions.

Intercountry Adoptions

International adoptions enabled many vulnerable children to receive loving and permanent homes. Yet, documented occurrences of fraud and abuse such as child trafficking across a number of countries made abundantly clear the fact that the necessary safeguards had not been established to provide for the safety of children, their biological families, and prospective adoptive parents. For example, according to Fonseca (2009), articles appeared in Brazilian newspapers in the 1980s describing stories of children mysteriously disappearing from maternity wards and lawyers seeking to make extraordinary profits from prospective parents.

In response to these extremely serious problems, in 1993, 66 countries came together and signed *The Hague Convention on the Protection of Children and Cooperation in Respect of Inter-Country Adoption*. Although the United States signed the convention in 1994, the agreement did not enter into full force until April 2008. The treaty established the "best interests of the child" as the paramount concern in adoption decisions. It also established principles and processes by which adoptions would be conducted. According to this treaty, adoptions could be approved only after the biological mother had freely given her consent and in the absence of financial remuneration. To ensure compliance with the terms of the agreement, participating countries agreed to establish a central authority for the regulation and supervision of adoptions. The Hague Convention was designed to protect all members of the adoption triad. It offered the adoptive parent much more transparency in the adoption process. For example, it required that adoption agencies provide prospective parents with a contract that specified crucial elements such as an itemized fee structure and a specification of the relationship between the agency and the provider. The Hague Convention requires that adoptive parents obtain 10 hours of education on international adoption.

Although the Hague Convention undoubtedly helped to protect members of the triad, it has by no means eliminated all abuses. For example, the Schuster Institute for Investigative Journalism, headed by E. J. Graff, released a report (Graff, 2010) reflecting the analysis of evidence of why the United States needed to close adoptions from Vietnam. According to one investigation, women had been told that their children would be adopted domestically and would be returned to them when they were 11 years old. The evidence also suggested that the motive for these abuses was monetary and that essentially, children were being sold. Vietnam, like other countries such as Ethiopia and Liberia, is not a Hague convention country (U.S. Department of State, 2011).

Research Efforts in Adoption

In the past several decades, large-scale investigations have been carried out such as the National Survey of Adoptive Parents (NSAP, see Bramlett & Radel, 2010, for an introduction), a collaborative effort of multiple agencies of the U.S. Department of Health and Human Services based on data collected between April 2007 and July 2008, and the reader will see these projects described throughout the text. Such broad-based efforts provide a treasure trove of information capable of answering innumerable questions about the characteristics and outcomes of adoptive families.

Smaller-scale studies have addressed specific questions such as the effects of institutionalization and caregiver behavior on children in orphanages, some of whom would be adopted. For example, Groark, McCall, and Fish (2011) investigated three institutions for young children in Central America. The researchers found that the structure of care was not conducive to the children's forming a secure attachment with their caretakers. The caregivers would work extremely long shifts and then be off for several days. As children entered a new age group, as defined by that institution, they would receive a new set of caretakers. The focus of the caretakers was on physical ministrations to the children; although some affection and verbal interactions occurred, the demand of custodial activities limited them sharply. In their interactions with the children, the "caretakers displayed substantial detachment, lack of availability and receptivity to children, failure to respond to children's overtures, little support or empathy for children, and little animated or expressive interactions, all in a climate of low affect (both negative and positive)" (pp. 245–256). The children tended to demonstrate indiscriminant friendliness, noncompliance, and provocative behavior. They also manifested a low level of cognitive performance. Therapists working with adoptive parents benefit from knowing about such studies because it helps the therapist avoid making an assumption that was once commonplace: If the child is experiencing difficulties, something must be wrong with the family, or more specifically, the adoptive mother and father (Smith, 2010). The therapist who can realize that at times adoptive parents face extraordinary challenges based on a child's background is far more likely to show the adoptive parent empathy and respect for the complexity of his or her parenting challenges.

Heterogeneity in Adoptive Parents

Another trend in contemporary adoption is the broadening of who can adopt. Increasingly, adoptions are no longer the exclusive province of the married male and female who generally have considerable financial resources. Rather, adoptions are opening up to a greater range of prospective parents. A tax credit for adoptive parents, established in 1997 and renewed in 2010 in conjunction with health-care reform, has broadened the socioeconomic inclusiveness of adoption. Also, as of 2010, it is both a credit and a refund, and families adopting special needs children from foster care are not required to itemize expenses (North American Council on Adoptable Children [NACAC], n.d.). More is said about heterogeneity among adoptive parents in the next section.

CONTEMPORARY CONTROVERSIES

For those therapists and human service professionals working with adoptive parents, having a cognizance of the outline of the history of adoption helps in developing an appreciation for the current era in which adoptive parents perform their caregiving functions. The here and now of adoptive parenting is characterized by a number of controversies that represent different and sometimes colliding conceptual frameworks in understanding what adoption is and how the life of the adoptive family should unfold. Many of the issues that adoptive parents bring into treatment will have a connection to these controversies. For example, an adoptive mother and father may come into treatment because they disagree on what level of openness to have in their relationship to the birth parents. A gay man may enter treatment because of discrimination he has endured in his effort to adopt a child. In recent years, adoption stories have received a great deal of media attention (Pavao, 2005), and this occurrence has led the public to register reactions to adoption controversies. This attention has in some instances been useful in raising awareness of adoptive phenomena and has been instrumental in bringing about necessary reforms. At times, though, it has led to the escalation of tensions, making the development of constructive resolutions more difficult. Controversies are important to recognize because their resolution frequently leads to change in public policies in the short term, and societal attitudinal change in the long term.

The Openness Dilemma

One of the most controversial issues pertaining to adoption is what level of openness in the relationship between birth parents and adoptive parents is in the best interests of the adopted child, the relationship between the adoptive parent and the adopted child, the well-being of the adopted parent, the relationship between the birth parent and adopted child, and the well-being of the birth parent. Early in this chapter, we presented a vignette pertaining to openness. In this vignette, the birth mother had been making less contact with the adoptive family than either the adoptive mother or adopted child liked. As this example implies and as Grotevant and McRoy (1998) note, openness is not a binary concept (opened/closed) but rather a continuum from high to low with different families locating themselves at different points along this continuum. Over the centuries, societies could be characterized as residing at different positions along this continuum. For example, in the middle of the 20th century, society-at-large embraced a closed position in relation to adoption. A closed system was seen as protective of the birth parent in that it spared her the stigma associated with an out-of-wedlock pregnancy. It was designed to protect adoptive parents in that it hid fertility problems, and adoptive children in facilitating their seeing themselves as the same as other children. Psychological health would be promoted in all parties—so this position held—if the stakeholders proceeded as if the adoption had never occurred, a position Kirk (1964a & b) described as the rejection of difference (RD) attitude.

A Trend Toward Openness

More recently, movement has occurred within U.S. society toward a much more open position on the continuum of openness. Like all societal shifts, this transition has been spurred on by multiple factors. Increasingly, birth parents, particularly in U.S. domestic adoptions, have rejected the position that establishing an adoption plan for their children must entail a total break in their relationship with them. Adoption agencies supported the trend toward greater openness: Birth mothers who were uncertain about their capacity to raise a child but wished to ensure his or her well-being by selecting the adoptive parents would be better able to accommodate the demand for children to adopt. Some adopted children have railed against a system that denied them the information and contact opportunities to consolidate their identities and have relationships with their birth kin (Grotevant, Perry, & McRoy, 2007). Yet, others bear their lack of information about their origins in silence and, at least in some cases, suffer severe psychological consequences. As Betty Jean Lifton (1994) writes, "Having abandoned their need to know their origins for the sake of their adoptive parents, they are left with a hole in the center of their being. They feel they don't exist" (p. 7). Among adoptive parents are those who wish to maintain some level of openness because of a view that openness benefits their adoptive child, adds richness to their family's life, enhances their ability to obtain much needed information (e.g., medical), and satisfies their own curiosity about their child's origins.

Relevant Research Findings

One difference between past and present policy and practices related to openness is that whereas earlier in history, decision making vis-à-vis openness was necessarily rooted in supposition, today policy makers, families, and other stakeholders can inform their stances about openness, at least in part, by an accumulating base of empirical research on the effects of different levels of openness. Grotevant, McRoy, and colleagues (2007) interviewed 720 members of birth and adoptive families involved in adoption, drawn from 35 agencies across 15 states. Adoptions were classified into one of three types: confidential adoptions in which no information is shared between birth and adoptive parents; mediated or semi-open relationships in which some information is exchanged typically through the adoption agency, which serves as liaison; and fully disclosed adoptions in which information is exchanged directly by the triad members.

The investigators looked at outcomes for children, birth parents, and adoptive parents. They found that for children, the type of openness was not connected to curiosity, self-esteem, identity, understanding of adoption, satisfaction with their families' levels of openness, or socioemotional adjustment (Wrobel, Ayers-Lopez, Kohler, & Friedrick, 1998). For birth mothers, each situation was associated with a distinctive pattern of anxieties. In the mediated and closed situations, the birth mothers had greater unresolved grief. In the open adoptions, birth mothers struggled with their worries about how the children they had parented would be affected by knowledge of their sibling who had been adopted by another family, and by knowledge of the child's economic situation, one that might differ from that of the birth family. Across situations, adoptive parents felt satisfied with the level of openness, secure in their relationship to the child, comfortable with their sense of parental entitlement (the right to fully assume the role of parent; Reitz & Watson, 1992), but fearful that the birth mother would attempt to reclaim the child. On the other hand, individuals in the most fully open situation had greater empathy for the birth parent, and greater understanding of the child's interest in the birth family. They also had less fear that the birth parent would try to reclaim the child.

In a study of foster care adoptions over an 8-year period, Frasch, Brooks, and Barth (2000) found across different patterns of contact between the birth parent and adopted child, adoptive parents felt a high level of closeness to their adopted children.

Taken together, these results fail to show a clear overall benefit of one configuration over another although specific conditions carry particular benefits and drawbacks for adoptive parents and birth mothers. These findings are preliminary and bear replication. The research teams acknowledged methodological limitations of the studies—an aspect these studies share with others. With these caveats in mind, we might suggest that these findings point to the importance of an individualized approach to decision making in relation to degree of openness. The two facts—that no one configuration had a commanding superiority over others and that neither closed or open adoptions bring the harm forecasted by their opponents—give leeway to the individual family to make decisions in terms of their own values, personalities, and other circumstances. An example of such a circumstance would be a family structure in which two adopted children had different birth parents. The adoptive parents may wish to have a roughly comparable level of openness so that neither child feels deprived.

Openness as an Attitude

Brodzinsky (2005), one of the foremost contributors to the adoption literature, provides a reinterpretation of the concept of openness. He notes that where as historically openness was viewed as a structural arrangement, a potentially more heuristic perspective is openness as an attitude. This notion of openness may be more predictive of mental health variables than its conceptualization as absence or presence of communication in that it may better account for variation in adoption outcomes. An openness attitude incorporates an acknowledgment that the structure of involvement among members of the adoptive triad may be largely due to a variety of accidental factors. For example, in the adoptions in Haiti, some birth parents died. As Brodzinsky notes, in other cases the birth parent may not be found. Yet, in these circumstances the adoptive parent could demonstrate a willingness to acknowledge and celebrate a child's history with that child and others, and to enter into a relationship with the child's kinship, birth and adoptive. Openness also means a willingness to engage the child with difficult topics associated with the adoption. Many older children who are adopted have been subjected to trauma of different sorts (Gray, 2002), and parents are sometimes hesitant to approach this material lest the child be retraumatized. Although this concern is understandable, a commitment to openness entails securing the necessary professional help so that a revisiting of painful life events will be constructive and reparative. Levy-Shiff (2001), looking at openness in a way consistent with Brodzinsky's, contrasted the adult children of adoptive parents who show a high openness to discussion of adoption-related topics with the children of parents who are more closed. She found that the former had a higher level of adjustment than the latter.

The Status of Records: Open Versus Closed

A related issue is the closed versus open legal status of records. In consistency with the view that closed adoptions are preferable, society developed the structures to promote closed adoptions, and permanently sealed records were a core feature of this structure. As Pavao (2005) notes, when records are closed it denies adoptive parents the information they need to make plans for the child. Closed records deprive the adult adoptees information to solidify their identity, and the birth parents the chance to reassure themselves on the well-being of the child and satisfy their own longing for contact (Cornell, 2005). The closed record policy treats all adoptive families the same, not recognizing that each has its own pattern of informational needs. Today, all parties of the triad are seeking greater openness and yet, the closed sealed policy is still in force in many states. The effort to change the sealed record statutory policy is a major area of adoption advocacy (Pertman, 2011).

Transracial Adoption

Contemporary adoption practice has also been characterized by debate as to effects of diversity in the adoptive family, particularly between adoptive parent and child. As noted, any view that African American children would be severely harmed by being adopted by Caucasian parents was challenged by the research showing that these children were as well-adjusted as their peers in black families. In a meta-analytic study, Juffer and van IJzendoorn (2007) examined 18 studies and found that no difference was obtained between the self-esteem levels of transracially adopted children and children who shared their parents' race. Yet, as Roorda (2007) reminds us, level of adjustment does not capture all that characterizes a human being. For example, to what extent does the individual have an identity that comprehends all that they are— including those elements that distinguish them from the adoptive family?

Although major support for limiting adoptions based on race no longer exists, we need to know how transracial families can best promote the child's identity development. Adoption texts now address the important topic of how transracial families can best meet the adoptive child's need to maintain strong connections with his or her culture of origin. For example, adoptive parents are encouraged to live and school their children in communities in which the children will encounter individuals who are similar to them in all important respects. However, the consensus in the field seems be that much more work on this challenge should be pursued. At present, it should be noted that therapists who work with adoptive parents need an appreciation of the potential significance of the parents' approach to racial differences to parents and children's well-being and be encouraging of parents' attention to this dimension.

Gay Adoptive Parenting

Currently, society places formidable obstacles to those gay and lesbian couples who wish to adopt. Government entities, adoption agencies, and members of society who promote the notion that parenthood is the exclusive province of heterosexual individuals pose these obstacles. If a member of a gay or lesbian couple becomes a parent via adoption, surrogacy, artificial insemination, or other means, that individual receives full legal rights vis-à-vis the child (Pawelski et al., 2006). Yet, given current state laws, that individual's partner achieves formal legal parental rights with difficulty or not at all. Some states allow for same-sex couples adoption, some second-parent adoption, and others, neither possibility (Appell, 2012). When both parents are unable to adopt, role ambiguity ensues. In the instance of divorce, the non-adoptive partner has no legal access to the child regardless of the number of years he or she may have been involved in the child's life.

Multiple investigations (e.g., Farr, Forssell, & Patterson, 2010; Patterson, 1994, 1997) have documented that the children of gay and lesbian parents are as well-adjusted and healthy as children from heterosexual relationships. Gartrell and Bos (2010), based on a longitudinal study U.S. National Longitudinal Lesbian Family Study following children born to lesbian couples in the late 1980s and early 1990s, have found generally that these children are successful socially and academically. Some of these children reported experiencing peer teasing. Averett, Nalavany, and Ryan (2009) found that gay/lesbian and heterosexual adoptive parents encounter many of the same risk factors (for example, sibling adoption) for their children's psychological difficulties and protective factors (for example, financial resources enabling the purchase of therapy and medical treatment).

The obstacles to gay and lesbian individuals' adopting affect not only themselves but also children and communities. Kaye and Kuvalanka (2006) found that in jurisdictions in which gay and lesbian parental adoptions are permitted, the number of children in foster care is lower than where they are not. Consequently, a societal challenge is how to develop the protections and rights for these families as those enjoyed by all others. A challenge for the therapist is how to support the gay or lesbian prospective parent through what are often extraordinary obstacles in building a family through adoption.[7] However, as Brooks, Kim, and Wind (2012) note, this population of prospective parents is distinguished by resilience and persistence. Hence, the task of the therapist is to mobilize the strengths of these individuals.

PRACTICAL POINTS

- Therapists who provide treatment to adoptive parents should educate themselves on adoption theory and research and be aware of societal notions that may influence their views of their clients who are adoptive parents.
- Therapists should be aware of the historical context in which adoption occurs, and have a cognizance of the current controversies that may lead to changes in adoption practices.

- Therapists who work with adoptive parents should recognize the considerable strengths adoptive parents bring to the task of raising an adoptive child and be prepared to mobilize these strengths.
- Therapists should avoid the assumption that when adoptive children have difficulties, it is necessarily because the parents are doing something wrong. In other words, therapists should not blame adoptive parents for difficulties that arise.

CONCLUSIONS

Adopting a child can be a process fraught with many difficulties, and perhaps because of these difficulties, a natural screening occurs. That is, those who surmount all of the hurdles often have considerable resources to offer their child—physical, psychological, educational, and financial. These resources are often much needed in raising an adopted child who may bring to the family challenges that will reveal themselves over time. Therapists aware of these resources will be in a position to help clients to summon them. Therapists also must be aware of the stressors and difficulties adoptive parents face because the alleviation of these are likely to be goals of therapy.

In the next two chapters, we offer two therapist tools in working with the adoptive parent—theory and research. Theories allow conceptualization of the developmental processes by which adoptive parents and children forge relationships over time and research enables the testing and enrichment of those conceptualizations.

NOTES

1. Although this text addresses kinship adoption, it does not take up adoptions by stepparents for two reasons. First, to do justice to this topic, it's necessary to talk about the dynamics of stepparenting, which would take us too far afield in this text. Second, the literature is simply insufficient to ascertain whether these families are best understood as subgroups of stepfamilies, adoptive families, or a third broad classification. The small amount of empirical work (e.g., Bramlett, 2010; Stewart, 2010) that has been done in this area suggests that adoptive families launched by stepparenting have characteristics of both. Although this area has major methodological challenges, we would hope future investigators could surmount them to shed light on this population of adoptive families.
2. Novy (2004) observes that literature has often focused on the topic of adoption because adoption raises fundamental questions such as "What is a family?" through the lens of a particular society. Along these lines, another important Dickens (1852–1853) novel, *Bleak House*, entailed a characteristic type of caregiving relationship in England, the guardianship. John Jarndyce became the guardian of Esther Summerson, an orphan, when she became a young adult. Esther was installed at Bleak House where she served as a kind of domestic manager. Although Mr. Jarndyce was portrayed sympathetically, the potential confusion of this type of caregiving role is seen in the fact that eventually Mr. Jarndyce proposes marriage to the much younger Ms. Summerson. Esther accepts his proposal—largely due to her gratitude for his munificence and her admiration of his character. When Esther's relationship with a more age-appropriate, less parental candidate blossoms, Mr. Jarndyce relieves her of her obligation to marry him.
3. Briggs and Marre (2009) note that this practice was not unique to the United States. For example, beginning in 1618, the United Kingdom sent children to its settler countries (for example, Australia, the United States, and New Zealand), a practice that could be seen as a forerunner of transnational adoption.

4. The reader can obtain a picture of the experience of a child adopted via the orphan trains by reading Moriarty's *The Chaperone*. The novel also provides the reader with an empathic grasp of an adopted child's intense longing to learn about his or her birth parents to achieve a sense of wholeness.

5. It is estimated that more than 98,000 Koreans were adopted by U.S. families between 1955 and 1998 (Freundlich & Lieberthal, 2007; Holt Korea, 1999; S. Korean Ministry of Health and Welfare, 1999; U.S. Department of State, 1999).

6. According to a research review by Triseliotis (2002) on long-term outcomes associated with adoption versus long-term foster care, adopted children experience a stronger sense of security, belonging, and sense of well-being. Yet, Triseliotis is careful to note that the individual needs of a given child and family may be best accommodated by long-term foster care.

7. Brodzinsky and Pertman (2012) edited a volume, *Adoption by Lesbians and Gay Men: A New Dimension in Family Diversity* that provides an in-depth treatment of this topic. Also adding to this literature is Goldberg's (2012) *Gay Dads: Transitions to Adoptive Fatherhood*, which reports on the experience of 35 gay couples prior to the adoption and 3 to 4 months post-placement.

Chapter 2

THEORETICAL CONTRIBUTIONS TO THE UNDERSTANDING OF PARENT-CHILD BONDING IN ADOPTION

April E. Fallon and Barbara L. Goldsmith

The psychoanalytic literature offers a plethora of theories that richly detail human intrapsychic and social development based on clinical observations with patients and clients in which normal development has gone awry. As is the case with most of our knowledge about developmental processes, much of this literature is based on observations of patients who began life and grew up with their biological parents. Nevertheless, psychological theories influence our current thinking on the adoption process, the child's healthy psychological development, and successful integration of the child into the family.

In this chapter, we examine an array of psychological theories and their most central constructs that in our experience shed light on our understanding of the development of the relationship between the child and adoptive family. To this, we add our own observations and examples of how this might apply and unfold in the process of adoption and thereafter. Although the adoption process involves both mother and father, precious little theory has been written about father. Thus, our focus primarily is on the mother (Chapter 5 incorporates theoretical contributions to our understanding of adoptive fathers). We begin first with prenatal psychic reorganization. Bowlby's theory of attachment and the concomitant mirror process of the caregiving system offer important contributions concerning the impact that age of adoption may have on the normal predetermined biological process. The child's attachment system is complemented by the caregiving system and George and Solomon's work is explored. Next, we discuss the human characteristic of adaptation in the context of ego development. We then describe Winnicott's contributions of the holding environment and the importance of the transitional object. Fonagy's work on reflective function also is highlighted as we see the significance of the parent's capacity to reflect on the child's internal experience. This is followed by a discussion of the importance of ongoing attunement in the mother-child interaction. We then discuss the importance of mirroring and development of healthy self-esteem. Finally the central tenets of Mahler's separation individuation are described.

BEFORE THE FAMILY BECOMES A UNIT: DANIEL STERN AND INTRAPSYCHIC REORGANIZATION

The scaffolding for healthy development commences long before the child arrives. It is ensconced in the genetic and cultural structures of generations that came before and is most dramatic prior to the entrance of the first child into the family. A woman's view of her relationship with her future child begins in her early relationship to her own mother and her internal representation of the way in which she was parented. This pattern of relating is re-created and practiced with dolls, animals, and toys in the form of "play-mothering." Such incomplete and fragmented expressions of mothering evolve and become more realistic with further biological and psychological development and life experience. At the same time, the woman's schemata of herself in relation to another (such as a daughter, a sibling, a friend, a wife) are refined as a result of both internal psychological models and environmental circumstances (Stern, 1995). Her schema of connection with close others becomes the backdrop and springboard for her interaction with her future child.

For the biological family, pregnancy becomes the "dominant organizing axis for the mother's psychic life" (Stern 1995, p. 172). The prior primary identity organization of the woman as a daughter and wife transitions to an image of herself as a mother and caregiver. Though biological in origin, girls learn caregiving from their own mothers through modeling, identification, and internalization. However, it is the mother's narrative view of her mother, rather than the actual history, that determines her capacity to mother. If a woman develops a view of her mother that is realistic and balanced even if it involves a troubled past, then likely she will have the capability of providing good enough maternal care (Fonagy, Steele, Steele, Moran, & Higgitt, 1991). Fraiberg in her work with mothers from traumatic backgrounds described it this way, "Access to childhood pain becomes a powerful deterrent against repetitions in parenting, while repression and isolation of painful affect provide the psychological requirements for identification with the betrayers and the aggressors" (Fraiberg, Adelson, & Shapiro, 1975, p. 420).

In the case of the biological family, the physical growth of the fetus parallels a mother's developing schema of her baby (Stern, 1995). A shift occurs in the "expectant" mother as she moves from being cared for to being a provider of care and protection (George & Solomon, 2008). During the waiting period, all expectant mothers experience a vacillation of anxieties and richly positive fantasies. Winnicott's (1956) term "primary maternal preoccupation" described a period of necessary absorption (the mother's natural absorption in her baby) beginning in the last trimester of pregnancy and continuing throughout the first several months after the baby's birth. For an adoptive mother, maternal preoccupation can begin with the adoptive mother's attachment to a photograph of the child she is planning to adopt (Fallon & Brabender, 2012). During this maternal preoccupation, the good enough mother puts her own needs on hold in order to focus on the needs of her baby. Stern (1995), incorporating some of Winnicott's work on maternal preoccupation, characterizes four themes: wishing to help the baby grow and fear about its health; a "maternal preoccupation" in dyadic solitude acknowledging and loving her baby; creating an environment to enable the child's growth and development; and transforming her self-identity. According to Stern (1995) these states decrease in the latter part of the pregnancy as the mother shifts away from daydreams to the real situation so that she and her actual baby can start to bond. Many doubts remain about one self as a parent, which may be essential for the mother's self reorganization (Bibring, Dwyer, Huntington, & Valenstein, 1961).

The significance of the mother's internal self-schema reorganization to the mother-child bond is paramount. Biology allows the space of 6 to 8 months for transformation; other circumstances, such as when parenting occurs through adoption or foster parenting, may not offer this same schedule of anticipatory opportunity. The evolution of parental representations is largely unknown and we suspect more varied depending on the circumstances. Adoption differs from pregnancy in that the waiting period is often longer and the result is uncertain (Fallon & Brabender, 2003, 2012). Yet, this psychic reorganization does occur and to varying degrees the same themes that Stern describes exist in the narratives of adoptive parents as well. In kinship adoptions, obligation and anxiety may truncate the role of positive images and reverie; yet the promise of a stable/better environment can fuel the identification as a caretaker whose relation to the child will be a positive force. We have posited elsewhere that for the adoptive mother, the attainment of the picture or video of the child instigates the construction of a maternal representation of the child (Fallon & Brabender, 2012.). Her anxieties center on the health of the child and the fear that the proposed family unit will not come to fruition, rather than the fear that the child will not grow inside her. For the majority of adoptive parents, at least some years of longing for a child have preceded a decision to adopt, or to begin the formal process of application for adoption. Thus, the extra time and longing provide the resources for the transformation from an identity of someone who is cared for to someone who is caring. Being an adoptive parent requires planning and realism; creating a growth environment for the child, at least physically, has often been a way to bind the other anxieties. Psychologically, the same doubts about the capacity to mother as captured by Winzinger (2010) in her interview with an adoptive mother still lurk, "Liz recounted her thoughts, hope and daydreams after seeing the picture of the infant with a mix of joy and fear. 'I was scared because I never was a Mom before . . . Am I going to be a good mom? Am I going to do the right thing?'" (p. 143). Maternal preoccupation and positive reveries are the predominant retrospective memory of that waiting period and transformation in identity. The photos concretely appear to fuel this process, although the visual reality may circumscribe the fantasies to some degree. Adoptive mother Sandra gave evidence of this image construction process in describing her reaction to seeing her daughter's photo for the first time. "She looked like a pistol . . . she is a tough strong kid . . . my view of her when I saw the picture was this is a tough girl. This is going to be one of these in your face kids" (Winzinger, 2010, p. 142).

We believe that Stern's construct of intrapsychic reorganization of the maternal representation is a meaningful and useful notion applicable to all adoptive parents and is essential to developing a healthy connection with the child. It cuts across the biological divide as prospective parents additionally consider notions of family in a non-biological, often cross-cultural context. To that end, receiving information about the child provides environmental priming for this reorganization and may be a powerful stimulus to catalyzing the parents becoming absorbed in caregiving activities.

THE CASE OF DORA

We offer the case of Dora and her adoptive family, to which we refer throughout the chapter. Dora had been left at a hospital in a large urban area. She was placed immediately with a single elderly foster care mother where she remained until she was placed with her adoptive family. Her biological mother, however, reappeared to social service and saw Dora twice in the first year and once in the second. After her third birthday the birth mother terminated her parental rights and Dora was placed in a permanent home. By age 4, she was legally adopted. When she was moved from the foster care placement she cried and clung to her foster mother. "No adoption," she cried. Initially her new parents offered to have Dora sleep on a mattress next to their bed. She refused, although they found that in the morning she was asleep on that mattress. In subsequent months her parents would find her in their bed in the morning. This pattern continued for about a year. During the day Dora appeared to make a good adjustment, rarely offering resistance, crying, or complaining. The mother noted that although Dora was pleasant, she did not seem engaged. As an example, the mother reported that when she hugged and kissed Dora, she received little response back. When Dora played with her dolls, she often pulled them apart, ripped their clothes, and used marker on their faces. By the time she was 5 this behavior subsided.

Dora began kindergarten without any overt anxiety at the separation. Her academic and social skills were within normal limits. Dora's parents worked during the day, but they spent all of their weekends together. Dora preferred to be at home rather than visiting others in their homes, even relatives. When Dora was 6, her mother needed to go out of town for a week. Dora remained home with her father and grandmother. When it was time for good-byes, Dora pushed away her mother's attempts to hug and kiss her. The mother called every day after school, but Dora did not want to talk with her. The mother allowed Dora to discontinue the conversations but experienced it as a rejection. The grandmother noted that while the mother was away, Dora took a doll to bed with her and filled the baby bottle with water. In the morning, the water in the bottle was gone. During the mother's absence the father noticed Dora seemed without much energy and appeared down. When her mother returned late in the evening, Dora still awake offered only a brief verbal greeting when her mother checked on her. The next morning the mother presented Dora with several gifts that she was sure the child would like. Dora pushed the gifts aside and demanded a new American Girl doll to add to her collection.

The mother attempted to talk with Dora about her absence and associated feelings. She articulated her own feelings about the separation and how she was able to live with them. The mother and Dora played dolls together re-enacting the separation. The mother let Dora direct the separations and verbalized what the babies felt and what the mother felt. With subsequent separations, the child was less overtly rejecting of the mother before leaving and after returning. In the evening the child filled the mother's favorite coffee cup with water and took it to her room. Sometime after lights were out and before morning Dora drank the water. However, while the mother was away, Dora still preferred to have little contact. The mother developed the strategy of texting once a day rather than calling, which allowed Dora control over whether she responded. During grade school Dora developed several friends, but still preferred to entertain at home. After fifth grade her two best friends were going to an overnight camp for 2 weeks, and Dora's parents wanted her to attend, too. Her mother spoke fondly of her own first experiences with overnight camp, but Dora was insistent on not going.

BOWLBY AND THE IMPORTANCE OF SECURE ATTACHMENT IN HEALTHY DEVELOPMENT

The infant is born with a biological proclivity to develop an enduring and unique "affectional bond" for survival (Bowlby, 1956, 1958). According to Bowlby (1988a), this attachment offers a secure base from which the infant can explore the world. Such a consistently available and supportive relationship serves as the template for other intimate relationships and provides the foundation for healthy biological, cognitive, social, and psychological development across the lifespan. Secure connections to parental figures help the child to regulate emotion, establish basic trust, and develop social skills and a positive identity. A disrupted early relationship to an important figure is likely to result in at least temporary and sometimes more long-term attributes of deprivation. Bowlby elaborated on this sequence of reactions by the infant to separation—first protest, then despair, and finally detachment (Bowlby, 1969/1991, 1973, 1980). In the case of Dora we see the initial attachment to the foster mother, not to the birth mother, as her infrequent appearances in Dora's life did not allow an attachment to occur. There is initial protest when separation is imposed by the permanent placement and some evidence over time of a detachment, but little evidence of despair as she appears to be engaged with her family and at school.

The attachment caregiving interactions complement and compensate for the child's lack of physical, cognitive, and social capabilities, yet permit as much freedom as possible to develop those skills. Bowlby (1969/1991) detailed how the attachment bond develops and interacts with the behavioral systems of attachment, fear, exploration, and sociability.[1] In the case of Dora, we can see how the disrupted attachment with the foster mother affected her sociability and exploration long after the traumatic event of her removal from foster placement occurred. Her compliance but lack of engagement at school signals Dora's disconnection with others at a time when sociability is important. Her preference to remain at home, rather than visit or attend camp is evidence that there are underlying anxieties about attachment which inhibit sociability and exploration.

The child is prewired to maintain a comfortable distance and connection to the caregiver and his or her behaviors are activated or terminated to attain this homeostasis (Cassidy, 2008). As the child grows the systems become more elaborate and mental representations of the attachment figure, the self, and the self in relation to that figure develop. Bowlby terms these representations *internal working models*.

Bowlby categorized the ontogeny of attachment into four phases that unfold and transform over the preschool years. As Bowlby conceptualized attachment, it becomes a characteristic of the child. Yet, its form is not merely an unfolding of a biological process. Rather, its properties emerge out of a co-constructed experience with the prominent caregivers in his environment and environmental circumstances. The first phase, lasting approximately 3 months, entails the infant's use of crying and grasping to elicit caregiver attention. In an increasingly attuned dance, the caregiver's efforts are met with the baby's reaching and smiling, which kindle positive caregiver reactions. A multitude of these daily exchanges keep the caregiver close and solidify the predictability to both mother and child. When a child begins life in an orphanage, caregivers are less available for this kind of interaction. When adoption occurs, regardless of their age, they need these kinds of intensive exchanges with the caregiver that young infants ordinarily receive. Children placed in foster care awaiting adoption are much more likely to have this stimulation available to them.

In the second period, which terminates in the 6- to 9-month range, the baby directs increasingly more elaborate behaviors to the most familiar caregivers. Ainsworth observed that Uganda infants differentiated their vocalizations, gestures, and exploratory behavior differently to their mothers even though many often had multiple caregivers. They "know" their mothers. Bowlby (1958) noted that the quality of attachment is affected by the "the extent to which the mother has permitted clinging, and following, and all the behavior associated with them or has refused them" (p. 370). Children in orphanages with multiple caregivers are further disadvantaged as these institutions prioritize physical care over psychological.

The third period lasts until age 4. During the first portion of this phase, attachment efforts are focused on the primary figures. Increased locomotion enables the child to have more control over proximity to the mother. At the same time, burgeoning cognitive development allows for an internal representation of the mother independent of her physical presence. This new internal working model allows for interactions to be categorized symbolically (Marvin & Britner, 2008). Bowlby wrote, "In the working model of the world . . . a key feature is his notion of who his attachment figures are, where they may be found and how they may be expected to respond . . . whether he feels confident that his attachment figures are in general readily available or whether he is more or less afraid that they will not be" (1973, p. 203). Although physical distance remains important, it is "felt security" that determines that distance (Sroufe & Waters, 1977). With Dora, particularly at night, the need for greater proximity to her parents and new attachment figures was apparent as she slept on the mattress in their room, despite her initial protest.

Bowlby notes that felt security is the result of the primary figure's sensitivity in responding to the child. "The mothers whose infants are more securely attached to them are mothers who respond to their babies' signals promptly and appropriately, and who engage in much social interchange with them—to the delight of each party" (Bowlby, 1969/1991, p. 316). Bowlby's personal and professional experiences led him to postulate that disruption of the bond after the 1-year mark increased the possibility of long-term negative effects (Bowlby, 1973, 1980, 1969/1991). It is also a sensitive time with increased attachment toward primary figures and heightened wariness toward those unfamiliar. The four behavioral systems become more coordinated, stable, and enduring. Bowlby articulated four attachment styles or strategies with secure being the ideal: the child being capable of exploration and sociable behaviors in the safety of his mother's view (see Chapter 3 for a more detailed discussion). As the child grows physically, cognitively, and emotionally, greater flexibility exists in how he or she maintains security. Yet, a forced separation often results in a regression requiring physical contact (often brief) with the mother (in Dora's case she pushed her mother away after returning from a brief absence).

In the final stage of attachment, a goal-corrected partnership with the mother is achieved—the capacity to have and negotiate a mutual plan for proximity with her (Bowlby, 1969/1991). The child appreciates that others have internal thoughts and feelings, separate and distinct from his or her own, and is capable of evaluating whether these perspectives match. Thus under normal circumstances, physical connection is no longer central for the child to feel secure; rather it is perceived availability of the primary attachment figure. Bowlby (1988a) also emphasized that parents' open dialogue about emotion and advocacy of their child's efforts to explore their inner worlds help to change their representational attachment scripts. If the child does have a history of loss, ongoing parental discussion about (attachment) trauma and deprivation with the child and with each other may enable the child to alter and revise his previous internal working attachment models.

THE PARALLEL CAREGIVING SYSTEM: CONTRIBUTIONS OF GEORGE AND SOLOMON

If healthy development is to proceed smoothly, a seamless interface with the parental caregiving behavioral system must occur (Bowlby, 1969/1991, 1988a). In the biological family (and we posit those adoptions that occur at birth), the mother's representation of herself with her child seems to be the most central force in achieving a healthy attachment (George & Solomon, 2008). Similar to the child, the parent, too, has a parallel repertoire of behaviors that facilitate relationship development. These include "retrieval, maintaining proximity, carrying, following, signaling the child to follow, calling, looking and in humans smiling," and which are activated when situations are perceived as dangerous or stressful (George & Solomon, 2008, p. 835). Care as manifested through the behavioral system is elevated through the earliest years, but requires less direct supervision as the child's internal working model is strengthened and a goal-corrected partnership is elaborated. Psychological processes of separation-individuation further affect the later toddler years.

There is no single way for a mother to provide the child with felt security. Caregiving behaviors take a multitude of forms among mothers of similar and different cultures and even among siblings with the same mother. Consistency and sensitivity to the child's individuality facilitates the evolution of an internal working model of the caregiver as trustworthy and the self as worthy of the caregiver's support (Ainsworth, 1954, 1985, 1989). The importance of sensitive parental input is revealed in the significant concordance between the mother's attachment pattern and the child's (van IJzendoorn, 1995; see Chapter 3 for further detail).

George and Solomon (2008) suggest that the concepts of coherence, balance, and flexibility capture the important elements of the caregiving behavioral system. The representations of mothers of secure children are flexible, balanced, and integrated and mothers of insecure children are more likely to have caregiving representations that are not flexible, sensitive, integrated, or insightful (see Chapter 3). Bowlby (1980) conceptualizes the underlying processes in producing these differences as a result of specific and consistent unconscious methods of excluding the processing of relational information and the maintaining of related memories. He refers to these as defenses which he defines as "an exclusion from further processing of information of certain specific types for relatively long periods or even permanently" (p. 45).

There are three forms of exclusion relevant to attachment: deactivation, cognitive disconnection, and segregated system (Bowlby, 1980; George & Solomon, 2008). In deactivation the mother uses repression to reduce anxieties about safety and loss in a relationship by attenuating the importance of the relational connection. This mechanism entails a depreciation of the importance of both the mother's caregiving and the child's attachment. Although these mothers can be responsible and view themselves as caring, they often oversee their children from a psychological distance and feel more comfortable allowing others to care for their children. This is a mother who may emphasize the negative aspects of the relationship and readily admits, "I am not a good mother," "This child is doing horribly." Mothers of avoidant children use defensive exclusion heavily.

Cognitive disconnection separates events from affect (Bowlby, 1980). The event and accompanying affect are neither fully remembered nor excluded. Ambivalence in the mother-child relationship is handled by denying anger toward the child and acknowledging only the loving aspects. Negative affect (anger) is directed toward herself or another caregiver, such as a teacher. These mothers assert close physical and psychological oversight; this allows for closeness and the positive aspects of the mother-child connection. However, they cannot psychologically separate from their child's discomforts or their own parenting failures in that process. They often express intense guilt and anxiety over the child's safety and lament their inability to control situations to ensure the child's safety (George & Solomon, 2008). Mothers who use cognitive disconnection prominently in their attachment to the child are more likely to have children with anxious ambivalent attachment styles.[2] Mothers of avoidant children often invest in exploratory and affiliative systems, encouraging personal achievement and/or being with friends and spend less time in more intimate caregiving interactions. In comparison, mothers of ambivalent children are overly focused on caregiving activities at the expense of allowing the exploratory and affiliative systems to flourish (George & Solomon, 2008).

The most pathological exclusion is the use of segregated systems (Bowlby, 1980). It involves a traumatic history that has resulted in the repression of these memories and/ or their associated emotions from conscious awareness. Sometimes a mother may be very aware of traumatic memories, but have no control over their intrusion into consciousness and into relationships (Fraiberg et al., 1975). Chaotic external environments also can accentuate the mother's feelings of being overwhelmed and she abdicates caregiving responsibilities almost entirely. These mothers are unable to protect their children physically and psychologically, leaving these children vulnerable for a disorganized attachment and at risk for later emergence of psychopathology (George & Solomon, 2008). Often kinship adoption comes about through the abdication of caregiving by the biological mother. These children need a great deal of help from adoptive parents and other professionals to compensate for effects of the biological mother's abdication.

In the traditional stable nuclear family the infant initially appears to attach to the mother. However, Bowlby recognized that the child had the capacity for multiple attachments, although these are hierarchically organized with distinct preferences particularly when distressed. This hierarchical arrangement with preference for a primary attachment figure if available is referred to as *monotropy*. From an evolutionary perspective monotropism is adaptive in that it often "takes a village" to keep a child safe (Cassidy, 2008). The loss of a primary attachment figure, either temporarily or permanently, allows for substitution without significant disruption to ongoing development, as demonstrated in Anna Freud's and Sophie Dann's (1951) experiment with the orphaned Holocaust children.[3] The monotropic child when in danger can have an automatic reaction to seek the primary attachment. Bowlby's model suggests some plasticity in the child's ability to overcome the deprivation of attachment figures and be receptive to multiple caretakers in institutionalization. The theory also accounts for how a child can form a new primary attachment when moved from a foster placement to a permanent adoptive family. It offers us considerable hope in the child's capacity to tap available attachment figures to achieve safety and provide healthy models for appropriate relationships and intimate connection. Although not without sequillae, Dora appears also to utilize her adoptive parents to form a new somewhat secure attachment.

Bowlby's theory incorporated his (and Ainsworth's) observations of stable families and speculation gleaned from his experience with institutionalized children. Together they provide a backdrop for understanding the ontogeny of attachment and the outer limits of its plasticity. We can make some generalizations about the timing of adoption and how the various arrangements prior to adoption might affect the child's ability to develop secure attachments to the adoptive family and later healthy representations of intimate relationships. Utilizing Bowlby's model, George and Solomon's caregiving system, and our clinical experience we offer our advice in considering the impact of two important variables, the timing of adoption and the pre-adoptive caregiving arrangements (institutionalization and foster parenting).

Bowlby offers a model for the significance of the timing of adoption. While even an adoption at birth involves a disruption of relationship, the effects in terms of attachment are less significant than if the adoption occurs later. Bowlby's theory and observations suggest that the earlier the adoption, the better chance that the child will have in developing healthy attachments. Sometimes the professionals and prospective adoptive parents have some options in terms of the adoption timing; for example, the benefits of early placement should be recognized in this regard. Bowlby's theory suggests that it is incumbent on us to advocate for the earlier date, to make a fuss when administrative delays might be avoided or overcome irritation to complete those additional forms expeditiously despite the appearance of duplication. In that period from nine months on, every month of delay adds further risk for greater difficulties in the attachment process. In the second 6 months of life the child is attempting to attach to a primary figure. Loss of that figure is akin to the death of a parent, which we know has significant and long-term psychological effects. Around the 1-year mark, patterns of attachment become more enduring. If the child has formed a secure connection, the possibility of another is more likely. However, if an alternative or less secure attachment style becomes preferred, it will take considerably more work to help the child alter it.

Timing generally interacts with type of placement prior to adoption. The most common arrangements for the infant after birth and before adoption are institutions and foster care. Most of the time prospective parents do not have choices about where the child is placed and are generally helpless to alter what other governments have sanctioned. However, with private adoptions both domestically and abroad, often some choice exists. At the point of a specific match, adoptive parents may be able to persuade involved lawyers and social agencies of their wishes and willingness to pay for private foster care, which is almost always superior to institutional care in terms of nurturing secure attachment.

This advantage is particularly significant if children are likely to remain in that arrangement after the 6-month mark. Large institutional settings have multiple care workers each of whom care for many infants. Physical care is a priority with little time to acknowledge the child who reaches out, smiles, or vocalizes. Plagued with too many duties, workers may subtly reinforce the child who needs little. They also may ignore the child who appears not to be satisfied. They do not have time to encourage those subtle and interactively reinforcing interchanges that occur a multitude of times during the day between mother and child or to quell the anxiety of a fussy child. Children adopted from an institutional setting need adoptive parents who recognize and acknowledge the emotional deprivations that this child had to endure. The kind of attachment strategy that the children developed was most adaptive given their temperament and environmental circumstances. This developed style then interacts with parents' attachment styles.

Professionals can be helpful in this regard aiding parents to recognize the co-constructions of attachment. For example, with an adoptive child, such as Dora, who has an avoidant style, the parents may mistake her lack of emotion over separations as a healthy development. The usual markers of overt anxiety and crying that alert the parent to the child's internal anxiety are missing. Dora's parents appeared to be sensitive to this, when they offered her a mattress in their room, despite her initial refusal and allowed her use it on her own terms. Likewise parents who themselves embrace more avoidant (deactivation) defenses concerning impending separations may become frustrated or impatient with an older child who comes to them with an anxious resistant attachment style. They may wonder why the child fusses over even brief separations when the child can cognitively appreciate that the parents will return in a few hours. Frank and Rowe (2000) suggested that parents can benefit from experiential training about the manifestations of various attachment strategies (Bonovitz, 2000; also see Chapter 8 for further discussion).

Foster care offers the possibility of caregiver-infant mutual exchanges. Toddlers coming from these settings fare far better than those coming from institutions. As Bowlby would predict, foster care offers more opportunity for the child to experience parental sensitivity and to be reinforced for healthy age appropriate interactive strategies. These infants are most often able to form secure attachments to their caregivers, although the child could develop a proclivity for avoidance or ambivalence. As with Dora, the problem is more often that the loss of an attachment figure when adoption occurs will lead to a depressive state with the child manifesting protest and despair. Adoptive parents will need to be patient with mourning the loss of this connection. Some adoptive parents attempt to deal with this loss by maintaining a connection with the foster parent. While there are many reasons why this may be a good idea, adoptive parents should not underestimate the intensity of the loss no matter what efforts are made to maintain this connection. Occasional contact cannot obviate the loss of the primacy of this relationship.

EGO PSYCHOLOGY AND THE SIGNIFICANCE OF ADAPTATION

Ego psychologists such as Heinz Hartmann (1958) focused on *adaptation*, or the way a child's innate potentials or *autonomous ego functions* (perception, language, attention, memory, concentration, motor coordination, and thinking) naturally unfold when nurtured in a suitable environment; an infant is born with the ability to adapt. Although Hartmann did not make any reference to adoption per se, his theoretical focus on adaptive capacities laid important groundwork for viewing the child's adaptation to his environment. The concept of ego strength, or resiliency, became the benchmark in assessing competence or mental health by evaluating a person's ego functioning. A child who is less caught up in conflict from trauma, anxiety, or depression is better able to adapt to his or her environment. Through Hartmann's lens, the critical goal with any child, but particularly with an adopted child, is to increase adaptation to his environment. When a child loses all that is familiar, the child struggles to adapt to the new situation. Luckily, we are wired to seek the best adaptation possible, even though any given response may not be the best from an outsider's perspective. A child's response to the loss of the familiar environment may be to turn inward, which might happen when a child is placed with a new family. In the case of Dora, we see her psychological disconnection as an adaptive protective response to the fears of further loss. When she enters school and is still not engaged this previously adaptive response is no longer one that is conducive to learning and connecting with her peers.

Anna Freud (1963) added another perspective: She assessed ego functioning from the vantage point of a *developmental line*, or a continuum that had endpoints for such traits as self-reliance, responsibility, and sociability. Unevenness in a child's development might result from points of regression or arrest, which was considered a risk factor for any child. The goal then is to get such a child "back on track" of normal development (Kennedy & Moran, 1991). Stress is often the culprit causing regression, which is most often considered to be pathological. Many late-placed adopted children, who have weathered the stressors of mistreatment and neglect prior to their adoption, may appear quite regressed or younger than their chronological age. It is important to understand this regression as a manifestation of the psychological deprivation that the child endured in his past environment, along with the impact of the dislocation from being moved from one placement to the next. An example of this type of regressive experience is illustrated in the example of Dora. Separations were difficult for Dora, who declined to go to camp and preferred to be mostly at home, and during one long separation from her mother at age 6, Dora's regression took shape in her pretending to be a baby and drink from a baby bottle. She also resisted contact with her mother. Likely this avoidance allowed her to deny her fears of loss. In later separations, Dora was able to transform that regression into a more adaptive response using her mother's coffee cup as a transitional object—a symbolic soothing emotional link to her mother that helped her cope.

Anna Freud and her colleagues studied children in their natural settings before and during World War II. One of the most interesting of these naturalistic "experiments" referred to earlier in this chapter was the study of a group of six young concentration camp orphans who lost their parents soon after their birth. These orphaned children adapted by becoming attached to their companions and not any adult. Freud and Dann's (1951) experiment points to both the adaptive resiliency of these children (who later went on to have their own families) and the strength of sibling attachment. This study supports the importance of keeping siblings together in foster care and adoption placements.

CONTRIBUTIONS OF D. W. WINNICOTT

Winnicott believed "if an adoption goes well, then the story is an ordinary human one, and we must be familiar with the upsets and setbacks of the ordinary human story in its infinite variations if we are to understand the problems that specially belong to adoption" (Winnicott, 1954b, p. 53). For Winnicott, the human story begins by accommodating to the infant's needs by a good enough mother.

The Good Enough Mother

No parents, whether biological or adoptive, are always able to know exactly what their child needs or how to provide a perfectly safe environment. Winnicott believed that when the environment is good enough in providing an infant with "good enough mothering" the infant's healthy development is facilitated. He held that an infant's primary needs were for relatedness and emotional responsiveness. These needs were considered to be central and it was the parent's responsibility to accommodate to the needs of the infant. Winnicott viewed the emotional development of the infant exclusively in terms of the child's relationship with his mother. He is most often quoted for his famous saying "there is no such thing as an infant" without its mother, meaning that "the infant and the maternal care together form a unit" (1960a, p. 587).

Holding to Provide Good Enough Maternal Care

Winnicott's term "good enough mother" describes the natural parenting function of responding to the baby. He believed that the foundations of the baby's mental health are initially laid down through the mother's ordinary devotion to her baby's physical needs, through holding, feeding, changing, and bathing the baby. According to Winnicott (1960a) the physical holding of the infant is a form of affectionate loving that helps the infant feel a basic sense of protection, safety, and security. Swaddling infants tightly allows them to feel held and safe. To feel held has both literal and figurative meaning. Holding is an essential part of bonding that fosters the baby's integration and a solid sense of self. A basic function of the "holding environment" is to reduce "impingements" coming from the outside world in order to protect the baby from feeling overwhelmed (Winnicott, 1960a).

Holding Adopted Children

Applying Winnicott's idea of holding to an adopted family, Nickman (2004, pp. 337–339) described four ways that parents can "hold" their adopted child. His helpful suggestions are summarized below:

1. It is important for adoptive parents to recognize and understand what their child may be communicating by means of a "symptom" or some action such as running away. In that case, holding becomes the parent's way to contain their child's anger, which might be manifested in stealing or any kind of destructiveness that can be understood as a result of the adopted child's deprivation. For example, Dora initially rejected her parents offer to stay in their room. By allowing Dora to use or not use the mattress next to their bed, they recognized and held both her anger and fear over losing her foster mother, while supporting the attachment to her new adoptive parents.
2. Because many adopted children anxiously "test" their parents to be sure they are wanted, the adoptive parents' continued determination not to be discouraged by their child's expressions of rejection, anger, and/or confusion is considered an important form of holding.
3. It is imperative for the adoptive parent to be able to hold the "discontinuities" of an adopted child's life until he or she is able to later integrate them for him- or herself and form a meaningful coherent narrative. Nickman compared this type of holding to "applying a plaster cast until the bones heal" (p. 339).
4. Holding may take the form of "affect tolerance" whereby the adoptive parents carry on a continuing "dialogue" with their child over the years about the various aspects of their adoptive experience. An example of this is when an adoptive parent comforts and talks with her adopted child about her fears about being "kidnapped" by her birth parents.

Holding serves a critical function for all babies, but especially for an adopted baby who may be more vulnerable to difficulties in forming a strong and cohesive self. A good enough mother provides an emotionally responsive holding environment that nurtures and fosters a firm and solid sense of both the baby's ego and the baby's body (Winnicott, 1960a). Once the child has developed a basic feeling of trust and safety in his environment, he is then later capable of being psychologically alone, which is essential to a healthy sense of self. Paradoxically, the ability to be alone develops through the very experience of mother and baby "being together" (Winnicott, 1958).

The Importance of the Transitional Object With Adoptive Children

Clare Winnicott worked with homeless children during the war. Kanter (2000) brought to light her unpublished 1947 case notes detailing her work placing a foster child in an adoptive home. Her notes illustrated how she supported the child's use of a toy duck in the transition to a new home. She described this phenomenon in detail below:

"The moment of uprooting is just when a skilled child-care officer is needed to see that what a child clings to in the past is brought with him and accepted in the new environment . . . there are many stories, which now, it is hoped, belong to another era, of children clinging to their own clothes and being given an anesthetic to enable the clothes to be removed, or favourite but filthy teddy-bears and other possessions being taken away and burned, but these did not belong to the past, and something became damaged and lost when the familiar things were taken away. These possessions stood for everything the child brought with him from the past and he could not afford to lose so much." (Kanter 2000, p. 255)

Donald Winnicott (1953) alerted us to the importance of the "transitional object." The most well-known transitional object is a child's teddy bear or security blanket. Winnicott observed that the transitional object develops between 4 and 12 months of age and allows the baby to increasingly engage with the outside world, helping the child cope with and master the crucial task of separation. The child often develops an intense attachment to his blanket or stuffed animal because it helps him feel more control over anxiety as he moves from one emotional stage to another. The teddy bear or blanket provides soothing comfort to the child, and can serve as a protection against anxiety or loneliness especially when the child is falling asleep. Attachment to these objects diminishes gradually as the child begins to internalize a capacity for self-soothing, safety, and symbolization. The child's special attachment to his or her teddy bear or blanket needs to be accepted and understood by his parents as symbolically representing the child's emotional tie to his mother. As the child increasingly separates from her mother for longer periods of time, this special object helps the child evoke and maintain a mental image of her mother in her absence. Paradoxically, the transitional object can best be understood as the child's attempt to stay connected to her mother while also trying to separate. The blanket or teddy bear serves as a tool to help the child be alone in her mother's absence. The use of a transitional object (coffee cup) was an important coping strategy for Dora during her mother's week-long absence. Each night, Dora filled her mother's favorite coffee cup with water and took it to her room.

The importance of transitional objects for the late-adopted child cannot be overestimated as it serves a critical function, especially in the case where there are multiple caretakers or when the child is transferred from one placement to another. Parents should refrain from taking away this important object from their children, who might become distressed if their favorite blanket is even washed or changed in any way. The need for a transitional object can reappear at any age when stress or deprivation threatens, because these objects represent a way to recapture the safety and security of childhood and provide a special way of coping especially during times of upheaval. For the adopted child who has lived through the turmoil of multiple placements and severed connections, fears of rejection can intensify anxiety and insecurity and result in the reappearance of transitional objects past the chronological age at which these objects are usually relinquished. It is imperative for parents to resist the pressure to take away the child's special object so he can "grow up and stop acting like a baby" and insist that she give up that teddy bear or thumb sucking. Usually, when the child feels secure the need for the object will disappear. Thus when Dora's mother returned she no longer needed to drink out of her coffee cup.

Holding and Surviving Hateful Feelings

As a pediatrician, Winnicott wanted to free mothers from feeling guilty over expected hostile feelings or resentments they might harbor toward their babies. Winnicott (1949) spelled out the many reasons why a mother would come to have "hateful feelings" toward her baby. Like Klein and Mahler, Winnicott highlights the critical function that aggression serves in the process of separation. After being moved from her foster placement to her adoptive home, when Dora played with her dolls she often pulled them part and ripped their clothes enacting her anger and helplessness over the loss of her foster mother.

Winnicott understood the importance to the child of his mother's serving as a target for the child's aggression ("object mother") and then surviving the child's aggression. Survival is crucial. A mother who cannot tolerate her child being angry with her and consequently withdraws, or retaliates in response to her child's anger, leaves her child vulnerable to feeling too powerful, too aggressive, and fearful about his or her own destructive potential. A child needs to be aware of his impact on others, but should not have to worry about his mother's survival. Paradoxically, a mother's ability to withstand her child's hateful feelings actually allows for a healthier connection between them. Winnicott (1949) believed that only by finding and reaching the mother's hate could her child be convinced of her love. This idea is most applicable to the dilemma of the adopted child about whom Winnicott (1949) felt would inevitably "test" the adoptive parents' limits in order to seek *proof* that he or she would still be loved and wanted. Dora pushed away her mother's attempts to hug and kiss when the mother was leaving to go out of town and then rejected her gifts when the mother returned.

Winnicott understood the difficulties of adopting a child with a prior history of problems. In the case of late placement adoptions, he was concerned that adoptive parents would blame themselves and feel responsible for the environmental failures that occurred previous to the child's adoption. For an adoptive parent of a late placement child whose early environment had not been good enough, Winnicott (1954b) felt that the mother becomes more like a therapist to a deprived child. In other words, the adoptive parents are "called upon to provide treatment rather than ordinary child care" (1954b, p. 55). This is certainly not an easy task for any parent to take on.

Similar to a therapist, the adoptive parent of a child raised in an orphanage or who has been through multiple foster placements offers herself to be "used" in order to provide her child with the environmental experiences that he or she initially missed. An adoptive parent of a late placement child is afforded an opportunity to provide her child with a new facilitating environment with good enough mothering and holding that the child missed in his earlier environment

The Role of Mirroring

Winnicott (1971) coined the term *mirroring*, which is a crucial aspect of a mother's responsiveness to her baby—and fundamental in the development of the self. In mirroring, the baby looks at the mother's face and sees herself and then feels recognized. For Winnicott the mirror symbolizes the loving gaze of the mother and for Kohut (1971) the "gleam in the mother's eye." The good enough mother's pleasure in her baby is reflected in her face, so that the baby sees the mother's loving expression and consequently feels loveable and good. Through mirroring, the baby looks into the mother's face, a kind of mirror, and sees itself. The mother's role is to give back to the baby the baby's own self. "*When I look I am seen, so I exist*" (Winnicott, 1971, p. 114). It would be a rarity for an adopted child who started her early life in an orphanage to be mirrored in the way Winnicott described.

KOHUT AND THE DEVELOPMENT OF SELF-ESTEEM

Heinz Kohut (1971, 1977) focused on relationships and the development of a cohesive sense of self, with an emphasis on understanding the development of healthy self-esteem and pathological narcissism. Kohut believed that all of us have normal "narcissistic" needs for recognition and that *selfobjects* (persons or things "used" to foster self-esteem and a sense of well-being) are needed throughout life to help in the maintenance of self-esteem and self-cohesion. Kohut (1971) believed that parents served special functions as selfobjects for their developing child, and that a *cohesive self* can only emerge from a relationship with empathically responding selfobjects. Empathy is a central Kohutian concept. Problems in empathy can arise from a parent's own self-deficiencies or when the ability to parent is excessively strained or overwhelmed by their child's needs. This can easily happen with a physically handicapped child, or with an adopted child whom the parents feel is too challenging or difficult, especially when the child continues to test whether his adoptive parents will reject him. Kohut believed that the need for empathy and recognition continues throughout life, not just childhood. Like Winnicott, Kohut linked the development of the self to maternal responsiveness and mirroring, but he added twinship and idealization as two additional functions essential for self-development. For a child to develop healthy self-esteem and a healthy sense of self, the child needs to have their self-worth mirrored and reflected back by an empathic caregiver (selfobject). A child's joy in riding his tricycle should be recognized and enjoyed by her parent (mirroring). A child also needs to feel connected to others who are similar to her (twinship) and to be able to idealize and identify with admired figures. Kohut (1977) believed that there needed to be a crucial balance or *optimal frustration* (a kind of optimal responsiveness) to a child's needs. In other words, it is essential to have a *balance*, neither chronic misattunement nor failure to meet a child's needs nor an overindulging gratification of the child's needs.

A core sense of the child's self is thus formed through the responsiveness of the parents (selfobjects), similar to Winnicott's idea of the holding environment and good enough mothering. Parents who are chronically indifferent or unresponsive to their children create lower self-esteem and narcissistic problems in their children. Kohut emphasized the importance of mirroring, idealizing, and twinship. The empathically responsive parent/selfobject mirrors by approving and admiring their child (Kohut & Wolf, 1978). Children who have been raised in orphanages are not likely to have been mirrored and so there is a real hunger for it from the adoptive parents. Every child needs to look up to a parent who he admires and feels protected by. Adoptive parents should permit and enjoy their child's idealization, because it is an important emotional experience for a child to feel that his mother or father is "perfect" and that the child is a part of that perfect parent. This connection is critical for an adopted child who is more vulnerable to feeling different from his parents. Physical dissimilarity between a child and his adopted parents can lead to a feeling of alienation. A crucial role for the parent is to empathically respond to *both* the child's needs for mirroring and idealizing. The third function of twinship is the need to be connected to someone the child feels is just like themselves—for example, a kindred spirit, soul mate, or twin.

In adopted children the twin fantasy is especially potent: The child longs to have somebody he or she resembles, a person to whom the child is genetically linked. In older childhood and adolescence, the yearning for a biological connection intensifies. For the adopted parent, coming to terms with issues surrounding "difference" is also important as these feelings are often related to loss. According to Watkins & Fisher (1993), "Adoptive parents do not have the experience of seeing themselves "physically mirrored"—seeing their own traits and talents as they would with a biological child. However, as Watkins and Fisher point out, through the "identifications that [naturally] emerge with love and attachment," the emphasis on physical resemblances begins to fade and other attributes such as a similar laugh or smile or sense of humor are shared between adoptive parents and their children" (p. 16).

The unmirrored (unrecognized or unadmired) self of childhood, from which so many children in orphanages suffer, continues in the form of a desperate search for someone to admire and affirm them and this someone could be the adoptive parent. Adoptive parents can serve the selfobject function of the mirroring and idealized parent, addressing the child's unfinished developmental needs for mirroring and affirmation. The child can now have another chance to get the things he or she may have missed. For the adopted child, however, there often is a double task: The child not only searches for a perfect parent to admire and be like, or for the perfect twin to feel connected to, but also in some cases, he or she may actually search for his or her birth parents and/or biological siblings whom he or she in reality resembles and to whom he or she is genetically connected.

MENTALIZATION: HOLDING THE ADOPTED CHILD IN MIND

The capacity for mentalization defined by Peter Fonagy and his colleagues evolves out of the secure attachment relationship between mother and child as well as the child's exploration of the *mind* of the caregiver. In other words, the mother's capacity to keep her child "*in mind*" then makes it possible for her child to discover his own mind. Another way to think about mentalization is holding mind in mind, as well as the "need to feel that one exists in the other's mind" and as "a need to feel that the other in whose mind you exist is also emotionally responsive"(Stern, 2009, p. 706). Children who are securely attached to their parents learn naturally about their caregiver's intentional stance and mental states.

Fonagy, Gergely, Jurist, and Target (2002) stress both the capacity to *mentalize* and regulate emotion as two important factors in determining successful development of the child. They define mentalization as a *theory of mind*, usually developed by age 4; it is the ability to make and use mental representations of their own and other people's emotional states. Recent neuroscience research has linked *mirror neurons* with "mind reading," or how one understands the mental states of another person. "In a kind of unconscious communication, mother and child unconsciously pick up and respond to subtle cues from each other which activate the neural patterns shared by both" (Gallese, Eagle, & Migone, 2007). Peter Fonagy and his colleagues (2002) further elaborate on mirroring by describing the importance of *contingent and marked mirroring* as part of establishing a secure attachment bond with the mother. Gallese et al. (2007) caution that the term mirroring can be misleading because the mother does not literally mirror the baby's behavior. If she sees her baby crying she does not also start crying (an "unmarked" response that reflects contagion rather than the empathic attunement the baby needs). In other words, it is best for a mother not to show her baby her own feelings; but instead strive to reflect her empathic awareness of the baby's own experience. A mother's ability to "match" her infant's mental states allows her infant to develop an understanding of its own mind as well as the minds of others. The biological basis for this matching or attunement is the mirror neuron system. Although the mirror system is a *hardwired universal* process, Gallese and others (Gallese et al., 2007) believe that there is a wide range of individual differences in the capacity to understand and empathize with others. Severe deprivation or trauma experienced by an adopted child in her early environment can undermine the acquisition of mentalization, just as inadequate parenting can lead to an insecure attachment style that leaves the child unable to either modulate or interpret his own feelings or the feelings of others (Fonagy, 2001).

Gilmore (2008) believes that adoption can interfere with the development of mentalization and in a striking overgeneralization, compares adoption with abuse and neglect. She states that "adoption poses the impossible challenge of thinking about unthinkable decisions by the people who are assumed to unconditionally love and cherish the child" (p. 380). She believes that the absent biological mother, a kind of "*hole object*," is both "present yet absent, incomprehensible and inexpressible" (p. 381). She implies that "reflection is *not* possible because the abandonment exceeds comprehension and containment. In other words, she concludes that the absent biological mother creates forever a "black hole" in the mind of the adopted individual. Gilmore believes that a major source of anxiety for the adoptive parents is their fear that their adoptive child will seem "alien" to them, manifesting traits from the birth parents and not them. More specifically, Allen, Fonagy, and Bateman (2008) found that it was mismatched mirroring (rather than adoption per se) that could generate an alien internal experience in a child, which could contribute to a fragmented sense of self. The problem with Gilmore's assertions is that she is positing that deficits in mentalization exist in an entire population of adopted children. She ignores the fact that most adopted children (especially those adopted at birth) have already formed an attachment to their adoptive parents by the time they grasp the reality of their relinquishment and this attachment helps provide a "container" for their pain and sadness surrounding loss.

Fonagy et al. (2002) believe that difficulties in mentalization result from an absence of *contingent* and *marked* mirroring by caregivers during the child's early development, referred to previously. Mirroring can go awry when the mother fails to "mark" her baby's feeling state, or incorrectly mirrors the baby's experience (noncontingent mirroring). They give the following example of noncontingent mirroring. A mother notices her baby's frustration, but expresses her anger at the baby instead of responding to the baby's frustration. Her anger overwhelms the baby and increases the baby's arousal instead of the more helpful response of containing and soothing the baby. Another example of an inaccurate reflection of the baby's experience or a noncontingent response is when a mother inaccurately interprets her baby's excitement as anger. Parents who are themselves lacking in the ability to mentalize may easily become dysregulated by their infant's distress and then fail to distinguish between their own feelings and those of their children (Allen et al., 2008).

Developing a secure attachment is of primary importance for all parents, but especially for adoptive parents and their children. Fonagy and colleagues (Fonagy et al, 1991) believe "that this sense of safety, which evolves as part of an initially shared mental process between infant and caregiver, stays with the child as a relatively stable aspect of his mental functioning (p. 215). Allen and his colleagues (2008) believe that secure attachment can be enhanced through the establishment of a safe, consistent, and secure relationship and through the teaching of self-reflective or mentalization skills. Teaching mentalization or reflective functioning can be accomplished by helping the child make connections between his experience of relationships and the actual representation of these relationships, and by helping the child learn how to recognize, name, and regulate emotions. In his theory of pedagogy, Fonagy believes that mentalization skills could be adapted to help parents and children who have deficits in mentalization. For instance, a "mind-minded" parent is attentive to her child's feelings and is someone who helps reassure a child who is frightened in a way that helps restore a sense of safety for her child (Allen et al., 2008).

Fonagy viewed the transmission of trauma as an "interactive process whereby patterns of behavior are learned and re-enacted across generations . . . perpetuated by mentalizing failures that cascade across generations" (Allen et al., 2008, p. 347). Mentalizing is compromised in moments of high negative arousal which can "set in motion interactions characterized "by mutual efforts at control and coercion rather than cooperation and mutual recognition" (Slade, 2008, p. 318).

As mentioned previously, abuse and neglect undermine mentalization, and late placement children with a history of attachment trauma, disorganized attachment, and/or "mindblindness" are likely to experience "profound difficulty developing and making use of what they need most to heal: secure attachments" (Allen et al, 2008, p. 212), which is a secure attachment bond with an adoptive parent. Although there may be obstacles in a traumatized child forming a secure attachment bond with an adopted parent, there may still be room for optimism if the adopted child has not given up hope. Sharp and Fonagy (2008) developed ways to teach mentalization skills to parents. These particular skills are also referred to as maternal mind-mindedness, reflective functioning or parental mentalizing and focus on the parents' ability to treat their child as a "psychological agent." Sadler, Slade, and Mayes (2006) found that parents high in reflective functioning are able to see their child "as having needs, desires, and intentions that are different than [their] own" (p. 275), and can separate themselves from their own projections.

To help adoptive parents promote mentalization in their child, they first need to develop an interest and curiosity in understanding how their child's mind works and be able to make sense out of their child's experience, by drawing links between their child's behavior and his mental states. Parents need to be able and willing to reflect on their own intentions and to understand the motivations guiding their own behavior as well as their child's. Helping parents of adopted children learn how to apply mentalization skills in order to hold their adopted child in mind can be accomplished by what Slade (2008) described as helping parents "develop a reflective stance in relation to their child and to their own experience as parents, which will aid in fostering a stronger attachment between parents and their child" (Slade, 2008, p. 307). For example, adoptive parents can provide a safe, contained holding environment for their adopted child to be able to think, feel, and talk about their adoption experiences. Children who have been raised in orphanages or multiple foster placements with the help of their parents can begin to process their traumatic experiences of loss (e.g., hold trauma in mind). Dora and her mother were able to play with dolls as a way to help Dora mentalize her mother's absence. Similarly, in the adoption situation, Nickman (2004) found that "families in which parents were able to carry on some dialogue with their children about the various aspects of their adoptive experience were better able to equip them to deal with the world in which they were growing up (Nickman, 2004, p. 340). This open dialogue creates a mentalizing and holding environment that also helps a child tolerate affect.

SEPARATION-INDIVIDUATION AND THE CONTRIBUTIONS OF MARGARET MAHLER

Margaret Mahler, like Bowlby, was interested in the development of the child's representations of the self in relationship to the primary relationship and in how adaptation influenced these mental representations. Both Mahler and Bowlby (like Winnicott and Kohut) acknowledged the importance of the environment. However, whereas Bowlby placed more significance on how the external reality influenced the development of these representations, Mahler felt that the child's characteristics or temperament was important too (Coates, 2004). In her classic book *The Psychological Birth of the Human Infant* (Mahler, Pine, & Bergman, 1975), Mahler postulates three phases of development that emphasize the child's burgeoning internal capacity to differentiate herself from her maternal representations: autism, symbiosis, and separation-individuation. This process that spans the first 3 or 4 years of life permits development of object constancy, an internal psychological state that enables the child to have and hold an image of the primary caregiver in his or her physical absence. Since Mahler's original theory postulation, the existence and timing of the first two phases, autism and symbiosis, have become controversial and seem to be in direct contradiction to the wealth of empirical information from current infant research on attachment theory (Blum, 2004). Thus, we focus only on the last phase, separation-individuation, as it is grounded in her detailed observations, is conceptually useful for the adoptive parents in understanding the behavior and struggles of their growing child, and provides understanding beyond what attachment theory offers. In particular, we concentrate on the practicing, rapprochement, and object constancy subphases.

Mahler assumed that the process of separation was psychologically and physically ensconced within the unfolding of attachment and connection. The child's accomplishment of this process occurred as a result of a mother-child negotiated dance with goals of autonomy and intimacy. Both parties would be required to compromise wishes, but the child most probably would be capable of more significant adaptation than the mother. "The child molds and unfolds in the matrix of the mother-infant dual unit. Whatever adaptations the mother may make to the child . . . the child's fresh and pliable adaptive capacity and his need for adaptation (in order to gain satisfaction) is far greater than that of the mother" (Mahler, 1963, quoted in Mahler et al., 1975, p. 5).

In Bowlby's model of attachment, the exploratory and attachment behavioral systems are in dynamic equilibrium with each other. A wariness of attachment security would inhibit exploration. In Mahler's conceptualization of the practicing subphase, exploration is a more articulated phase-specific set of behaviors ushered in by the development of locomotion. Walking allows for physical separation and exploration that had not been previously available to the child. The delights and hazards of this new accomplishment were also not contemplated by the mother. Thus a new equilibrium of mutual regulation must be negotiated (Blum, 2004). In this period from 9 to 18 months, the child is less focused on the mother and experiences effects of elation and joy. There is intense focus on physical skill mastery and exploration (Bergman & Fahey, 2011). Periods of momentary contact with the mother occur: The child fills up with maternal supplies, emotionally "refueling," and then turns attention again to the exciting and new world (Pine, 2004). The mother's task is to oversee the environment for safety. She then must accept her child's seeming dismissal of her importance and take pride in his or her exploration. Yet, she must remain psychologically available without intruding and ready in a flash to step in if real physical danger emerges. Some mothers are better at this than others.

Children adopted before 6 months are likely to be close to a normal schedule for the practicing subphase. However, children adopted after 1 year are likely to be delayed in their timetable for practicing. They are likely to require more security with their new primary caregivers before they revisit the practicing subphase. As the child physically matures he or she becomes capable of more extensive exploration and locomotion. If parents are older (see Chapter 6) or in some way less capable of keeping the bigger, quicker, stronger child safe, the parent may have anxiety and the child frustration. Thus, the practicing subphase may not be as joyful for either party as might normally be the case.

The obliviousness that the child exhibits during the practicing subphase is replaced by a more clinging and demanding demeanor as rapprochement commences. Vacillation between the child's "shadowing" the mother and darting away from her often makes it appear to the mother that the child is sending mixed messages. It seems as if the child wants to involve the mother and share with her, but only on his or her terms. The child wants to recapture the relatively symbiotic form of intimacy previously enjoyed with the mother but fears the loss of autonomy and the emerging separate identity; this is the intrapsychic conflict behind the toddler's opposing behavioral vacillations. Over the course of 18 to 30 months, despite coercive efforts to maintain the mother as a narcissistic extension of the self, he or she also learns the "mother tongue," by becoming aware that the mother has her own independent interests and wishes (Blum, 2004). It is a stressful and distressing period for both the mother and child. Although this behavioral ambitendency of clingy distress and rejection of the mother's efforts appears similar to Bowlby's anxious/ambivalent attachment, Mahler conceptualizes this pattern as an age-related developmental phenomenon necessary for the resolution of the conflict of a need for oneness and a desire to cling and the push for autonomy and maintenance of the perception of separateness (Pine, 2004). With the affectionate and empathic respect for separateness and yet availability to intercede for safety, the mother and child will survive the experience and the child will attain a sense of separateness even in the presence of the mother.

Dora exhibits many aspects of a child struggling with rapprochement. Even though 6, her late adoption would predict this delayed developmental trajectory. While the initial separation leads to regression (drinking the bottle), in later separations, Dora pushes away attempts at contact, yet drinks from the mother's favorite coffee cup. The child's overt rejections of the mother's affections, calls, and gifts at the same time as she incorporates her mother's habit of drinking water in a favorite item of her mother's are signs that the child is either reliving or still experiencing the conflicts of rapprochement. The rapprochement "challenge" is to endure the omnipotent aggressive responses while sustaining love for the child (Blum, 2004; Parens, 1980). The child's incorporation of the mother's habits and use of her things, yet rejection of her gifts reveal a new level of "I and you and I versus you" (Bergman & Fahey, 2011). She wants to be close to the mother, but only on her terms as she demands a specific doll. Although the mother initially felt rejected, she worked with her own therapist around this issue. Once the mother understood the meaning of the mixed messages and the child's struggle she was able to deal with her own rejection and be available to Dora.

The child's capacity for language is helpful in this case. Despite the child's rejection, the mother attempts to talk with Dora about her absence and associated feelings. She articulated her own feelings from the separation and how she was able to live with them. The mother and Dora played with dolls together, reenacting the separation. The mother let Dora direct the separations and verbalize what the babies felt and what the mother felt. With subsequent separations, the child was less rejecting of the mother before leaving and after returning. However, while the mother was away, Dora still preferred to have little contact. The mother's texting strategy allowed Dora control over whether she responded. As Bergman put it, "The shared moments of mother's understanding and acknowledging the child's burning desire to be present in the mother's mind help to bridge the gap of separateness" (Bergman & Fahey, 2011, p. 21).

The final stage of separation-individuation is object constancy, the capacity of the child around 3 years of age to engage in autonomous activities and carry the mother with her. Both affectionate and negatively charged aspects of maternal representation are integrated into the mother's image. The relationship is not severed because of maternal disappointment or frustration. The explosion of language development and fantasy formation concomitant with object constancy enable the emergence of new levels of reciprocity and mutuality (Blum, 2004). Secure attachment is necessary but not sufficient to achieve individuation. Achievement of object constancy aids the child in the resolution between connection and attachment and autonomy and individuation.

PRACTICAL POINTS

- It is extremely important that prospective parents understand the usual time frame and nature of attachment and how the child's connections with the former and new family may be affected by the timing of the adoption.
- Transitional objects are particularly important for adoptive parents. During stressful times, attachment to a certain object like a teddy bear or blanket can help an adoptive child cope by recapturing a feeling of safety and security. Understanding the soothing function of a child's attachment to this object provides the rationale for the parents to allow them to persist even when children seem too old to have one. When a child is feeling more secure the need for this object will usually disappear.
- Depending on the age of adoption, children may be struggling with issues of attachment when peers are pushing for more autonomy. This may affect adoptive children of grade school age, wanting to have play dates at home instead of at others' homes. If the child is struggling with issues of attachment whether they are toddlers or of school age, they are not likely to be psychologically able to engage in exploring their environment.
- When a child whose attachment is less than secure pushes away, the natural tendency for a parent might be to similarly withdraw and feel rejected. This reaction is not helpful to the adopted child. Such behavior may represent the child's testing out whether he or she is wanted. It is best for the parent not to withdraw but to remain psychologically available and positive.
- Children who have been raised in orphanages have likely not had the critical experiences of mirroring and a secure attachment bond that promote mentalization. Teaching adoptive parents how to mirror and hold their child in mind would be important parenting skills, especially with adopted children who have suffered neglect and abuse.

CONCLUSIONS

In this chapter, we have outlined how some theoretical aspects of child development influence the mother-child relationship. The constructs of attachment, adaptation, holding, transitional objects, self-esteem, mentalization, and separation-individuation enable adoptive parents and their therapists to understand what underlies some of the child's behavior. These theories are important in helping therapists work with adoptive parents around developmental delays and in understanding how and why age of placement might disrupt the developmental trajectory. In the next chapter, some of the theoretical constructs discussed in this chapter, such as attachment, are given empirical validation with respect to their importance in healthy child development. Research on adoption outcomes and age of child adoption are explored.

NOTES

1. The exploratory system allows the child to learn about the environment. The fear/wariness system protects the child by eliciting fright when confronted with certain stimuli such as darkness and loud noises. The sociability system encourages the child to seek affiliation, not necessarily those figures with whom an attachment has developed. Interplay within these systems impinges on the attachment behavioral system. For example, when the attachment and wariness systems are minimally engaged, the exploratory and sociability systems can be activated.
2. In this strategy, the child's attachment and wariness behavioral systems are amplified as the child ambivalently vacillates between seeking close proximity and resisting it at the same time.
3. Freud and Dann worked with a group of children who had lost their parents before 1 year of age and had been living in Thereseinstadt at the end of the war. These children were cared for by multiple caretakers in the concentration camp who themselves were starved and tortured. In a remarkable story of the human spirit, these children survived and appeared to develop strong attachments to each other, which lessened the effect of loss as multiple caretakers cycled through their early lives.

Chapter 3

USING RESEARCH TO INFORM BEST PRACTICES IN WORKING WITH ADOPTIVE FAMILIES

Hal S. Shorey, Sanjay R. Nath, and Meridith Carter

As highlighted in the previous chapter on theoretical considerations in adoptive parent-child relationship formation, much of our understanding of the processes through which relationships are formed and children bond to their parents, whether the parents are biological or adoptive, comes to us through attachment theory (see Bowlby, 1988b). Yet, attachment and other theories relevant to the field of adoption have been studied by researchers with varying and sometimes discrepant perspectives, assessment tools, and research methodologies (Shorey & Snyder, 2006). Having an understanding of these methodologies is important to mental health professionals who operate as "local clinical scientists." From this perspective, using research to inform practice, professionals working in the field of adoption can (a) form tentative hypotheses about adoptive parents and their children, (b) test those hypotheses in the course of their intervention/placement efforts, and (c) use feedback to reformulate their decision making and interventions based on relevant data.

In considering how we frame problems and approach developing solutions, it also is important to consider the underlying biases and research preferences in our theoretical orientations and our professional disciplines. Theoretical orientations (e.g., psychodynamic, developmental, cognitive) influence our willingness to use research and what data we consider meaningful. In relation to our disciplines, the medical community focuses mainly on health and physical growth-related outcomes in adoption research whereas social scientists generally attend to cognitive, psychological, and behavioral factors. Even among social scientists, there are differences. Social psychologists tend to favor variable-centered research approaches (i.e., the relationships between constructs) using self-report instruments (see Sperling, Foelsch, & Grace, 1996). Clinical psychologists, in turn, emphasize the use of person-centered approaches including structured clinical interviews and behavioral observation and coding systems (see Main, 1996). These differences have resulted in what can be a disjointed literature that is difficult to put to use in applied settings. In this chapter, we address this issue by (a) reviewing the historical development of knowledge in the area of parent/child attachment, (b) exploring the research methods used and the conclusions that can be drawn from them, and (c) selectively reviewing research that is central to understanding the adoptive parent-child bonding process and outcomes for children and their adoptive parents.

THE HISTORY OF RESEARCH ON ATTACHMENT
AND PARENT-CHILD INTERACTIONS

The history of research on child outcomes relating to adoption, bonding, and attachment starts with the genesis of attachment theory (see Bowlby, 1969). In contrast to the theoretical perspective framed in Chapter 2 of this volume, our present discussion is designed to highlight the research methods used to derive the theory and generate knowledge in the field. This material should help mental health professionals become part of the tradition of generating meaningful knowledge and informing best practice through their regular interactions with children and their adoptive families.

Bowlby and the Observational Method

John Bowlby was a child psychiatrist who trained at the British Psychoanalytic Institute during a time when Melanie Klein and supporters of object relations theory were a dominant force (see Bretherton, 1992). In the course of his training, Bowlby became disillusioned with traditional psychoanalytic theory, which asserted that child psychopathology had its genesis in internal aggressive fantasies and libidinal drives. Bowlby countered that parental behaviors have a direct impact on the developing personality of the young child and that the resultant dispositions become imprinted within the structures of the central nervous system to become stable and enduring characteristics that shape thoughts, feelings, and behaviors across the lifespan.

An early exemplar of applied research was Bowlby's classic "44 Thieves" (1944) study. In this research work, Bowlby endeavored to identify the parental roots of childhood delinquency. The study demonstrates how objective measures can be combined with clinical records and observations to derive meaningful inferences on the causes and outcomes of childhood maladjustment: an approach that should be easily adopted by most mental health professionals working with adoptive families. In the study, children aged 5 to 14 were given the Stanford Binet intelligence test, along with a thorough psychiatric evaluation. A detailed social history was obtained through interviews with the child and the mother or mother substitute. School and other records also were considered and follow-up therapy notes were examined. The data gathered reflected Bowlby's advocacy of intensive investigation of intrapsychic and ecological factors, such as home conditions, in understanding any given individual.

Bowlby also used behavioral descriptions of each child (obtained from teachers, parents, etc.) and clinical data to facilitate a "rough" clinical classification of children in terms of *character types*. Because he had a control group, Bowlby was then able to differentiate the delinquent youth from nondelinquent youth in terms of the relative distribution of these character types. The most striking finding was that all of the 14 (of 88) youth classified as *affectionless* fell into the delinquent group. Bowlby described affectionless youth as lacking in affection or warmth for anyone, being solitary, undemonstrative, and unresponsive (either to kindness or to punishment). Of primary relevance to adoption, an examination of these children's life histories indicated a common theme wherein they experienced complete emotional loss of their mothers or mother substitute for an extended period of time during infancy.

In reflecting on these findings, Bowlby suggested that applied qualitative research is needed if we are to "tease out" the subtle outcomes relating to child/parent/environment interactions. Bowlby pointed out that large scale "academic" investigations using statistical analyses may overlook the many heterogeneous causes of maladjustment and artificially lump a group of behaviors into one category (e.g., "externalizing behaviors"). In support of larger studies, however, Bowlby also cautioned against making inferences from research that lacked comparison groups.

Early Measurement Issues in Attachment Research

Although statistical analyses were not used to test hypotheses in Bowlby's "44 Thieves" study, quantitative measures such as the Stanford Binet were used to match the research and control groups. Bowlby's study also highlighted the need for valid measures and measurement systems to accurately classify cases in terms of personality dispositions. In comparing groups, qualitative data is only as good as one's confidence that each group truly represents a discrete entity. Bowlby himself readily pointed out that his classification was "rough" and should be interpreted cautiously. He also recognized that personal interview data and self-reports obtained from maladjusted children were of questionable validity. Accordingly, Bowlby paid increasing attention to the reliable and detailed collection of observational data.

Bowlby's desire for methodological rigor grew in response to widely publicized works that did not adhere to scientific principles. In 1947, René Spitz galvanized public attention to the treatment of institutionalized children with the release of his silent film titled *Grief: A Peril in Infancy*. The film documented the experiences of hospitalized/institutionalized young children who developed "anaclitic depression" (lethargy, wasting, and retarded physical, psychomotor, and language skills) in response to a prolonged lack of social contact with a mother or mother surrogate. Although it garnered a great deal of public attention, Spitz's film was not influential from a research perspective because it lacked careful control or documentation of the conditions under which the filming took place. These latter criticisms were, however, addressed in a 1953 film by one of Bowlby's associates, James Robertson (see Bretherton, 1992).

Robertson was skilled in naturalistic observation because he had worked at Anna Freud's Hampstead residential nursery where he and all staff were required to take detailed notes of the children's behaviors (see Bretherton, 1992). When he was hired by Bowlby in 1948 to assist in observing hospitalized children who were separated from their parents, Robertson convinced Bowlby to let him film a documentary about the children's experiences. In anticipating criticism of their methods, however, Bowlby worked with Robertson to implement careful controls and document the filming/data acquisition process. For example, the filmed child was chosen at random and filming of the clock on the wall was proof of regular interval-time sampling.

Parent/Child Interactions as Predictors of Child Adjustment

When Mary Ainsworth came to London in 1950 and took a position as a researcher under Bowlby, she was charged with analyzing Robertson's data. Ainsworth was highly influenced by Robertson's observational abilities and records of the children's behaviors. She later applied these methods to her own pioneering research on how children bond to their parents (Ainsworth, 1963).

When she moved to Uganda after her time working under Bowlby, Ainsworth expanded the research and methods used to study parent/child bonding. She recruited 26 families with infants aged from birth to 24 months and observed them for 2 hours every 2 weeks for a period of 9 months. In her narrative account of this research, Ainsworth (1963) described how suspicious and reluctant her initial Ugandan participants were and how she interacted with them in a reciprocal fashion (providing nutritional and medical aid) in order to gain their trust and cooperation. Nevertheless, her efforts paid off and she eventually had more willing participants than she could accommodate.

Ainsworth's study holds many other lessons for adoption research. She demonstrated how to combine behavioral observations and interview data from the mothers to derive ratings of maternal sensitivity. Concurrently, she coded infant behaviors in interactions with their mothers. This enabled her to determine that in the course of 9 months of observation, 23 of the 28 infants became "attached" to their mother (i.e., the infant responded differentially to the mother relative to others in the environment). When Ainsworth returned to the United States, she built on her experience in Uganda through initiating a larger systematic research program that became known as the *Baltimore studies*. In Baltimore, she recruited families before the birth of their child and followed each family with regular home visits (18 in all) until the child was 54 weeks old. Rather than recording frequency counts of behavior, as is common in some forms of observational research, Ainsworth emphasized carefully documenting meaningful behavior patterns as they occurred in context. In this way, she identified striking individual differences in how sensitive, appropriate, and prompt mothers were in attending to their infants' signals and how the infants responded in turn to the mothers.

As a result of the aforementioned research, Ainsworth went on to develop the well-known Strange Situation Procedure. This procedure, with its standardized protocol and coding system, facilitated the reliable classification of the three attachment "styles" commonly known as *secure, anxious-ambivalent*, and *avoidant*. In the Strange Situation, children are categorized as having one of the styles based on coding how they: (a) interact with parents in play and exploration, (b) react to bids for affiliation by a stranger, and (c) respond to their parents over a brief separation and reunion. Ainsworth's securely attached infants acted somewhat distressed when their mothers left, but greeted them eagerly and warmly on their returns. Anxious-ambivalent infants were distraught and protested when their mothers left; on their mothers' return, these infants continued to be distressed and protested even though they wanted to be comforted and held. Avoidant infants, in contrast, seemed relatively undisturbed both when their mothers left and returned (see Ainsworth, Blehar, Waters, & Wall, 1978). Main and Solomon (1990) later identified a fourth, "disorganized" style characterized by chaotic and conflicted behaviors in response to the *Strange Situation* task. Such behaviors involve alternating approach and avoidance behaviors, wherein the child may approach the parent upon reunion only to freeze in a catatonic-like stance, or retreat only to approach the mother again.

Research has revealed that each of these styles corresponds with both (a) specific parenting behavior patterns and (b) long-term mental health and achievement outcomes for the children. The parents of secure children are consistently available, warm, and responsive to their children's dependency needs while simultaneously holding high expectations for the children's behaviors. Thus, secure children come to view themselves as lovable and efficacious, others as available to provide support when needed, and the world as a safe and predictable place. Secure children typically evidence the best mental health, cognitive, and achievement-related outcomes of all the attachment styles (see Bowlby, 1988b).

The parents of avoidant children also are consistent in how they respond to their children, but rather than displaying warmth and meeting their children's dependency needs, they tend to reject their children's neediness and discourage the overt display of negative emotions (e.g., sadness and anger). At the same time, they readily encourage autonomy and high achievement. It follows that these children learn to forgo asking for reassurance, suppress or deny negative emotions, and become goal-oriented strivers who put achievement ahead of relationships. Relative to secure children and anxious children, avoidant children display higher frequencies of externalizing problems including aggression (Burgess, Marshall, Rubin, & Fox, 2003) and are the least empathic (more hostile, disconnected, and isolated; Sroufe, 1983).

On the opposite end of the spectrum from avoidant children, the parents of anxious-ambivalent children are inconsistent in their response patterns. Sometimes they are warm and accepting, while at other times they are cold and rejecting. In behavioral terms, this amounts to a variable reinforcement schedule that accentuates children's approach behaviors. Thus, anxious-ambivalent children develop a pattern wherein higher relative anxiety (compared with the secure and avoidant children) leads them to become hypervigilant for rejection cues so that they can maintain close proximity to the parent while simultaneously minimizing the chances of rejection. By extension, they tend to give up some of their autonomy in the interest of maintaining a focus on trying to attain a sense of security and reassurance in relationships. Because of this preoccupation, these children score highest in behavioral inhibition relative to those with secure and avoidant styles (Burgess et al., 2003). They also have been found to manifest higher levels of hostility and depression than either their avoidant or secure counterparts (Cooper, Shaver, & Collins, 1998; Roberts, Gotlib, & Kassel, 1996).

Finally, the parents of disorganized children often are characterized as "frightened of frightening." When children try to gain comfort or reassurance from such a parent, anxiety and fear are not ameliorated and may even be accentuated. This situation can occur when the child is being abused by an attachment figure, when the primary caregiver suffers from a severe substance abuse or mental health disorder, or when the primary caregiver herself is being abused. In this latter case, the child cannot gain a sense of comfort from someone who herself is terrorized and frightened. Of all the attachment styles, the disorganized style is associated with the worst mental health and achievement-related outcomes. Jacobsen, Edelstein, and Hoffman (1994), for example, found that relative to secure and avoidant children, they scored significantly lower on measures of cognitive ability. Moreover, their lower performance appears to have related directly to their low feelings of self-worth and confidence. Carlson (1998) found that they had behavior problems in preschool, internalizing problems and dissociation in elementary school and high school, psychopathology at age 17½ (based on a 7-point rating of number and severity of K-SADS diagnoses), and evidenced signs of dissociation at age 19.

Helping Children by Studying Attachment in Adults

The extension of attachment research into adulthood has had wide-ranging implications for the field of adoption because it identified the parenting behaviors that facilitate optimal and suboptimal bonding. In 1984, George, Kaplan, and Main developed the Adult Attachment Interview (AAI) to mirror Ainsworth's childhood attachment styles. The AAI is a semi-structured clinical interview that pulls for narrative descriptions of childhood relationships with parents and then codes both the content and the structure of verbalized responses to yield attachment classifications. It is beyond the scope of the present chapter to delve deeply into the AAI classifications or descriptions and excellent resources are available to inform the use of attachment styles and the AAI in practice (see Shorey, 2010; Steele & Steele, 2008; Wallin, 2007). Even based on the information presented in this chapter (and in Chapter 2), however, the astute mental health practitioner should see the benefit in being able to form tentative hypotheses about both the biological and adoptive parents' attachment styles.

There is a high likelihood that any given child will come to exhibit the same attachment style displayed by the parents that raised him (whether biological or adoptive). This "intergenerational transmission of attachment" has profound implications for the adoption field. A qualitative study by Steele, Hodges, Kaniuk, Hillman, and Henderson (2003) assessed 43 mothers and their adopted children who had been exposed to pre-adoption aversive experiences including physical and sexual abuse and neglect. The mothers were administered the AAI and the children were then given a set of story prompts that asked them to describe what they expected in family roles, attachments, and relationships. Comparing this narrative data with results for the AAI, Steele et al. (2003) found that the children's play stories were linked directly to the adoptive mothers' scores on the AAI. For example, aggressiveness in children's stories was related to mother's use of denial/repression on the AAI.

A quantitative meta-analysis by van IJzendoorn (1995) indicated that there is a 70% probability that any given child will have the same attachment style (assessed with the Strange Situation) as her or his parent (as assessed with the AAI). Even when the AAI was administered prior to the birth of the focal child, a 69% concordance rate was still found (van IJzendoorn, 1995). These findings demonstrate how the personalities and emotional states of the adoptive parent should have a direct correspondence with outcomes for their adopted children as attachment style is determined through interaction with parents in early childhood.

RESEARCH ON ADOPTION

As the title of this chapter indicates, our primary goal is to review the adoption research in a way that it will inform best practices in adoption. Accordingly, in the sections to follow, we go far beyond merely reporting research findings. Rather, by highlighting areas of congruence between studies, inconsistencies, and methodological issues that bear on the reported findings, we identify key areas that should be attended to by the human services profession working in the adoption field. This review and associated summaries also should help the reader identify priorities to be considered in advancing the welfare of the adopted child and his or her adoptive parents.

Age at Adoption

Given that the young child is likely to take on the personality characteristics of the primary custodial caregiver, it stands to reason that the age of the child at adoption should have an impact on children's attachment styles, behaviors, and psychological adjustment. Ainsworth (1963) had observed that most infants become "attached" to a primary caregiver during the age range of 4 to 12 months. "Attached" in this sense means that they respond differentially to the primary caregiver relative to other adults in the environment (e.g., will stop crying only when picked up by the mother). If a child is adopted before this attachment differentiation takes place, then the primary attachment pattern should theoretically come to approximate that of the adopted parent. If adoption takes place after such an attachment has formed (to a biological mother or foster parent, for example) or has not formed (as with some institution-alized children), then there should be less of a correspondence with the adoptive parent's attachment style.

Overall, results for the impact of age at adoption are mixed. Andresen (1992) and Jerome (1993) found no correlation between children's age at adoption and their behavioral and school outcomes. Similarly, and in relation to attachment, Marcovitch et al. (1997) assessed 56 3- to 5-year-old Romanian children adopted in Canada and found no correlation between age at adoption and children's levels of attachment security. Veríssimo and Salvaterra (2006) also failed to find a relationship between attachment security and age at adoption in children aged from 10 to 69 months. Finally, Niemann and Weiss (2012) assessed 22 mother-infant dyads and found no relationship between attachment security and age at adoption (average age at adoption was 13 months).

In interpreting results from these studies, however, the reader should be aware of several notable limitations to this research. First, most of the studies lacked statistical power (the ability to detect an effect when an effect really exists) because sample sizes were too small. Second, only one study assessed the attachment style of the adoptive mothers. Niemann and Weiss (2012) determined that 86% of the adoptive mothers in their sample had insecure attachment styles. If we combine this finding with the aforementioned research on the intergenerational transmission of attachment, then we would have to concede that the younger children were at age of adoption, the longer they would have been raised by these insecurely attached mothers, and the more likely it would be that the children themselves would develop insecure attachment styles. In this latter case of insecurely attached mothers, attachment theory would predict that age at adoption would not be related to secure attachment in adoptees.

It may simply be that levels of secure attachment in the adopted child differ as a function of more or less time spent in institutional care. Niemann and Weiss (2012) found that children who had fewer pre-adoption placements had higher levels of attachment security. Marcovitch et al. (1997) similarly found that children who had 6 months or less of institutional care had better outcomes relative to those who had more than 6 months of institutional care. These findings notwithstanding, the age at adoption hypothesis generally assumes that the adoptive parent is securely attached. This suggestion is supported by Veríssimo and Salvaterra's (2006) finding of a positive correlation between secure attachment indicators in the adoptive mother and attachment security in the child. The expectation of a correlation between age at adoption and secure attachment also assumes a "linear relationship" between the age at adoption and secure attachment. A linear relationship means that as children's ages at adoption increase, secure attachment should get incrementally lower. This linear relationship expectation, however, goes against Bowlby's theorizing that attachment behaviors in the child develop in phases (see Chapter 2, this volume).

Phases can be studied by comparing age "groups" at time of adoption and looking at outcomes across longer time periods, rather than viewing age at adoption as a continuous variable and assessing outcomes around age 4 or 5 as in the preceding studies. Habersaat, Tessier, and Pierrehumbert (2011) studied levels of secure attachment and behavior problems among internationally adopted youth aged 12 to 18, and found that children who were adopted before they were 6 months old, relative to children adopted when they were 24 months or older, evidenced fewer behavior problems in adolescence across a range of indices (lower anxiety/depression, social problems, withdrawal, attention problems, rule-breaking, and aggressive behaviors) and had higher levels of secure attachment. These findings corroborate other research suggesting that children fare worse when they have been adopted at later ages (Sharma, McGue, & Benson, 1996b; Tizard, 1991; Verhulst, Althaus, & Versluis-Den-Bieman, 1990). Not surprisingly, analyses conducted by Haversaat, Tessier, and Pierrehumbert (2011) also indicated that the levels of secure attachment in the adopted child predicted the intensity of behavior problems in adolescents. Accordingly, secure attachment in the adopted child should be viewed as a protective factor even though such attachment cannot necessarily be attributed to the adoptive parent unless that parent has a secure attachment style.

Overall, the research on age at adoption can be summarized in stating that adopted children will be positioned to realize the best possible outcomes when (a) the adoptive parent is securely attached, and (b) adoption occurs before the child is 1 year old. A 2009 meta-analysis by van den Dries, Juffer, van IJzendoorn, and Bakermans-Kranenburg indicated that children adopted before they were 1 year old (as opposed to children adopted later) were comparable in attachment security to their nonadopted peers.

General Outcomes for Adopted Children

Research conducted over the past four decades on international and domestic adoption has shed light on a host of outcomes using a wide range of research methodologies. The reader should not always interpret outcomes at face value, however. De Verthelyi (1996) suggested that what defines a "good outcome" is socially constructed and culturally bound. Some researchers, for example, conclude that any shift toward maladjustment (e.g., externalizing behaviors) is evidence of a negative outcome, even though such a shift may result in adopted children more closely approximating same age peers and behavioral norms for their new host cultures. Thus, mental health practitioners should be discriminating when it comes to accepting at face value the conclusions that any given researchers derive from their data.

The tension between general versus specific outcomes and between research conclusions and the data on which it is based harkens back to Bowlby's (1944) assertion that general outcome measures (such as one measuring delinquency) tend to obfuscate subgroup differences that might be observed at a more domain-specific level or in a different context (e.g., assessing delinquency in relation to theft). Moreover, research with children generally, and with adopted children in particular, poses unique methodological challenges including the establishment of baselines and using appropriate comparison groups and group norms (see Bowlby, 1944; Freundlich, 2002), the need for long-term follow-up, decisions about relevant outcome variables, and the development of valid measurement tools (De Verthelyi, 1996).

Research on Cognitive and Psychomotor Development

The most valid and accepted measurement tools are those that reflect objectively observable and quantifiable phenomena. In adoption research, such measures typically relate to medical status and cognitive or psychomotor development. Children internationally adopted from institutional settings, for example, consistently have been found to exhibit delayed physical, cognitive, psychomotor, and language development and lower academic achievement. Research also indicates that after being adopted, many of these children make significant gains, for the most part catching up with their nonadopted peers (Brodzinsky, Smith, & Brodzinsky, 1998; Cohen, Lojasek, Zadeh, Pugliese, & Kiefer, 2008; van IJzendoorn & Juffer, 2006; Wilson & Weaver, 2009).

Children who experienced significant early institutional deprivation also seem to catch up with their peers in height and weight, but not as frequently in head circumference (van IJzendoorn, Bakermans-Kranenburg, & Juffer, 2007). Children adopted from institutional settings at older ages, however, exhibit less plasticity or ability to catch up with nonadopted peers on indices of physical growth (Groza, Proctor, & Shenyang, 1998; Judge, 2003; van IJzendoorn et al., 2007).

Research on Behavioral and Emotional Adjustment

Research on behavioral and emotional adjustment of adoptees yields a similar pattern of results as reported for cognitive and psychomotor development. Increases in internalizing behaviors have been observed for adopted children (Rijk, Hoksbergen, & ter Laak, 2010; Tan, 2011; Tan, Marfo, & Dedrick, 2010) but generally these children stabilize by the time they reach school age. Despite stabilization in status, however, these children still lag slightly behind their same-aged peers. A meta-analysis conducted by Wierzbicki (1993) of 66 studies found small to modest effect sizes for greater behavior and school problems among adopted children as compared to a general population of nonadopted peers. A large, epidemiological study by Sharma, McGue, and Benson (1996a) similarly indicated that relative to a matched control group of same-age peers, adopted children exhibited a pattern of poor adjustment in relation to drug use, antisocial behavior, negative emotionality, school adjustment, and ratings of parental nurturance. Similar findings of slightly poorer rates of overall emotional and behavioral functioning have been found in relation to increased rates of referral for special education, hyperactivity, delinquency, and lower school performance (Feigelman, 1997; van IJzendoorn & Juffer, 2006; Verhulst, Althaus, & Versluis-den Bieman, 1990a).

Overall, adopted children have been found to be overrepresented in clinical psychiatric populations (Brand & Brinich, 1999; Kim, Davenport, Joseph, Zrull, & Woolford, 1988; Sullivan, Wells, & Bushnell, 1995; van IJzendoorn & Juffer, 2006; Wierzbicki, 1993), with as many as 2 to 5 times more referrals for psychological services relative to nonadopted peers (Grotevant & McRoy, 1990). This phenomenon appears to occur among child and adolescent adoptees, but not among adults who had been adopted as children (Feigelman, 1997). There is increasing evidence that adjustment problems in adopted children all but disappear among adult adoptees, with few differences noted on any outcome variable generally considered as markers of positive adjustment in industrialized Western societies (Brodzinsky, Smith, & Brodzinsky, 1998; Feigelman, 1997; Haugaard, 1998). One study even found that adult adoptees fared better on measures of educational level, job status, and marital stability than nonadopted peers (Feigelman, 1997). By extension, many authors have critiqued the proposition that adoptees are at significantly higher risk for long-term maladjustment.

In his 1997 review, Haugaard concluded that data from nonclinical samples show a risk that is "modest or nonexistent" (p. 47). He and others suggest that positive findings relating to psychopathology may be the result of a small number of particularly troubled adopted individuals, who skew the distribution of adjustment problems among adoptees (e.g., Brand & Brinich, 1999; Miller, Fan, Christensen, Grotevant, & van Dulmen, 2000). Additionally, many authors have suggested that adoptive families are more likely to seek help for their adoptive children because they are highly vigilant for any signs of maladjustment or delayed development (Brand & Brinich, 1999; Fisher, 2003; Haugaard, 1998; Kim, 1995).

Comparing International Adoptees With Country-of-Origin Peer Groups

The studies reviewed so far compared adoptees in relation to peers in their adoptive communities. When compared with same-age nonadopted peers from their birth countries/cultures, however, adoptees appear to have significantly better outcomes. When using these latter comparison groups, adopted children had higher IQ scores, better school performance, higher self-esteem, and exhibited fewer behavior problems (van IJzendoorn & Juffer, 2005, 2006). Positive findings regarding the emotional and behavioral adjustment of adoptees also have been found in transracial domestic adoptions (e.g., Alexander & Curtis, 1996), international adoptions (Tizard, 1991), and open adoption (e.g., Brodzinsky, 2006), as well as in adoptions into single-parent families (Groze, 1991; Haugaard, Wojslawowicz, & Palmer, 1999) and adoptive families with same-sex parents (Averett, Nalavany, & Ryan, 2009; Stacey & Biblarz, 2001). Children who are adopted along with siblings also tend to have better outcomes than when siblings are placed apart (Hegar, 2005). Adoption into families with a mixture of birth and adopted children, however, has been found in one study to predict slightly poorer adjustment for adopted children (Barth & Brooks, 1997; see also Chapter 6 in this volume).

In sum, the research to date indicates that in nonclinical samples adopted children fare similarly to their nonadoptive peers. This is consistent with Brodzinsky's (1987) conclusion that "most adopted children are well within the normal range with respect to behavioral, emotional, and academic adjustment" (p. 29). When children adopted at older ages and clinical samples are considered, however, adopted children fare somewhat worse. Nevertheless, most adoptees cannot be differentiated from their peers in adulthood. This may be at least partially attributed to adoptive parents generally being older and higher in socioeconomic status relative to biological parents in most comparison samples. Older, better educated, and more affluent parents may simply be able to provide their children with more opportunities and better remediation.

Longitudinal Studies of Adoption

Longitudinal research designs are optimal for assessing changes over the course of adoption, the impact of pre-adoption risk factors on later development, and the degree to which adoptive parents shape postadoption adjustment. It should be pointed out, however, that most of this research has been conducted in the realm of international adoptions that may accentuate differences with comparison groups that are from the adoptive, rather than the birth, cultures.

Pomerleau et al. (2005) compared health status and physical and cognitive development among 123 Chinese, East Asian, and Eastern European children adopted to Canadian parents before 18 months of age. They assessed the children shortly after arrival in their host communities and 3 and 6 months later. Results indicated that at their first assessment, the adopted children presented with health problems and physical (weight, height, and head circumference) and cognitive and psychomotor delays. It should be noted, however, that Pomerleau et al. (2005) were comparing these children against North American norms. The only way to truly determine if delays were significant would be to compare adopted children's outcomes to norms from their birth cultures. This shortcoming notwithstanding, Pomerleau et al.'s (2005) adopted children, as a group, evidenced marked improvement in health status and cognitive and motor development through the 6-month assessment period, with Chinese and Russian children improving more than children from other Asian countries who started off with better statuses.

Cohen, Lojkasek, Zadeh, Pugliese, and Kiefer (2008) conducted a longer 2-year longitudinal investigation of physical, cognitive, psychomotor, and speech development of Chinese girls adopted to Canadian parents and derived similar findings. Chinese girls started off delayed in relation to physical and developmental measures but improved drastically across the 6-, 12-, and 24-month follow-ups. They did not, however, reach developmental parity until the 2-year mark and they remained delayed in terms of smaller size, weight, and head circumference. This study was an improvement methodologically over the study by Pomerleau et al. (2005) who made comparisons in relation to U.S. norms. In contrast, Cohen et al. (2008) used a matched control group of nonadopted Canadian peers. Although this control group is clearly more appropriate to the conclusions being made, it still leaves open to debate the cause of the observed differences. The research did not assess the Chinese sample in relation to a matched group of nonadopted Chinese girls living in China. It could be that differences relative to the Canadian group are partially due to phenotype and not exclusively due to poor conditions in Chinese orphanages as the researchers assumed.

Although very informative, Cohen and Farnia's (2011) study of a subset of the Cohen et al.'s (2008) sample also makes causal inferences that do not fully follow from the research design. Cohen and Farnia examined the attachment styles developed by 31 of the adopted Chinese girls and their nonadopted Canadian counterparts as assessed in the *Strange Situation*. Results indicated that the majority of adopted infants had secure attachment styles (71%, $n = 20$), while 21% ($n = 6$) were disorganized, and 7% ($n = 2$) were anxious-ambivalent. The matched control group was 80% ($n = 24$) secure, 7% ($n = 2$) disorganized, 7% ($n = 2$) anxious-ambivalent, and 7% ($n = 2$) avoidant. Based on this data, the authors concluded that the adopted sample was more disorganized and that this constituted evidence of pre-adoption abandonment experiences or deprivation.

Although it may appear from reading the preceding paragraph that the difference between 7% disorganized versus 21% disorganized is large, in actuality this amounts to a difference of just four girls. This exemplifies why percentage data from small samples simply cannot be presumed to generalize to large samples that would be representative. Moreover, because the sample size was small (fewer than five participants in some of the categories), no statistical analyses were conducted to determine if this was more than a chance occurrence. In terms of the general U.S. population, the percentage of disorganized attachment is approximately 15%. As such, it may simply be that Cohen and Farnia's (2011) comparison group was less disorganized relative to the general population *and* the adopted group. It also could be that neither group differed, outside of chance probabilities, from the normal population.

This critical analysis of Cohen and Farnia's (2011) study was put forward to illustrate the problem of attempting to generalize data reported with no statistical analyses. Cohen and Farnia's (2011) premise that insecure attachments are a product of the pre-adoption environment also cannot be supported because the adoptive parents' attachment styles (which are known to have strong effects on children's attachment styles) were not assessed or controlled. Although we are speculating, it may be that the sample contained a higher than expected number of adoptive mothers with unresolved attachment classifications (the adult corollary of child disorganized attachment). It also was not clear if Cohen and Farnia's Strange Situation raters were blind to the adoption classification. Given the apparent bias that adoption researchers generally have that adopted children experienced deprivation and experienced abandonment prior to adoption (see Tan, 2011), they may have a tendency to overpathologize adopted children's behaviors.

Tan (2011) also conducted a 2-year longitudinal study with Chinese girls adopted in Canada. This study recruited adoptive families through adoption groups and agencies, including groups "for specific areas of development (e.g., attachment, special-needs, identity) or general postadoption adjustment" (p. 16). The authors reported an increase in maladjustment among the Chinese girls overall across the 2 years of the study. But this finding has to be interpreted with caution. Because the group started off with lower levels of externalizing behaviors relative to the general population, increases in scores could simply reflect a statistical artifact known as regression toward the mean (on retesting, originally high scores will almost always move more toward the mean of the population). For Tan's (2011) research to have supported his conclusions, he would have needed to recruit a matched (in terms of age and socioeconomic status) sample of Canadian girls and administered the same measures at the same time points to determine if the Canadian girls evidenced the same trajectory as the Chinese girls over time. Even then, results could be posited to reflect normal enculturation (i.e., becoming more like the Canadian girls in the adoptive culture) independent of the effects of adoption.

In discussing his results, Tan (2011) reported that because adjustment problems got worse as this population of adopted Chinese girls got older there is a "critical need for early detection and early treatment" and that "mental health professionals should work closely with these children to process their experience of early abandonment and to adopt a positive attitude toward being adopted transracially" (p. 20). It is important to point out that in their research on Chinese infant girls adopted in Canada, Cohen and Farnia (2011) stated that "they had relatively favorable early conditions prior to adoption placement and less exposure to the severe forms of deprivation and neglect typical of some other international adoptees, such as those adopted from Romania" (p. 2345). Cohen and Farnia pointed out that these children were usually abandoned because of the "one child rule" in China and not because of maternal risk factors and that there was anecdotal evidence that these infants had formed attachments with their caregivers in their pre-adoption institutional settings. This is not to say, however, that most adopted children (both domestic and international) have not experienced attachment disruptions or related behavioral and mental health issues. Accordingly, there is a strong need for empirically supported interventions as reported in the section to follow.

ATTACHMENT-BASED INTERVENTIONS FOR USE IN ADOPTION

Theoretically, bonding to new attachment figures (the adoptive parent, a caring teacher or coach, or a therapist) in later adolescence or adulthood should serve a reparative function and facilitate building more secure attachment schemata in children (Bowlby, 1988b; Mikulincer & Shaver, 2003). Such reparations should be facilitated best through adoptive parents providing a consistent secure base, and being available, warm, and responsive to the adopted child as he or she explores the new family/social environment and experiments with new and hopefully more adaptive/positive behavior patterns.

Because adopted children are in the process of developing (for infants) and/or modifying (for older children and adolescents) their attachment styles, it should be possible to promote greater attachment security by focusing on the adoptive parents' parenting style (see Shorey, Snyder, Yang, & Lewin, 2003). Mental health practitioners working with adoptive families can optimize outcomes for their children by focusing on: (a) enhancing adoptive parents' sensitivity to the child's emotional cues, (b) changing the parents' attachment styles in the direction of security, (c) providing and enhancing social support for parents, or (d) combining these three approaches to enhance parental mental health and well-being.

Parental sensitivity can be enhanced by providing adoptive mothers with videotaped feedback of interactions with their adopted children (see Black & Teti, 1997). Parents also can be helped to promote their own secure attachment by helping them reconstruct their early relationships with their own parents, which, in turn, should free them to create new models in their interactions with their adopted children (Cicchetti, Toth, & Rogosch, 1999; Toth, Rogosch, Manly, & Cicchetti, 2006). Other interventions can include building stronger social support networks and providing adoptive mothers with experienced mother mentors (Barnett, Blignault, Holmes, Payne, & Parker, 1987).

In their meta-analytic review, Bakermans-Kranenburg, van IJzendoorn, and Juffer (2003) found that three basic intervention types—behaviorally changing parental sensitivity, modifying parents' internal working models, and increasing parental social supports—all were effective in increasing parental sensitivity. Interventions that are effective in increasing parental sensitivity also are effective in increasing attachment security in children (Bakermans-Kranenburg et al., 2003). Nevertheless, it is more difficult to change attachment security than it is to change parenting behaviors, and recent clinical interventions using combined approaches have yielded the most success in this area.

THE CIRCLE OF SECURITY

In their *Circle of Security* intervention, Hoffman, Marvin, Cooper, and Powell (2006) use a group format to change young children's attachment classifications. Although not designed specifically for adoptive families, this intervention should be equally effective for this special population. The first aim of the intervention is to establish the (parent) group as a secure base for parents to explore their relationships with their children. The intervention then uses educational and therapeutic formats to increase parents' (a) sensitivity and understanding of childhood attachment needs, (b) empathic attunement and capacity to provide reflective functioning, (c) empathy for the self and the child in understanding defensive reactions, and (d) awareness of how their own developmental histories and attachment styles affect their behaviors in relation to the child.

Over the course of the 20 weeks of the *Circle of Security* intervention, 69% of those children originally receiving a disorganized or insecure-other classification changed to a more desirable (organized) attachment classification (secure, avoidant, or anxious ambivalent). Overall, 44% of children initially classified as insecure changed to a having a secure attachment style by the end of the intervention.

Toddler-Parent Psychotherapy

In a similar but longer (58-week) treatment program known as Toddler-Parent Psychotherapy (Cicchetti et al., 1999; Toth et al., 2006), clinicians meet with mothers and their toddlers in conjoint therapy sessions. The therapist helps the mother to modify her attachment representations and distorted perceptions and behavior patterns, which are thought to directly affect how she will interact with her child. This attachment style modification is accomplished when the mental health professional helps the mother become aware of the interpersonal patterns that are observed, and provides a corrective emotional experience through showing her empathy, respect, concern, and positive regard. Toddler-parent psychotherapy is effective in changing attachment classifications in children from insecure to secure and is also effective in decreasing rates of disorganized attachment. Toth et al. (2006) found that 58.8% of toddlers originally classified as disorganized changed to a secure classification across the course of their intervention. Although this intervention was not designed specifically with the adoptive child in mind, the prevalence of disorganized attachment in some adoption samples should make this approach particularly attractive as a treatment option.

Dyadic Developmental Psychotherapy

Other researchers have also found children's insecure attachment styles can be moved in a secure direction by increasing healthy parental behaviors. Dozier, Stovall, Albus, and Bates (2001) found that when children are placed in foster care, their attachment classifications come to resemble those of the foster parent after 3 months in placement. Building on these findings, Becker-Weidman (2006) implemented an attachment-based intervention, Dyadic Developmental Psychotherapy, with adopted and foster-care children aged 6 to 15 years (mean = 9.4 years). The aim of this intervention is to modify children's attachment styles through therapists working directly and simultaneously with the children and their adoptive/foster caregivers. In this treatment modality, mental health practitioners foster secure relationship formation among parent-child dyads through establishing an emotionally attuned relationship between the caregiver and child, the therapist and child, and between the therapist and caregiver. In this protected environment, children can experience many of the processes inherent in normal secure development.

Dyadic Developmental Psychotherapy also necessitates a focus on caregivers' attachment styles because insecure styles can interfere with caregivers' abilities to enact secure attachment principles. In a typical session, the therapist spends time alone with the parents, instructing them in "attachment parenting methods," and, if needed, helps the parents work through their own insecure attachment issues. Work with the child then involves the therapist and parents together (a) being affectively attuned and validating of the child's subjective experience, (b) implementing cognitive behavioral techniques to help the child make sense of and modify maladaptive behaviors, and (c) facilitating cognitive restructuring of past experiences to increase malleability of relational schemas.

Through parents' use of empathic attunement in a structured environment provided by the therapist, the child can feel safe and remain emotionally engaged while reprocessing distressing emotions associated with past traumas (such as those often attributed to pre-adoption environments). In this work, the child also is repeatedly cycled through the fundamental caregiver/child attachment pattern of (a) sharing emotional experiences, (b) experiencing a breach or separation in the relationship, and (c) reconnecting and realigning caregiver/child emotional states. As these cycles repeat across the course of treatment, just as they do in normal development, the child comes to construct a new working model of the self in relation to others, which then facilitates healthy bonding with the caregivers, enabling the secure attachment dynamic to continue after treatment ends.

Becker-Weidman (2006) provided evidence for the efficacy of this 23-week intervention, finding that children in the active treatment group ($N = 34$) were rated by their adoptive or foster care parents as having significantly lower levels of attachment disorder and fewer behavior problems after the intervention as compared to a pre-intervention assessment. The treatment group also had significantly better outcomes across these same indices than a treatment-as-usual group, which did not show significant improvements in pre- to postintervention assessments.

PRACTICAL POINTS

- Bowlby's early research should serve as a reminder that when making judgments about the health or biopsychosocial adjustment of adopted children and families, we should take care to be cognizant of the reference groups to which these individuals are being compared. Whether we are conscious of it or not, all of us use reference groups (e.g., same age peers in the host culture versus culture of origination) when arriving at conclusions (e.g., better adjusted or less well adjusted). Remember that all conclusions relating to adjustment are relative.
- Ainsworth's research methods demonstrate how researchers and mental health professionals become a part of the systems they are studying or working to change. Rather than ignoring this relationship, researchers as well as mental health practitioners should use this position to improve outcomes for children and their families.
- Mental health practitioners should learn about and get comfortable with the child behavior pattern associated with each attachment style and the associated parenting practices. This will enable them to form tentative hypotheses about a child's developmental trajectory and areas of vulnerability and choose the best possible interventions.

CONCLUSION

The research on adoption and the related topics of parent/child bonding, attachment, and interventions for children and their families is vast and our hope was to have captured what we believe is a small but representative and useful sample of the available literature in this area. What was not covered here, however, is covered with even more specificity in the other chapters in this volume.

Research findings are an important consideration when it comes to implementing best practices in adoption placements and interventions. As highlighted in the preceding section, such interventions also feed back in important ways to inform research and developments in the field. It follows that all researchers in this area impact and become a part of the systems they study. By extension, they have an obligation to work toward improving, directly and indirectly, the lives of the children and families they study. Similarly, even if they have no intention of contributing to the field through scholarship, we believe that all mental health practitioners (and parents) are researchers who continually collect data, analyze it, and use the insights garnered to intervene or make the adjustments needed to help adopted children realize the best possible outcomes.

Our hope is that the readers use this chapter and the research information presented as a launching pad to directly access the many valuable resources and interventions presented. We also hope to have laid a solid foundation for making the most of the research findings and recommendations contained in the subsequent chapters of this volume. Whether we approach this topic from a research or a practitioner perspective, we should all be unified in our dedication to the parents we work with and their adopted children.

Chapter 4

THE ADOPTIVE MOTHER

Virginia M. Brabender, Amanda Swartz,
Mary Winzinger, and April E. Fallon

When a woman becomes an adoptive mother, all elements of her internal life—her emotions, cognitions, fantasies, impulses related to her child—are likely to influence not only her own well-being, but also that of her child. Her experiences as an adoptive mother are also likely to affect all members of the family—her partner, the other children in the family, her own parents, and her broader social network. Knowledge about factors determining the mother's confidence in her role, her sense of being bonded to her child, her attitude toward different facets of her child's identity, and her satisfaction in her relationships with her parents and her parenting partner is likely to benefit all members of the kinship network.

Yet, the literature has minimally addressed both stable and changing aspects of her experience. Perhaps this neglect is because of the paramount character of the needs of the child. Although the research on the adoptive mother is sparse, over the past decade or so, researchers and clinicians have conducted qualitative and quantitative studies that provide a window into the adoptive mother's experiences. In this chapter, we integrate the findings from these investigations with our own semi-structured interviews of 26 women (Swartz, 2010; Swartz, Brabender, Fallon, & Shorey, 2012; Winzinger, 2010), all adoptive mothers of internationally adopted young children. From our own practices and those of other contributors to this text, we also draw clinical examples of women who have participated in other types of adoption—domestic, foster, and kinship, national and international. As others have found (Gailey, 2010), adoptive parents are generally extremely eager to share their experiences. The literature, too, has been helpful in providing additional anecdotal observations on women's experiences with building families through adoption.

The texture and intensity of a woman's experience is influenced by a host of variables—the type of adoption, the level of family support, the quality of her alliance with a parenting partner, the reactions of any siblings, and the community response to adoption in general and this adoption in particular, to name a few. We employ a developmental perspective in examining these variables. That is, we explore the mother's experience from the time she first begins to contemplate the adoption, to the waiting period, through the initial stages of forming a relationship with the child, and beyond. Chapters 8 and 9 on parenting the child and adolescent respectively supplement the material in this chapter. The emphasis of this chapter is on the mother's sense of herself as a mother and felt connection with the child rather than particular parenting behaviors.

THE ERAS OF ADOPTIVE MOTHERHOOD

In a mother's relationship with her adopted child, all that goes before creates a foundation for what occurs within the present, and certain developments require developments that have occurred earlier. Yet, we avoid using the terms *stage* or *phase* because they suggest invariance and universality. From our own clinical work, our conversations with many adoptive mothers, and our reading of the literature, we believe that although both men and women mature as parents, how they do so—the exact course this maturation process takes—is variable. At the same time, we have discerned some common reactions at certain phases of the adoption process and particular periods of the adopted child's life. Given the variability we see and its connection to contextual factors, no adoptive parent should feel that his or her course is a lesser one simply because it does not fit our description. The uniqueness of each adoptive family is as valuable as that which each family shares with others.

Before the Baby Arrives

The scenario that is initially addressed in this section is most descriptive of the circumstance in which a parent adopts a very young child, a child less than 2 years old. However, parents who adopt an older child share in many of the reactions that we outline. This latter group of parents has additional challenges and reactions, which are considered subsequently.

Contemplating Adoption

A moment occurs when adoption becomes a glimmering of an idea in the mind of an individual. A few mothers in our sample told us that they had always hoped to adopt a child, and this idea seemed natural because one or more members of their families were adopted. One mother wrote, "My husband and I knew that we would adopt. He has friends growing up that were adopted. And my father was adopted and my grandmother on my mom's side was adopted. And so I always knew from a kid that this was something I wanted to do." Yet, for the majority of individuals, the plan to adopt is wrought with uncertainty, and emerges from the failure to carry to term a biological child. To contemplate adoption requires acknowledging a loss—the vanquishing of the dream of having a biological child.

The Psychology of Loss in Adoption

The loss that individuals contemplating adoption experience is multifaceted, and for different individuals, certain facets—based on their circumstances and personality dynamics—may be more salient than others. One facet is the loss of a sense of genetic continuity and the preservation of the biological family line.[1] Another is the loss of predictability in the person that child would be, physically and psychologically, even if the predictability is exaggerated in the minds of the parents. Infertility represents the loss of what many societies deem to be a normal family, a unit based upon biological ties (Wegar, 1997). Associated with these facets are the emotions of mourning. Although sadness is often especially prominent, other affective elements may be present as well. For example, when a woman defers childbearing to pursue her career, and then has fertility difficulties, a phenomenon occurring with increasing frequency (Smock & Greenland, 2010), guilt often ensues. Partners in a relationship may experience anger toward one another, as each perceives the other as having created an impediment to a successful pregnancy. An example is the case of one partner resenting the other's insistence on a high level of financial security before attempting to conceive a child. Some individuals will take advantage of support groups such as those sponsored by RESOLVE to sort out and cope with these various feelings.

As individuals begin to explore adoption, further opportunities for loss arise. For example, a single woman seeking to adopt through the public system may discover that she is regarded as undesirable by public agencies, and may be informed that she will qualify only for children with particularly great challenges (Gailey, 2010). For her, the loss is of the fantasized child, unfettered by significant physical or cognitive difficulties. For a gay or lesbian couple pondering adoption as a means of building a family, learning that only one individual will have legal status as a parent, a reality in a number of states, precipitates a loss in both prospective parents but especially the person who will forgo legal parental rights. Individuals who consider adopting a child who is not a newborn face the loss of the time the child lived apart and knowledge of the child's early life. When the child's circumstances during that time apart had toxic elements, the loss of being able to offer the child a healthy start is present. At times, these different sources of loss can enter an adopting or adoptive parent's consciousness unexpectedly. The therapist aids a parent by preparing him or her for these unanticipated loss reactions (Eldridge, 2009).

Women in this contemplation state may harbor common misconceptions about the loss reactions they face at this time. The first is that having loss reactions disqualifies them from being good candidates for adoptive parenthood. In fact, the mere recognition of such difficult psychological contents can be an aid to coping with the demands of adoptive parenting. Another assumption is that because adoption is commonly viewed as a positive event, painful feelings in relation to it are irrational (Russell, 2000). Adoption is a complex event: Different facets beget different emotions. A variation on this assumption is that grieving for the biological child is disloyal to the adoptive child. This is no truer than the idea that a parent's grief for a child who has died constitutes a betrayal of the surviving children. Another misconception is that once the decision is made or once the adoptive child enters the family, loss reactions will dissipate. Throughout an adoptive parent's life, different feelings connected to that loss are likely to surface and can exist amid a variety of positively toned experiences. Sometimes adoptive parents will experience a period in which few thoughts about the infertility arise. Then, some circumstance will activate that constellation of thoughts and feelings, which can be experienced at a fairly high level of intensity. For example, Russell (2000) shares an example of an adoptive mother who found that the process of searching for her child's birth mother caused feelings of loss to bubble up at a level of intensity that surprised her. On the other hand, some unexpected feelings can be positive. For example, adoptive mothers who discover later in their lives that they have health problems with a genetic underpinning are grateful for their freedom from worrying that their children will succumb to the same diseases. One of the mothers in our sample noted that her first child appeared to have been hardwired for the family neurosis of obsessive-compulsive tendencies, but she had hope that her child of a different genetic make-up would be free of this affliction.[2]

Psychological Interventions

Clinicians and other professionals working with a woman contemplating adoption can be maximally helpful when they invite the expression of the full gamut of feelings associated with this important decision. Facilitating women in grappling with reactions of loss is the awareness that their ability to recognize these feelings will be of benefit to their adoptive child given that adoptive children also have losses to bear (Warshaw, 2006). The clinician should also be careful to recognize the variability in loss reactions that women have and be attuned to his or her client's specific reaction.

Both the profundity and the character of the loss reaction can vary greatly. For example, a woman with secondary infertility (failing to conceive a second child after having had one biological child) may genuinely have a minimal reaction to her circumstance. Women who are in communities in which adoption is regarded favorably may have an attenuated response to particular aspects of infertility. For example, Pakizegi (2007) observes that in many African American communities, kinship adoptions are common and more highly valued than in White communities. This differential social valuation is likely to shape the parents' responses to infertility and the perceived viability of adoption as an alternative. Clinicians should be aware of this contextual variation. As in all matters, clinicians should develop an understanding of a woman's internal life based on the material she presents rather than assumptions of how she must feel. Certainly, too, the clinician should cultivate the awareness that loss is not unique to adoption, but is inherent in being alive. Clinicians should also help the aspiring parent to recognize that alongside of loss-related emotions are joyful feelings that, rather than being obliterated by sadness, are often made more acute by the acknowledgment of psychological pain. Too vigorous of an effort to defend against sadness, anger, guilt, and so on, typically leads to the suppression of all authentic feelings.

At this time, adoption professionals can make an important contribution in helping the pre-adoptive parents to form realistic expectations of the challenges that are likely to emerge with whatever form of adoption they consider. Palacios and Sanchez-Sandoval (2005) provide a summary of their own large-scale research study that is consistent with the vast majority of studies in the field, stating that "adopted children are well integrated into their families and schools, show good psychological adjustment, and are comparable in psychological outcomes to nonadopted community classmates, at least for those youngsters adopted at birth or within the first year of life" (p. 125). They acknowledge that as the age of adoption increases, adjustment problems increase. Still, they note that the problems observed are generally in the mild to moderate range. Of particular importance is their finding that the more accurate the expectations, the greater the psychosocial adjustment for parents and children as the children mature. If the child has certain health challenges, the parent benefits from knowing how these may play out over time (see Chapter 7). One important contribution of a psychotherapist who is not an adoption specialist is helping his or her client to know that adoption specialists can provide assistance in looking down the road to ascertain what might lie ahead.

Applying to Adopt and Waiting for Assignment

Once the prospective mother has made the decision to adopt, she must then embark upon the arduous activity of completing the adoption application. For all aspiring adopters, this process is time-consuming and fraught with uncertainty. Candidates ask, "Will I be found to be adequate or lacking by the professional who is evaluating me and my application?" Provocative questions about that parent's background (for example, "Did your parents ever use corporal punishment?") can provide further basis for concern. Such thoughts not only evoke anxiety but also resentment over the loss of privacy. Prospective parents reasonably wonder, "Why is the evaluative process so thoroughgoing for us, and altogether absent for biological parents?" (Fallon & Brabender, 2003; Russell, 2000). For some prospective parents, the period is especially fraught with anxiety. For example, same-sex couples or older adults may worry that they will be rejected by pregnant women and therefore will be waiting forever (Goldberg & Gianino, 2011). Unwelcomed feelings of inadequacy, long since buried from earlier life struggles, now reappear.

When an adoption initiative follows extensive treatment for infertility, the intricate and lengthy process of preparation can lead to intense frustration and impatience (Pavao, 2005). One mother in our group explained, "[We] decided to adopt after we couldn't have our own children. So that [attempting to get pregnant] went on for years. And after we finally decided that wasn't going to happen, it took another three years because we had some obstacles that came up." This mother further explained that due to criteria in the country from which they were attempting to adopt, the "paperwork kept expiring and we had to redo our paperwork three times. And it was hard work getting all the paperwork together and we went and got three physicals . . . and the criminal background check." Nonetheless, this time allows for the internal and external preparation necessary for adoption. The tiresome paperwork and other hurdles can provide a service to the parent who might understandably jump into adoptive parenting in a headlong fashion. Still, for some parents, the duration of the waiting period is beyond what can serve any useful purpose and leads prospective adopters to question whether they will ever receive an assignment.

Maternal Feelings During This Period

From the time the prospective mother (along with her partner) decides to move forward with an adoption application until the time in which she receives an actual assignment of a child, particular thoughts and feelings are characteristic. She has made an affirmative decision to adopt and a joyous anticipation begins to build. Alongside positive feelings, specific fears about adoption emerge. These fears may play a role in shaping the mother's decision about the type of adoption that will be pursued. Swartz et al. (2012) noted that a subgroup of women in their sample claimed that they pursued an international adoption in large part because they feared that within a domestic adoption, a birth mother could have a greater opportunity to make contact with and even reclaim the child. Some research (for example, Viana & Welsh, 2010) suggests that during this period, high levels of maternal stress—created in part by this raft of worries—affect parental well-being following the adoption.

Recent work within the attachment literature discussed in Chapters 2 and 3 describe how during a pregnancy, the mother's fantasy activity about the child performs an important function in building the bond. A pre-adoptive mother's ability to imagine her child establishes a foundation for the construction of a caregiving system in which the child attaches to the mother who lovingly provides a set of essential parental functions such as protection and encouragement of exploration. Swartz, Brabender, Fallon, and Shorey (2012) found that the mother's preoccupation with the details of preparing the adoption application did not contribute to her ability to fantasize about the child and actually appeared to interfere with it. The mothers we interviewed seemed to be more focused on whether they would be approved to adopt, a concern that left little mental space to picture the child. Some mothers conveyed a sense that it was hubris or an invitation to disappointment to think about their eventual child until the adoption application was approved (Swartz, 2010).

Psychological Interventions

At this juncture, pre-adoption counseling can be extremely useful. Prospective mothers can gain awareness of the different types of adoption and make a more informed choice than they otherwise would have. Exposure to research findings on the experiences of adoptive families can be useful. For example, parents may become acquainted with the research finding that as the child advances in age, worries about reclamation diminish (Grotevant & McRoy, 1998) and that in fact, efforts at reclamation are relatively rare. They may also test specific hypotheses in light of additional data. For instance, they might consider whether with greater accessibility of the Internet, the international aspect of some adoptions truly protects an adoptive parent from the birth parent's efforts to obtain information about the adopted child. Contact with couples with older adopted children can also be useful. As Pertman (2011) points out, parents often begin feeling threatened about the specter of contact with birth parents, but later wish that greater openness were possible.

Prospective parents may be greatly helped by developing their own support groups for waiting parents. The waiting situation can be painfully isolating, but hearing about the struggles of other families aids the prospective family in recognizing that this extended uncertainty simply goes with the territory of adoption. Waiting parents are likely to be heartened by hearing of the progress other families have made. Other prospective parents, too, may have suggestions for how to cope with some of the practical problems that arise such as talking to a waiting sibling about the process. A group established during this period may continue to provide emotional sustenance long after the adoption has taken place.

Adoption Within the Public System

For foster-to-adoption parents, the process is different during this period in which the adoption application is being completed. When a woman aspires to be the mother of the child she fosters, the real child rather the fantasized child activates the maternal caregiving system. She also need not anticipate problems about her child's background that never materialize. These women can engage in actual caregiving behaviors such as acts of maternal attunement and protection, and can focus on actual rather than imaginary problems. Also, the extensive training that is made available to foster parents is likely to enhance their confidence in their caregiving roles and to cultivate particular competencies such as the capacity to help the child cope with loss and grieving. Even in this situation, however, the difficulty in obtaining comprehensive assessments for children can lead to the emergence of a variety of behavioral and health difficulties (Grimm & Hurtubise, 2003a, 2003b), and prevent early intervention.

Waiting for the Child

Once the pre-adoptive parents are referred a child, the mother's internal experience shifts dramatically. Now that a particular child has been identified, the mother gives way to fantasizing her future life with that child.

The Role of Fantasy   Catalyzing fantasy is the mother's receipt of a photograph of the child (Swartz, 2010; Swartz et al., 2012). A number of our interviewees—including ones who have biological children—saw the photograph as akin to the ultrasound in pregnancy. One mother's expression of her reaction on seeing the photo was characteristic of our other participants, "You immediately think of the future for your child, that you want to give them absolutely everything in the world. You just want them to be healthy. You want them to be happy; you want them to be fulfilled as a person. You want them to develop." Another mother, describing the intensity of feeling upon seeing the photographs said, "We were puddles of mud, all we did was cry . . . we just thought she was the most beautiful thing we'd ever seen! So we couldn't wait to go get her. We didn't know how long it was going to be."

The external stimulus of the photograph fosters a process that has been described by Winnicott as *primary maternal preoccupation* (1956/1992), entailing a lessened focus on her own needs and the world outside of her and a heightened focus on her infant. Others indicate that a woman's sense of self will develop to incorporate the concept of herself as a mother (Ilicali & Fisek, 2004). We believe that this period marks the beginning of the bonding process as the mother now contemplates the child as an individual with unique characteristics. As the mother invests more heavily in thinking about her child, mundane activities become irksome. Yet, the goal of adoption prevents the mother from immersing herself too completely in her internal thoughts; the adoption demands the performance of practical tasks. For example, for international adoptions, the assignment often brings with it the necessity of planning a trip abroad including the potential for an extended stay.

The overall emotional climate of this period is positive, but certain negative affects crop up. The relief that is experienced in obtaining the referral of a child is accompanied by new anxiety: The mother has a real child to lose. The assignment of a child does not preclude legal challenges and the adoptive mother is acutely aware of this fact. Small snags in the process are now experienced as major setbacks; these events evoke anger and even despair, as the mother fears that the adoption could be derailed. She may fear this loss not only for herself but also for any other children in the family. As the following mothers noted, the other emotional challenge is the increased difficulty of having to wait to be with the child (Swartz, 2010):

> I just fell in love with this little baby. I would get these pictures every month from the doctor. And I just want to . . . it was very, very hard. That process was hard.
>
> We had seen pictures of her and that was torture, because you wanted to hold her so bad. You know, I was mad, because I wasn't the one caring for her. One of my friends said, "When you get her, she'll be sleeping through the night. You're so lucky." I wanted to smack her.

Ultimately, when an individual receives a referral, he or she must make a determination whether to accept it. Sometimes prospective parents are presented with a decision that they did not expect. For example, they may have been informed that the child potentially assigned to them has a particular physical vulnerability such as low birth weight. Often, the parent must make a decision in an extremely short period of time. Some of the fantasy activity that would otherwise occur is supplanted by consultation with various professionals to ascertain the significance of the information about the child.

Psychological Interventions

Maternal fantasies are precursors to the mother-child bond. The therapist's recognition of this connection helps him or her to be supportive of this vital internal activity, which sometimes becomes externalized within the session. That is, the mother's felt safety within the session may allow her to share her musings with the therapist, which can be joyfully received by the therapist. Sometimes clients need permission to fantasize. They may believe—consciously or unconsciously—that fantasizing suggests a hubris, the punishment of which could be denial of the child. The identification of this dynamic enables the mother to bring her reality-testing resources to bear in challenging it. Through such a process, fantasy becomes liberated and bonding can begin.

Transition

The transition period refers to the segment of time in which the parents bring their adopted child into their home. For international adoptions, it typically entails a trip abroad, although occasionally, the country will have the child sent to its future home with an escort. For domestic adoptions, the transition period may involve being present at the hospital when the biological mother gives birth. For kinship adoptions and foster care adoptions, the process may be similar to the international and domestic adoptions or it may be far more gradual, making the transition time less distinct. However, as McGinn (2007) points out, for some, kinship adoption is precipitated by tragic circumstances such as the death of a parent. In these instances, the transition may be quite abrupt and at the time the child comes into the home, it may not clear how long the child is staying. Furthermore, the expansion of the family may be borne out of obligation rather than desire.

Initial Encounter

For parents who are meeting the child for the first time, this period is one of excitement, trepidation, and uncertainty about how the process will unfold. One mother described it this way:

> We didn't know when we would get to actually meet our daughter. We got off the plane, and thought perhaps she would be there with her foster mother but instead we had a team of agency personnel—a social worker, a lawyer, and a translator—drive us to our hotel. Even they were unsure exactly when we would see her. They left us in our hotel room and an hour later she arrived. It was almost dizzying.

Upon finally seeing their child in flesh and blood, many mothers reported a rush of intensely positive feelings. One mother observed, "I just loved her from the second I picked her up. I just can't explain it, but I can't imagine loving a baby more if I had given birth to her." The majority of mothers we interviewed saw their feelings on meeting their child as very positive. Still, a substantial subgroup described the formation of a positive bond as a slow process. For some mothers, a perceived discrepancy between the photo and the real child interfered with the quick emergence of positive feelings toward the child. It was almost as if the mothers had bonded with another child who only faintly resembled the child before them. In other cases, mothers were confronted with aspects of the child's appearance that suggested illness. Even when the parent had been warned, it did not seem to eliminate fully anxiety about the implications of the evidence of some physical weakness. In still other cases, the strength of the child's rejecting behavior toward the parent dampened the parent's positive feelings. Finally, some parents were overwhelmed with sadness by seeing the conditions in which the child spent his or her early life. One mother said, "She wouldn't eat unless she was like laying down. It was obvious she had never been held while she was eating . . . I remember putting her in the tub and it was like she was a jellyfish." Another mother expressed the common worry about experiences of emotional deprivation, "M was in no way upset about leaving the caregiver so she obviously never really felt like anybody was, you know, her own, or any kind of close attachment." This mother was representative of all of the mothers in our sample in having a keen attunement to bonding and attachment issues.

In summary, then, the reflections of our mothers revealed a great range of feelings upon meeting and getting to know their child. It is important to note that all of the parents who initially struggled with the absence of positive feelings or the presence of negative feelings went on to form an intense connection to their children. Instant rapture is not the *sine qua non* of bonding.

Journeying Home

In international adoptions, the trip home often has the admixture of feelings characteristic of the earlier phases of the adoption process. On the one hand, exuberance abounds as the adoptive parent realizes at long last, the hard-wrought goal of consummating the adoption and bringing the child into his or her permanent home has been achieved. On the other hand, trepidation of potential interferences with the process continues. This anxiety also pertains to domestic adoptions and is made particularly acute by the seeming unpredictability of how the birth mother will feel when she sees her child and how those feelings may shape her decision making. Another source of anxiety is self-doubt about the adequacy of one's caregiving as small or large crises occur during the transition period. One mother describes events that occurred on the trip in which she and her husband brought their child home from an eastern European country:

> It's the sixth day into our intercontinental trip to St. Petersburg, Russia. We are about to, finally, and officially, receive our new son, now 12 months old, and become first time parents! First, I feel excitement, and then some panic creeps in. I remind myself that my husband and I are older than most first-time parents, and that between us, we have several advanced degrees. So how hard can this be?
>
> Flash forward 36 hours and no sleep. We are flying home to Pennsylvania through London's Heathrow Airport. We are waiting to go through customs, and I REALLY need to use the restroom. There are hundreds of people scurrying about and we don't want to get separated from our group, so I leave my husband holding our new son at a designated place and run across the entire holding area and into the Ladies Room. Finally, I can take 60 seconds for myself! (Lesson One: NEVER plan that things with a young child will go smoothly.) I immediately, and distinctly, hear my husband yell at the top of his voice, "BECKY! He's PUKING!!!" I hurry out and there's my husband holding our son. . . . at arm's length. . . . while the poor little guy is vomiting all over himself, and my husband, and the floor. Okay . . . grab the baby wipes. Reassure our son (and my husband) that all is going to be all right. Do we have a change of clothes (for both of them)? No, of course not. (Lesson Two: ALWAYS have an extra pair of clothes with you. . . . at least for the baby.) Maybe some apple juice will settle his stomach? Oh, the apple juice . . . maybe the six bottles of juice we gave him on the airplane wasn't the best idea . . . maybe he wasn't crying because of the change of pressure . . . maybe there was some other reason for him to be crying? Maybe he was crying because he had a stomachache from all the apple juice we were feeding him! (Lesson Three: Never assume that advanced degrees prepare you for parenthood!)

As this narrative suggests, another important commodity during this process is a sense of humor. Questions about one's parental competence may be accompanied by apprehension about the adoption itself. Mothers may wonder, "Is this child still crying after all of my efforts to console him because I am not the birth mother? Might she have done it better?" At the same time, these experiences are formatives in demonstrating to the mother that she can in fact be an effective caregiver. Often, the more challenging the incidents, the more compelling the evidence of her maternal resources.

In kinship adoptions and adoptions from foster care, the children are often older. In these cases, the adoptive parents may observe behaviors that are worrisome. Frequently, a belief is harbored that once the child is safely lodged in the adoptive parents' home, those behaviors will, if not vanish, diminish significantly (Hodges, Steele, Hillman, Henderson, & Kaniuk, 2005). As we see, when problems are not lessened to the degree anticipated, adoptive parents are at risk for making highly negative self-attributions that can affect their own well-being and that of their child.

In the transition period, the mother's bonding to the child intensifies and she begins to engage in those behaviors such as soothing and protecting the child that are part of the maternal caregiving system, behaviors that will gradually promote the child's attachment to her.

Psychological Interventions

Parents' self-consciousness about their own feelings in this often novel situation will give rise to fears, as the following example suggests:

> Penny adopted her third cousin, now 4 years old, who came to her from a distant country. The child was extremely guarded and her ways were strange to Penny. Penny had a limited understanding of the child's language. With much anguish, she confessed to her therapist that she feared she might never love this child as intensely as she loved her other three children, none of whom were adopted.

This parent's level of vigilance about her sense of connection could interfere with developing a sense of connection. The therapist's task here is to reduce the intensity of the client's self-evaluative activity. Many therapeutic strategies exist for how to do this and therapists will generally select those that are compatible with their theoretical orientations. Some questions that might lead to productive introspection are the following. Does she love her other children the same or are there important qualitative differences in the texture of her affection for each? Does what she sees as the slowness of growth of tender feelings make sense in terms of the entire context of this adoption? Is her fault-finding a manifestation of a more general or schematic view of the self as "not making the grade" in some respect? Often, a parent's concern about not loving enough or not loving at all is associated with intense shame. The opportunity to express such a worry with a therapist who demonstrates acceptance and understanding has the potentially to be enormously beneficial to the parent.

Nesting

This period corresponds to the first days in which the child is in the home with the parents. For some adoptive parents, especially those who adopt internationally, this step offers permission for parents to feel less anxious about the reality of the adoption. Now that the child is in their home, parents' trepidation that some external force could circumvent the adoption lessens greatly although may not be altogether absent.[3] For many parents, though, apprehension has become such a regular part of adoption that they identify new targets for its placement. For example, some mothers worry greatly about signs of developmental progress and may spend much of their early days with the child obtaining various professional consultations about the significance of any perceived difficulties.

Other painful feelings may also occur. For example, in international adoptions, some mothers feel sadness at taking the child away from his or her culture of origin. One mother said "[she] felt guilty about taking away from the people that she knew . . . even though I knew in my heart that her growing up with a family was much better than living in an orphanage." This mother also described thinking a great deal about the birth mother during this period and feeling sadness for her loss. Other mothers described experiencing loss in connection with having been denied the opportunity to be part of their child's early years. However, for other adoptive parents, a sense of falling in love with the child's culture or country of origin and an immense sense of gratitude may be salient.

A pleasure of this period for adoptive mothers across the different types of adoption is the opportunity to fall into routine. As mothers resume their daily tasks, they can begin to see how their newly adopted child fits into the family, and gradually a rhythm of interaction between mother and child develops. The mother's awareness of this *pas de deux* further fortifies her bond to her child and her child's attachment to her. For example, if a mother is successful in soothing her child when he or she cries, then her confidence as a caregiver increases. Reciprocally, when the mother's regular caregiving responses in relation to the child are met with indifference or even withdrawal, maternal self-esteem is in jeopardy and mothers are at risk for responding in ways that do not support the attachment process. We see this phenomenon of the mother responding to the child's disrupted attachment behavior in Chapter 8.

Another aspect of this period is the mother's realization of the change in her lifestyle that is necessitated by having a child enter the family, particularly if the child is very young and requires constant vigilance and attention. For example, if the child is 14 months old and mobile, the mother must shadow the child from moment to moment; otherwise, the consequences can be perilous. Even though the mother has yearned for this child, the radical abridgement of her freedom may easily feel like the fourth day of a snowstorm and can engender a variety of reactions including surprise, anxiety, restlessness, and resentment. This latter feeling may be directed toward her partner or spouse if that individual is not as affected by the transition. The mother is also likely to have guilt in relation to these feelings on the notion that "This is what I wanted. Why then do I feel so shut in?" The mother's need for periods of relief from childcare is one that she easily may not have anticipated. It is here that postadoption counseling can be extremely useful. The counselor, for example, may point to the usefulness of the partner's assuming responsibility for the child at regular blocks during the week so the mother can attend to other needs. On the other hand, the mother may be pleasantly surprised at the role her partner takes in childcare:

> Sandra's husband brought back their internationally adopted 1-year-old daughter while Sandra remained home with their 6-year-old son. During the first several months, Sandra was taken aback that her husband was extremely active in the child's care, more so than he had been with her son. Gradually, Sandra came to realize that his participation gave her an opportunity for refueling that served the well-being of all members of the family.

Once the child is brought into the family, others will naturally want to welcome this child. Should only the nuclear family be present for some initial period? Should invitations to care for the child even briefly be accepted? What flow of guests is likely to overstimulate the child? These and a host of other questions concern the boundary that parents must establish between the child and the external world in order for the child to feel secure and to begin to recognize his or her new attachment figures. How the mother and her partner answer these questions will depend on a variety of factors such as the age of the child and the child's prior living situation. For instance, a 4-year-old child raised in an orphanage may find his or her status as an only child strange and unnerving. Introducing cousins at an early point may soothe the child and soften the transition. Conversely, a 1-year-old who has lived in foster care as an only child may be alarmed by the presence of older rambunctious cousins competing for his or her attention. Conflict may arise if either the mother and her partner believe that their efforts to protect their child will be construed as rejections of members of the extended family, the neighborhood, or the community. As is discussed in Chapter 11, the importance of anticipating this interpretation and educating critical others prior to the child's entrance increases the parent's freedom to favor the child's security in parental decision making.

Establishing the Rhythms of Daily Living

Following the settling in period is one in which the mother and child each come to anticipate one another's behavior, enabling a pattern to emerge in their interactions. For infants, the pattern is as simple as "crying leads to feeding and soothing." The simplicity of this connection belies its power. For the infant, its regularity strengthens the child's sense of security and attachment to the mother, and the child's manifestation of being soothed fortifies the mother's confidence in her caregiving capabilities. Older children will send more complicated signals, some of which will require all of the attunement the mother can summon. For example, some children will send signals that they do not wish to be approached, when the opposite is the case. The mother's recognition that the child's standoffish attitude is only a veneer covering a longing for mutual involvement advances the relationship and the well-being of both parties. If after several weeks the child does not settle into regular patterns of sleeping and eating, maternal stress rises. One mother, for example, described a situation in which her older biological child, destabilized by the adoption, would frequently and uncharacteristically enter her bedroom in the middle of the night, while her new adopted child vomited any food she took in. She summarized this experience by saying, "I felt like I was just in combat." The older sibling's difficulty in settling on the arrival of a new family member is not unusual. All members of the family, but particularly children, are vulnerable to destabilization at this time.

The potential for such circumstances to compromise the mother's resources for and confidence in parenting is great. Hence, it crucial that others in her life, but especially postadoption counselors and pediatricians, nonjudgmentally assist her in identifying ways to help the child settle into the home. For example, Dozier and colleagues (e.g., Dozier, Higley, Albus, & Nutter, 2002) have developed an intervention package helping very young children to achieve biobehavioral regulation. The goal of regulation is important because dysregulation has been shown to be associated with atypical patterns of cortisol production and higher stress. The caregiver learns to create for the child a predictable environment, which in turn, allows the child to develop self-regulatory capacities. The growth of these capacities diminishes not only the infant's stress, but also that of the mother.

During this period, the child's relationship with the outside world intensifies. The mother naturally feels an increased closeness with those who partake in the joy of the child's entrance into the family. However, she may confront attitudes (even on the part of very close friends and relatives) that are disturbing and serve as a harbinger of challenges that will arise in later stages of parenting. For example, on meeting her new niece adopted from Haiti, a great aunt expressed delight and warmth. However, once the child had been placed down for a nap, the great aunt questioned her niece concerning the decision to adopt internationally rather than domestically. The adoptive mother politely answered her question; yet, her recognition of the underlying question—"Why would you adopt someone outside of your own race and culture?"—incited anger and hurt. Early experiences with subtle racism can induce parents to deny racial and cultural differences to avoid the pain that attends prejudice and discrimination. Alternatively, these moments can serve an educational function for the parent helping her to appreciate what the child is likely to experience as she advances in age.

Postadoption Depression Syndrome

Although for most mothers, the pleasures of this period predominate over any disturbing or painful aspects, for some, the negative reactions reach a level of intensity akin to postpartum depression in women who have recently given birth. This phenomenon, labeled *postadoption depression syndrome* (PADS) by June Bond (1995), has been studied in a series of recent investigations. Such studies have provided different pictures of the frequency of depression as well as the factors associated with it. For example, Senecky et al. (2009) found that 15% of all adoptive mothers exhibited at least mild depressive symptoms 6 weeks after the completion of the adoption, a percentage roughly equivalent to rates of postpartum depression. Interestingly, they found that the rate of depression declined from pre-adoption levels, an intuitively reasonable finding given that mothers had now accomplished their all-important goal of adopting a child. Those mothers whose depression appeared to be affected by an existing condition rather than environmental stress. However, Payne, Fields, Meuchel, Jaffe, and Jha (2010) obtained higher levels of postadoption depression (for example, 26% at 5 to 12 weeks) and found it to be attributable to circumstances within the immediate familial environment.[4]

Although many questions remain, it does appear that a significant subgroup of mothers experience depression after adoption. Although future research is likely to be helpful in elucidating the vulnerability and protection factors, it is likely that both characteristics of the mother and the child, as well as other environmental factors, all make a difference. For example, the mother's own attachment style (see Chapters 2 and 3) is likely to affect how she experiences the child's attachment behaviors. For a mother with a fearful attachment style, interactions with a child showing withdrawal behaviors could be much more stressful than for the mother with a secure attachment style. Foli (2010) identified unmet expectations as another factor linked to post-adoption depression. From her interviews with 21 adoptive parents and 11 experts in the field of adoption, she found that the depression adoptive parents experience is related to the felt demand upon pre-adoptive parents to persuade others of their potential to be super parents. After the adoption, they inevitably confront their limitations, and the recognition of the disparity between their ideal and real parenting selves leads to a precipitous drop in self-esteem.

Psychological Interventions

Although adoption specialists are likely to be aware of the potential for depression during this period, this realization may elude the general mental health professional, who could think that the mother's achievement of the goal of adoption would preclude serious psychological symptoms. Evidence of suffering may be construed as a minor stress reaction. Whether a mother has minor adjustment problems or major difficulties with depression or other negative emotional states, a major impediment to her obtaining the assistance she needs is the anxiety that the adoption evaluation is likely to generate in her. Evaluation is necessary: Certainly, the establishment of parental fitness prior to placement is crucial. Yet, good things can have bad consequences: The requirement to prove herself can be felt long after the requirement is lifted. If a mother has a proclivity toward self-critical introspection, the pre-adoptive evaluation is likely to intensify it. Also, in pronatalist cultures, some people in the mother's life are likely to have taken a naysaying attitude toward the adoption (Fallon & Brabender, 2003). By admitting that she is having difficulties, the mother may feel that she is confirming their negative pronouncements and predictions. For all of these reasons, it is imperative that those who work with the adoptive mother convey an attitude of reassurance and acceptance. They must strive to normalize her array of feelings and cultivate recognition that introduction of a child—adoptive or biological—into a family is a momentous event and that a lengthy period of acclimation is needed.

Early Childhood Years

When we meet the preschool child, he or she may have been adopted in early infancy, in early childhood (years 2 to 5), or any time in between. In this section, we see that some issues are particular to the length of time the child has been in the home, and others are simply characteristic of this developmental era.

Adoption of the Preschool Child

The mother who has adopted the older child has the same task of forming a strong emotional bond with her child. Yet, she is likely to experience greater challenges. The child's capacity to form an attachment undoubtedly has already been shaped by many factors, known and unknown (see Van den Dries, Juffer, van IJzendoorn, & Bakersmans-Kranenburg, 2009 meta-analysis; Ward, 1997). Whereas the infant will engage in behaviors to evoke caregiving responses, the older child may have learned a repertoire of behaviors that convey rejection of, or indifference to, caregivers. In a sibling group adoption, the older child may be competing for attention with a much younger child who is doing all the right things to elicit it. The seemingly disengaged child may be actively mourning the alteration of his or her tie with prior caregivers, birth parents, foster parents, and other important figures in the child's life (Melina, 1998). To protect that tie, the child may take on a closed stance in relation to the adoptive mother. Also, he or she may manifest a host of difficulties in the areas of affect regulation, cognition, interpreting social cues and *mentalization* (as described in Chapter 2, the ability to recognize and understand the emotional states of others; Fonagy, Gergely, Jurist, & Target, 2002) as a response to earlier trauma, severe emotional deprivation, or both (Shapiro & Shapiro, 2006).

Although generally the literature speaks to the difficulties of adopting the older child, Krementz (1982), based on her study of adoptees from 8 to 16 years of age, makes the valuable point that those children who have had a fairly long history of living with their biological families (not true in all children adopted at an older age) have memories that can be incorporated into the formation of their identities.

Psychological Intervention

For the well-being of all family members, significant parental struggles in helping the older child adapt to his or her new family should not be negotiated alone. Rather, parents should tap the expertise of an adoption specialist who is knowledgeable about and experienced in addressing the wide variety of critical areas such as trauma, developmental psychology (particularly attachment theory and research), family dynamics, and so on (Pavao, 2005). This professional can make a significant contribution in alleviating the maternal[5] distress that is rooted in worry about the child's well-being and ability to forge a deep and loving relationship with her and the other members of the family. At times, the distress mothers experience may be due, at least partially, to the activation of their own conflicts, areas of tension that in their earlier adult lives remained submerged. The conflicts and problems that may arise are various. The child's difficulties with attachment may bring to the surface any residual attachment issues of her own. For others, the child's struggles may beget a self-punitive response in the mother in the form of harsh self-criticism ("It must be all my fault"). For still others, the child's difficulties may renew the mother's sense of loss in relation to infertility ("I probably was never meant to have a child"). These examples are a mere sample of the ways in which adoptive mothers may respond to the child's difficulties in adjusting to the adoptive family.

Mothers may have resistances to seeking assistance for the family. As Foli and Thompson (2004) note, "There is a real, perhaps irrational fear in most adoptive parents that the social worker [or other professional] will hold our imperfections against us and even take steps to remove the child from our home" (p. 167). Those professionals who work with the adoptive mother, particularly one who is parenting a child with significant challenges, should anticipate her reluctance both to disclose problems and to pursue their alleviation. That professional should take special care to provide abundant reassurance that strong emotional reactions can easily arise in such a parenting situation, but that their examination is likely to benefit both the child and the mother. Their study benefits the child because when the mother is assisted in recognizing the conscious and previously unconscious elements of her reaction, she gains fullest access to all of her psychological resources—her reflective capacity, her attunement to the child, her conveyance of empathy—to assist the child with developmental struggles. In fact, research shows that the mother's psychological status with respect to particular critical functions strongly affects the child's well-being. For example, van IJzendoorn (1995) looked at a variable referred to as *parental state of mind*. This feature relates to the capacity of the mother to reflect upon her own attachment experiences. Van IJzendoorn found, in reviewing a set of 18 samples, that parental state of mind was associated with the security of the infant.

Through her examination of her own areas of difficulty, the mother benefits herself because those issues activated by the adoption are ones that in all likelihood have affected adversely various areas of her life, even if she has enjoyed a relative sense of well-being. The developmentalist Erik Erikson (1950/1995) explained that throughout life, human beings receive opportunities to renegotiate conflicts that emerged at earlier points in development. Although these conflicts may have been resolved somewhat satisfactorily at an earlier point, new opportunities create potential for a more thorough resolution than achieved in the past—a resolution that enables her to pursue more successfully her current developmental tasks.

Because of these multiple advantages of the mother's self-examination, the adoption professional should strive not only to acquaint her with the importance of this process, especially if she is manifesting or reporting difficulties, but also to aid her in accessing services. As various chapters in this text point out, postadoption services, such as support groups in which mothers can share common problems, are inadequate (McDonald, Propp, & Murphy, 2001) and those that exist may not be easily accessed. Therefore, whatever the adoption specialist can do to aid mothers in securing these services will be of immense service to the family.

The Effects of Trauma

The discussion here of the mother's concerns and areas of conflict should in no way be construed to suggest that the parenting challenges she experiences are due exclusively or even primarily to her inner psychology. Mothering children who have experienced trauma and neglect is a hugely daunting task. Shorey, Nath, and Carter (this text) describe Steele et al.'s work in Chapter 3, but it bears reconsideration in the present context. Steele, Hodges, Kaniuk, and Steele (2010), in an important investigation, looked at the narratives of children who were adopted as young infants versus those who had been adopted between 4 and 8 years and who had two or more types of physical or sexual abuse or severe neglect. They found that children who were adopted later showed a greater proclivity to themes of extreme aggression and unusual patterns of thinking. Although 2 years later these differences were still present, the investigators found that the late-adopted children created narratives that were now more secure and positive.

This pattern of findings is important in two ways. First, it shows that the effects of prior abuse and caregiver instability remain even after the child has been placed in a more stable and nurturing environment. We would expect that the behaviors that are connected to these malignant inner working models would have staying power. Hence, parents must expect that the modification of the child's views of others is going to be a long-term project. Second, the new environment does allow the child to begin to construct alternate, healthier models that seem to exist alongside the earlier schemas. As time goes on, then, the adoptive parent is likely to encounter great variability in the child's behavior. Increasingly, the parent may notice that the child has made major strides, and it may even seem as though the effects of early trauma have been obliterated. Yet, particularly when the child is under stress, the early behaviors can return in full force. Adoptive parents should expect such occurrences. Steele et al. (2010) note that those adoptive parents who are well able to mentalize and thereby to convey to the child their grasp of the child's still all-too-present pain can teach the child that repair of interpersonal breaches and strains is possible. Although the child's negative inner model may not be eradicated, it increasingly loses the competition with the more robust secure models in shaping experience and social behaviors.

Special Parenting Issues With the Preschool Child

During this developmental period, whether the child has recently entered the family or did so as a young child (or infant), the parent will encounter issues that require active decision making. A very partial sampling of the issues with which the parents must grapple is the following:

• At this time, parents approach the issue of when to begin to reveal to the child that he or she was adopted. As the American Academy of Child and Adolescent Psychiatry (2011) notes, experts agree on a variety of points concerning adoption disclosure. The child should be told he or she is adopted and the parents should make this communication. Moreover, the information the child receives should be pitched at his or her developmental level. For example, according to Pavao (2005), what is important is that the young child hears the word "adoption" from his or her parent. Yet, the considerable common ground among adoption writers and specialists does not remove from the parent considerable leeway in precisely when and how certain bits of information about the child's history are communicated. These related decisions include how the parents will talk about the birth parents with the child, how they will nurture the child's identity formation, and how the parent responds to any emerging behavior problems.

• How will the parents handle differences, when present, between child and parent in race and culture? During this era, children begin to see that parents are physically dissimilar from themselves in certain respects. Others may also comment on these differences. Parents can place themselves anywhere on the continuum from strongly emphasizing the differences to ignoring them altogether. How these differences are discussed is another decision-making point: Are they seen as a source of enrichment or as a threat that must be minimized? Chapter 6 explores this issue further.

• Parents must ascertain how they understand and wish to respond to any behavioral disruptions occurring during this period. Unlike the child who has been subjected to multiple traumas, some adoptive children will show mild behavioral problems. Parents vary in terms of the extent to which they acknowledge the problems and the attributions they make about them. For example, the parents may identify their own parenting practices or that of their parenting partner as contributory. Alternately, they may see the fact of the adoption, or the child's innate qualities, as the key causal agents. Still other parents may identify a complex set of interacting factors as relevant. Gailey's (2010) interviews of adoptive parents revealed that factors related to race, class, and gender were associated with which perspectives adoptive parents assumed. For example, she found that wealthier parents were more likely to attribute problems to the innate characteristics of adopted children rather than their own parenting behaviors.

Defining the Problem

How parents understand the problem will affect what they do about it. For example, if they see a confluence of factors—including some pertaining to them, to the child, and to the broader environmental context—as responsible for the child's adjustment, then they are likely to embrace an intervention that both addresses the entire kinship system (including the birth parents) while also homing in on individual family members. Again, social class makes a difference in what the adoptive parent may define as the problem and what is done about it. For example, Gailey (2010) found that working class families placed much more emphasis on children observing rules, and rule breaking more often led to punitive forms of discipline. Within upper-class families, more of a focus on children presenting well outside of the family was present, and these parents were more likely to emphasize medication as an intervention than their less affluent counterparts. Her work suggests that adoptive parents would be well-served by thinking about how their own status on crucial demographic variables affects their parental philosophies and practices emanating from these philosophies.

Psychological Intervention

Those professionals working with adoptive parents would do well to recognize that adoption can beget an array of challenges to the parents' self-esteem (Hushion, 2006). For example, the child's behavioral difficulties may make the parent feel inadequate ("If only I were skilled enough, my child would be doing fine"). Mental comparisons the parent may make between the fantasized, idealized biological child and the real adoptive child may beget shame. Like all human beings, adoptive parents are likely to be motivated to find means to preserve self-esteem in the face of these assaults. Frequently, the parents' efforts to defend their levels of self-esteem are predicated on the use of differences between their family and other families, between the adopted child and themselves.

Adoptive parents can embrace the often-unconscious strategy of denying or exaggerating differences (Kirk, 1984). Ignoring differences permits parents to deny the challenges that place parental self-esteem in jeopardy. For example, by failing to recognize the child's behavioral difficulties, the parents can avoid questioning whether their own behaviors contribute to them. By exaggerating differences, for example, by seeing all the difficulties that the child manifests as attributable to adoption, the parent can avoid acknowledgment and exploration of the co-constructed dimension of the child's difficulties. These defensive maneuvers limit the parent's ability to support the child in performing the tasks of this developmental stage. For instance, the child needs to begin to construct a healthy identity comprehensive of all-important aspects of his or her person. The parent who exaggerates differences fails to support the child in establishing his or her adoptive family membership as a key element of identity. Likewise, the downplaying of differences leads the child to inadequately incorporate his or her own ethnicity, race, and heritage as key identity facets. For this reason, it is crucial that therapists working with adoptive parents provide them the opportunity to grapple with any self-esteem concerns so as to make the use of defenses less necessary. For example, within a cognitive behavioral therapy, the parent may identify automatic thoughts and ultimate schema that constrict the parent's identity, for example, "I am good only if I am exactly like my parents." The therapist can work with the client to challenge such notions. The process of examining identity benefits not only the child but also the parent in that it places parental self-esteem on a more solid, reality-based footing.

Later Childhood Years (5–12 Years)

The parenting challenges that occur during this period are rooted in the child's greater cognitive maturation and more substantial immersion in an interpersonal world outside the home.

Common Challenges

Three areas of concern are likely to be salient during this era:

- As the child proceeds through these years, he or she possesses the cognitive resources to grasp much more fully than previously what it means to be adopted. Juffer (2006) found that the majority of 7-year-old children understood the difference between being a birth child versus an adopted child. This realization often begets complex reactions on the part of the child, many of which are painful. The child now "gets" that he or she has another set of parents who did not choose to raise him or her,[6] an understanding that typically evokes conscious or unconscious feelings of rejection and notions about the self as defective. The child also recognizes that families exist in which children are raised by their biological parents; his or her family is different from this mainstream familial context. Envy and curiosity about this alternate situation can be presences in the child's emotional life. Envy may also extend to any biological children of the adoptive parents, children whom they see as having a privileged position. Anxiety may also be stimulated as the child worries that the adoptive parents will abandon him or her (Rosenberg, 2010). Many of these reactions tend to be unacceptable to the child because they seem at odds with their loyalty to their adoptive parents. These feelings readily go underground and achieve expression in behaviors that mask their origins. The mother's empathy for the child may lead her to unconsciously identify with the child's self-devaluation, an assessment also rooted in her incapacity to be the child's birth mother and to parent the child within the context of a traditional family. For some mothers, a lessening in self-regard also occurs when efforts to address the child's behavioral difficulties fail and when she senses that the child is experiencing psychological pain, the source of which she may not be able to access.

- During these years, the child becomes ensconced within a school system, an involvement that is like to spawn a variety of problems. As suggested in the prior point, adopted children carry a very significant psychological burden during this period, the burden of making sense out of being adopted. In addition, they are expected to acquire a set of academic skills in a range of areas. The former frequently interferes with the latter (Pavao, 2005), leading adopted children to manifest an array of academic difficulties. Additionally, adopted children may have difficulty in school because of the effects of prior trauma, prenatal drug exposure, prenatal malnutrition, maternal stress in pregnancy, and lack of sensory and social stimulation early in life (Gunnar & Kertes, 2005; van den Dries et al., 2010). Problems may also be created for adopted children and children from other nontraditional families (for example, children in blended and divorced families) by a message given that only one type of family is acceptable or through the use of hurtful language such as referring to the child as "given away" (Rosenberg, 2010). Such communications occur through assignments, through incidental communications, and through a lack of understanding when the child has reactions related to the adoption. Witnessing these problems, the adoptive mother must contend with her own pain when, for example, she is repeatedly contacted by school administrators reporting various problems the child is showing at school (see Evan B. Donaldson Adoption Institute report [Smith & Riley, 2006] on school-related issues and their effects on the parents). In fact, the mother may feel shame and embarrassment and worry that the child's behavior suggests that her mothering is inadequate. Also, many adoptive mothers must assume a potentially new and uncomfortable role— that of advocate for her child (Chapter 11). Support groups are especially helpful in enabling mothers to recognize that such struggles are common. She also may learn about approaches other parents have found to be successful in working with the school and dealing with issues such as how much information to give the school about the adoption.

- Children may encounter their first experiences of discrimination from their peers. A key task for the adoptive parent is to assist the child in handling these disturbing events. As Eldridge (2009) notes, the parent can make a tremendous contribution to the child's well-being by helping the child to recognize that he or she can respond to these provocations in different ways (for example, laughing rather than getting angry) and that the offending comments reflect on the person delivering rather than receiving them. She also suggests that the child can come to understand that these difficult moments represent growth opportunities.

- Although identity will be a much more prominent focus in adolescence, much of the infrastructure of identity is laid during these years. As the child becomes aware of the meaning of adoption, the opportunity is created to integrate this facet with other aspects of his or her self-representation. How the parents regard the adoption will bear upon the child's view. If, for example, the mother sees her child's adoption as a trivial part of his or her history, then the child will be likely to minimize its importance, and thereby lessen the significance of others in the kinship network who have had a key role in the child's life, such as the birth parents. Conversely, when the mother regards the adoption as the key, defining aspect of the child, he or she will undervalue other aspects in the construction of identity. As with many other aspects of parenting, a sense of balance enables the child to construct a sense of identity that is broadly incorporative of all-important aspects of his or her being. Critical, too, is what the parent conveys about the child's race, ethnicity, and culture, as well as her own (and that of her partner), areas that will be explored further in Chapter 6 on diversity.

Psychological Interventions

Therapists working with adoptive parents may find that these parents are confronted with a variety of situations that seem novel and disturbing:

- Dora came in to her session in tears. The third-grade teacher said that Daisy, her 8-year-old adopted daughter, had been hitting other children. The teacher acknowledged that as of late, the children had been teasing one another, but she noted that Daisy's response to the teasing was unacceptable. She also noted that Daisy had participated in the teasing.
- During an annual parent-teacher conference, the teacher asked parents Mike and Cindy if they had 10 cats at home. They laughed and said they had no cats. The teacher did not laugh but with eyebrows raised said that their adopted Tammy had insisted on multiple occasions that they had a house filled with cats. She noted that she had been worried about Tammy lying on a regular basis.
- Agatha received a call from the mother of a child at her school. This mother complained that Agatha's 10-year-old daughter, Lilly, had been taking control of the playground and dictating who could play with whom. This mother said her classmates at the direction of Lilly had shunned her daughter. She referred to Lilly as a bully. Agatha noted to herself that this girl was in a special education class with Lilly in reading.

Unsurprisingly perhaps, research suggests that the kinds of difficulties seen in these vignettes compromise parents' sense of well-being and satisfaction in parenting (Castle et al., 2009). In all of these situations, parents are likely to say to the therapist, "What did I do wrong?" The question is typically accompanied by a great deal of self-recrimination. Parents may assume that the identified problem must be rooted in deficiencies in the home environment because the child did not manifest difficulties earlier. The therapist has several important responsibilities. The first is to make clear to the parent that although no one's parenting is optimal at every moment, the identified behaviors can have multiple roots including the child's reaction to his or her progressively greater understanding of what it means to be adopted or the effects of experiences prior to the adoption. Certain trauma such as pre-adoptive child sexual abuse can lay dormant during the early years (McKay, Ross, & Goldberg, 2010). By helping parents to avoid self-blame, therapists empower them to use all of their energy for problem solving. The second is to encourage parents to use the same analytic skills that they have developed in relation to their own issues and conflicts to gain insight into their child's experiences. Behavior has meaning. What is Tammy saying in creating a picture of a house filled with cats? Why does Lilly specifically identify another child in special education as being the brunt of her aggression? What does it mean to Daisy when the other children tease her? More important than answering any of these questions in a definitive way is an attitude of reflection and calm that promotes empathy for the child's experience. The third is to help patients to access resources (see Child Welfare Information Gateway's fact sheet on this topic, 2005) for assistance with their child's problem behaviors and the issues to which they are attached.

ADOLESCENCE

The adoptive mother is likely to have an array of challenges during adolescence, many of which are created by the important tasks of adolescence, which include becoming an independent person and consolidating a robust sense of identity. Many of the challenges of mothering the adoptive adolescent occur with both sons and daughters. For example, Dolan (2012) found in her study of adopted Asian children that both adolescent sons and daughters were more reticent to talk about race-related tensions with their parents than they had been as children or pre-adolescents. Still, some issues take different shape with sons and daughters.

Mothering Adolescent Daughters

During early adolescence, it is common for daughters to turn away in some fashion from their mothers in order to establish more firmly their own identities, become self-reliant, and achieve a sense of autonomy (Graber & Brooks-Gunn, 1996). They must supplant a relationship of dependency on the mother with an identification with her (Besser & Blatt, 2007). Adoptive daughters are no exception. Consider, for example, the case of Camilla and Adrienne:

> Camilla's 16-year-old daughter, Adrienne, was adopted from Ecuador as an infant but she had an uncanny resemblance to Camilla. Throughout her childhood, Adrienne had been told, "You look just look your mother." On such occasions, Adrienne and Camilla would exchange a knowing smile. Camilla saw herself as being extraordinarily close to Adrienne. While Camilla loved her sons (one biological, one adopted) immensely, she felt a special bond to Adrienne born out of what she saw as stronger attunement to one another and a number of common interests such as ballet and theater. Camilla had had trouble with both of her sons in different ways during their childhood years and beyond. Adrienne—she believed—was the one without the problems, save an occasional report of a teacher that Adrienne was writing mean notes to her friends about other girls in the class. In each case, Adrienne successfully convinced her mother that the offended girl was overly sensitive or that her role in the rejection had been exaggerated. Camilla found her daughter's explanations compelling.
>
> One afternoon, Camilla was cleaning out Adrienne's closet and she found an expensive piece of jewelry that she believed had been stolen. All of the family members had participated in looking for the piece of jewelry and had engaged in discussion about whether particular individuals who had visited or worked in the home had taken it. Camilla had been suspicious of friends of each of her sons and they had expressed indignation at her suggestion that these individuals had committed this act of thievery. To Camilla, it was evident that the piece of jewelry was not misplaced but stolen. Upon discovering the missing item in Adrienne's position, Camilla was so flooded with feelings of anger and hurt that she felt dizzy.
>
> When Camilla confronted Adrienne, she insisted she had forgotten that she had taken it to merely look at it. Camilla was shocked at Adrienne's transparently untrue statement, but also wounded that Adrienne would allow her mother and other family members to go through the steps of accounting for the necklace without revealing that she in fact possessed it. When Camilla went to bed that night, she sobbed while repeatedly uttering in an imaginary conversation with Adrienne, "Who are you?" Her husband attempted to console her but she dismissively told him that he could not possibly understand.

Some mother-adoptive daughter pairs experience little discord in their relationship until adolescence, although typically forerunners of eventual conflict appear, as they did in Adrienne's case. The strong connection that developed between Camilla and Adrienne was built both on the strong attachment Adrienne formed with Camilla in her early life and their continuing development of shared interests in values, part of which were rooted in a common femininity.

Yet, Adrienne's behavior and Camilla's shock suggests that the foundation of their relationship may not have included the ways in which they differed from one another and the differences created by Adrienne's status as an adopted child. Quite often, even if differences and uniqueness have been downplayed or denied prior to adolescence, the natural developmental striving to consolidate a sense of identity will foster the clearer emergence of such elements. When they do, they can seem to shake the foundation of the relationship not because of what they are but because of the separateness they signify. Camilla was upset that her daughter had stolen her jewelry and lied about it. But the greater source of distress was in her awareness that she did not know all there was to know about her daughter. This recognition made her daughter seem like a stranger to her. What Camilla had not realized is that her daughter had aspects of her that belonged to her alone. Acts such as Adrienne's often represent an effort to make concrete those separate parts.

Such discoveries can foster growth in mother and daughter and put their relationship on more solid footing. As Camilla acknowledges Adrienne's push to be separate, she should also see that Adrienne is intimately tied to her. After all, it was her necklace that Adrienne appropriated to herself, briefly or permanently. Integrating both sides of the conflict—the longings for connection and separateness—will enable Camilla to act in ways that will further her relationship with her daughter. For example, Adrienne at this time may welcome more deeply exploring her adoption with her parents as well as thinking about her country of origin and her birth parents. Such discussions could reveal Adrienne's longings to have contact with her birth parents, a process that would be likely to contribute further to identity consolidation. On the one hand, recognizing and exploring Adrienne's distinctive background affirms her separateness, but on the other, doing so within the familial context also underscores the connection among family members. In helping her daughter to build her identity, Camilla would be serving as an *identity agent* (a term coined by Schachter & Ventura, 2008), a collaborative role crucial for the adoptive parent to fulfill given the complexities faced by the adoptive adolescent in pursuing this developmental task (Von Korff, Grotevant, Koh, & Samek, 2010).

The separation process may have implications for how the daughter grapples with the challenges of high school:

> During Annie's middle school year, she frequently asked her mother for assistance with various academic tasks. Because of Annie's organizational difficulties, she benefited from this help greatly, and seemed to enjoy the time she spent with her mother after school each day. However, when she went to high school, she began to refuse any maternal help in this area, and her grades plummeted. Her mother became apprehensive, but realized that Annie's reaction was congruent with a natural developmental push. The mother recognized that Annie's becoming more independent was constructive and healthy. She found a young woman to tutor her, a solution Annie accepted because the tutor seemed more like a peer than an authority figure.

Academic challenges intensify in high school, and they can be especially so for those adoptive children whose early lives failed to support their cognitive development fully (Smith & Sherwen, 1988). By taking into account the natural developmental push of this period toward separation, mothers and the therapists who work with them can identify viable solutions to supporting the adolescent's needs in both realms—the academic and the socioemotional.

Mothering the Adolescent Son

Adoptive sons, too, can show an exaggerated lessened dependency on their mothers in early adolescence. This movement may be accompanied by an increased interest in spending time with their fathers. At work here is the son's natural developmental impulse to identify with his father as a means to consolidate his identity. Also driving the retreat from closeness with their mothers may be the very force that influences adoptive daughters to do so at this time—the need to crystallize identity by allowing for the emergence of all parts of themselves including those residing outside of the family. With sons, the challenge can be greater than with daughters in one respect: The former may show less of an inclination to engage in discussions about identity including their adoptive identity (Skinner-Drawz, Wrobel, Grotevant, & Von Korff, 2011).

Adoptive mothers understandably sometimes experience hurt in response to their sons' distancing:

> One adoptive mother had taken her son on a special mother-son trip since he was 5. Her husband stayed home with the younger children. She found it to be a valuable opportunity to hear about aspects of his life he did not typically share. However, she was nonplussed when he came to her at age 15 and said he really did not want to go on the trip anymore.

This hurt may re-evoke early reactions when the child (particularly if he or she was adopted at an older age) entered the family and may not have been manifestly eager to engage with the adoptive parents. As in that early period, the inclination to protect the self by backing off from the adolescent may be great. However, parental remoteness, if sustained or intense, is likely to activate for the child many of the early feelings associated with the losses of adoption. What is important is the mother's allowing the adolescent the space to individuate while maintaining emotional availability. In the next chapter, we see how the son's (or daughter's) father can play a role in reducing tensions and hurts in the adolescent's relationship with his mother.

Searching

The process of identity consolidation occurs throughout adolescence into at least early adulthood, and as noted previously, often eventuates in a more active and focused desire on the part of the adoptive child to search for his or her birth parents if the circumstances of the adoption prevented the child from knowing them. When family discussions about adoption have occurred throughout adolescence, this yearning will emerge organically and be part of the social fabric of the family. At this juncture, mothers are confronted with a variety of issues: Will my child be helped or hurt by additional information and potential contact with the birth parents? Will my child be able to absorb the disappointment of having a search fail? Will our family be able to constructively handle any complexities created by ongoing contact with birth parents? Adoptive mothers also have questions about their own ability to cope with the search. They may question: "Why aren't I enough?"; "Will she like her birth mother better?"; or "How much will I now have to share my child?"

Petta and Steed (2005) conducted semi-structured interviews with 21 adoptive parents (16 of whom were mothers) whose children had engaged in a search, a reunion, or both. They found that "adoptive parents experience very real and significant psychological responses as their adopted child engages in searching and a reunion relationship. With regard to the range of issues experienced . . . , the fear of losing the child seems primary and underpins other themes, such as entitlement and identity as a parent" (p. 240). However, they identified a variety of factors that influence their level of comfort with the process. For example, participation in counseling or support groups lessened the parents' anxiety. The extent to which the adoptive parents perceived their children as ready for the process was the extent to which those parents enjoyed freedom from distress. Both of these factors would speak to the importance of an adoption specialist working with a family embarking on a search or when the family learns that a birth parent is searching for the adopted child. The adoption specialist can help the family with its decision making such as the timing of the search. He or she can also aid the adoptive parent in ascertaining whether her fears of the outcome of a search and reunion are warranted and in creating a foundation for new relationships should the search be successful.

Therapists can provide psychoeducational information to adoptive parents that can allay particular anxieties as their child explores the possibility of a search. Adoptive parents benefit from understanding that generally, the desire to search has to do with the adolescent's wish to consolidate his or her identity (Melina, 1998) and achieve a sense of wholeness. Rarely is it a reflection of dissatisfaction with the adoptive parents or a sign of maladjustment in the adolescent (Wrobel, Grotevant, & McRoy, 2004). It is part and parcel of the natural developmental process of defining oneself, a necessary precursor to becoming an adult.

Reculturation

Baden, Treweeke, and Ahlewalia (2012) have recently identified the concept of *reculturation* as the process by which transracial and international adoptees reclaim their birth cultures through a process of immersion. These authors point out that the adoptee's wish to identify more fully with his or her birth culture becomes more intense in late adolescence and early adulthood, often leading to activities designed to support this wish. Examples are traveling to the birth country, learning one's natal language, or establishing stronger friendships with one's country of origin. The adoptive mother may feel that these reculturating activities constitute a rejection of her, and therapists can be helpful in educating both parents on the vital nature of these pursuits for their child's identity consolidation (Baden et al., 2012).

The therapist can also be helpful in the circumstance in which the adolescent is not showing an interest in his or her cultural heritage. Although the parent may perceive the adolescent's indifference as a manifestation of being at peace with who he or she is, generally, this stance is often rooted in unarticulated apprehensions about reckoning with his or her background. Sometimes, assisting the adolescent in addressing prejudices and racism that he or she perceives to be associated with minority status may be crucial in helping the adolescent in moving toward a full integration of all parts of the self (Gill, 2012). Alternatively, the reluctance may be rooted in the adolescent's sensitivity to any conscious or unconscious fears that the parent may have about the adolescent's identity exploration.

PRACTICAL POINTS

- Both parents and therapists should expect significant changes with each developmental stage due not only to increased cognitive and emotional maturation, but also to the child's increased ability to grasp the meaning of adoption.
- Parents should strive during the pre-adoptive period to form accurate expectations of their lives as adoptive parents, and therapists treating pre-adoptive parents should assist them with this process.

- Therapists make a contribution to adoptive families by assisting adoptive parents in grappling constructively with differences and using mentalization to understand the child and adolescent's mental states and their linkages to behavior.
- Therapists can help adoptive parents of adolescents by fostering a realization that ultimately, the identity that his or her daughter or son constructs—a process that can go well into young adulthood—fosters well-being when it is inclusive of all facets of his or her past and present contexts. As this identity begins to include the individual's goals, it may encompass his or her future context as well.
- General mental health professionals can make a contribution to adoptive families by helping them to access adoption specialists when difficulties arise. If the general mental health professional continues to see the adoptive parent, he or she should actively collaborate with the adoption specialist treating the family.

CONCLUSION

The adoptive mother experiences a complex odyssey as she moves from the contemplation of adoption through the waiting period, the momentous event of meeting the child, the early nesting period, and the subsequent stages through young adulthood. Her experiences during all of these maternal eras are shaped both by her own psychology, her relationship with her partner, the dynamics of the larger kinship network, and of course, the personality features, special needs, and developmental stage of her child. Although research has only begun to explore the interrelationships of these factors and how they bear upon the mother's well-being and maternal behaviors, enough clinical observation and research has accrued to conclude that although the overlap is considerable with biological mothering, distinctive aspects are present as well at many stages of the mothering process. Adoptive mothers, like adoptive fathers, also have special needs—such as, in some cases, assistance in dealing with the diverse reactions of relatives toward the adoption—that should be recognized and addressed by the mental health community.

NOTES

1. A novel that beautifully depicts the excruciating decision to give up efforts at conceiving a child and moving toward adoption is Jennifer Handford's *Daughters for a Time*. This novel also illustrates how complexities in the adoptive parent's life such as divorce and illness color the contemplation of adoption.
2. Some adoption writers would see such reactions as a defensive retreat from loss of the biological child. We suspect that such automatic interpretations constitute the imposition of the pronatalism of many Western cultures (Wegar, 1997). For some mothers, this behavior may indeed be defensive, but for others an authentic expression of an embrace of adoption.
3. Adoptive parents are well aware of, and alarmed by, those cases in the news in which biological parents reclaim their children after they have become part of the adoptive home. Baby Veronica in which the father reclaimed his baby girl is an example of such a case (CNN, 2012). Baby Veronica left her adoptive parents at 2 years of age after having been with them from birth.
4. One difference between the two studies is cultural. The Senecky et al. (2009) study was done with Israeli mothers, and the Payne et al.'s (2010) study with U.S. mothers.
5. The focus of this chapter is specifically on the mother. However, both parents can and do experience distress when the child shows adjustment difficulties, and our recommendations for the father are the same.
6. This statement is made from the standpoint of the child. The birth parent may not feel that he or she had real choice, a perception often aligned with his or her actual circumstances.

Chapter 5

THE ADOPTIVE FATHER

Rao Gogineni and April E. Fallon

There are 5 million adoptive fathers. They have been present throughout history and come from all walks of life and from all socioeconomic circumstances. Among them are notables such as Bob Hope, Paul Newman, Ronald Regan, John McCain, Willy Mays, Burt Reynolds, George Lucas, Prophet Muhammad, Alexander the Great, and Julius Caesar. Then there are the rest of us who aspire to make a difference in at least one child's life.

Adoptive fathers are a diverse group. They can be part of a heterosexual two-parent family, be single or divorced. Or they can be gay, single or part of a gay couple. They can be a stepfather or a grandfather or uncle from a formal or informal kinship arrangement. Despite the commonalities in gender and parental status among all of these men, significant differences also exist in the social and legal context in which they provide for the child, their experience in the world, and society's acceptance of their arrangement and place as an adoptive father (Baumann, 1999; Schwartz & Finley, 2006). In this chapter we bring varied strings of theory, clinical observation, and research together to offer a sequel to the Adoptive Mother chapter. First we outline paternal functions. We then present the father's journey from prior to adoption through the adopted child's adolescence.

IMPORTANT ROLE FUNCTIONS OF THE FATHER

Popular media have provided models of adoptive fathers, such as Brad Pit, Adam Pertman, and Scott Simon, who have offered narratives on their experiences. The synergistic effects of the women's, gay, and single fathers' rights movements have heightened awareness of father's significant role in the well-being of the family throughout childhood.

In the past two decades, theory and research supporting the important role that a father has in a child's development and in the family's well-being has burgeoned (Coley, 2001; Lamb 1986, 1997a, 1997b; Ross, 1994a, 1994b; Silverstein & Auerbach, 1999; Trowell & Etchegoyen, 2002).[1] However, there has been little application of theory and even less research specifically related to adoptive fathers; most of what has been written concerns a narrow demographic range of adoptive fathers. We describe eight important functions of all fathers. In examining these eight functions, we include studies, examples from others' writings, and our in-depth interviews of 10 adoptive fathers who have children ages 1 to 17.

Early Support of the Mother

Although many mothers are more directly involved with infants than are fathers, the role of offering emotional support to the mother both prior to and after the entrance of the child into the household is extremely important. Support can be physical, as when a father handles some of the household chores or cares for the child to give the mother freedom to pursue her own needs. Involvement in household chores and child care changes the family dynamics and eases the mother's workload (Lamb, 1997a). The effect of such a contribution also can be emotional. The father's support of the mother before and after the birth or adoption of the child promotes both mother and child well-being. By supporting the mother, a more effective mother-infant relationship can occur, which facilitates positive adjustment in children (Yogman, 1994). Although the father may be away for most of the day, his entrance into the home in the evening provides psychological relief for a mother who has struggled that day with a fussy or oppositional child. The father's arrival can signal a reduction in anxiety as the mother views his presence as a sharing of the day's difficulties. The father, not part of the symbiotic dyad, can also serve a containment function for when the mother has difficulties controlling her feelings (Emanuel, 2002).

Adoptive fathers play a pivotal role in nurturing and supporting the mother with special needs children. In fact, fathers are key in preventing adoption disruptions. A nurturing husband/father helps ease the stress of the mother and is very helpful in high-level management of the needs of these special children (Westhues & Cohen, 1990).

The "Second Other"

In the traditional family, the father is the second stable object in the child's internal world. Stanley Greenspan referred to the father's early role as "The Second Other" (Greenspan, 1994a, 1994b). Knowing there is a father, or someone else thinking of the child, frees the mother from the infant; fathers provide the infant and mother with some relief from each other (Davids, 2002). The father offers "an antidote to too much mothering" (Marks, 2002, p. 97). A great deal of intensity is present in the mother-child early bond (see Chapter 4) and both mother and infant often need a Second Other to keep them from getting stuck in an overinvolved, claustrophobic relationship. The additional person provides greater emotional stability for the family and helps the child to integrate affective and behavioral polarities. As the infant moves into the toddler stage, the father provides a second significant other, which enhances the toddler's sense of security in moving away from and back to the base of security, which is usually the mother. Research has shown that infants can identify pictures of their fathers earlier than they can identify pictures of their mothers (Marks, 2002). This finding suggests that the father's lesser physical presence encourages the child to develop a capacity to symbolize earlier than might be the case if all-important figures were always physically present to the infant. The Second Other remains important throughout the child's development, particularly when mother-child conflicts involve projections from past traumas. Shacochis, an adoptive father involved in a formal kinship arrangement, describes how his very presence as the Second Other ameliorated and diffused some of the intense conflicts between his daughter Samantha and his wife. "I found myself the patriarch of a family that most resembled a storm-tossed life raft, its jury-rigged sails filled with the winds of loss and mourning . . . for C [my wife], Samantha's (adopted child) blameless presence was a bleeding reminder she would never have her own biological child. . . . From the minute Samantha unpacked into her new life, the psychic polarity between Samantha and my wife began to use up a lot of oxygen in the house. . . . I was the good time Charlie who could be co-opted as a witness for the defense" (2005, pp. 179–182).

An Alternative Attachment Figure

Essential to healthy functioning is the development of a secure attachment (see Chapters 2 and 3 for additional discussion). Although mothers are usually the first and primary attachment figure, most fathers around the world provide an important and alternative attachment even though they do not spend as much time with their infants (Grossman, Grossman, Kindler, & Zimmerman, 2008). During the first 18 months, the child establishes an independent attachment relationship with both parents. When caregiving is equally shared, almost no difference is present between child's attachment to the mother versus the father by the time the child is a toddler. The father's representation of his own history of attachment is almost as influential as the mother's in helping the child develop a secure attachment (Steele, Steele, & Fonagy, 1996). The father's attachment contribution to the child's development is additive and unique and is best captured in the father's sensitivity in play with the child. A longitudinal study showed that when the attachment to the mother is secure, the child's development is even further enhanced if attachment to the father is also secure (Steele et al., 1996). The child's early security of attachment to the father also predicts more positive behavior at school and in interactions with peers (Suess, Grossman, & Sroufe, 1992) as well as enhanced overall mental health (Howes & Spieker, 2008).

In our sample of 10 fathers, 2 traveled to the country of the child's origin without their wives to pick up their daughters. Both felt comfortable in doing so and perceived this journey as the basis for their continued close connection to their child. In one case, for almost a year after coming home, the daughter continued to prefer her father when he was available. As the girl grew, she developed a tremendous interest in playing sports, which pleased her dad. He continued to take primary responsibility for her athletic development, often leaving work early to travel to games. The adoptive father's initial early physical contact served to foster the strong attachment. Sometimes countries' policies convey to the father that he is far less important than the mother, thereby interfering with the father's construction of identity as an attachment figure.

Introduction to the External World
With Encouragement of Self-Determination

Many fathers engage in a qualitatively different way of interacting with infants than mothers do. Fathers love to play with their children. Although certainly much variability exists, developmentalists have noted that mothers and children play in a more conventional manner with games and toys, whereas fathers' play is more unpredictable and creative, with a greater range of arousal and excitement (Lamb, 1997b). Mothers are generally more rhythmic and containing, holding their infants more for caregiving activities and to restrain them from unsafe activities. In contrast, fathers hold their infants as part of play, engaging in staccato bursts of both physical and social stimulation (Yogman, 1994). Mothers hold the baby facing them, whereas fathers hold baby facing out to the world (Emanuel, 2002). The father involvement with the child in play becomes the child's bridge to the external world. In the case of the adopted child, this includes thinking about the child's personal history and biological origins (Flynn, 2002). The greater the involvement of the father, the more rapid the development of the infant, and the greater their ability to withstand stress and be more socially responsive (Pederson, Anderson, & Kain, 1980). These noted differences refer to groups and not individual mothers and fathers. Certainly in some families, fathers will show a strong proclivity to engage in caregiving activities and mothers will be more adventuresome and unpredictable in their play. In a single-parent family the caregiver is likely to have a more expansive repertoire of play behaviors.

The father's playful interactions with the child serve several functions. One, they assist the child in developing a sense of identity in the first years of life separate from the mother (Target & Fonagy, 2002). Second, much of their play has elements of separation and return, which helps with affect management. The difference in each parent's interactions with the child exposes complementary cognitive and affective organizations of the world. The father's form of play requires the child to learn to adapt to him because he presents novelty (Gunsberg, 1994). Third, the push toward exploration of surrounding space independent of the mother and a sense of bodily competence encourages self-determination. Mahler refers to this stage as the practicing subphase (Mahler, Pine, & Bergman, 1975). Fourth, the "good father's" mentorship aids the child in discovering his skills and areas of competence and encourages creative expression (Ross, 1994a, 1994b). Fifth, the early positive quality of interactive play with fathers uniquely promotes peer sensitivity, peer acceptance, positive attachments, and social adaptation and competence even through adolescence (Grossman et al., 2008).

Promotion of Separation and Individuation

Once the child has developed a secure attachment and is confident in his exploratory skills and social competence, the next task in development is achieving comfort in the world without the physical secure base of the mother (and father). Mahler provides detailed descriptions of toddlers attempting this task; it is often accompanied by an almost simultaneous painful push away from, followed by a pull toward the mother, who represents safety. This starts in the preschool child and continues until early adulthood. The father provides the important function of encouraging this separation and individuation.

In his book *The Hidden Wisdom of Parents*, Osherson eloquently captures this important function of the father.

> The father beckons to the child at many different ages. For the baby who only has eyes for mother and is disconsolate when she leaves the room, for the toddler who wants to explore the world beyond mother's lap yet timidly wonders if safety lies only in her arms, for the school-aged child taking the school bus for the first time wondering if it's better to stay home with mommy, for the normal teenager tottering on the edge of adult sexuality and power—for all of these children, father's attention and interest are a bridge away from the comfort of mother toward the comfort and challenge of the larger world. (1999, p. 216)

Thus, the father not only introduces the infant, and later toddler, to a stimulating, varied, and larger world, but also encourages differentiation and individuation, while the mother provides a safe haven when fear is too great (Gunsberg, 1994).

Individuation cannot occur before attachment is secure and the child has competence in exploration. When adoptions occur after nine months to a year, these earlier developmental milestones may not have taken place. The sensitive father will intuit this developmental misalignment and not prematurely encourage individuation. This need is more easily fulfilled for girls whose fathers are less bothered by anxious and clingy behavior. For boys, clingy behavior may stimulate paternal anxiety. For example:

> Robert, adopted at 5 years of age, was placed in full day kindergarten after two months in his new home. He showed little anxiety or distress when dropped off. This "stiff upper lip" attitude was encouraged by his father as good adjustment and mature behavior.

Robert was little problem in the classroom, although his teachers felt that he was not engaged with either the staff or other children. However, at home, his sleep became increasingly disturbed with nightmares and inability to return to his bed during the night. With the help of a therapist, the father recognized the child's difficulties in not being securely attached and his reinforcement of a pseudomaturity. They moved the child to half day kindergarten and the mother made arrangements to work from home. The father stopped praising the child for "being a little man" when it came to leaving. While initially the parents were encouraging of the "mature" response to separation, they began to recognize it as a maladaptive and avoidant reaction to attachment security.

Development of Gender Identity

Fathers can help with the development of sexual and gender identity, although writers offer different emphasis on the nature of this contribution (Johns, 2002). Freud was the first to theorize about the crucial role of the father in boys' and girls' development with his well-known "Oedipus complex" (Freud, 1905). Clinical case reports provide detailed examples. For example, Tyson (1994) describes how the father plays a crucial role in the boy's establishment of core gender identity, gender role, and the foundation for sexual partner orientation. Ross (1994b) recounts a case in which a boy's perception of his father and his attachment and identification with the father contribute to unfolding identity and eventually sexual identity. In contrast, others raise doubts about the direct impact of the father's role in the development of gender and sexual identity (Block, 1976; Lytton & Romney, 1991).

From empirical work, we do know that fathers play differently with female and male children; they are much more active with male than female children, whereas mothers' play is equally active (Gunsberg, 1994). Children who have lost fathers at a young age struggle more with self-development and sexual identity (Burgner, 1985). We also know that when fathers are active and involved, less gender role stereotyping occurs (Pleck & Pleck, 1997). Hence, fathers can offer an alternative to the cognitive, social, and emotional organization of the mother. Identification and disidentification with each parent is likely to impact the development of a mature gender identity (Johns, 2002).

For example, a couple adopted a boy at 4 years of age. Although he had ADHD and nocturnal enuresis (bedwetting), he appeared to make a good adjustment at home and then in school. When the child was 8 years old, the parents began an acrimonious divorce, which took several years to resolve and resulted in the child living with the mother. The child began to have significant mood lability, temper tantrums, encopresis (soiling in the pants), and behavioral inhibitions. After working with both parents and child for 6 months, the counselor suggested that the child stay with the father, in part because the mother appeared to need a break. In addition, as the child entered adolescence, the counselor felt that the boy needed the father to more prominently identify as a boy developing into a man. Over the course of 6 months, the boy's self-esteem and self-concept improved dramatically, as did the behavioral inhibitions, mood, and encopresis. It is likely that the late adoption did not allow for solid early gender identification. Thus, when he no longer had his father physically present all of the time, his incomplete identification caused ruptures in his self concept, which manifested in mood lability, behavioral inhibitions, and the regressive encopresis.

Development of Social Competence

The father's involvement with his children in middle childhood is important in their development of problem solving skills, memory, and social competence (Biller &

Kimpton, 1997; Sarnoff, 1994). Children who experience their fathers' positive interest are likely to develop their personal resources and social competence, whereas those who are paternally deprived are at risk for suffering psychological problems, including a poor self-concept, insecurity in peer relationships, and other psychological dysfunctions.

The father's positive presence is seminal during adolescence for continuing development of social competence. With involvement, the father can be helpful in the development of skills relating to the handling of conflict and power, completing school, decisions about life course transitions, careers, sexual activity, marriage, and financial independence (Hosley & Montemayor, 1997).

The Adoptive Father's Centrality in the Child's Psychic Formation and Psychosocial Life

In the past, discussion of the adoptive father's role has been almost nonexistent (Flynn, 2002). Yet, it is clear that adoptive fathers play a significant role in the sociopersonality development of their children, both in concert with and complementary to the child's mother. Adoptive fathers who are older than their nonadoptive counterparts are in general actively involved in their adopted children's lives. Those who have self-doubts about their importance, in part due to the silence in the literature, may be timid about their involvement, which can affect the child negatively. Steve Jobs said it well, when asked by New York Times writer Steve Lohr (1997) what he would want to pass onto his children. Jobs said, "Just to try to be as good a father to them as my [adoptive] father was to me. I think about that every day."

BECOMING AND BEING AN ADOPTIVE FATHER

Becoming a father is important in the life cycle (Gurwitt, 1994). However, unlike motherhood, fatherhood is generally not rehearsed or practiced as a child. It most often does not become a central or pivotal part of the male identity until fatherhood status is anticipated or achieved (Osherson, 1999). Pertman (2005), the executive director of the Evan B. Donaldson Adoption Institute, writes of his life and focus before and after adoption in this way, "I don't think I gave adoption a second's thought until Judy and I were in our early forties, confronted the aching reality that we could not create a family the old fashion way. I was a happy, professionally satisfied, well compensated journalist . . . (today) it is all adoption all the time" (pp. 207, 216).

Wish to Become a Father

For a man, the readiness to parent often is preceded by the question: Can I adequately provide for the child within my own social context? This question is posed by both straight and gay males (Goldberg, Downing, & Moyer, 2012). The desire to parent is not just a relational dynamic. It involves transition from thinking about me (or us) to the notion of a family. However, with each adoption story, it is clear that every man makes this psychological transition in his own unique way. Hood, a single male, involved in the delivery of health services in underdeveloped countries, writes of his transformation differently, "A woman in Nicaragua patted her swollen belly and asked 'Do you want this baby?' . . . I had seen a lot of kids with bleak futures. . . . But I had never had an offer to take one. After a sleepless night I realized I had an answer to that woman's idle desperation: yes. . . . The seed that had been planted in Nicaragua had taken root. . . . Despite self doubt, my dream was to adopt an orphan and it wouldn't go away" (Hood, 2005, pp. 226–228).

Opportunities to become a father as a single man have been limited. Traditional societal beliefs about routes to fatherhood constrain fantasies about becoming a father. When involved in a gay relationship, the pressures of the societal norms of heterosexuality complicate the struggle to transition this identity. Jesse Green (1999) writes of his partner's struggles in deciding to become a parent (and adopt).

> [T]oo much child-lust in a man made him a freak: a possible pedophile, or at least homosexual. . . . A man who wants to adopt a child is often seen . . . stealing from a woman. . . . Was it finally unnatural—that is, unhealthy—for a man to raise a child without a woman? Was it selfish? . . . these ideas influenced Andy's thinking . . . instead with some money that he had earmarked for a child, he bought a small summer house . . . that's what gay men did instead of having children . . . or they gardened . . . or they collected . . . or they traveled or cooked . . . but it is in the nature of substitution manias that the substitutions never suffice. . . . Ask a gay man why he might want to have a child and you're likely to get an uncomprehending stare. For it cannot be overstated how hamhandedly American culture pushes parenthood on heterosexuals and how stingily it withholds the idea from gay men. . . . Are you unable to afford a meal, let alone a child? . . . Are you 14 years old and illiterate? . . . Are you miserable in your marriage? . . . good have a baby. Are you mature and well off and responsible, but gay? Good collect Roseville. (pp. 22–37)

Berkowitz and Marsiglio (2007), in their study on childless gay men and gay fathers, suggest that the biggest loss in coming out is the realization that they will not be fathers. Over time and with awareness of opportunity, many see that they may not have to abandon their dreams of fatherhood. Psychologically, the transition to achieving procreative consciousness was precipitated by caring for a child, being exposed to adoption, interacting with lesbian mothers, death of a partner or family member, and encountering other gay men who chose to father.

Effects of Infertility

Some estimate that approximately 15% to 20% of couples in the United States are infertile, with approximately 60% of them involving a male component (U.S. National Library of Medicine, 2012). The CDC analyzed data from the 2002 National Survey of Family Growth and found that 7.5% of all sexually experienced men reported a visit for help with having a child at some time during their lifetime (Anderson, Farr, Jamieson, Warner, & Macaluso, 2009). This equates to 3.3 million to 4.7 million men. Approximately one third to one half of the infertile couples seek adoption. Ninety percent of those who adopt have had difficulties with infertility (Baumann, 1999). The majority of non-kinship adoptions occur either as a result of infertility (medical condition or natural aging) or a status that precludes conception (e.g., gay couples or being single).

Most boys grow up assuming fertility and were taught to place controls on it. The ability to procreate is central for most men's sense of identity and for masculinity. Learning of their infertility, particularly when it is due to a male biological insufficiency, is a shock. "Someone has said his sperm are no good!" (Becker, 1997, p. 61). Sexuality and virility are closely linked to the ability to procreate. Most of the self-help literature is geared toward female infertility and so men have few role models to manage this news and are often alone and isolated with their feelings. Feelings of fear, humiliation, sadness, and anger are common responses (Fleming & Burry, 1988). Webb (1999, 2000) and Becker (1997), in their interviews with infertile men and infertile couples, identified themes of profound grief and loss over not being able to father a biological child. They experienced disbelief, anger, a sense of injustice, and numbness around the loss. Inability to have a biological child was of major significance in their lives. Listening to well-intentioned relatives and friends who imply that control over infertility is a matter of knowledge and secret tricks exacerbated their sense of powerlessness. These men reported feeling like a failure, defective, "a loser." One of the men stated, "I felt unmanly, inadequate and powerless. . . . I felt inadequate sometimes when my performance as a sexual partner was not perfect. And that I imagine that my infertility might have something to do with this" (Webb, 1999). Men often equate infertility with prowess and sexual interest (Kupecky & Anderson, 1998). For some men it is the ultimate humiliation, like "cutting off your balls" (Becker, 1997, p. 1). These men often ended up feeling isolated and betrayed, even by their spouses, and inhibited to share. Men are more likely than women to keep their infertility a secret (Becker, 1997). Distancing from others increases the isolation. Men and women often respond to the news of infertility in different ways. Schalesky (2001) provides a good example of this in Michael's story, "No matter how much I studied the subject, no matter how many websites I visited, I couldn't seem to find a logical series of steps towards our final goal . . . whenever I talked to Shannon about the subject our conversations would always end in turmoil. Nothing I said helped. I tried to be positive, I tried to suggest solutions I thought might work, but it only seemed to make her angry."

Working Through Psychological Effects of Infertility

A process of mourning must take place. The men in Webb's (1999) study expressed their need to move forward—to take something painful and serendipitous and find new and positive meaning from it. This frequently involved helping them reprioritize their goals and values. Redefining masculinity was also necessary. It meant moving past their isolation to share with wives and sometimes other friends and family. This sharing can lead to bringing couples closer, although each spouse has his or her own timetable for grieving and accepting infertility. Friction and resentment in the relationship can develop when one spouse attempts to rush the decision to adopt or remain childless. When this happens, Webb advises on the importance of focusing on feelings and meaning of the loss rather than solutions to it. Conway and Valentine (1988) found that multiple losses, existing supportive relationships, and the perception of being a victim or causing the loss mediated the mourning process.

Long-term plans to cope and adjust to the infertility helped (Fleming & Burry, 1988). The quality of the grieving did change over time. However, the impact of the loss—of fantasies, genetic continuity, and fertile self image—never disappeared (Conway & Valentine, 1988). It was reexperienced throughout the life cycle, particularly during the adoption and cohorts' celebrations of their children's life events. Fleming and Burry (1988) likened it to dealing with a chronic illness: One can be proud of the adaptation, but the loss remains. Thus, although a mourning and adaptation is necessary, adoption is the not the resolution to infertility. As Webb indicates, "Children of adoption can never take the place of the biological children you could not have. It simply is not fair to the child" [to place this demand].

Male experience of infertility differs from female experience. Becker (1997) found that when fertility is not the man's problem, he initially ignores it, while the woman becomes absorbed and preoccupied with it. Wives are interested in overcoming infertility; husbands are more interested in returning to normalcy (Golombok, Cook, Bish, & Murray, 1995). She becomes angry that he is not involved and he becomes defensive and feels that she is too enveloped in it; herein are the seeds of threat to the relationship. The loss of fertility becomes the lightening rod for polarization. Working through this involves deciding and agreeing when to acknowledge that infertility will preclude having a biological child, and an agreement on if and when to engage in reproductive assisted technologies. For the man, telling others including family is a significant step in acknowledging the loss.

Contemplating Adoption

Although grief work may never be complete, recognizing the loss of one's biological fantasy child is essential before a couple can move forward and pursue adoption. Although some couples and singles move at a similar pace to accept adoption as the only viable alternative to having a family, a significant number of couples are divided over the decision to adopt a child (Smolowe, 2012). Most adoption specialists and social workers agree that it is usually the men who are reluctant (Smolowe, 1998). This difference may, however, be a timing issue, as Becker (1997) found that men may require a longer time to move to the next step of adoption. Although somewhat tongue-and-cheek, this account written by Smolowe's husband captures a good range of many men's anxieties and initial attitudes about adoption.

> There is a reason men hesitate just a tiny little bit before plunging into adoption . . . time, money career, age, sleep, diapers, and control of the remote. . . . Where are you going to get time for a kid? You don't have any time as it is. If you had a kid you wouldn't get to do anything—even go to the gym. . . . No more winter vacations to Caribbean islands with topless beaches. . . . And what about money? . . . no community college for your kid. . . . How are you going to afford the Ivy League? . . . Do you really want to work at McDonald's in your golden years? . . . You think some boss will put up with your having to stick to a schedule, having to go home at night to feed the baby instead of finishing important projects. . . . You'll be out on the street. . . . How many homeless people send their children to Princeton? . . . You think you'll get to watch *Meet the Press* Sunday morning when Teletubbies is on at the same time? We're not even talking about your own flesh and blood. . . . Weren't we at war with one Asian country or another . . . now we want to raise their children? (Treen, 2005, pp. 199–200)

As the last statement indicates, men more than women place value on the importance of biological heirs (Prager, 1999b). For the next step to occur, men need to relinquish that dream and come to terms with the inability to conceive biologically (Daly, 1988). Parenting and nurturing have to become significantly valued. Severson (1994) feels that because of the importance of the biological bond for the father, they need a "fire in the belly" to proceed on to adoption. The adoptive process requires that both partners must achieve a consensus to move toward that goal. In addition, they must face the societal remnants of adoption stigma (Miall, 1987; Wegar, 2000).

In all male couples, this emphasis on biology may be attenuated. Interests such as valuing family ties, enjoyment of children, and desire to use resources to benefit a child's life were of paramount importance to gay men in their motivation for pursuing parenthood (Goldberg et al., 2012). Generativity by genetic lineage did not appear on their lists.

Waiting for the Child and Transition

For many prospective adoptive fathers, the transition to becoming a father involves a three-step process. First, like the biological father, the initial step entails a general acknowledgment that in the context of this relationship, he has the desire and resources to welcome a child. For an adoptive father, a second step involves an affirmation again that he is willing to utilize additional resources to have a family even without the connecting genetics. Thus, adoptive fathers must affirm twice their parenting interests, which frequently expands and extends the usual time frame. This step, though, may have considerable value; it may help to decrease the ambivalence most prevalent in prospective biological fathers during pregnancy. Once the second decision is made and the paperwork is submitted, an open-ended waiting time ensues. This segment from one of our interviews aptly captures the father's experience during this period.

> [W]e liked the agency and their domestic adoptions were open . . . and that sounded like a nightmare, I guess we were emotionally immature . . . so we went to do an international adoption . . . that didn't work out . . . over Human Rights and we waited for 2 or 3 years . . . we had grown up emotionally and decided open adoption was a good idea . . . the only thing about domestic adoption is . . . it could take a month or it could take forever because you have to be chosen . . . we just really wanted a kid. . . . I hoped that the kid would be intelligent enough . . . maybe just wanted to play football . . . as a man you think about practical matters, whether you earn enough money and whether you will be able to provide . . . if the house is ready . . . I didn't have any emotional feelings . . . it's quite hard. If you are pregnant, you have 9 months . . . so you want to protect yourself from fantasizing because you don't know if you are going to be in this for 9 months . . . or 2 years.

Our adoptive fathers focused on preparing and doing rather than imagining. Another father said, "I didn't daydream. I was thinking, 'now we have to plan like what we're going to do.' I was teaching. . . . I've got to scramble my schedule. . . . I had to get my knee scoped . . . our house was being renovated."

Once assignment has been made, visual aids, a picture or video, are often sent to the prospective parents. In our research, it is apparent that mothers use such resources to begin a bonding process (see Chapter 4). Most of the adoptive fathers in our study seemed to have a more abbreviated response to the visual image, either not remarking on them at all or with brief statements such as "cute," or "a neat personality." This response is more similar to the biological father who also does not use the time during pregnancy to begin the bonding process. However, some are articulate about an immediate connection. NPR host, Scott Simon in his book, *Baby, We Were Meant for Each Other* (2010) provides such an example of an immediate and intense bond. "My wife and I knew that Elise and Lina were our babies from the moment we received their postage-stamp portraits. Logically, I know that's not possible. But I also know that's how my heart, mind and body—my very chromosomes, I am quite sure—reacted to their pictures . . . I suddenly felt the tugging of some huge extraordinary cord from the other side of the globe. . . . We would kick down the Great Wall of China to get to her" (pp. 150–151). Adoptive parents endure an additional third decision. Once the assignment is made, adoptive parents must accept a specific child with the potential for a vague imperfection. Parents are often assigned children older than their preference stated. Children from China often are delayed in walking because they have been swaddled. A host of other physical and psychological traumas judged to be minor by the agency are often implied in the information that arrives (see Chapter 7). Will this affect the child long term? Will taking this risk ruin our lives and our families? If we refuse, will the agency allow us another chance?

Jess Green (1999) gives us a wonderful account of his partner, Andy's, transition. Andy receives a call from the social worker who states that a boy had been born a few days ago: Did he want him? The child had "the shakes," the mother who had denied drug use had tested positive and another couple declined. Andy had a day to decide.

> [H]e sought information that might help him . . . "non-optimal" (a social worker's euphemisms for the circumstances surrounding the birth). . . . Andy's mood . . . from elation to terror to confusion to paralysis—and only a few hours left. . . . Adoption gives you a choice that biology reserves for itself, but in doing so it exacts a price . . . panic of having to make a decision without knowledge. . . . Biological parents . . . don't get to say, "no, I'll wait for the next one" . . . he now resented the choice. . . . Andy spoke to the wife, who told him that the boy was slightly fussy but delightful and handsome. . . . Andy began to think he was Erez. *That's Erez down there waiting for me, calling for me: He wants me to come and get him.* (pp. 54–56)

When the adoptive fathers are presented physically with the child, any ambivalence and distancing dissipates. Most biological fathers report initial elation and exhibit absorption and preoccupation with the infant, which has been termed *engrossment* (Greenberg & Morris, 1994; Lamb, 1997b). The first intimate moments of contact with the child are also intense for adoptive fathers, whatever the age of the child. This adoptive father's expression of his feelings when he first saw his daughter at 3 months of age (writer, Pia Savage) in the foster mother's house echoes the elation and engrossment reported in biological fathers.

> She was a beautiful baby—her blue eyes pierced our hearts. . . . We loved her immediately. . . . She smiled at us—and we cried inwardly. Such joy we have never experienced or ever anticipated. . . . We were frozen with happiness afraid that anything we may say or do will melt some of it. . . . I took the baby from Marion and held her in my arms an exquisite sensation went through my body. She was so warm, easy to handle, so clean, so smooth, so very good. (Savage, 2011)

Men have strong desires to hold and touch their babies regardless of whether they are biological progeny or adopted. Fathers are often surprised at the degree of their involvement with their children from the beginning. Here's how one of our fathers described it, "It's probably the most unique experience a man can have. It's like I gave birth to our daughter . . . as they handed her to me, it was just a remarkable transformation . . . as I put my arms out and grabbed her. I knew that she was mine. . . . Whatever doubts I had to begin with just dissipated within nano-seconds. . . . It's a phenomenal experience."

Establishing New Rhythms

Men envision themselves as fathers based on their early memories of their fathers, wishing to emulate them or attempting to compensate and redo their inadequacies (Lamb, 1997a). Alongside these aspirations are the demands of relationship adjustment, childcare duties, which often involve sleep deprivation, and a general sense of ineptness when it comes to taking care of the child (Osherson, 1999). Research with biological fathers has noted a decline in health status, more disagreements with their spouse, and a decrease in marital satisfaction in the first 18 months after birth (Ceballo, Lansford, Abbey, & Stewart, 2004; Ferketich & Mercer, 1989). Our interviews suggest that these issues are less troublesome for adoptive fathers. Surveys support our perceptions; in comparison with biological parents, adoptive parents have more positive expectations and more satisfying experiences in their transition to parenthood (Ceballo et al., 2004; Levy-Shiff, Goldschmidt, & Har-Evan, 1991). With regard to the quality of the marital relationship, similarly to biological fathers, adoptive fathers experience an initial dip in marital quality. However, 4 to 5 years later adoptive fathers reported a higher quality than biological fathers. Adopting a child may put less strain on the marriage than a biological birth. Our fathers tended to see their children as "easy going" and "mellow," perhaps because they are older or their commitment to adoption has included recognition and acknowledgment that these issues could arise. Also, adoptive fathers have to plan in a way that biological fathers do not.

Like Me

Lamb (1997b) notes that when a baby is born, fathers frequently see the physical likeness of themselves in their child. A similar process, referred to as *claiming* in the literature, appears to unfold in the adoptive father shortly after the child has joined the family. Adoptive parents begin to focus on the similarities between their attributes and the child's characteristics—appearance, personality, talents, or behaviors. The actual physical characteristics and similarities may not be very important (Baumann, 1999). Parents' identification of these parent-child similarities permit them to feel more secure in their connection to the child. For example, one father in our study noted:

> We have the same sense of humor. She's quick like me when it comes to humor. She gets my jokes more than my wife and son and she has a great comeback. One time, I was playing with her and saying that she was so sweet and I was so hungry I was going to eat her up. She looked at me and said, "But Daddy I thought you were a vegetarian?"

With adoptive parents, the greater the identification of similarities, the higher the attachment levels reported between adoptive parents and their children (Baumann, 1999).

High Level of Involvement

After the initial frenzy of visitors abates and the family settles into home life, a renegotiation and assignment of duties at home and a rebalancing of work-home priorities occurs. Men's level of participation in their children's lives is much more variable than a mother's involvement, depending on the negotiation of home and childcare duties. While all mothers have more interaction with their infants and young children than fathers, adoptive fathers, compared to biological fathers, manifest higher levels of interaction, feeding, holding, body contact, looking, and touching (Holditch-Davis, Sandelowski, & Harris, 1999). Thus, adoptive mothers and fathers are dividing their time more equally in childcare than are biological parents. Perhaps, the infertility struggle and the requirement of active engagement may contribute to a man's commitment to fatherhood and thus, his role in childcare distribution. Part of this disparity might be due to an age factor; adoptive fathers are older than their biological counterparts. Those men who postpone fatherhood until after 35 tend to be more nurturing. Adoptive fathers also are inclined to be more educated and financially able, and may be equipped to strike a better time management equilibrium between childcare and professional activities. Completion of the adoption process has required fathers to articulate their commitment to fatherhood. In this process and through meetings with other prospective adoptive parents and the required educational activities around adoption, they have come to view fatherhood as an enriching experience, which contributes positively to higher levels of involvement (Pleck & Pleck, 1997).

Unmet Expectations and Postadoptive Depression

In our interviews with fathers, almost all fathers expected that the process of integration into the family and caring for the adopted child would be more difficult than it turned out to be. Our fathers were incredibly enthusiastic about their experiences, which are in part related to the nonrandomness of the sample (who else would agree to hours of interviewing). However, similarly in a national survey of adoptive parents, 86% reported that the experience was better than expected and only 14% felt that it was more difficult than expected (National Center for Health Statistics Division for Health Interview Statistics, 2009). Although the majority of fathers are managing the challenges of fatherhood and adoption, some are struggling to cope with situation stressors. Adoptive fathers, like adoptive mothers, can experience postadoptive depression. Life stress, depression before and during adoption, difficulty with child temperament, childcare stress, and lack of social support including family and peers have been found to be contributors to postadoptive depression in adoptive fathers (Foli, 2010; Foli & Gibson, 2011). Further, examination of these fathers reveals their unfulfilled expectations in domains of self, child, family, and friends (Foli, 2010). These fathers are more educated and have greater resources, so they often have the expectation of being superparents. They have assumed their children will be similar to them in terms of talent and will readily connect to them and the family. In contrast, these fathers feel that they were often not given accurate information about what their children would require and what effects orphanage life may have on the child's development. The expression of depression often takes the form of feeling overwhelmed and expressed anger toward the adoption agencies at not informing or helping them; these fathers do not feel prepared to navigate solutions to managing their children's difficulties. They often do not feel supported by their larger social network, which views the problem as less of a mental health issue and more as an issue of faulty judgment or hasty action on the part of adoptive parents. One of the adoption workers in Foli's (2010) study observed, "Adopting a child was similar to an arranged marriage and that the assumption of a 'perfect match' was only an assumption" (p. 393).

Research points to ways in which the risk of postadoption depression can be attenuated for adoptive dads. Prospective fathers need to be proactive in pursuing specific information about the proposed adopted child (i.e., their delays, disabilities). Evidence exists that after assignment and prior to adoption, prospective parents experience low levels of psychological stress and express few worries about the child; yet, they are most often lacking in critical information about the child's background (Welsh, Viana, Petrill, & Mathias, 2008). Fathers and mothers need to have information about early deprivation, life in an orphanage, and loss of a primary caregiver (foster mother). It is a myth that a child can quickly be integrated into family routine at an age-appropriate level and that all the child needs is love (Narad & Mason, 2004). Second, prospective fathers should examine their expectations of a child in light of the information they have learned specifically about their child, beliefs and expectations of their own role in helping the child, and expectations of their family and friends. For adoption workers, it would be important to identify prospective fathers (parents) who might be vulnerable to postadoptive depression. These prospective parents particularly need to be apprised and educated about common and potential issues that might initially arise when they return home. In addition, they need to be given potential resources that could aid them if they have problems and honestly let them know what they can expect from the agency after the adoption has been completed. They should be encouraged to reflect on their own hopes and dreams for the child and their families. When adoptive fathers come for treatment, it is important to be aware that this syndrome may present differently in men than women, particularly with anger. The therapist will need to work most closely with the adoptive father around unrealistic and unfulfilled expectations in relation to his own life, the life of his child, and his social supports.

The Adoptive Father in the Early Childhood Years

Bonding and Attachment

Attachment is most often discussed in the context of the mother-child dyad. We know that attachment occurs to the father, even though the mother usually remains the primary attachment figure (Bowlby, 1969/1991). The father-child attachment is particularly important, especially when there are prior difficulties in the mother-child relationship.[2]

The father-child bond is a product of the child's temperamental characteristics, previous experiences with the environment in connection with the child's critical periods of attachments, and the adoptive father's own attachment style and response to the child's characteristics. The adoptive mother interviews were characterized by effusive, lavish, and detailed language about their bonding attempts. In contrast, in our interviews with fathers, the articulation of feelings about bonding and connection was brief, although it was clear that all of them felt a strong sense of connection. One of our fathers who had adopted a girl at 9 months had this to say about the transition, "It was just so exciting and she was screaming her head off at the time . . . she was terrified, poor little thing . . . she calmed down. It took her maybe, I think the first day, she hated both of us. The second day she liked (my wife) and then the third day she liked me. She was a really quick transition . . . reaching out for you to get held and not like crying all the time . . . crying a lot because she was you know so scared . . . she bonded with us really fast."

When the child is adopted after 1 year of age, often attachment becomes a critical variable in the relationship. One father who adopted a girl at 5 expressed these feelings:

> In the first 2 years, it was clear that S (child) preferred my wife. It felt as if she avoided me when she could. When I would come home from work, if S was watching TV or playing and I greeted her, she would not even look up. She never kissed or hugged me. When I attempted to touch or hug her she would pull away or tolerate it with a stiff body. I knew about attachment and tried not to take it too personally, but occasionally it would get to me. I knew I had to reach out to her and would sit with her when she was watching TV. It was still hard not getting anything back for years. There have been small but incremental changes over the years which keep me hopeful. When my wife is not available, she will approach me for things she needs, although she has a clear preference for my wife. She will even spontaneously greet me when she comes home. She will occasionally tolerate a hug, though not much is reciprocated. I am committed to her for life and want to do what I can so that she will be able to love someone intimately. I don't always know how to do that and I wonder: Is it me or is it her?

In a biological family, the attachment connection is often taken for granted, which is likely the result of the genetic connection and togetherness from the beginning. The child reaches out and the parents respond. In the adoptive family, the delayed placement and lack of genetic connection make salient the initial separateness of the child and parents. The older the child when placed, the less likely the child is capable of reaching out in an age-appropriate way and the greater difficulties in attachment. The father's experience of rejection can lead to a protective withdrawal. It can also lead to feelings of guilt—what have I done wrong to cause this? Both of these reactions can be further damaging to the father-child relationship. Removing blame from both sides of the equation is key to the father and child's well-being as is highlighting for the father the child's contribution (personality, environment, and timing) and the salubrious effects of the father's responses. Responsibility without guilt or blame is the ideal adaptive response for the father.

Activities, Involvement, and Independence

Compared to biological parents, adoptive parents report greater satisfaction with their family life and greater family cohesion (Ceballo et al., 2004). Likewise, their children view them more positively (Lansford, Ceballo, Abbey, & Stewart, 2001). During the preschool and early school years, adoptive fathers are recalled by their children as being more involved and displaying closeness than were biological fathers (Sobol, Delaney, & Earn, 1994). Adoptive children remember their fathers as displaying the most closeness and seeking out opportunities for affiliation. As one of our fathers said, "(when) push comes to shove . . . she'd rather be with mom unless she just wants some quiet time because I'm more of a cuddler . . . (wife) S is also really physically active with the kids, but she's not as much put a kid on your lap and watch TV . . . if I have to go away for work for a couple of days, they're like, 'Daddy! Daddy!' Because you know they miss me and just because they have I guess a different relationship with S than with myself . . . yesterday she's exhausted, she's miserable and you know what she wanted? She just wanted to plop on me . . . and it calmed her down right away after she had a little bit of time on my lap."

Fathers' involvement with children in the early years is differentiated from mothers' interactions in their activities; fathers tend to love to play games. Fathers are playmates and encourage creative and more flexible play. Game playing is the only activity that consumes more of the adoptive father's than mother's time (Holditch-Davis et al., 1999). One dad made this observation, "She's just really connected to her mom and in the ways daughters are to their mom. And to me, in the ways . . . you know, the Dad, being the one that pushes her and has her take risks and stuff like that."

The Adoption Story

During the preschool period, a most important task for parents is telling the adoption story. At a time when parents are just beginning to find routine in their roles as parents and comfortable connection with their child, they must present the child with information that highlights the difference and separateness from them. The adoption story emphasizes for both the parents and child the unique way in which the family was formed. As the child matures psychologically and cognitively, the meaning of this for the child deepens. It also comes at a time when an individuation process is beginning to occur. Yet, in retrospect, adoptive families are viewed by their children as more cohesive and adaptable (Sobol et al., 1994). Perhaps it is this fact of biological difference that enables the child to achieve individuation without losing the recognition of togetherness. One father talked about his daughter's unfettered acknowledgment of this, "and she'll acknowledge that she is different from us and we don't look very much alike . . . people look at (child) and say, 'well you don't look like your parents' . . . and (child) would just say, 'Well I'm adopted' . . . we've told her from day one . . . it's not even an issue. She's all . . . 'You know, well obviously, I'm adopted.' "

Fathering During Adolescence

During adolescence the task is to individuate further from the parents and develop a separate and authentic identity. The adopted adolescent must take a "voyage backward" in order to put into perspective his or her biological origins and adoptive family, and find a deeper connection between past, present, and future (Brodzinsky et al., 1998). In that process, adolescents must further grieve the loss of birth mother and father and potential self (Brodzinsky, 1987). Adoptive parents must distinguish between typical adolescent struggles for autonomy and identity and specific adoptive identity issues. In transracial adoptions the adoptive family also must cope with ethnic and racial issues and differences that bubble up during adolescence (Rosnati & Mart, 1997).

Adoptive fathers and adoptive stepfathers are rated significantly higher in nurturing and involvement than stepfathers or biological fathers, suggesting that the more intense involvement in the family at the start of family life, the greater the participation through the tribulations of adolescence (Schwartz & Finley, 2006). The higher the functioning of the young adult, the higher the perceived involvement. Involvement and nurturing seem also to be related to the quality of communication between adoptive parents and their child. In a large Italian study, internationally adopted adolescents reported a higher quality of communication with both parents than adolescents living in foster and biological families (Rosnati, Iafrate, & Scabini, 2007; Rosnati & Marta, 1997). Even if it is true that adopted adolescents may have additional difficulties during adolescence that are not present for nonadopted adolescents, this study suggests that adopted adolescents feel that they can talk to both mother and father about it.

This period of time is tremendously tumultuous in any family. It is often difficult to discern whether the issues are more than just adolescent struggle and strife. One father said this about his adolescent daughter.

> The other day my wife and I caught our daughter lying to us. She had been skipping her after-school activities and meeting up with friends, something she knew that she would not have been permitted to do. When I found out, I felt such anger and humiliation. How could she have been lying to us for weeks? . . . She had shamed our family. When confronted, she continued to attempt to deceive. . . . I wondered, is this just an adolescent let's see how far I can push this? I also had the fleeting thought does this have anything to do with her being adopted? What did I do wrong that she seemed to be so brazen in continuing to misrepresent? . . . Does she not feel a sense of connection and responsibility to the family? Is this normal?

This father's concerns about the meaning of this event are a good example of the struggle that adoptive parents face during the adolescent years. Normal adolescents refuse, rebel, and deceive and eventually outgrow it to laugh about it years later. It is important not to misconstrue the adolescent's poorly designed attempts for independence as the failure of the adoption. Professionals can be helpful in determining whether this is something about the child, an aspect of character that requires modification, an ill-conceived attempt at developing some autonomy, inadequate parenting, a problem at the relational interface, or some combination of these.

As the mother and adolescent continue often to share a more intense and intimate connection, the adoptive father has the additional assignment of helping the adolescent break from this intense bond nondestructively. The following way in which this may emerge during adolescence is classic:

> My wife and C (child) were arguing about something in the next room. That was pretty typical for the last couple of years. They fight over clothes, grades, chores, her room etc. I think this was over watching TV. My wife said something about the effects of too much TV watching. C said, "I don't have to listen to you, you're not my real mother." My wife left the room and came into the room I was in. I couldn't tell whether she was angry or hurt. She sat there silently for a while and finally said, "I can't handle this." I don't like to get into these fights, but I could see that it was important to just keep talking so I asked C to come in and questioned her about the comment. She denied it meant anything. I told her how I would feel if she said that to me. I put on my therapist hat. I could understand why she might have said it. Then I went through all the reasons, I could think of, including Erikson, why she might have said it. C did not have much to say when I finished. I could see my wife felt better, like she had gotten herself out of her feeling and was able to empathize with C and see it more as just an angry push away. . . . It must have worked because a few hours later C was talking to my wife about some of her friends at school.

In this example, the mother and daughter were embroiled in a disagreement in which each had established a position. The adolescent felt considerably threatened and responded in a hostile and distancing manner. This adoptive father saw a rupture in the connection between his wife and daughter, which he felt would be detrimental to their relationship. Although he does not normally get involved in their disagreements, he did in this instance, attempting to articulate the adolescent's motives for her comment, and was able to pull his wife away from her distancing affect and renew her empathic connection to their daughter.

PRACTICAL POINTS

- When potential or current adoptive couples present for treatment, whatever the reason for presenting to therapy there may be ongoing psychological effects of infertility long after successful adoption. Resolution of these elements is an ongoing process that may never completely resolve for many couples. Men in particular may have difficulty in expressing feelings about it and difficulty in understanding that their wives/partners may have a different process and timetable for dealing with the loss.
- Adoptive parents may need help in acknowledging that they may have unrealized dreams for their adoptive children. They may need support to deal with their unrealistic expectations of the adopted child.
- Adoptive fathers are often more active and involved in their children's lives. They play a particularly crucial role in diffusing the intensity of mother-adolescent negative interactions so that the mother may regain her compassion for the adolescent's struggle for identity.

CONCLUSION

We have reviewed the roles and tasks of a father in the context of a man's transformation to becoming and being an adoptive father, which are based on the literature, both theoretical and empirical, our interviews, patients' struggles, and our personal experiences as adoptive parents. This role is important and warrants its own extensive consideration separate from the role of the mother. This is an underexplored area in the clinical and research literature. Over time, the adoptive father's responsibilities and activities are necessarily going to change and therefore longitudinal investigations are crucial to the further understanding of his role. The diversity of arrangements for fathers in a parenting context creates a need to examine adoptive fathers in different situations, whether the parenting configuration is solo, male-female, or all male. What may be an applicable description of one group may not pertain to all. This segues us into the next chapter, which considers issues of diversity in the adoptive family.

NOTES

1. Parenting involves a potpourri of caregiving functions that are accomplished within the parameters of the bioecological context in which the family is embedded. Research suggests that neither parent necessarily starts out as competent. Mothers often appear to be more skilled because after a year's time, they have spent considerably more time with their infant (Lamb, 1986). When fathers have assumed the primary caregiving role, they are as competent and sensitive as mothers (Pruett, 1987; Russell, 1999).
2. The measurement of attachment between the father and child has been elusive, as the same instruments used in mother-child research appear not to be a valid measure of bonding and connection between father and child.

Chapter 6

RECOGNIZING DIVERSITY IN ADOPTIVE FAMILIES

Virginia M. Brabender, April E. Fallon, Alicia Padovano, and Phil Rutter

Throughout this book, our authors have attempted to characterize the dynamics, internal experiences, and behaviors of the adoptive parent, and sometimes it may seem as if this group is largely homogeneous. This is far from the truth. Adoptive parents vary from one another in myriad ways, ways that are likely to shape their experience of being an adoptive parent, their interactions with their child, the stressors they face, and their reaction to such issues as openness in adoption. In this chapter, we attempt to both capture this diversity and identify the gaps we have in our knowledge of how adoptive parents differ from one another, especially those gaps related to parents' or children's adjustment.

A universe of variables distinguishes adoptive parents from one another. The adoption scholar and mental health professional must identify those variables within that universe that are likely to have the most substantial role in accounting for critical differences in how adoptive parents feel about themselves as parents, how competently they discharge their responsibilities as parents, and how deeply they bond with their adopted children. One place to start is through an exploration of those variables that tend to be highly linked with individuals' identities. These variables contribute both to self-definition and frequently to the individual's regulation of self-esteem. One system that has been proposed to classify identity variables is Pamela Hays' (2008) ADDRESSING framework. She has assembled a group of identity variables that have shown to be influential in affecting individuals' behaviors and experiences, and may often be the targets of other biases. Hays' ADDRESSING scheme is an acronym with each letter standing for an identity class of variables. Within this system, A refers to Age and Generational influences, DD to Developmental and Acquired Disabilities, R to Religion and Spiritual Orientation, E to Ethnicity, S to Socioeconomic Status, S to Sexual Orientation, I to Indigenous Heritage, N to National Origin, and G to Gender. This scheme, while having heuristic value, is, like all classification systems, incomplete. Lamentably, adoption or other non-traditional means of building families are not included in this scheme. Yet, this conceptual tool has relevance for adoptive parent and mental health professionals who work with them in at least two ways. It captures the status of any member of the adoptive triad, a status that may influence on the adoptive parent's experience.

Relevant also is the similarity or difference in status of two or three members of the triad on a given dimension. For example, the adoptive parent may be residing in an upper socioeconomic tier and be aware that the birth mother occupies a much lower tier. The awareness of this disparity could give rise to a range of feelings such as guilt and the guilt itself may precipitate a defensive response such as annoyance or devaluation of the birth mother. Such feelings are unlikely to be hidden from the adoptive child.

This chapter addresses a subset of the variables in Hays' framework from both vantages—individually and relationally. Some variables are not covered because they are investigated in another chapter. Other variables are discussed minimally because of a paucity of research in relation to them. As elsewhere in this book, our attempt is to characterize both what exists in the theoretical and research literature and what are the significant gaps. Although the Hays scheme provides us with the means to organize a great deal of material concerning diversity, it must be supplemented with other conceptual tools. For example, within this chapter, we use Baden and Steward's (2007) Cultural-Racial Identity model to expand on Hays' discussion of particular dimensions.

IDENTITY VARIABLES WITHIN THE ADDRESSING FRAMEWORK

Now let us take a closer look at the variables of age and generational influences, disability status of the parents, religion and spiritual orientation, the ethnicity, race, culture complex, socioeconomic status, sexual orientation, and gender.

Age and Generational Influences

Adoptive parents vary in age and this variation may be related to parents' motives for adopting, their experience of the adoption, and their parenting behaviors. For example, some parents adopt after they have raised one or more biological children perhaps because a relative is unable to care for a biological child. Almost half of the domestic adoptions are formal or informal kinship adoptions. The 2005 Census Survey revealed grandparents who were functioning legally or informally as parents are raising 6 million children (Stritof & Stritof, 2012). These individuals may be in their 50s, 60s, or even older. A second group of parents may simply desire to continue parenting even after their children have left home or may wish to start another family after remarriage. Those within this category are often motivated by the desire to respond to children in need. The primacy of this motive often leads to a willingness to bring special needs children into the home. For a majority of people pursuing adoption, a biological child is not possible because they are single, are in a same-sex relationship, or have infertility issues. Adopting a young child or infant is their very natural wish.

The Pew Research Center report indicates an increasing age trend for all parents, although adoptive parents tend to be older than biological parents (Morello, 2010), in part because adoption is not constrained by the biological clock. Yet, social restrictions and agency limitations on parental age may exist. Most agencies involved in domestic adoptions will accept applicants who are over 25 and under 45 for newborn infants. Many other countries have no age limit on adoptions, and may accept prospective parents who are well beyond 45 (Adamec & Pierce, 2000a, 2000b). India has the lowest age limit of 40 with China following at 50 and Cambodia at 55 (Benoiton, 2007). Maternal age limits are a factor in individuals' decisions to pursue international adoption (Momaya, 1999; Yu, 2000).

Surveys reveal that about one third of the adult population still disapprove of women having babies after 40 (Morello, 2010). The social stigma is real. Many adoptive parents report comments from well-meaning friends and relatives, "Do you really think you should be taking this on, a child from who knows where, at your age?" Leishman (n.d.) who writes a Super Dad Column on *Community Blogs* gave this example:

I put my 3-year-old in her car seat the other day and as I was buckling her in I said to her in the way Dad's chat to their little daughters about nothing in particular, "So how are you, young lady?" There was a pause and Rosie replied, "Fine . . . how are you, old man?" She laughed along with me . . . I might say I felt well and truly put in my place. . . . I guess when your hair is gray you just have to take it on the chin."

Many older parents report being mistaken for grandparents and describe feeling isolated among other parents who are younger. They also worry that they may not have the needed energy and stamina. Indeed, it is hard to volunteer for the fundraising parent-faculty basketball game when you have just had a knee replacement. Older parents feel a pressure to look and act younger than they are. One adoptive mother said, "I'd like to stop coloring my hair, but I don't think it's fair to Jessica to have an older looking mother." Yet, significant advantages attend being an older parent.

Advantages of Midlife Parenting

The social stigma of older parenting was fueled by a study of 22 nonrandom students of older parents who articulated their negative perceptions of the their parents' age (Morris, 1988).[1] This finding has been contradicted by a study of several hundred college students who, when compared with their cohorts of younger parents, reported that little difference in affective quality of parenting (Finley, 1998).

Older parents have greater economic security, are more established in their careers, and have the potential for more professional flexibility (Thompson, 2011). They have previously achieved a number of personal goals. Older parents have more stable marriages and are less likely to divorce; they have a greater ability to communicate and have learned the value of compromise and establishing a consensus (Ashe, 2011; Panaccione, 2011). They have had a chance to travel and spontaneously take off for unknown destinations with friends (Thompson, 2011). These parents have committed more time to their marriages and careers before focusing their energies on children. They bring emotional maturity, patience, flexibility, and good organizational skills to the child rearing process (Ashe, 2011). Indeed, if you are an accomplished individual, refraining from projecting your own longings onto your children to fulfill your own needs is easier (Frankel & Wise, 1982). Older parents expose their children to more varied experiences (Kern, 1982). According to Jerome Kagan of Harvard, many older mothers are calmer and more rational with their children (Yarrow, 1987). They express a greater satisfaction with parenting than their younger counterparts (Ragozin, Basham, Crnic, Greenberg, & Robinson, 1982). Their communication with their infants is richer, more responsive, and more abundant than younger mothers (Bornstein, Putnick, Suwalsky, & Gini, 2006). Older fathers are less traditional in their child rearing practices and more sensitive during play (Recker, 2007). Overall, negative effects of increased parental age on the well-being of the child seem to be few (Boivin et al., 2009).

In addition, many parents experience psychological benefits of being a parent in midlife. They report that it pushes them to develop and maintain a youthful perspective and to have a daily life that is more energetic. At a time in life when social isolation may increase, it encourages intense connection in a relationship. Also, children provide moments of intense joy and enliven even well-worn activities (Arnold, 2011). Finally, young children are fearless and push parents toward new pursuits. All parents get tired, and the older parent may be less able to stay up all night and perform at full capacity the next day. The "challenge is to be a parent, not an 'old' parent" (Recker, 2007, p. 2).

When the Grandparent Becomes the Parent

In the past 100 years life expectancy has increased from 47 to 76 years (He, Sengupta, Velkoff, & DeBarros, 2005). Medical technology has enabled older adults to maintain good health. As a result, relatives—grandparents, great aunts and uncles, and even older siblings—are often available to care for young children when parents are disabled or have died. A third of the children in foster care are cared for by formal kinship arrangements in which, typically, a grandparent has responsibility for the child (Child Welfare Information Gateway, 2012a). In addition, the largest portion of substitute caregiving is children living informally with grandparents, aunts, and uncles. Overall approximately 2.4 million grandparents have provided parental or primary care for grandchildren (Population Reference Bureau, 2012). In a qualitative study, Metcalfe (2010) explores the experiences of this older group involved with primary caregiving responsibilities. This group is altruistically motivated to contribute to future generations and desire to help their families. Especially helpful in such circumstances are the grandparents who step in when their teenagers have given birth to children and lack the psychological readiness to be parents. They view being older as an asset, drawing on previous life lessons for guidance and internal support.

A major concern for the older adult is how she will manage physically and psychologically if she took on such responsibility. Several studies have examined the effects of caregiving on physical and mental health in the older population. The good news is that three quarters of grandparents raising grandchildren report their health to be the same or improved compared with prior to their caregiving (Gibbons & Jones, 2003). Relative to a normative sample, the life stress of raising a grandchild does not detrimentally affect physical health (Leder, Grinstead, & Torres, 2007). In fact, some have reported weight loss and improved health as a result of the increased demands of caring for a young child (Musil, Gordon, Warner, Zauszniewski, Standing, & Wykle, 2010). The increased responsibility often makes it difficult to keep medical appointments or engage in self-care, problems that can negatively impact health. Other factors also negatively affect health. First, if there are prior medical issues, such as diabetes and heart disease, the stress of caregiving can exacerbate them (Minkler, Roe, & Price, 1992). Stress can be intensified by having to care for more than one grandchild and the presence of behavioral problems or other disabilities in the child (Leder et al., 2007). Thus, a healthy grandparent caring for a normal child should not expect to have additional physical problems compared with his age cohort.

More of a problem for grandparents is the psychological impact of having parental responsibilities for a child: "I thought I was done with all of this. Can I really be changing diapers again?" "What happened to 'Happy when they arrive and happy when they leave'?—These kids never leave!" Studies show that grandparents who have full-time responsibility for their grandchildren have decreased psychological well-being when compared to those grandparents who do not have full-time care (Dolbin-MacNab, 2006). They experience increased depression, loss of social networks, and strain in their marital relationship (Robinson & Wilks, 2006). The particular context that accompanies the new role of primary caregiving also influences how the grandparent views the task. Those grandparents who provided care through formal kinship agreements were much happier than those who provided informal kinship care (Bunch, Eastman, & Griffin, 2007). The latter arrangements have less role clarity, more ambiguous boundaries, and are more likely to produce feelings of entrapment in grandparents as they feel forced to assume the primary role of parenting rather than the expected role of grandparenting.

What can help? The following are a few suggestions for adoptive or primary caregiving grandparents, or therapists working with them.

Establish clarity of the expected role. Grandparents do not pursue a formal arrangement for many reasons, including difficulties in directly confronting the parent about defining his or her role in the care of the child. When possible, a formal arrangement is likely to provide clarity for both the caregiver and child; it increases the child's psychological safety and decreases depressive symptomatology in the caregiver. With a formal kinship arrangement, local and state financial assistance may also be available if needed.

Make peace with the situation. This situation arises because of some life difficulty, often unforeseen. Choices are limited and a family member needs help. Grandparents desire to aid, but psychologically they were planning to do so in a more limited grandparent role. If they are to be effective caregivers and not compromise their psychological health, they will need to come to terms with the ambivalence around the desire to help versus the resentment experienced as a result of feeling as if the golden years of life have been stolen.

Make personal health a top priority. This new situation often requires a reprioritization of activities and responsibilities. One's own medical appointments should continue to be a top priority.

Seek support. Finding social support is key to a successful arrangement. Family and community support for this role makes a considerable difference in the psychological well-being of the grandparent (see Chapter 12 for a further discussion of support groups). The capacity of friends, neighbors, and church to offer the caregiver time off for refueling is an enormous psychological lift (Metcalfe, 2010). Support groups can combat the sense of isolation and help with feeling understood. Formal group, family, couples, or individual therapy may help resolve the ambivalence, reduce family conflict, and provide additional support (Metcalfe, 2010). Workshops on parenting improve confidence in making difficult decisions. Parent training and parent-child groups such as the ones originally designed by Henri Parens (2010; Frank & Rowe, 1986) enable the grandparent to appreciate developmental milestones and provide support for healthy parenting practices.

Disability Status of the Adoptive Parent

With the *Adoption and Safe Families Act* of 1997, the door is no longer closed to people with various physical disabilities to become parents. Increasingly, the recognition exists that while all adopted children need love, empathy, and understanding, other needs are more specific. For example, a parent with severe arthritis who may be unable to adequately shadow a toddler may be fully able to parent an older child. Also important is the entire web of support that a parent with disabilities can muster. For example, the proximity of grandparents, aunts and uncles, and close friends can be helpful adjuncts to parental activity.

Religion and Spiritual Orientation

There are more than 50 formal religious traditions in the United States (Pierce, 1999b). In addition, many individuals view themselves as spiritual without identifying with a particular religious affiliation. Although all the major formal religions in the

United States have great concern for the care of children and those of orphan status, they differ significantly in how they define adoption, the importance of ethnicity or bloodline, and the religious rites associated with adoption.

Christian Doctrine of Adoption

According to the American Religious Identification Survey (ARIS), 75% of Americans identify themselves as Christians (Kosmin & Keysar, 2009).[2] For many, the Adoption Doctrine is the foundation of Christianity. For Christians, salvation is a matter of being adopted and entering the family of God (Marshner, 1999). Theologically, then, the act of adoption "most directly mirrors God's actions toward us" (Olsen, 2010). Christians point to the stories of Moses and Esther in the Old Testament as signs of the acceptability and virtue of child adoption. In the book of Ruth, Noemi took upon her own knees the baby, Obed, born to Ruth and Boaz (Marshner, 1999). The baby became an Israelite, despite Ruth's foreign blood. Obed begat Jess who begat David. The royal status of David and his heirs was the result of David and his house being adopted by God. In 2 Samuel 17:4 God said, "I shall be the father to him, and he shall be a son to me."

Christian groups have also promoted child adoption of less "desirable" orphans (Barnhill, 2010). Project Wait No More initiated in Colorado Springs at the New Life Church to aid in reducing the foster children who were eligible for adoption. They cut the number of foster care children eligible for adoption in half as a result of this project (Draper, 2010). The efforts of an African American Roman Catholic Priest, Father George Clements, to find homes for Chicago children of color was the start of the One Church One Child Program and resulted in more than 100,000 children being adopted (Fr. George Clements, 2003). Similarly, the wife of a minister of the Bennett Chapel Missionary Baptist church in Texas felt spiritually called on to adopt a child in need and led friends and members to adopt 70 children of color (Belanger, 2009). Although some of these couples come to this route because of infertility difficulties, many do not. They specified that central among their reasons for adoption was their intent to fulfill God's plan (Belanger, Copeland, & Cheung, 2008).

Jewish Views of Adoption

The first commandment in the Torah, "Be fruitful and multiply," places having children as an obligation of the couple and children at the center of family life (Gold, 1999). Yet a higher proportion of Jewish couples are unable to have biological children (Brodsky & Rosenfeld, 2005).[3] Most Jewish couples who adopt see this route as the only alternative to building a family. In practice, they adopt children from a variety of religious and ethnic backgrounds and, with the support of their religious community, raise them as Jews. Still, within traditional Jewish law and in contemporary religious practice, contradictory views regarding adoption seem to exist. The Bible and Talmud are filled with many beautiful examples of respected people who parent children born to others. In Genesis, Abraham adopts his servant Eliezer. The most famous, Moses, is found and raised by Pharaoh's daughter. The Talmud is unequivocal in maintaining that parents are those that parent, not give birth to a child (Prager, 1999a). Gold (1999) quotes from Exodus Rabbah, "He who brings up a child is to be called its father, not he who gave birth" (p. 5).

At the same time, Jewish law emphasizes bloodlines in establishment of identity. Many rabbis, particularly orthodox, strongly encourage adoptive parents to obtain documentation of the birth parents' Jewish status. When the birth mother is gentile, a conversion is required. How formal this is varies by Rabbi and congregation. Formal conversion to Judaism is accomplished by ritual circumcision (even if already circumcised) for a boy and a mikvah, a ritual bath, for both boys and girls. The Bar/Bat Mitzvah becomes a very important celebration for the child to reaffirm or protest the conversion. Adoption makes salient an unresolved issue in the Jewish community of who is Jewish, with many rabbis not recognizing the Jewishness of many adopted children (Gold, 1999). The importance of lineage can be seen in Israel's unparalleled public funding for procreative technologies (Birenbaum-Carmeli, 2009). In contrast, domestic adoption entails a 5- to 7-year wait and numerous adoptive parent requirements (income, schooling, same religion, etc.). International adoptions are constrained by bureaucratic intricacy and cost more than the average yearly Israeli salary.

Jewish families have found ways to resolve this conflict. For example, Rabbi Gold (1999) advises Jewish families to regard as the true parent the one who teaches culture and values, recognizing that each adopted child comes with a history and never loses his or her birth identity. That Jews on an individual level have resolved conflicting notions about adoption within Judaism is seen in the fact that adoptions are very common and the communities celebrate them (Brodsky & Rosenfeld, 2005). Undoubtedly, how nurturing the religious community is of the new adoptive family depends on the community itself (as is true of the communities of other religions). One single mother who adopted a Chinese daughter described her Reformed synagogue as having a wholly welcoming response. She noted that the acceptance of differences was a hallmark of this religious institution, one she carefully selected as the spiritual home for her adoptive family.

Islamic Views of Adoption

The most well-known orphan in Islamic culture is the Prophet Muhammad who lost both parents and grandparents before he was 8 and was subsequently raised by an uncle. He is to have said that a person who takes care of an orphan will be next to him in Paradise (Huda, n.d.). The importance of caring for orphans is well established in Islam and the role of the guardian is an important one. Yet, specific rules in the Qur'an about the relationship between an orphan and the adoptive family have led some to proclaim that adoption is prohibited in Islam. The relevant Qur'an verse is: "God has not made . . . . your adopted sons your sons. . . . . Call them by the names of their fathers" (Ahmad, 1999, p. 246). Adoption as we know it in the United States does not exist within Islam. Islam allows for a guardian/child relationship. The term used is *kafala*, which means to feed or sponsor, which is more similar to our notion of foster parent. That is, a caretaker agrees to take this role of educator and protector "as a father would do for his son" (Ahmad, 1999, p. 245). Adoptive families are trustees and caretakers of someone else's child (Huda, n.d.). Identity, established by bloodline, is never denied. To that end, these children retain their biological family name and inherit from their biological parents, not necessarily from the adoptive parents. The trend in U.S. adoptions to have continued involvement with the biological parent is more in line with Islamic law than the previous practice of hiding the identity of the birth parents. As U.S. practices and law do not entirely overlap with the teachings from the Qur'an, the adoptive couple needs to face two issues, the first of which is the issue of family name. Most U.S. adoptions involve acquiring the adoptive family name whereas the Qur'an encourages the child to keep his or her biological name. Although legally, the biological family name can be kept, such a practice calls attention to the child's status such as when in school; other children, Teachers, and administrators routinely ask for documentation or proof of the relationship when the name is different. It also can create an identity challenge for the child and undermine his or her sense of connection to the adoptive family. Given that the predominant practice is to take the surname of the adoptive parents, the child having been exposed to the values of Western culture may question his or her status and security with the adoptive family. Second, when it comes to marriage, U.S. law is more restrictive in not permitting marriage to biological and adoptive siblings and often first cousins, whereas Islamic practice allows the adopted child certain marriages within the adoptive family. Lastly, U.S. law for the purposes of inheritance treats adoptive children with the same accord as biological children. U.S. law, however, does recognize the validity of wills that use a distribution based upon Islamic law (Ahmad, 1999). Thus, the traditional Islamic allocation of assets would need to be spelled out in a will or U.S. guidelines will apply.

Hindu Law of Adoption

The Shastric Hindu Law views adoption as sacramental rather than secular. The purpose of adoption is to secure a son to perform funeral rites for the father and to continue one's lineage. Traditionally Hindus believed that a father who died without having a son would go to hell, *poota*. Only a son could save the father (Agrawal, n.d.). Accordingly, traditional Hindu Law allowed only the adoption of a boy who was from the same caste as the father, was not an orphan, did not possess an infirmity or whose mother the adoptive father could not marry (Aktar & Abdullah, 2007). All rights and restrictions applying to the natural family were equally in force with the adopted child, although all rights of the biological parents were replaced with adoptive parent rights (Onsker, 2011). These traditional Hindu laws have been updated such that a Hindu female can adopt if she is not married. However, adoptions for both male and female Hindus are possible only if the adoptive parent has no child or grandchild of that sex. Thus, traditional Hindu thought considers adoption a method to complete the family structure and ensure the family future. Practicing Hindu Americans are likely to seek to adopt only Hindu children. In India, many informal adoptions take place among relatives for the purposes of inheritance, heirs, and attempts to provide advantageous marriages. However, given our immigration laws, it is difficult for many Hindus to continue this tradition in the United States.

Religion, Law, and the Practice of Adoption in the United States

Although a great deal of open controversy over the practice of racial matching has occurred, much less has been said about the role of religion and the practice of *religious matching* (pairing parents and children who have the same religion) in determining suitability for adoption (Modell & Dambacher, 1997; see Chapter 1 for the early history of religious matching). Public agencies are governed by the "best interests of the child" doctrine, which is delineated in the Standards of Excellence for Adoption Service (Child Welfare League of America, 2000). This document in all of its revisions explicitly allows for the right to be placed into a family that reflects their racial or cultural heritage unless this interferes with an expedient placement. Under certain circumstances, the best interests of the child have been judged to be determined by a racial or ethnic group regardless of expediency as in the case of *Mississippi Band of Choctaw Indians v. Holyfield* (Goldsmith, 1990; Strong, 2005). Procedure and protocol are made in state-by-state laws and court decisions, but agencies have enormous flexibility and some believe that matching has been more driven by agency policy than by law (Modell & Dambacher, 1997).

Several states have religious matching statutes, which allow for a child to be placed with adoptive parents of the same religion unless it would substantially delay placement. At the same time, a number of states have indicated that religion may not be the sole determinant of a placement (Beschle, 1989). As is established in our constitution, the government cannot prefer one religion over another; it cannot endorse an action that either advances or inhibits religion.[4]

Ethnicity, Race, and Culture

Throughout the history of adoption, the ethnicity, race, and culture of all members of the adoptive triad have given rise to a host of issues, which have been the object of heated rhetoric and serious investigation. Among the identity variables explored in this chapter, probably no others have received so much attention, and for good reason. Adoption and culture are inextricably tied because each culture defines what families are, and how they are created. Within some cultures, adoption is seen as a very natural way of building a family, and within others, much less so. How adoptions occur also is culturally rooted: Does adoption require a formal legal process or is it simply a family's taking-in of a child in need (see Schachter's [2009] discussion of *hanai*, a Hawaiian form of adoption whereby a child who needs a home is welcomed into a family and cherished)? Cultures also differ in the value placed on adoption: To what extent is adoption perceived as a valued means of building a family? Although cultural perspectives on adoption may not be evident, on a day-to-day basis they bear critically on the adoptive family's experience. To the extent that the adoptive parent ascertains these cultural values, assumptions, and beliefs related to adoption, to that same extent his or her experiences as an adoptive parent interacting with those in the broader community are likely to be coherent.

Race, ethnicity, and culture also figure prominently in adoption because individuals adopt children who differ from themselves on these dimensions. Children adopted internationally often differ from their parents in terms of ethnicity and culture, and frequently in terms of race.[5] According to the *2007 National Survey of Adoptive Parents*, 28% of all adoptions from the foster care system are transracial, transethnic, or transcultural (U.S. Department of Health and Human Services, 2011). The variation between the adoptive child and parents on these dimensions molds the identity of each member of the family system and the family system as a whole. That is, a transracial or transcultural adoption creates a transracial or transcultural child, parent, and family.

Any discussion of race/ethnicity/culture requires definitions of these variously used terms. Here, race is seen in consistency with the American Psychological Association (APA) Guidelines: "Race, then, is the category to which others assign individuals on the basis of physical characteristics, such as skin color or hair type, and the generalizations and stereotypes made as a result" (American Psychological Association [APA], 2003). Likewise, we embrace the definition of culture offered by this group: "the belief systems and value orientations that influence customs, norms, practices, and social institutions, including psychological processes (language, care taking practices, media, educational systems) and organizations (media, educational systems; Fiske, Kitayama, Markus, & Nisbett, 1998)" (APA, 2003, p. 380). Finally, ethnicity refers to "the acceptance of the group mores and practices of one's culture of origin and the concomitant sense of belonging" (APA, 2003, p. 380).

The reader interested in exploring the writing that has been done on this congeries of identity facets will quickly discover that the literature is vast. Important volumes have been devoted to this topic such as Steinberg and Hall's (2000) *Inside Transracial Adoption*, Simon and Alstein's (2000) *Adoption Across Borders: Serving the Children in Transracial and Intercountry Adoptions*, Marre and Briggs's (2009) *International Adoption: Global Inequalities and the Circulation of Children*, and Gailey's (2010) *Blue Ribbon Babies and Labors of Love: Race, Class, and Gender in U.S. Adoption Practice*, to name a recent few. This treasure trove offers readers a wealth of information and has implications for many areas, including public policy. Our focus is on those studies that illumine the adoptive parents' experiences and that have ramifications for their parenting activities.

"How should I parent my adopted child who differs from me in race/ethnicity/ culture? And does it make a difference in how my child develops?" Although the research literature cannot yet answer these questions comprehensively and certainly not definitively, findings do suggest that these are very good questions for three reasons. First, simply the fact of being different from the other members of the family in appearance or cultural background can be challenging to a child. In a study of Dutch 7-year-old children adopted from Colombia, Korea, and Sri Lanka, Juffer (2006) found that children from Sri Lanka and Colombia who experienced distress over being different also had more frequent behavior problems.

Second, the adoptee's race, natal culture, and ethnicity are facets of his or her identity, facets that must be nurtured and integrated with all else that defines the child, including the parents' ethnicities, cultures, and races. In Chapter 1, we discussed the finding that children who were raised by parents of a different race demonstrated a level of adjustment comparable to that of children raised by parents of their own race (McRoy, Zurcher, Lauderdale, & Anderson, 1984; Silverman & Feigelman, 1981). However, these early findings also suggest that the adoptive parents' provision of regular opportunities for the child to interact with individuals within his or her own race make a difference in the child's construction of his or her own identity. McRoy et al. (1982) found that when the transracial family ensured that their children had substantial exposure to others of their own race, their black adoptive children identified themselves as being black and saw this identification positively. Conversely, when children lacked contact with individuals of their race, their notions of black people were stereotypic and they saw themselves as faring better being lodged in a white family. Essentially, by failing to have access to a black community, black children were prone to engage in self-disavowal. DeBerry, Scarr, and Weinberg (1996) found that adoptive parents were more likely to create a bicultural environment for young children but half ceased to do so when the adoptees reached adolescence. This lessening emphasis was also accompanied by the adolescents' diminished identification with African American culture. Yoon (2001) observed that Korean-born adolescents whose parents who fostered interest in their natal culture had a more positively toned racial/cultural identity and better adjustment than parents who ignored this facet of the adoptee's identity.

Third, in some cases, children's race, natal culture, or ethnicity are associated with lack of privilege and discrimination, beyond that attached to being an adoptee (see Chapter 11 for an elaboration of this point). The responsibility of helping their children to respond constructively to expressions of prejudice that they may encounter outside of the home falls heavily on the adoptive parent.

Contemplating the special needs of the adopted child within a transracial/ transcultural family bespeaks of a parental sensitivity and reflectiveness that is likely to benefit children regardless of the specific approaches the parent takes. Nonetheless, currently, research is underway that will shed light on how parents can use their sensitivity and reflectiveness to best effect. Baden and Steward (2000, 2007) proposed the *Cultural-Racial Identity Model*, a theoretical framework designed to capture variation among adoptive individuals in the structure of their identifications. By looking at the diversity among adopted children, Baden and Steward address a fundamental limitation of most research in this area. Most typically, studies examining adoptive child adjustment entail comparisons between adopted and nonadopted children. Such contrasts fail to illumine what attitudes and psychological features of adopted children are most associated with higher levels of socioemotional adjustment. In contrast, Baden and Steward's model, by looking at different identifications adopted children have, can see which identifications serve their well-being.

The Baden-Steward model (Baden & Steward, 2000; Baden, 2007; Baden, 2008) consists of two identity axes, one of which is race and the other, culture. By separating these axes, Baden and Steward enable investigators to examine the individual and overlapping influences of race and culture. The definitions of race and culture appear largely consistent with those we have offered in this section. The model builders are careful to stipulate their use of race as a sociocultural construction rather than a biological phenomenon. Residing within the Cultural Identity Axis are the *Adoptee Culture Dimension*, capturing the extent of the transracial adoptee's identification with his or her natal culture, and the *Parental Culture Dimension*, which pertains to the adoptee's identification with the parents' culture. Identification in this model is seen as manifesting itself in knowledge, awareness, competence, and comfort with a particular culture (e.g., natal, parental, other cultural groups, no social group). These dimensions can be factorially combined. For example, an adopted adolescent could be low in both parental culture and adoptee culture dimensions, and Baden and Steward would see this combination as a status of culturally undifferentiated identity. Another adolescent low in parental culture identification and high in adoptee culture identification has a pro-self identification, according to the model. The *Racial Identity Axis* provides the same information for race, and once again, when the adoptee race and parental race identifications are examined together, four different identity statuses emerge. When the racial and cultural axes are combined, 16 statuses are yielded, providing a nicely differentiated picture of adoptees' identities.

Investigators are beginning to use the Baden-Steward Identity model to determine whether particular identity statuses are associated with different levels of adjustment in adopted individuals. In one study of this model, Baden (2007) looked at the adjustment levels of transracial nonwhite young adult adoptees,[6] all of whom had been adopted by White couples as a function of cultural/racial identity. One major finding was that participants did show a great deal of scatter in terms of identity statuses. This finding revealed that the Baden-Steward Identity model captures the variability among adoptees in this important area of identity. It also makes the obvious but still important point that transracial adoptees develop various identification configurations. A second finding was that the only dimension within the model that predicted adoptee adjustment was parental culture: Being able to identify with their parents' culture appeared to be a protective factor in relation to distress. Baden speculated, "identification with one's parents may indicate more secure levels of attachment, so that those who share similar values, traditions, beliefs, and practices (i.e., culture) with their adoptive parents may be more likely to report less psychological distress" (p. 373). Although this finding is intuitively reasonable, it does suggest that parents could go too far in linking the child to his or her natal culture to the extent that the child does not feel part of the parents' culture. However, the linkage may also be a manifestation of the child's feelings about the parents. The child may not identify with the parents' culture because of some negative element, transient or chronic, within the relationship.

As more research accrues on the Baden-Steward model, a question of special concern for adoptive parents and the therapists who treat them is how their own communications with respect to race and culture influence the identity the child builds. Baden and Steward (2007) dug the theoretical groundwork for this exploration by describing parents as having four potential styles of thinking about race and culture. They indicated that parents can either affirm or discount the parents' racial or cultural group, the children's racial and/or natal culture, or some combination of affirming and discounting. For example, in a parent-affirming, child-affirming environment, the parents create a social world filled with individuals representing the parents' culture(s), the child's culture, the parents' race(s), and the child's race. Acceptance is established as a core family value. The challenge in this context is to assist the child in coping with an external social environment that may be far less embracing of differences than the home environment. Another example is the parent-discounting, child-affirming environment in which the parents provide role models of individuals representing the child's race and natal culture affiliation but not their own. We would wonder whether the child could experience this kind of parental stance as a manifestation of self-rejection (i.e., the parents rejecting parts of themselves). Also, children identify with parents. If parents have a negative self-identity, the child may internalize this view.

Future research revealing how parenting style affects the child's racial/cultural identity, and how the latter affects adjustment, will be a helpful resource for adoptive parents in transracial/transcultural families. Not only will it be important to look at parental styles but also at particular decisions they make in relation to their adoptive child. For example, what are the benefits to a transracial/transcultural family of living in a community in which a child can interact with individuals of his or her race or natal culture within a wide age range? Some families may live in suburban communities in which the broader composition of the community does not constitute a resource to the same degree that it would for a child living in a town in which people of different ages come together regularly. Also, what are the differential consequences of parents' providing a light exposure to, versus immersion in, the child's natal culture?

Although we have much to learn in this area, the research that does exist and the accumulation of clinical and anecdotal data suggest five points that can have usefulness for adoptive parents and their therapists:

1. First, the adoptive parent is likely to have a variety of reactions to the fact that the child's race and culture of origin is different from his or her own and that over the course of life together, these feelings may wax and wane. At times, these feelings may be celebratory, at other times, mournful, and at still others, at points in between these emotional poles.

2. Second, if the parent does not adopt the child as an infant and that child's early life (whether in weeks, months, or years) was spent in the natal culture, that child will have a memory, conscious or unconscious, of that early life—a memory from which working models of human interactions are constructed (Lapidus, 2006). The adoptive parent's lack of knowledge can give rise to intense feelings of loss in that parents yearn to be a part of all phases of their children's life but particularly the early ones.

However, this history can also engender perplexity in adoptive parents when knowledge of that history is necessary to decipher certain of the child's responses. Lapidus tells the story about the grandparent who was puzzled over the adopted 14-month-old child's adamant refusal to stay within his crib at the time of his afternoon nap. He would walk to the bathroom and point to the tub. Apparently, the model he had built from his past experiences was that the afternoon nap was to be preceded by a bath. Once this connection was identified and he was bathed before the nap, his protests ceased. One important contribution of child therapists and adoption specialists is to help the parents appreciate how the child's prior life might be affecting his or her current moods and behavioral patterns, particularly when the parent finds such moods and behaviors disturbing, chaotic, and incomprehensible.

3. Third, the decision to adopt transracially, transculturally, or both presents parents with a large responsibility and a great opportunity. On the one hand, the parents take on the important, multifaceted task of enabling the child to recognize, explore, and integrate all aspects of his or her cultural and racial identity. On the other, as the family-at-large becomes transracial and transcultural, it offers all of the family the opportunity to expand their identities. In one recent study, parents who observed a child's racial/ethnic holidays and chosen multiracial/multicultural entertainment felt closer to their children (Vonk, Lee, & Crolley-Simic, 2010).[7] Identifying with one's race or culture is not a singular activity—the identification is with a group, and requires contact with members of that group. Parents, then, must organize their lives to enable this contact on a regular basis. Sometimes, this contact may require considerable restructuring of the family's life such as moving to a different neighborhood to ensure that the child will be among others who look like him or her (see vignette concerning the decision to move in Chapter 1). In other cases, it may require small but important acts to help that child make use of the resources his or her community offers. For example, one of the authors (VB) who with her husband had adopted a 1-year-old girl from Honduras lived in a small university town, which was highly diverse in terms of the race and cultural background of its inhabitants. Although many Hispanic families lived in the community, the author's family had not gotten to know them by the time their daughter was around 2 years of age. The parents maintained watchfulness for chances they might have to establish such relationships. One day at the playground a father and a daughter who appeared to be Hispanic were cavorting on the jungle gym. The author casually approached the dad and chatted as the two daughters played together. For the next year, the families got to know one another through casual encounters at the swim club, the park, and community events. The eventual deepening of the relationship enabled the author's family to be included in a host of cultural events and for their daughter to have an intimate friend whose background reflected part of her own, an intimacy that perhaps was deeper because it developed from such an early age. The benefits for the adoptive family went beyond the opportunities it afforded the adopted daughter to experience an affirmation of her identity.

4. Fourth, parents should regularly discuss issues of racism, privilege, and discrimination and how they manifest in family members' everyday lives. This engagement often entails that those parents who are members of the majority group understand their own privilege and the subtle ways in which it operates. This awareness establishes a foundation for appreciating instances in the child's life when he or she must contend with being denied privileges. The home should be an open environment for the child to talk about difficult experiences. Also, parents who have not experienced the denial of privilege need to call upon those who have, members of the child's own racial group, to share strategies and coping behaviors for contending with racism (McGinnis, Smith, Ryan, & Howard, 2009).

5. Fifth, adoptive parents do well to recognize that identity is a dynamic phenomenon. From moment-to moment, time-to-time, individuals vary in terms of what elements they see as critical to their identity. Perhaps as the complexity of identity increases, as in the case of a person who shares in the identities of the adoptive parents as well as his or her own, the potential for variation is greater than a person who has a less complicated circumstance. Adoptive parents who know that such variation can occur can take with equanimity those times when their children veer in one direction or another. That's not to say that each of these times is a mere phase. Rather, what it may represent is a showcasing of an aspect of identity to reserve its place among other aspects (Butler-Sweet, 2011). Furthermore, when an identity is complex, its crystallization may continue well into adulthood.

Socioeconomic Status

Over the past decade and a half, the range of individuals in different socioeconomic strata who are able to afford adopting a child has expanded greatly (Pertman, 2011). Whereas upper middle-class and upper-class adoptions tend to be private adoptions, domestic or international, working-class adoptions generally occur within the public sector. Only recently has information been provided on the question of how a family's socioeconomic status influences the experience of adoptive parenting. Gailey (2010) carefully examined the role of social class in adoption in a qualitative investigation in which she conducted, over a 13-year period, semi-structured interviews with 131 adoptive parents. The study had a longitudinal aspect in that she interviewed approximately half of the participants 5 years subsequently. The interview topics were far-ranging and included the pre-adoptive experience, meeting the child, the child's entrance into the home, the child's adjustment throughout the years, and many other areas.

A central finding of Gailey's (2010) is that social class figures substantially in many aspects of adoptive parenting. For example, Gailey found that whereas working-class couples were not inclined to discuss problems in front of their children, middle-class families did pursue such conversations. She found that working-class parents were likely to establish clear boundaries, be directive, and in some cases, use physical punishment more than middle-class parents, who tended to be more democratic and indefinite about family rules. As a consequence of this difference, children in her middle-class families were more likely to engage in behaviors that tested the limits of acceptability. She makes the interesting point that for children who are adopted from foster case, the working-class family provides a much easier adjustment because it resembles more closely the foster care environment. She also found that working-class families were more likely to have expectations that the child contribute to family life by sharing in tasks, whereas upper-income parents expected the child to meet particular academic standards. When the child failed to do so, the parent struggled with disappointment.

Despite these general trends, Gailey (2010) also found that class interacts with many of the identity facets we describe in this chapter, such as the effects of class interacting with those of race and gender. Gender roles were observed to depend on social class. Whereas wealthier fathers involve themselves in their children's lives through spectator activities (e.g., attending a ballgame), middle- and working-class fathers are more actively engaged in childcare. Differences in the ideology of what constitutes family depended both on social class and race. White working-class parents, relative to other groups, ascribed to the notion that family ties are genetic ties, and African American working-class parents were least likely to embrace this idea.

Social classes also define therapists working with adoptive families. As in his or her work with nonadoptive families, the therapist's view of the family and intervention is likely to be affected by the match between the socioeconomic status of the family and that of the therapist. For example, an upper middle-class therapist may perceive a lower middle-class family's strong rule orientation as an indicator of a desire for excessive control over the child. In such a circumstance, the therapist is more likely to have difficulty conveying empathy for the parents' struggles. Although some behaviors (e.g., abuse) are clearly unacceptable, therapists do well to recognize that all families have their own cultures, and attached to these cultures are diverse patterns of parent-child interaction.

Sexual Orientation

The sexual orientation of the adoptive parent has a unique impact on a parent's experience of the adoption process, particularly given the existence of heterosexism and homophobia in our current society. Here we focus on the experiences of sexual minority (gay or lesbian) parents to highlight how their experience of adoption is distinctive.

As noted earlier in this chapter, many parents adopt due to an inability to have biological children, often after attempting to create a family through biological ties. Options for building a family for gay and lesbian individuals are more limited. Although various avenues exist for gay and lesbian individuals to become parents, including foster parenting, adoption, donor insemination, egg donation, and surrogacy (Chan, Raboy, & Patterson, 1998; Telingator & Patterson, 2008), same-sex couples never begin with the potential of having a child that is biologically related to both parents. Many of the available options afforded to lesbian or gay parents entail a variety of complications that include financial and emotional risks (including potentially unsuccessful medical procedures, complex parental constellations, or fostering children with the intention of eventually adopting, only to have the child return to his or her birth family). In the *Velveteen Father: An Unexpected Journey Into Parenthood*, Jesse Green (1999) tells of his partner's attempts to team up with a lesbian couple in order to become a parent. Eventually, Green's partner recognized that should such a plan have been carried out, the complications would have been enormous. Savage (2000, p. 29) describes a similar effort. He indicated that the lesbian couple with whom he hoped to collaborate could not decide if the time was right: "They'd been together ten years, and parenting was the only new territory they could explore together. But then the talk of kids, the future, and the rest of their lives made mortality a little too palpable, I guess." Savage goes on to adopt a male child with his partner. Like all prospective adoptive parents, forces outside of Savage's control influenced his ability to adopt a particular child. For same-sex couples in particular, although they may have the biological capacity to conceive children individually, adoption is often a preferred method to create a family because it affords both parents equal connection to the child (Goldberg, 2010).

As discussed earlier in the chapter, adoption is fraught with loss on multiple levels. Abby Ruder,[8] a therapist specializing in supporting and educating adoptive families through the adoptive process, suggests that for adopted children, the experience of loss is multifaceted. She underlines the therapist's important role in assisting adoptive families to ensure that all aspects of loss are explored and addressed for the adoptive child and parents alike. Clinicians can assist adoptive parents in understanding the losses the child experiences, so as not to personalize the natural feelings and reactions children have throughout the adoption process but instead differentiate these reactions from reactions to the family's minority statuses. It can be especially difficult for adoptive families to understand and navigate reactions that occur around developmental milestones and identity development. Children may be more likely to express negative emotion about themselves or their family during these periods of transition as they attempt to make sense of past events or current relationships.

When 14-year-old Tricia tells her adoptive lesbian mothers, "I hate you and I hate this family. I wish you weren't my moms," she may be expressing frustration with her mothers' strict limits in not letting Tricia stay out past her curfew with friends—a normative desire for increased freedom and independence as part of her adolescent individuation. She could also be experiencing an unconscious reaction to being the same age as her birth mother when she had Tricia. Tricia may be expressing feelings of wanting to enjoy the "freedom" her mother had at the same age to "make decisions for herself." Her mothers, Judy and Carol, may be highly sensitive to Tricia's comment, having experienced micro-aggressions (see Chapter 11 for a more in-depth discussion and explanation) related to their sexual orientation in the past. A therapist can assist Judy and Carol in being sensitive to the array of possibilities that Tricia may be reacting to as well as assist Judy and Carol in processing their reactions to Tricia's statement. Another possible reason for Tricia's statement is that she experienced discrimination such as name-calling or others assuming her own sexual orientation and using derogatory terms or phrases with her based on her family structure or her mothers' sexual orientation. She may have had difficulty articulating her emotional reactions to being criticized, leading to a desire to distance herself from what others identified as the cause of her or her family being, "different." Padovano (2012) found that some of the young adult women she interviewed who had been adopted and raised by lesbian mothers reported not always sharing instances of discrimination they experienced with their mothers in an effort to "protect" their mothers. Nonetheless, these young women did have strong emotional reactions to the discrimination.

Clarification of why Tricia made the comments she made could be important for both Tricia and for Judy and Carol. Therefore, clinicians can assist in exploring the possible reasons for adopted children's reactions. Often reactions are complex and could be influenced by all factors discussed, including developmental time frames, reemergence of a sense of loss, or specific encounters with discrimination. Therapists can play an important role in supporting gay and lesbian adoptive parents by allowing a space to voice and address concerns about discrimination and homophobia. Clinicians might role play with parents various scenarios that may arise in anticipation of how they could guide and counsel their children and/or reflect on ways they have previously reacted when their child has informed them of instances of discrimination. Interviewees in Padovano's (2012) qualitative study indicated that their mothers' ongoing open dialogue both about issues surrounding loss in adoption and strategies for responding to instances of discriminations as being very helpful. They contributed to the women having a strong sense of self and openness to difference. The following type of experience is all-too-common in children of same-sex parents:

> When Bobby and Parker went with their fathers to a science museum, the museum staff member would not allow their fathers, Jack and Matt, to receive the "family discount" since they must "obviously" be two separate families. Jack asked to speak

to the manager while Matt wanted to leave the museum. Bobby and Parker began to ask questions about why they could not enter the museum "like everyone else." They had been looking forward to going to the museum for weeks. Bobby and Parker later expressed confusion and disappointment about not going to the museum after Matt insisted that they leave. Jack wrote a letter to the museum about the discrimination they experienced, however, Jack and Matt never provided an explanation to their sons. Instead Bobby and Parker remember their fathers arguing about the museum "not being a good place."

A therapist could be someone to assist Jack and Matt in processing the differences in their ways of responding to discrimination as well as identifying ways to explain to their sons, in an age-appropriate manner, what occurred. A therapist could point out the strengths in each type of response and help Jack and Matt to model to their sons that there is not one correct way to react or respond. They might note that in different circumstances, advocacy or being completely disclosing may not in fact be safe. Some therapists assume that being open and honest would be the best policy; however, parents can model both advocacy and discretion within different contexts.

In addition to specific instances of prejudice, Brodzinsky et al. (1998) identify a major challenge for same-sex adoptive parents known as *institutional discrimination*, in particular, *heterosexism*. Heterosexism refers to the belief that heterosexuality is the norm and/or is superior to all other sexualities. Depending on the laws of the state in which families reside, same-sex parent couples must often decide who will be the adoptive parent, while the second parent must become a legal guardian or go through second parent adoption. No matter what the route to adoption, Mallon (2000) notes that these processes lead to an asymmetrical relationship between an adoptive child and each parent. Therefore, despite adoption being a means of having equal connection to each parent, when states limit the legal ties between family members, it can be reflected in something as simple as the titles a child uses for each parent. Green (1999) discusses that some children call the parent who adopted them first Mom or Dad and the second parent by their first name. This inequality can lead to feelings of jealousy or insecurity among parents or an inability to fully function in the role of an "official" parent in important instances (e.g., picking a child up from school, signing permission slips, or even seeking necessary medical care). In addition, Ross et al. (2008) articulate the impact of homophobia and heterosexism inclusive of potential derogatory verbal assaults, violence perpetrated against those who are (or presumed to be) LGBTQ, or through perpetuation of hurtful myths about LGBTQ people (e.g., as child molesters).[9] Sam Abel (2000) gives a poignant example of this in the adoption of Adam with his partner Craig Palmer:

We've been visiting family in Boston. On the way home, as we're driving on the interstate, a car pulls up alongside us. The two teens inside shout something. Craig opens his window. They yell, "Hey faggots—it's Adam and Eve, not Adam and Steve" then laughing speed off. Apparently, they'd seen the rainbow sticker—the gay pride symbol—on our car window. Adam sleeps through it. Craig and I have heard this kind of thing often enough, but this time we're really shaken. Eventually we realize Adam is going to be harassed for having two dads.

Similarly, Abigail Garner shares her personal experience as well as those of other children of gay and lesbian parents in her book, *Families Like Mine* (2005). She cites specific strategies that gay or lesbian parents use to avoid outing their family as having gay or lesbian parents by talking "about both parents interchangeably as if they were one person" (p. 116). A clinician working with a couple like Sam and Craig might help them explore what their own coming-out process had been like and how this may translate to what their son, Adam, might experience. Although Sam and Craig may have particular hopes about how Adam will react, a discussion that recognizes Adam's need to find his own voice and way of coming out about his fathers' sexual orientation may be helpful. Again, clinicians could assist gay and lesbian parents in recognizing that children may respond differently given their developmental context and that these responses will likely shift over time given the context. Tricia may not feel safe to be "out" about her family given her strong desire for peer acceptance during adolescence as she attempts to define her own sense of identity, especially within the context of adoption or other minority identifies such as race and culture. Goldberg (2010) describes children of lesbian or gay-parented families as perceiving the need for secrecy to protect themselves or their parents, which can lead to feelings of isolation and stress. They may ask their parents to limit their openness about their sexual orientation or displays of affection. Therapists can normalize this request for parents, and help them to identify ways of discussing disclosure.

Another example of institutional discrimination has been documented within the adoption process itself. Shelley-Sireci and Ciano-Boyce (2002) found that compared to heterosexual adoptive mothers, lesbian mothers perceived significantly more discrimination in the adoption process as well as feeling that they had to be more evasive or less open about certain aspects of themselves, namely feeling as though their approval to adopt (by an agency or the birth parent) would be hindered by being open about their sexual orientation and relationship status. Ross and colleagues (2008) reported that lesbian adoptive mothers experienced stress over the decision to disclose their sexual orientation in the adoption process, feeling a need to conceal their identity particularly in international adoption. Similarly, Matthews and Cramer (2006) conclude, based on qualitative data, that gay and lesbian adoptive parents often face unique obstacles in the adoption process surrounding "don't ask don't tell," unspoken policies in the home-visit process, application, and review processes. Additionally, Matthews and Cramer note that gay and lesbian adoptive parents face discrimination in the child-parent match and are often matched with more challenging children. At an information session directed at potential gay and lesbian adoptive parents in the suburbs of a large Northeast metropolitan area, current gay and lesbian adoptive parents spoke about how it had been "easier" for them to adopt children who were older and or had "special needs," meaning that they either had physical or mental disabilities or emotional disturbance. Results from Tornello, Farr, and Patterson's (2011) study on parenting stress among gay adoptive fathers demonstrated that gay adoptive fathers experience significantly more stress when they report less social support, less of a positive gay identity, and higher levels of stigma sensitivity. These findings suggest that therapists could assist gay or lesbian adoptive parents in further processing their own reactions to stigmatization and discrimination, in increasing their sense of positive identity around sexual orientation, and in seeking out supportive communities and relationships.

Finally, with regard to the legalities of same-sex couples adoption, Appell (2012) points out that although the legal system continues to move toward acceptance and accommodation, many gay or lesbian adoptive parents, lawyers, and other professionals involved in the process are not familiar with and inconsistent rulings of particular courts because the laws are varied and constantly changing and because adoption is both confidential and local. Brodzinsky, Green, and Katuzny (2012) highlight various factors in addition to the constraints of the legal system, including the policies, practices, and religious affiliation of individual adoption agencies as well as the attitudes of birth parents toward gay and lesbian parents in choosing the families who adopt their child.

As discussed in Chapter 1, recent research has discounted any detrimental direct effect of parental homosexual orientation on their children and minimal significant differences between the development and functioning of children of gay and lesbian parents versus children of heterosexual parents.[10] Researchers have also found children in lesbian families to be as well adjusted as children in heterosexual families (Gartrell, Rodas, Deck, Peyser, & Banks, 2006) and children in gay fathered families to have equal well-being compared to children fathered by heterosexual fathers despite facing stressful conditions (Bos, 2010; Patterson, 2000). Some research has demonstrated that children raised by lesbians possess even greater mental health (Gartrell et al., 2006) while young adults raised by adoptive lesbian mothers reported personal strengths such as being more open to difference (Padovano, 2012). Gianino (2008) echoes common themes among extant literature regarding gay fathers (including adoptive gay fathers) in their "tenacity and resilience in their pursuit of parenthood; dedication to the care of their children; investment in parenting roles that challenged patriarchal norms, and shifts in support networks to include involvement with heterosexual parents" (p. 207).

Emerging research has demonstrated that family process variables, including strength and quality of parent-child relationships, as opposed to sexual orientation of the parent, are associated most with a child's positive psychosocial and school adjustment (Patterson, 2000; Wainright et al., 2004). Therefore, although parent sexual orientation may affect a family's experience of the adoption process, it is important to support adoptive families both during and after the adoption takes place. In a recent interview (September, 2012) on National Public Radio, Adam Pertman of the Evan B. Donaldson Adoption Institute spoke about the importance of viewing adoption as a process that develops over time as opposed to a single event. Therapists can work to foster strong parent-child bonding by encouraging gay and lesbian parents to share how they have navigated their minority status and discrimination with their children, who may face adoptism (see Chapter 11 for further discussion), racism, and heterosexism among other forms of discrimination. Additionally, mobilizing change at the institutional level is imperative. Pertman and Howard (2012) identify ways in which legal, political, and organizational action can reduce barriers for gay and lesbian adoptive parents including providing adoption professionals with accurate information about lesbian and gay adoptive parents to correct any misunderstandings or stereotypes perpetuated by society. We would argue that general psychotherapists would also benefit from having ready access to this information. Clinicians might also help parents considering adoption identify local or national organizations committed to diverse families such that they are both supportive and inclusive of sexual minority status in their trainings and attitudes.

Farr and Patterson (2011) investigated co-parenting in adoptive families, comparing families by sexual orientation of the parents. Results indicated that lesbian couples were more supportive of each other in their co-parenting and showed the least undermining of each other as compared to heterosexual and gay male adoptive couples. While families that used supportive co-parenting had children who exhibited fewer behavioral problems, sexual orientation and gender of parents in adoptive families may be linked to co-parenting styles. The unique aspects of lesbian and gay adoptive families are examined in greater depth in *Adoption by Lesbians and Gay Men: A New Dimension in Family Diversity* (Brodzinsky & Pertman, 2012). Some lesbian and gay parents may at times be so wearied by discrimination that their self-confidence wanes. Therapists can perform a service by being knowledgeable about the strengths gay and lesbian parents bring to relationships and conveying this information. Therapists can also encourage these parents to join a support group with other gay and lesbian parents, another venue in which members can gain feedback that is less likely to be affected by negative social biases.

As discussed with race and culture, therapists can also explore options with gay and lesbian adoptive parents in seeking out supportive communities that are open to and welcoming of individuals with diverse identity characteristics. Again this may involve parents making structural changes such as relocating or choosing new schools, doctor offices, or religious communities that affirm a variety of family structures and relationships.[11]

Gender

Gender has been a focus throughout earlier portions of this text, particularly in Chapters 4 and 5, and in the last section of this chapter. However, several points still need to be made about parental functioning in the context of gender role stereotypes. The adoptive family is by definition a variant of the non-traditional family in that it departs from the family model, born of 1950's demographics of a mother-caregiver, father-breadwinner, and biological children (Mallon, 2000; Walsh, 2012). Although the non-traditional aspect of adoptive families creates special stressors such as a vulnerability of family members to discrimination and prejudice, it also provides particular opportunities. One of these opportunities is greater liberation relative to the traditional family from stereotypic parental role assignments, especially in the area of gender. Adoptive fathers, for example, seem to exhibit a readiness to take the nurturing functions often perceived as the mother's domain in traditional families (see Chapter 5 for an expansion of this point). Their involvement in all aspects of child-rearing bespeaks not only of the father's willingness but also of the mother's openness to this level of paternal activity (Volling & Belsky, 1991). Breaking with the family framework of traditional mother-father roles allows for the development of co-constructed parental roles with greater fluidity and flexibility.

Despite this greater perceived role flexibility, adoptive parents as members of the society are subject to broad societal views on parenting. Miall and March (2003), based on their study of both adoptive and biological parents, found that these groups are similar in seeing caregiving as a natural, instinctual maternal function with fatherhood having greater foundation in learned experiences. Their participants described fathers as "leaders, guides, and breadwinners responsible for the financial and economic security of the family" (p. 19). These perceptual differences are accompanied by behavioral differences. For example, in initiating discussions about adoption, adoptive fathers are more active and involved in early years when children are more curious, whereas mothers are consistent communication brokers. They tend to communicate with the child at a high level across situations and child characteristics. They are more likely to narrate to the child his or her birth story and to talk about the birth mother (Freeark et al., 2005). A critical research question is whether adoptive parents who more readily embrace gender stereotyped parenting roles versus those with a constructivist framework have greater parental satisfaction and greater effectiveness in parenting adopted children. In other words, what attitudes about gender are helpful to both adoptive parents and adopted children?

Presumably, those families who differ from the traditional family in multiple ways enjoy the greatest freedom in role assignments. These families seem better able to write their own rulebooks. Sutfin, Fulcher, Bowles, and Patterson (2008) found that lesbian parents were less likely to create gender-stereotyped physical environments for their children. They also found that lesbian parents held more flexible views about issues related to gender than did heterosexual parents. Adopted children of same-sex parents testify to this attitudinal openness. Young adult daughters of adoptive lesbian mothers described their mothers as encouraging them to engage in any activity they wanted to try regardless of the gender norms surrounding the activity (Padovano, 2012). In this way, the mothers supported their daughters in developing their own unique interests and identities.

Therapists of adoptive parents should think about how the client conceptualizes gender and parenting roles as a potential contributor to stress. For example, the adoptive mother who perceives her husband's high level of parenting activity as an indictment of her own maternal shortcomings may be helped to consider what the child, her husband, and she gain from having two highly active parents and the long-term effects of this configuration on all members of the family.

FAMILY STRUCTURE

Hays' (2008) ADDRESSING framework was designed to capture the variability among individuals. In taking account of the diversity among adoptive families, we also must consider the ways in which systems or family configurations are diverse from one another.

Single-Parent Families

Although the most common type of family configuration has two parents (Smock & Greenland, 2010), single-parent families are becoming more common among the general population and the population of adoptive families. Possibly because of their increased presence, this family structure has been compared to the traditional two-parent situation. Lansford, Ceballo, Abbey, and Stewart (2001), using data from the National Survey of Families and Households, compared five types of families to see what determined family well-being. One configuration was the single-parent family. The investigators compared adoptive families, two-parent families with biological children, families with stepparents, and single-parent families with biological children in terms of whether some configurations led to a higher level of well-being of the children or parents than others. They found that far more important than family structure were the processes within the families such as the degree of conflict among family members.

Single adoptive mothers, according to Gailey (2010), have a distinct set of challenges given that they generally rely on only a single income and have a greater burden of childcare relative to two-parent families. Gailey indicates that they respond to these challenges by energetically tapping community resources. Middle-class single mothers are especially active in developing networks of neighbors, friends, and others outside the family, the members of whom provide mutual support in myriad ways. Working-class and middle-class single mothers in particular saw the boundaries of the family as permeable and were open to admitting as kin others, especially friends and other adoptive parents, who were willing to enter into a mutually nurturing relationship.

Pakazegi (2007), based on her review of the literature, notes that single parents have an ability to take life challenges in stride.

The aforementioned are all strengths that should be mobilized by the therapist in working with single adoptive parents. However, during the time when single individuals are contemplating adoption, they are likely to be beset by a host of negative reactions from friends and family, for example, "Don't you think it's selfish of you to do this?"; "Don't you think every child deserves two parents?" As Pakizegi (2007) notes, the single adult person is often stigmatized in our society and such questions can be manifestations of the stigma. What is important is that the therapist not participate in the stigmatization. Instead, the therapist makes a valuable contribution in helping his or her client to differentiate between his or her own beliefs and those of important others. Helping the client to formulate responses in relation to these challenges also is useful to the contemplating individual. Having responses "at the ready" is in general a valuable resource for adoptive parents.

Sibling Constellations

Adoptive parents often wonder how siblings might affect the adopted child. There are various sibling configurations that could potentially impact both parents and children. Agencies often have an informal algorithm for how to handle siblings in adoption, although there are only a few empirical studies that speak to this issue. We discuss the effects on adoptive parents and children in two family arrangements: when the adoptive child is part of a sibling group; and when biological children are born either before or after the adoption.

When the Adoption Package Includes Siblings

Sibling placement is typically the result of a crisis in the family of origin. Agencies often attempt to discern whether sibling placement together will be a source of support for the children or will be an unhealthy, even tormenting interaction for one of them. Most prospective parents who begin their quest for adoption prefer to adopt a healthy, young single child, although two thirds report that they would accept siblings (Geen, Malm, & Katz, 2004). Some prospective parents prefer a sibling group because of their age or because of the reduction in cost, particularly in international adoptions. That family connections should be preserved when possible is generally assumed. Siblings ripped away from their family of origin can provide solace to each other even at an early age. Anna Freud's observations of the orphans from concentration camps provide support for how siblings separated from parents before one year have increased chances of survival if they have each other (Freud & Dann, 1951).

Previous notions that adoption of sibling groups resulted in a greater possibility of adoption disruption are unfounded. A large study in the Netherlands found that adoptive children placed with a sibling had fewer behavioral problems than children adopted alone and that 10 years after adoption, sibling adoption afforded no increased risk of adoption disruption than if adopted alone (Boer, Versluis-den Bieman, & Verhulst, 1994). In general, sibling adoption has a protective function for the adoptees. As birth records of adoptions become more accessible, the request for information about siblings exceeds those about biological parents, which suggests that even after years of separation many adopted children seek a biological connection (Pierce, 1999a).

In contrast to the positive effects for the adopted siblings, adoptive parents report lower family functioning and less satisfaction with sibling groups compared to a singleton adoption (Leung & Erich, 2002; Palacios & Sanchez-Sandoval, 2005). In a sample of gay adoptive fathers, reported parental stress was higher, the greater the number of children (Tornello, Farr, & Patterson, 2011). Therapists working with prospective adoptive parents should encourage them to get as much information as possible about the sibling group. They should ask the agency questions that would uncover the extent and nature of the sibling contact and relationship. For example, poverty and neglect can often result in siblings foraging in the streets with little connection to each other. Overcoming the history of maltreatment and neglect can often be too much for one adoptive family—particularly in the absence of strong supports (Boer et al., 1994).

When There Are Biological and Adoptive Siblings in the Household

According to 2000 Census, 2% of U.S. households have both biological and adopted children. This arrangement can be the end product of a remarriage, the desire for a larger family, a crisis in the extended family, or the wish to continue parenting as biological children become independent. Two important questions arise: How does the adopted child in this arrangement fare compared to one in which no other children are in the home? How do both biological and adopted children adjust?

Previously, the presence of biological children was thought to be associated with an increase in adoption disruption, although more recent work suggests that the adopted child's adjustment is based upon other factors as well (Boer et al., 1994). Overall there is a small but significant difference at least during adolescence for adopted compared to their nonadopted siblings (Sharma, McGue, & Benson, 1998). Being the only adoptee in a family of birth children appears likely to increase maladjustment in the adopted child (Brooks & Barth, 1999). The more stepsiblings in the family, the more behavioral problems the adopted child has. However, when adopting a sibling pair, the presence of stepsiblings does not increase behavioral problems of adopted siblings (Boer et al., 1994). In addition, placement is more successful when stepsiblings are at least 3 years older than the placed child.

When a new child is added to any family, the older children can feel envy as the parents must at least temporarily shift their focus to the younger child. When an adopted child is added to an intact biological family, the adopted child could also experience a sense of isolation from the family group. In a large study of adopted and biological children, the adopted child's adjustment was predicted by the biological child's adjustment (Tan, 2008). This study suggests that the adopted child's adjustment is in part dependent on the adoptive parents preparing the biological children for the entrance of a new child. Older biological siblings can be given status as teachers and playmates of the adopted child. In a descriptive and detailed study of parents with biological children adopting a child older than the biological siblings, Bergel and Crymes (1990) found few maladaptive changes in family functioning. Marriages remained stable and biological children were not negatively influenced by the adoption. Children worked cooperatively with each other and the older adopted child felt valuable to the family. In general, nonadopted siblings benefit from the addition of adopted children (Ternay, Wilborn, & Day, 1985).

PRACTICAL POINTS

- In developing a case conceptualization of an adoptive parent, therapists should attempt to take into account the multifaceted identities of both the child and the adoptive parent. Both the similarities and differences in these identities are likely to play a role in shaping the parent's experiences.

- Therapists must recognize that an individual's demographic status and identity is likely to be associated with a particular set of stressors that arise in adoptive parenting.
- Therapists must also examine their own identity facets and how they affect their interactions with the adoptive parent.
- Therapists serve their adoptive parents well by helping them to develop parenting practices that honor the child's past, their own past, and their current lives together.
- When certain aspects of the parent's or the child's identity are associated with societal discrimination, these facets must be addressed over time in order to promote the well-being of parent and child.

CONCLUSION

Like every human being, the adoptive parent has a complex, multidimensional identity. The parent's ability to integrate all of the facets that define him or her, and to renounce none of them, would seem to foster the child's doing the same. That is, parental self-acceptance would seem to be a catalyzing force for the child's self-acceptance. However, parental modeling is likely to be an insufficient factor in the child's achievement of a positive identity and healthy self-esteem. The research supports the importance of the child having a sustained exposure to, and capacity to be immersed in, social networks that tap important aspects of the child's identity that may be different from the parents' identity facets. We need to know much more about what exposures and immersions are especially helpful in identity construction. Also, research shows quite clearly that identity facets such as gender, social class, and race interact with one another in complex ways in their effects on parents and children. Although it may be some time before we understand fully the intricate ways in which these variables interact to affect the psychosocial adjustment, self-esteem, and identity of parent and adopted child, at present, adoptive parents can contribute immeasurably to the well-being of their child, and quite possibly their own well-being, by having an awareness of their own identity facets, those of the children, and a readiness to explore, affirm, and rejoice in all of them.

NOTES

1. This section is derived from the broader clinical and empirical literature of effects of parent age on child well-being.
2. This percentage presents a marked decline over past decades. In 1990, as the ARIS report shows, 86% identified themselves as Christian.
3. This may be the result of factors such as delayed marriage, pursuit of additional education, or women's desire for a professional career.
4. As implied above, the state could endorse religious matching of a minority religious group in deference to the continuation of religious diversity (Beschle, 1989). At the same time, many courts have explicitly endorsed the child's spiritual welfare as an important consideration in that there does seem to be some evidence that religiousness is correlated with emotional mental health (Bergin, 1983; Bergin, Masters, & Richards, 1987).

5. Collard (2009) points out that intercountry adoptions are themselves becoming more diversified. She describes a type of adoption, the transnational adoption of a related child, in which cultural and racial differences do not exist. Within Quebec, Canada, this form of adoption is increasingly common and, as Collard writes, presents its own challenges and opportunities. For example, current Quebec regulations require the rewriting of birth certificates, thereby, in essence, nullifying the child's prior kinship connections, creating a discontinuity in the child's life history, and rendering ambiguous most of the child's kinship relationships. For example, as Collard states, "How are other members of the family inscribed in this new genealogy? If my half-sister is now my mother, is my full brother who has not been adopted by my half-sister now a half-uncle, an ex-brother, or still a brother?" (p. 130).

6. Baden's assessment of a sample of young adults also is a methodological advance in that much of the research on identity, as Roorda (2007) points out, has been done on children. Although some identity formation occurs in childhood, adolescence and young adulthood are the generally regarded as the crucial periods for identity formation.

7. Causality cannot be inferred from this relationship. It could be that the closeness parents feel for their children induces them to celebrate the holidays of the child's natal culture.

8. Personal communication, May 26, 2011, discussing her work and experience as a therapist working with adoptive families.

9. See Bos, van Balen, & van den Boom, 2005; Patterson, 2005; Stacey & Biblarz, 2001; Tasker & Golombok, 1995.

10. See Chan, Raboy, & Patterson, 1998; Fitzgerald, 1999; Flaks, 1995; Flaks, Fisher, Masterpasqua, & Joseph, 1995; Patterson 1992, 1994, 2001, 2006; Telingator & Patterson, 2008; Wainright, Russell, & Patterson, 2004).

11. Young-adult women in personal narratives from Padovano's (2012) qualitative research, from a panel of gay and lesbian adoptive parents who spoke at the Equality Forum held in Philadelphia, Pennsylvania (May 2011).

12. Please see Chapter 5 for further discussion of how gender roles manifest for adoptive fathers.

Chapter 7

ADOPTION OF CHILDREN WITH SPECIAL HEALTH CARE NEEDS

S. Ileana Lindstrom, Sonia Voynow, and Bret A. Boyer

This chapter examines the issues and challenges of parents who adopt children who have special health care needs. Throughout this chapter, we cast a wide net to define special needs to include physical, mental, cognitive, and developmental disabilities. We use current research, interviews with adoptive parents, and clinical experience to examine the factors that predict a successful special needs adoption. We focus on the issues, concerns, joys, and challenges experienced by these parents, in order to help adoptive parents and the professionals who work with them. The more we understand about successful adoptions, and about the experience of raising a child with special health care needs, the more we can validate and give hope to the parents who are considering taking this step, or who have already adopted a child with special needs.

For brevity and clarity, we use the phrase *special health care needs* and the abbreviation SHCN to denote children with "chronic physical, developmental, behavioral, or emotional conditions and who also require health and related services of a type or amount beyond that required by children generally" (McPherson et al., 1998, p. 3). You should note, however, that the diagnosis or health condition does not define who these children are, and that, above all, these children are unique individuals with special characteristics and talents.

SHCN would encompass, for example, attention-deficit/hyperactivity disorder (ADHD), autism spectrum disorder (ASD), Down syndrome, spina bifida, cerebral palsy, cystic fibrosis, diabetes, reactive attachment disorder (RAD) and other attachment-related disorders (e.g., due to primary caregivers' abuse or neglect, or maltreatment history during institutional care), developmental trauma disorder (van der Kolk, 2005), posttraumatic stress disorder (PTSD), fetal alcohol spectrum disorders (FASDs), depression and anxiety disorders, epilepsy, acquired immune deficiency syndrome (AIDS), asthma, and other disorders/syndromes.

Some research has suggested the usefulness of subcategorizing such disorders/conditions to note those with life-threat and foreshortened life expectancy (e.g., AIDS, cystic fibrosis), those with high needs for family self-management (e.g., diabetes, asthma), those affecting cognition and learning (e.g., Down syndrome, autistic spectrum disorders, ADHD), those influencing physical independence (e.g., spina bifida, spinal cord injury, cerebral palsy), and those shaping emotional and interpersonal functioning (e.g., RAD, depression, ADHD); as well as those that are constant (e.g., diabetes) as opposed to episodic (e.g., epilepsy) (Boyer, 2008; McCubbin & McCubbin, 1993; Rolland, 1987; Thompson, Gustafson, Hamlett, & Spock, 1992; Wallander & Varni, 1992). These differences in the onset of the condition, course of the symptoms over time, need for family self-management, and interference with life functioning and survival pose different coping challenges for parents (Boyer, 2008; Rolland, 1987).

THREE APPROACH CLASSES

Adoptive parents approach the adoption of a child with SHCN in one of three ways, with each way affecting greatly the experience of being an adoptive parent. These approaches are underappreciated in the research and literature addressing adoption of children with SHCN (see Table 7.1). *Approach Class 1* parents choose to adopt children with special health care needs, embarking on the journey of providing a family for someone in great need. These are parents for whom the decision to adopt a child with these needs has personal and philosophical meaning. *Approach Class 2* parents originally seek to adopt a healthy child, but encounter factors that persuade them to adopt a child with SHCN: They may experience difficulty in getting cleared for adoption or in finding a suitable child for their family, or they may encounter a particular child who happens to have SHCN. While Approach Class 2 parents do not initially intend to adopt a child with SHCN, they are made aware of the child's SHCN at the time of adoption.

Approach Class 3 parents adopt a presumably healthy child who later develops or manifests severe or chronic health conditions. Many pediatric disorders, such as diabetes, asthma, pediatric cancer, pervasive developmental disabilities, and ADHD, may manifest only after the family has adopted the child. Studies regarding the age of diagnosis for children in general populations (adoptive and nonadoptive, but primarily nonadoptive) indicate that many health conditions arise at ages that, for many children, would be postadoption.

One study (Mandell, Novak, & Zubritsky, 2005) found that the average age was 3.1 years for diagnosis of autism, 3.9 years for pervasive developmental disorder not otherwise specified, and 7.2 years for diagnosis of Asperger's disorder. Rates of type 1 diabetes for children under 10 years of age is 19.7 cases per 100,000, but rates are still 18.6 per 100,000 for children age 10 to 19 (Centers for Disease Control and Prevention, 2011). Although asthma is most often diagnosed by 3 years of age (Yunginger et al., 1992), a recent study found that 32.3% of 942 children were first diagnosed with asthma

Table 7.1.   Classes of Adoptive Parents' Approach to Adopting a Child With Special Health Care Needs

Approach Class	Definition	Prior Intent to Adopt a Child With SHCN	Knowledge of SHCN Prior to Adoption
Approach Class 1	Parents intentionally seek the adoption of child with SHCN	Yes	Yes
Approach Class 2	Parents seek adoption of healthy child, but concede to adopt a child with SHCN	No	Yes
Approach Class 3	Parents adopt a child presumed to be healthy; SHCN develop after adoption	No	No

between ages of 3 and 6 years (Lam, Leung, & So, 2007). The average age of onset of ADHD symptoms is typically between 3 and 4 years of age; however, age of onset is dependent on the type of ADHD, such that the onset of ADHD, combined type, appears to emerge in children between age 5 and 8 years of age, while ADHD, predominately inattentive type, is most commonly diagnosed between ages 8 and 12 years (see overview of studies in Barkley, 2003). These few examples highlight the possibility that someone adopted as an infant or young child may subsequently develop physical, behavioral, or developmental disorders.

We attest that these three groups of parents, by virtue of their different approaches to the adoption, vary in their experience regarding commitment, preparation for raising a child with SHCN, and the parenting and marital stresses that accompany raising a child with SHCN. Review of the psychosocial literature about adoption reveals that nearly none of published research articles delineate these distinctions and the potential impact of these Approach Classes on parenting a child with SHCN.

Problems in the Research About Adopted Children With Special Health Care Needs

Several problems characterize the research regarding adoption of children with SHCN. These problems are important to identify, as they affect some of the findings of the existing research, and hamper the ongoing research to understand the experience of families adopting children with SHCN.

Ignoring Approach Class Distinctions

Currently, the adoption research has not attended to the differences in parents' approach to the adoption of children with SHCN, as defined in the three Approach Classes of adoptive parents in Table 7.1 earlier. This has led researchers to draw conclusions about parents adopting children with SHCN that are only true of parents among certain Approach Classes but not others. In most studies, research appears to deal chiefly with the experiences of Approach Class 1 parents.

Ignoring Experiences of Biological Families

Another problem in the SHCN adoption research is that it has largely ignored what we know about biological families' experiences with raising a child with chronic or severe physical or mental health problems. Several models within pediatric psychology have articulated important factors regarding adjustment to pediatric diagnoses. These include categorical models (Rolland, 1987), which emphasize the differences among various health conditions; risk-resistance models (McCubbin & McCubbin, 1993; Rolland, 1987; Thompson et al., 1992; Wallander & Varni, 1992), which emphasize disease factors and family factors that pose greater difficulties or impede adjustment and factors that facilitate better adjustment; and models that have integrated the categorical and risk-resistance models to guide assessment and treatment planning (Boyer, 2008). Research into adoption of children with SHCN has seldom utilized these models to guide their investigation, thereby leaving the adoption literature divorced from literature regarding general parenting for biological children with SHCN. Parenting an adopted child may surely be similar to parenting a biological child with the same medical or psychiatric diagnoses in many ways, and research findings from nonadoptive families will be referenced throughout this chapter, when that research informs the overall experience of raising a medically ill child.

Failing to Consider the Adoption/Nonadoption Variable

A further dilemma is that general research into families' adjustment to pediatric illness seldom reports whether any participants in their research are adoptive families. Reports of medical or psychological research almost always describe the ages, gender, race, ethnicity, geographical location of residence, and socioeconomic status of the families studied in their research. Whether the children in their sample are biological or adopted, however, is almost never reported. As such, the reader is left to assume that the sample compromises entirely of biological families, with no way to ascertain whether that indeed is true.

COMPARISON TO CHILDREN IN THE GENERAL POPULATION

According to the 2007 National Survey of Adoptive Parents (NSAP; for key findings, see Vandivere et al., 2009), 85% of adopted children were rated by their parents as having excellent or very good health (Vandivere et al., 2009). However, 39% of adopted children have SHCN, compared to 19% of the children in the general population (Vandivere et al., 2009). In 2005, there were approximately 470,000 adopted children with SHCN in the United States (Bramlett & Radel, 2008), and adopted children with SHCN were more likely than overall populations with SHCN to need physical, occupational, or speech therapy; display behavioral, developmental, or emotional problems; require treatment or counseling; or experience limited activities (Bramlett & Radel, 2008). For example, 53.8% of adopted children with SHCN had ADD/ADHD, compared to 29.8% of all children with SHCN, and 8.0% of adopted children with SHCN had autism, compared to 5.4% of all children with SHCN (Bramlet & Radel, 2008).

DISRUPTION OF ADOPTION FOR CHILDREN WITH SHCN

Within the adoption research, the permanent continuation of the child's placement is regarded as the ultimate outcome, as the successful placement and ongoing care for the child is paramount. For all adoptions, placement disruption, in which the child is removed prior to the finalization of the adoption, varies by the age of the adopted child. Generally, rates for disruption over all ages range from 6% to 11% (Coakley & Berrick, 2008), while rates of 10% to 16% have been reported for youth over the age of 3 (Barth, Gibbs, & Siebenaler, 2001), and rates as high as 24% have been reported for adolescents (Berry & Barth, 1990). Dissolution, which refers to ending the adoption after it has been finalized, is less frequent, ranging from 1% to 7% of placements (Coakley & Berrick, 2008).

One might fear that the demands of caring for an adopted child with SHCN would result in higher rates of disruption. While some studies support this, they indicate that children with externalizing behaviors, emotional difficulties, and sexual acting out appear at increased risk for disruption (Barth, Berry, Yoshikami, Goodfield, & Carson, 1988; Berry & Barth, 1990; Rosenthal, Schmidt, & Conner, 1988; Smith & Howard, 1991), while children with physical and developmental disabilities have not been consistently shown to be at greater risk (Haugaard, Moed, & West, 2000; Rosenthal et al., 1988). Adopted children who exhibit verbal or physical aggression, defiance, stealing, property destruction, lying and manipulation, running away, hyperactivity, and peer problems show the highest rates of placement disruption (Smith, Howard, & Monroe, 2000).

These findings emphasize the importance of considering the specific symptoms for a special health care need, rather than assuming that all children with SHCN are at greater risk for disruption. It is also important to note that in these studies regarding adoption disruption, the Approach Classes for parents' approach to adopting children with SHCN was not considered.

WHO ARE THE FAMILIES WHO ADOPT THESE CHILDREN?

Overall, parents who choose to adopt a child with SHCN appear to be have more adaptive and cohesive family relationships (Cowling, 2003; Deiner, Wilson, & Unger, 1988); be more religiously or spiritually active (Glidden, 1986; Marx, 1990); and are older, more flexible and child-oriented, patient, tolerant, highly educated, and married longer (Glidden, 1990; Reid, 1983) than those who adopt children without SHCN. Such research indicates that parents adopting children with SHCN do not experience shock, denial, despair, or depression as do birth parents (Glidden, 1990), and that this spares them the guilt, bitterness, grief, and anger that biological parents experience (Glidden, 1986). For this reason, adoptive parents may exercise more problem-focused coping (Glidden, 1986), and compensate by creating a more positive experience of the adoption (Glidden, 2000).

In characterizing these adoptive families, investigators frequently make the assumption that those who have adopted children with SHCN all know and seek these types of adoptions. That is, all adoptive families are assumed to represent Approach Class 1 families. Perry and Henry (2009) note, "Most adoptive families who have a child with special needs made a conscious choice to adopt a child with a disability" (p. 549). Although this may be true for Approach Class 1, Approach Class 2 parents may experience guilt, bitterness, grief, and anger that their decision to adopt a child with SHCN has proven much more stressful than they anticipated. Approach Class 3 families adopt children assumed to have no SHCN, but who develop SHCN after the adoption. For Approach Class 3 parents, their experience of the onset of the child's SHCN may more closely parallel that of biological parents. This comparison has not been empirically investigated.

COMMITMENT

All parents who plan to adopt need to examine their level of commitment to the work of raising a child, and to accepting the change that it will bring to their lives. For a parent who adopts a child with SHCN, this level of commitment may need to be even higher. He or she should probably expect to invest a significantly higher level of resources, time, and patience into parenting than would the parent of a typically developing child. Glidden, Billings, and Jobe (2006) assert that, in addition to the daily tasks of providing for and nurturing their children, these parents must also accept the child's diagnosis and limitations, access resources, and plan for their child's transition into adulthood.

Commitment and Approach Classes

The literature concludes that a higher level of initial commitment may exist in Approach Class 1 parents, who set out to adopt a child with SHCN (Glidden, 1990).

However, it is unclear whether this initial commitment is different in Approach Class 2 parents, who may concede, rather than set out, to adopt a child with SHCN.

Also, the literature is silent about the factor of commitment in Approach Class 3 parents, who are not anticipating that their child will have special health care needs. In fact, these adoptive parents may have much more in common with the biological parents of children with SHCN, especially in terms of initial commitment. For these parents, raising a child with SCHN is not a "choice," but a necessity (Glidden, 1990).

Finally, while a high level of commitment to adopting a child with SHCN is acknowledged to be helpful in the initial stages of parenting, it is not clear to what extent the differences in the level of parental commitment may change over time. More studies are needed to assess how, if at all, the level of initial commitment predicts the ultimate success of the adoption over the long term.

The Case of Priscilla: Approach Class 1

To provide examples of adoptive parents' experiences, we intersperse excerpts from interviews conducted with adoptive parents of children with SHCN. In addition, these excerpts serve to illustrate the differences in these experiences among parents from different Approach Classes. We begin by introducing "Priscilla," who adopted a 6½-year-old girl named "Diane." Diane had been previously adopted, and brought to the United States from an orphanage in Vietnam. Totally unbeknown to her first adoptive parents, Diane had been sexually abused as a young child in the orphanage. Diane was diagnosed with reactive attachment disorder (RAD) after adoption placement. This first adoption was dissolved after Diane repeatedly threatened to kill the adoptive parents.

Priscilla was employed at the mental health unit of a hospital where Diane was admitted. She became deeply moved by Diane's trauma history and the failure of the first adoption. Priscilla began to make inquiries into adopting Diane. She felt confident and attributed this feeling to her husband's support and her success in working with children with physical and emotional issues. Also, she felt that she had successfully raised her biological children. Priscilla intentionally sought the adoption of Diane, a child with known SHCN, and, as such, Priscilla is an example of an Approach Class 1 parent.

Diane's therapist warned Priscilla that Diane would likely experience behavioral symptoms related both to the sexual trauma and to the trauma associated with the dissolution of the first adoption placement. Diane's therapist pointedly asked Priscilla, "Do you realize she may try to kill you?" Priscilla, however, remembers feeling a kind of "high": "It's like having a baby. . . . This is going to be your child." Looking back on her level of commitment to Diane and the challenges they would face, Priscilla recalled:

> I quit my job so I could be home with her 24/7 to do the attachment work [during the 3 years, postadoption finalization]. . . . We had to get back to square one [building trust] . . . you could start feeling the battle between good and evil and I was not going to give up. . . . I don't think I ever would think about giving up because you don't give up. . . . It's like . . . This is your child. You just don't abandon them [sic].

The Case of Mindy: Approach Classes 2 and 3

We next introduce you to "Mindy." Mindy had been deeply saddened by her experience of miscarriages. When she began to seek a child to parent through domestic adoption agencies, she discovered waiting lists of 2 to 3 years. Having learned about briefer waiting periods involved in international adoptions, Mindy and her husband pursued a child in a foster home in South America. They were informed before they embarked to meet "Kaitlyn" that she had been born prematurely. It was not until they met Kaitlyn, however, that they were told, and could see, that she was failing to thrive. Mindy had intended to adopt a healthy child. She decided, albeit with hesitation, uncertainty, and fear, to finalize the adoption based on her strong desire to be a mother, her husband's support, her training as a nurse, and her sense that she might be Kaitlyn's only chance to survive. Before Kaitlyn reached her second birthday, she came to live with Mindy and her husband.

Mindy, like Priscilla, was aware prior to the adoption that the child had SHCN. However, it was only after the adoption was finalized that Mindy learned the extent of Kaitlyn's health issues. Kaitlyn had cerebral palsy and other serious health issues. Mindy's approach to her adoption of Kaitlyn may be described as a blending of two approach classes: Approach Class 2 (i.e., parents who set out seeking adoption of a healthy child, but concede to adopt a child with SHCN) and Approach Class 3 (i.e., parents who adopt a child presumed to be healthy, but discover SHCN after the adoption finalization).

Mindy recalled her level of commitment and her relationship with Kaitlyn during the first few years as a family. She said, "Well, I was definitely attached. I mean, there was no sending her back!" She also remembered thinking:

> Oh, my goodness this [parenting a child] is not going to be typical. But I had so wanted a healthy child, and it was, it was by no means that way, so uh, I guess it was a feeling of, "All right. So this is it." I always do that. I'm a very loyal person, so whatever it takes, it takes, and I'm a parent for life. And, oh, I firmly believe it.

PREPARATION

The literature discussing adoptive parents' process of adoption is riddled with a dichotomous use of the term *preparation*. At some points in the literature, the term refers to formal services or information provided to parents in the process of adoption. At other points, the term preparation is used to describe the degree to which parents feel prepared for the experience, once the adoption has occurred, or parents' perceived readiness. Generally, research indicates that adoptive parents benefit from having complete and detailed information about their adopted child (Barth & Berry, 1991; Barth et al., 2001; Berry & Barth, 1989; Brooks, Allen, & Barth, 2002), including accurate health and birth history information (Peterson & Freundlich, 2000).

Preparation in Approach Classes 1 and 2

Approach Class 1 parents, who intend to adopt a child with SHCN, and Approach Class 2 parents, who at least have some advance knowledge that their child will have special needs, can prepare themselves in both concrete and more intangible ways prior to the adoption. Parents can investigate community resources ahead of time, as well as assess the time and money required to raise a child with SHCN (Perry & Henry, 2009). Parents can also consider the effect that raising a disabled child will have on the other members of the family, and try to envision challenges that will arise in the future, such as their child reaching school age, or what will happen when they can no longer care for their child due to old age or illness.

Mindy's main concern about her daughter, Kaitlyn, is her inability to live as an independent adult and how she will manage without Mindy's supervision should she survive Mindy:

> Well, I was worried that she [Kaitlyn] would never walk, I mean, it took her until she was almost three with a lot of therapy, so, the walking was a big thing. And even now, she doesn't have a perfect walk. . . . She's very intelligent, but [there are] . . . large gaps with Kaitlyn's neurological impairment. She acts emotionally much younger than her years. . . . So, I worry because she's not independent. She will always need some type of supervision. I don't see her living . . . on her own. So that's a worry, particularly after the ugly divorce, which was really painful for me, um, and painful for her, too. So, at this point in time, I am worried about it, what happens, and what's going to happen to her after I move on, because we all do move on. Um, I do have arrangements with the DDD, the Department of Developmental Disabilities in [name of her state of residence], but you know, that worries me, because that's not something that Kaitlyn is going to want or llike. . . . So, I guess independence is like my main, was my main worry all along from the very beginning.

Adoption service providers play a particularly crucial role in preparing parents to adopt a child with SHCN by providing detailed information about the prospective adoptee (Barth & Berry, 1991; Barth et al., 2001; Berry & Barth, 1989; Brooks et al., 2002). This information may include accurate health and birth history (Peterson & Freundlich, 2000), as well as resource options such as support groups (Perry & Henry, 2009). Pre-adoption preparation can be particularly effective for Approach Class 1 parents who adopt a child with clear treatment goals and expectations regarding their disability. For example, literature points to the positive outcomes for parents who adopt children with Down syndrome (Hodapp, Ly, Fidler, & Ricci, 2001), a disability in which the child does not usually display other emotional problems, and for which there is a wealth of information about progress, effective parenting, and prognosis (Perry & Henry, 2009).

However, the type of information that parents receive in advance about their child and the nature of their SHCN can vary widely. Most adoptive families report feeling well prepared (Berry, Barth, & Needell, 1996). Still, some studies have found that a significant proportion of parents, from one third (Rosenthal, Groze, & Morgan, 1996) to 58% (Reilly & Platz, 2003), feel that they had not been given sufficient input to form accurate expectations, particularly in terms of receiving adequate medical information about their adopted child (Rosenthal et al., 1996). One study (Wind, Brooks, & Barth, 2005), regarding the types of information received by adoptive parents, found that 72% received information about their adoptive child's birth history, 68% about family history, and 60% about medical history. However, only 11% received HIV test results, and 12% received information about early childhood history (Wind et al., 2005). Parents adopting a child with a history of environmentally or contextually based risk factors (e.g., disrupted attachment, inconsistent caregiving, or maltreatment within an institutional context) felt less prepared than those adopting children who did not have this history; however, those adopting children with biobehavioral risks (e.g., ADHD) did not feel significantly less prepared (Wind et al., 2005).

Preparation in Approach Class 3

For Approach Class 3 parents, who had intended to adopt a healthy child, pre-adoption information can feel misleading in what it omits:

Occasionally a child who is presented to prospective adoptive parents as being healthy is later found to have a mild or even severe disability. This is more often the case with international adoptions than with domestic adoptions; the diagnosis may have been missed in the child's country of origin, or the adoptive parents may have been intentionally misled in an effort to see that the child was adopted. Sometimes, a child's condition is thought to be temporary—the result of being in deprived conditions—and the parents later discover it is not. (Melina, 1998, p. 286)

Adoptive parents have also reported frustration and helplessness when healthcare professionals fail to explain, effectively communicate about, and/or resolve medical problems, and they cited professionals' lack of knowledge regarding adoption and adoption resources (Molinari & Freeborn, 2006) as a source of added stress.
Priscilla recounted this experience:

I felt like she [Diane] really needed someone who would meet with her and give that support . . . after a lot of research, I found the [name of clinic] . . . they were an hour and a half drive away . . . We just didn't have the money then. . . . And we had three children in college and we weren't really financially equipped to handle all the extra expenses. . . . At [name of psychiatric hospital], there was no one who seemed to have an understanding of RAD and childhood sexual abuse.

Priscilla also recalled the following frustrations:

[It was so hard] to find an institution (sighs) or a therapy group or even a therapist who would understand all that was going on in our home with all of Diane's issues . . . [they] would blame [her behaviors] on us, the things that we were doing; or [they] wouldn't understand. . . . But we did find a place [name of clinic where Diane received services] where everyone understood what was going on, plus . . . I did get services through the state then . . . that was offering respite [care for adoptive parents] and they would hand-pick a respite family that Diane would feel safe in . . . they [the state] also helped with some of the costs of therapy at that time [during first 3 years after Diane's adoption].

One way that some prospective adoptive parents become prepared for the adoption of a SHCN child is through the experience of being a foster care parent. In 2003, the Urban Institute reported that, of all types of parenting groups, foster care parents represented the largest group who adopted children with special needs, including SHCN (Geen, 2003). According to this report, the research suggests that foster parenting may constitute a positive antecedent to adoption placement of children with SHCN, and that, "For those wanting to adopt but not interested in foster parenting, agencies may want to create opportunities to volunteer with foster children so parents can better assess whether they are able to care for a special-needs child" (Geen, 2003, p. 2).

Across the Approach Classes

For all Approach Classes of parents, however, the best preparation cannot take everything into account. Health needs and other comorbid disabilities may not become clear until after a child has been adopted. Even when parents know about their child's SHCN, they may not be aware of their scope, or they may discover other behavioral or medical issues that occur later in the child's development.

In addition, all Approach Classes of parents may have unrealistic hopes for improvements in their child's condition. In such cases, the adoptive parent may experience the same shock and distress that biological parents face:

> The child with a grim prognosis will often rapidly improve soon after placement because she is receiving the love, personal attention, and treatment she has needed. So the child who had been diagnosed as severely mentally retarded advances to where she can be considered mildly [intellectually challenged]. Observing the effect of love and good quality care, parents may have the unrealistic hope that progress will continue until the child is fully able. When this expectation is not realized, adoptive parents may have to go through the process of accepting the child's limitations. (Melina, 1998, p. 286)

When adoptive parents do have prior knowledge about special needs, their preparation can help to immunize them against the stress inherent in providing extra resources, time, and energy. However, preparation and commitment, even in the best of circumstances, cannot fully shield parents from stress (Bailey et al., 2005; Center for Children With Special Needs, 2012). Priscilla, reflecting on her level of perceived preparedness, frequently employed words such as *commitment, hope*, and the *constant expenditure of energy*. She also made frequent references to her connections with extended family members, church friends, her marital relationship, and her religious faith and spirituality, and to her efforts to maintain those connections. Priscilla described herself as a "therapist mom" and, when asked to expound on that self-description, she responded that her parenting of Diane was very different from her parenting experiences with her two biological children: "There's nothing that can prepare you for adoption, I think." Priscilla was aware of much of Diane's history of abuse that took place in the orphanage, and the dissolution of Diane's first adoption. In addition, she had been cautioned by a therapist about Diane's threatening behaviors toward her previous adoptive parents. Nevertheless, Priscilla recalled thinking, at the time she and her husband decided to adopt Diane, "I didn't expect it [parenting Diane] to be much different than what we'd done before in our parenting."

Mindy compared the realities of parenting Kaitlyn as "different from my fantasy [of parenting a child]." She continued:

> I was totally unprepared. I was totally in denial. It took me years to realize that these are special needs that are life-long and she [Kaitlyn] wasn't going to catch-up. So, I guess that was really a process, a process of accepting. And Kaitlyn was doing the best she could, and I could not fix or change her into whom I wanted her to be. So, that, I can say, is [something] I've learned [through the process].

COPING AND STRESS

Simply put, increased levels of stress pose risks for multitudes of health, mental health, and performance problems among all of us (for a recent review, see Contrada & Baum, 2010). Indeed, the term *parenting stress* was coined as early as 1980 (Burke & Abidin, 1980) to capture the experience of parents' stressful demands in raising children with various needs. Children with chronic health conditions, conditions that require parents to serve as caregivers and primary agents for self-management of the disease process, or conditions that require parents to manage disruptive behaviors, all pose challenges with which parents need to cope. Glidden, Flaherty, and McGlone

(2000) argue that even the most prepared and committed caregivers may feel overwhelmed with responsibilities, leading to an increase in strain and maladjustment.

Coping refers to the methods a person uses to respond to stressful situations, particularly with the intention of making the situation less stressful and more manageable. For parents who are not adequately prepared to deal with SHCN, and for Approach Class 3 parents in particular, there may be more challenges for coping than for well-prepared Approach Class 1 parents. Coping may be generally better for Approach Class 1 parents, because they presumably have motivation and commitment to adopt a child with SHCN, and believe that they have the support system in place: "Without grief or guilt to interfere, these parents can effectively concentrate on the child's needs from the beginning" (Melina, 1998, p. 286).

However, "when a disability is unexpected, parents typically react with shock, denial, anger, and the other stages of grief" (Melina, 1998, p. 285). Many elements of this experience can contribute to elevated levels of stress, including grief over the loss of the "expected" child, relationship concerns, financial anxiety resulting from an increase in bills and necessary time off from work, the desire for acceptance by others, increased time demands and decreased personal time, loss of daily routines, and the process of navigating challenges in obtaining required services (Bailey et al., 2005; Center for Children With Special Needs, 2012).

Learning From the Broader Pediatric Literature

A vast literature has documented depression and anxiety among biological families experiencing pediatric health conditions. Although a full review of this data is beyond the scope of this chapter, a few examples highlight experiences among biological parents that may be very similar for adoptive parents, particularly Approach Class 3 parents. Mothers of children with cerebral palsy (CP) report spending an average of 6 to 8.3 hours per 24-hour day caring for their child's medical needs. These mothers' levels of depression were related to greater time pressure for child caregiving (Sawyer et al., 2011). Studies have found depression symptoms to be greater among mothers of children with CP (Ones, Yilmaz, Cetinkaya, & Caglar, 2005), with 30% of these mothers reporting clinically significant depression, with severity comparable to major depression (Manuel, Naughton, Balkrishnan, Smith, & Koman, 2003). Higher rates of depression have been documented among mothers of children with autistic spectrum disorders (Ingersoll, Meyer, & Becker, 2011), and difficulties in family adaptability predicted worsening of depression among mothers of children with autism, over a 3-year period (Baker, Seltzer, & Greenberg, 2011). Furthermore, mothers of children with autism who used avoidant coping (distraction and disengagement) were more likely to experience anger and depression than mothers who utilized positive reinterpretation and reframing (Benson, 2010). Studies of biological mothers, whose children have type 1 diabetes, have found that mothers became stressed by the vigilance required in caring for their diabetic child (Sullivan-Bolyai, Deatrick, Gruppuso, Tamborlane, & Grey, 2003), with 17% (Kovacs et al., 1985) to 22% or 24% (Jaser, Whittmore, Ambrosino, Lindemann, & Grey, 2008, 2009) reporting clinically significant depression. Mothers who reported more distress coping with diabetes-related stress also reported higher levels of anxiety and depression (Jaser et al., 2009), while mothers' depression was associated with their involvement in diabetes management and the child's depression over time (Wiebe et al., 2011). Consistent with the expectation that many demands of parenting an ill child are similar for biological and adoptive parents, it is reasonable to believe that parents adopting children with SHCN may also be at risk for increased depression, anxiety, and parenting stress.

EXISTENTIAL ISSUES

The difficulty in coping with parenting a child with SHCN is compounded by the *existential* issues with which such parents often need to deal, particularly when they do not know that their child will have SHCN. In their extensive examination of this literature, Perry and Henry (2009) reviewed research by Glidden, citing that, "Immediately after . . . the diagnosis of a child's disability, parents often experience a sense of despair and meaninglessness and begin to question their own identity and personal values, the meaning of life, and their religious beliefs (Glidden, 1986, 1990)" (p. 542). For most parents, the time of diagnosis presents a crucial period for adjustment, as the parents must cope with both the existential crisis and the proce-dural demands of caring for the child's illness (Glidden, 1990; Perry & Henry, 2009). Although current literature states that adoptive parents do not experience the same kind of existential shock as do biological parents, this literature does not distinguish between parents of different Approach Classes, and ignores the likely experience of Approach Class 3 parents.

Priscilla explained that when she and her husband decided to adopt Diane, they thought that consistent parenting, imbued with their love and compassion, would help Diane attach to them and overcome the negative behaviors related to her trauma history. However, in the first month or two after they brought Diane to their home, Priscilla remembered:

> I was getting worn down by all of Diane's fears, her anxiety . . . all of her inability to get past her fear of love and trust. . . . [Over the next three years] I was doing all that I knew to help establish that bond with Diane . . . and [up until then] I felt like I could connect with any child . . . I could reach any child to help calm them down, but [with Diane] I was definitely challenged!

Almost inevitably, parents feel a sense of isolation in such a circumstance, a pain that can be lessened via connection with other similarly situated parents. Support and self-help groups (see Chapter 12) offer mediums through which existential issues can be constructively addressed.

POSTTRAUMATIC STRESS

Posttraumatic stress (PTS) refers to a triad of symptoms that people may experience in response to overwhelmingly stressful incidents. The set of three symptom clust-ers includes: (1) intrusive thoughts, images, or dreams about the stressor; (2) anxious arousal when faced with these intrusive thoughts, images, or environmental reminders of the stressor, including hypervigilance, anxiety, exaggerated startle response, or difficulty sleeping; and (3) avoidance of, or attempts to avoid, the intrusive thoughts or reminders of the stressor (American Psychiatric Association [APA], 2000). Although these symptoms have been observed following combat stress, rape, violence, and severe motor vehicle crashes, they have also been documented after "learning that one's child has a life-threatening disease" (APA, 2000, p. 464). Among presumably biological families, PTS has been experienced by parents of children diagnosed with cancer (Alderfer, Cnaan, Annunziato, & Kazak, 2005; Kazak et al., 2004; Stuber, 2006), type 1 diabetes (Landolt et al., 2002; Landolt, Vollrath, Laimbacher, Gnehm, & Sennhauser, 2005), and pediatric-onset spinal cord injury (Boyer, Knolls, Kafkalas, Tollen, & Swartz, 2000; Boyer, Tollen, & Kafkalas, 1998; Boyer, Ware, Knolls, & Kafkalas, 2003). PTS has not been formally investigated among parents adopting children with SHCN, but these parents may be at the same risk for PTS as biological parents. Research needs to evaluate whether the risk for PTS may be different for adoptive parents, as well as for adoptive parents of different Approach Classes.

When one adopts a child with SHCN, and one's life changes include fear for the child's life or medical safety, loss of the expected parenting role, and threat of chronic stress to the parents' relationship (if partnered) and family, adoptive parents may be plagued with constant reminders and worries about the situation, anxiety, and failed attempts to avoid the distressing concern. These symptoms may rise to the level of PTS, or even posttraumatic stress disorder. More important, the stresses of caring for a chronically ill or developmentally disabled child are not a single event in the past, like a horrible car crash, but an ongoing stressor that poses new and changing demands on the adoptive parent. Some scientists, therapists, and parents may wonder whether parenting a child with SHCN is really the same as other traumas, especially if the special health care need is not a life-threatening condition. The stress of parenting such a child does, however, threaten the expected course of one's life as a parent, as well as the child's development—a topic discussed in the next section.

AMBIGUOUS LOSS

Even after receiving a diagnosis, some adoptive parents remain in a state of existential crisis, uncertain about what their child's diagnosis means for the future. O'Brien (2007) suggests that the term *ambiguous loss* can serve to describe the experience of such parents, who have children with "a lifelong and pervasive disability" such as autism spectrum disorder (ASD) (O'Brien, 2007, p. 135).

The term *ambiguous loss* originally referred to the experience of people whose family members were missing or psychologically changed (O'Brien, 2007). For adoptive parents whose child has a diagnosis like ASD, the prognosis is vague, involving unexpected changes in behavior and periods of regression, as well as other comorbid issues, including anxiety or other medical disorders. In these cases, parents remain uncertain about what their child will be capable of or need through adulthood.

To complicate matters even more, in the case of some disorders, such as ASDs, children are indistinguishable from their neurotypical peers. As a result, family and friends might discount the idea that something is wrong, and these messages undermine parents' self-confidence or certainty about the child's difficulties and, thus, increase confusion (O'Brien, 2007, p. 137). The story about the Row family (Weathers, 2007), set in the United Kingdom, touches on the challenges of parenting four adopted children, siblings from the same biological parents. When adopted by Sandy and Robin Row 21 years ago, the children ranged in age from 2 to 6 years. After the placement, the adoptive parents discovered that the children had been neglected by their birth parents, and that all exhibited, to different degrees, developmental delays. The four children were each diagnosed as having an ASD, the oldest three having been diagnosed with Asperger's disorder. The children received additional diagnoses, including attachment disorder, ADHD, dyslexia, auditory processing disorder, and dyspraxia (Row, 2005).

As the Rows recollected, "We were thrilled when we were accepted as their adoptive parents. Really, though, we had no idea what we were letting ourselves in for" (Weathers, 2007, p. 1). The Rows initially thought that they would be able to cope; however, they admitted that on many occasions, they despaired, feeling isolated and helpless. They, and the adoption agency, were not fully aware of the extent of the children's problems. For example, the oldest child was finally diagnosed with Asperger's disorder, but only after "ten years of violent tantrums and uncontrollable behavior" (Weathers, 2007, p. 1). Mrs. Row reflected:

> Had we known then all the problems and stress we would face, I doubt we would have gone ahead, because we wouldn't have considered ourselves equipped to deal with the challenges they presented. But we didn't know, and despite the mistakes we've made and the tears we've cried, we love them all to bits. We never felt that the adoption agency kept anything from us about the children, because back then techniques for diagnosing autism weren't so sophisticated. But what did make us angry was how hard it was to get the right help for them once they had been properly diagnosed. (Weathers, 2007, p. 1)

POSTTRAUMATIC GROWTH

Adequately supporting adoptive parents of children with SHCN would not be complete without a discussion of posttraumatic growth. Richard Tedeschi and Lawrence Calhoun (2004) have written a number of books and articles about this concept, which refers to the positive changes that individuals experience in their struggles with trauma. Adoptive parents who can successfully cope with the demands of raising a child with SHCN can experience such posttraumatic growth, which can include improved relationships, new possibilities for one's life, a greater appreciation for life, and a greater sense of personal strength and spiritual development (Tedeschi & Calhoun, 2004).

The positive aspects to the experience of parenting children with special needs must be kept in mind when assessing adequate support for adoptive parents of children with SHCN. Recognition of the contribution that a child with a disability makes to a family may result in less familial stress (Hastings & Taunt, 2002). The adopted child with SHCN may, for example, inspire other family members to reassess their life values and goals and their standards regarding the quality of life. This may result in the expansion and enrichment of their worldview, philosophy, and perspectives concerning their own personal challenges and those of others. The family of an adopted child with SHCN may discover that this child enhances family dynamics through his or her contributions of a particular sense of humor, innate wisdom, and unique perspectives on a variety of situations. Sometimes, this child may encourage other family members to take pause in their busy schedules and to reflect. As a result, family members may find that their patience and level of frustration tolerance increases, and that their skills in mindfulness and active listening have been enhanced. In light of these contributions, many parents do discover renewed strength to persevere in their care of their child with SHCN.

Priscilla recalled that when Diane was approximately 9 years old, Diane told her this story about herself: that when she was born, she held on to five strings—trust, belief, hope, innocence, (and one that Priscilla could not recall). Diane told her mother, "I lost four of those strings almost right away . . . and I've been hanging on by the string of hope ever since." Priscilla spoke about her own personal development, and the further development of her parenting skills, as some of the many benefits of her relationship with Diane. She was learning from Diane survival and coping skills, which Diane had in her "reservoir" (as Priscilla called it). Priscilla recalled thinking, "If she can do it [survive and cope], then we [Priscilla, her husband, and the other children] can do it, too." In terms of how she has benefited from her relationship with Kaitlyn, Mindy stated, "I always felt accepted and loved."

MARITAL SATISFACTION

The relationship of parenting a child with SHCN to parental and marital satisfaction was assessed in a direct comparison between families with biological children, adopted children, and with a mixture of biological and adopted children (Asbury, Cross, & Waggenspack, 2003). The degree of special needs among children showed an overall relationship to parental satisfaction, but only when there were adopted children in the household (adoptive families and mixed families). When length of marriage and husband's age were included as covariates, degree of special needs did not significantly relate to marital satisfaction. The authors note that Asbury et al. were not aware of the parents' Approach Class, and had not assessed whether Approach Class affected the relationships found in this study (Asbury et al., 2003).

Mindy's account of adopting Kaitlyn serves to illustrate some of the stressors exerted on the marital relationship, especially when each of the partners do not see eye-to-eye on parenting concerns. She described, for example, how she and her (now ex-) husband differed in their views concerning Kaitlyn's employment as a young adult:

> I totally accept Kaitlyn for who she is and for her strengths, but he does not understand the differences. He thinks that she should be more, you know, working a job 9 to 5. . . . [Her feet were] operated on . . . , so now . . . she's able to walk and stand better, but her feet ache. So she worked very, very hard [as a waitress], but she couldn't do it anymore. Well, he does not accept that. . . . He's very mad at me because she's now on Medicare because she's disabled. . . . And so, he doesn't get it at all . . . that there's limitations. But he feels that she could be more independent and he blames me for her lack of wanting to really grow, I guess.

PRACTICAL POINTS

In this section, we provide some suggestions and recommendations, beginning with those directed to therapists, counselors, and other helping professionals who work with adoptive parents of children with SHCN. These are followed by our suggestions and recommendations directed to adoptive parents of children with SHCN. In support of a maximally informed and unified effort, we encourage our readers to become familiar with *all* of these practical points.

For Therapists/Counselors and Other Helping Professionals

1. Inquire with adoptive parents and prospective parents about the history of their decision to adopt a child with SHCN (i.e., their Approach Class), as well as their expectations about what life will be like raising a child with SHCN.

Consider the potential psychological dynamics that may be at play, particularly for parents whose histories match Approach Class 2 and Approach Class 3.

2. Be aware of the research evidence pertaining to biological families experiencing SHCN, which demonstrates increased parenting stress, greater risk for depression and anxiety, posttraumatic stress, and marital stress. Adoptive parents may experience risk for these same difficulties.

3. Be aware that some adoptive parents may be reluctant to seek therapeutic services for stress related to raising adopted children with SHCN. These parents may fear that admitting to such stress may indicate their failure as parents. It may be helpful to educate these families about the experiences of biological families, as per number 2 above, to reassure adoptive parents that such stresses do not simply result from inadequate parenting skills.

4. Recognize the potential for multiple life-enriching experiences and personal growth, for parents and for the child. When they arise, affirm and celebrate them with your clients.

5. Continually assess for and discuss with clients symptoms of parental stress (e.g., burnout), anxiety, depression, insomnia, and other indicators of compromised health and mental health, as well as compromised health of clients' committed relationships (partnership/marriage) and family dynamics (as applicable). Balance this assessment with inquiry about strengths and growth (as noted in number 4, above), so as to decrease families' apprehension to seek appropriate assistance (as noted in number 3 above).

6. Become informed about available community services, such as parental respite services, adoptive parenting training/education classes, support groups, and outpatient therapy, in order to make referrals as needed.

We underscore the importance of assessment that is balanced in terms of a rigorous attention given to strengths as well as to symptoms and risks. Given the dynamic nature of interpersonal relationships and family systems, we also underscore the importance of assessment that is ongoing. Keeping in mind the results of the research discussed in this chapter, we encourage helping professionals to acquire as much information as possible pertaining to resources in their communities that are available for adoptive parents and families of children with SHCN. When these resources are not available, helping professionals might consider developing them or advocating for them.

For Adoptive Parents of Children With SHCN

1. The importance of pre-adoption preparation for parents of children with SHCN cannot be overstated: Obtain *comprehensive* information from adoption agency caseworkers about the history of the child (e.g., medical, developmental, educational, and mental health histories) as well as the social and placement history of the child. Consult the lists of suggested questions to ask caseworkers in "Obtaining Background Information on Your Prospective Adopted Child" at www.childwelfare.gov/pubs/f_background.cfm

2. Become, as much as possible, an expert about the child's specific SHCN(s). Becoming an expert not only entails becoming informed about diagnoses, course, and treatment of the disorder/condition, but also informed about the resources available to address your child's and your family's needs.

3. Become informed about available supportive services for you and your child. These may include (among many others): psychotherapy (individual therapy for the parent[s] and the child, couples therapy, family therapy), suppliers of special in-home equipment and devices, specialized modes of transportation (e.g., wheel chair accessible), educational accommodations, community respite programs, and federal and state adoption financial assistance/subsidy programs and eligibility criteria (see http://www.childwelfare.gov/adoption/adopt_assistance/).
4. A helpful introduction to postadoption services is provided at the following websites: http://www.childwelfare.gov/adoption/adopt_parenting/ and http://www.childwelfare.gov/adoption/adopt_assistance/
5. Intentionally construct a supportive network of professionals (e.g., therapists/counselors, health care providers, educators) who are well-informed about your needs as an adoptive parent of a child with SHCN.

CONCLUSION

In our endeavor to clarify the parenting experience of adoptive parents of children with special health care needs, we compared the literature to (a) results of research that studied the experiences of both biological and adoptive families with SHCN, (b) our interviews with adoptive parents of children with SHCN, and (c) our collective clinical experience. As a result, we found that there are three important issues that have not been previously addressed in the literature. What follows is a summary of these issues and our recommendations.

We found that there are three different ways that adoptive parents approach the adoption of a child with SHCN, here entitled *Approach Classes*. It is suggested that each Approach Class influences the commitment, preparation, challenges, and coping related to parenting an adopted child with SHCN. Further investigation of differences based upon these Approach Classes is warranted.

A second issue is the lack of clarity concerning the adoptive versus biological status among families in the broad body of pediatric research. Because this distinction is almost never made in the reports of these studies, it is not clear whether the data represent experiences of adoptive parents or biological parents. Whether the research findings are relevant to biological families, adoptive families, or both, therefore, remains unclear. As the pediatric and pediatric psychology literature continues to develop, the biological versus adoptive status of families in such studies should be routinely reported.

A third issue is the degree to which the type of special health care need of the adopted child (e.g., psychological, physical, or a combination of both) influences the quality of the relationship between adoptive parent and the child. Furthermore, distinctions between types of health conditions within each of these categories may be helpful in guiding both research and parents' readiness for coping with SHCN. Models to guide considerations regarding the interaction of family and psychological and physical factors related to SHCN have been articulated (Boyer, 2008; McCubbin & McCubbin, 1993; Rolland, 1987; Thompson et al., 1992; Wallander & Varni, 1992) and may be helpful in providing greater assistance to parents adopting children with SHCN.

As demonstrated throughout the literature, adoptive parents of children with SHCN have their own special parenting challenges and three in particular. According to these parents, (1) they have not received adequate information about their child's medical, mental, and early life history; (2) they experience a lack of continued support, postadoption; and (3) many helping professionals are not fully informed about and do not fully understand or appreciate their needs. We hope that parents, prospective parents, and the helping professionals who work with them will find the practical points presented earlier to be beneficial.

The pages that follow mark the beginning of the next part of this book—a move from theory and research to a focus on practical considerations for adoptive parents and for the helping professionals who work with them. This shift begins with Chapter 8, Parenting the Young Child, which highlights two aspects of parenting in particular: (1) the factors underpinning the adoptive parents' decision to adopt (e.g., issues of infertility, family and societal perspectives about adoption), and (2) the relationship between effective parenting and parent-responsiveness that is specific (i.e., appropriate) to each developmental stage of the child. The authors will elucidate the challenges that arise for adoptive parents, and suggest ways to meet these challenges. They will also emphasize the strengths that adoptive parents exhibit, and the resources that support them in successful adoptions.

Chapter 8

PARENTING THE YOUNG CHILD

Elaine Frank and Denise Rowe

In the ever-changing world of adoption, the need to understand the intricacies of building relationships becomes increasingly important. Thousands of adoptions take place every year and parents seem to have less information and time to experience becoming attached to their babies or children. Whether they are parents by birth or adoption, most parents are by nature or can become "good enough," and can learn to recognize and adapt to their ghosts, the issues they bring from their own upbringing to the raising of their children. Adoptive parents must almost always take on the identity of being "remedial parents" (Winnicott, 1954a, 1964), as most adoptions may be thought of as "special needs adoptions" (van Gulden & Bartels-Rabb, 1993) as far as parenting is concerned. Controversy exists in the field of adoption and probably among adoptive parents about the above; but for us (because parents and later their children have an added self-aware dialogue about adoption) it refers to the particular circumstances of each family's adoption that parents must understand in order to build the parent-child relationship from day one with their child. This relationship becomes the basis for the formation of each child's sense of identity and belongingness.

In birth families, knowledge of normal child development, physical, cognitive, and emotional, helps parents to develop empathy, patience, understanding, and acceptance of the child they have, which in turn enhances the parent-child relationship. Adoptive parents have the additional task of understanding how the adoption experience affects development at each stage from infancy onward. An extra measure of patience, empathy, and knowledge about child development is crucial for supporting the child's initial attempts during the attachment phase, as well as for accepting the temperament, history, culture, and country of origin of the child. This understanding allows parents to meet the emotional needs of the adopted child. Of utmost importance will be the adoptive parents' understanding that there will be differences between the chronological age and the developmental stage of their adopted child that will require them to respond to the latter and not the former.

We describe interventions and educational strategies for working with adoptive parents that we have developed and implemented through our parent-child groups and 25 years of "developmental guidance," parent-child groups, counseling, and therapy with these families.

GHOSTS IN ADOPTIVE FAMILIES

All people come to parenting with a given set of influences. What each person brings from the start—personality, temperament, emotional well-being, intellect, education, early experiences, and philosophy of parenting—affects the family in numerous ways.

This is what Selma Fraiberg, psychoanalyst and social worker, referred to as "Ghosts in the Nursery," the intrapsychic representations of past experiences and relationships that travel along with parents and children and have direct impact on the children's lives (Fraiberg et al., 1975). These life experiences are the ghosts born of a different time and place but very much a part of the present and affecting the whole adoption experience. Adoptive parents should be aware of these influences, both within themselves and in the children they adopt. The pediatrician T. Berry Brazelton (1992) stated that when parents are cognizant of their ghosts, they are able to be better parents.

For more than three decades, we have worked with both birth and adoptive families. Our experience has taught us that as much as there are differences in parenting between these two populations, many similarities are also present, and the latter may be more important. As we watched the attachment process, we saw that many factors affect whether the relationship becomes a good, growth-promoting one, or is derailed, deformed, or hindered by "ghosts" from the parents' or child's actual or fantasized past.

Identification of ghosts is more obvious when traumatic abuse has occurred, but is common in many minor situations. For example:

> A mother with straight hair who was jealous of her curly haired sister and who always had a permanent herself could not hide her disappointment in her daughter Carol's straight hair. Mother was unable to relate happily to her daughter because she projected her negative feelings about her sister onto Carol, who at 2 years was showing signs of depression and withdrawal. During a developmental guidance session, the therapist initiated a discussion asking why mother was so often angry with Carol for small things. By focusing on her childhood jealousy and hatred of her sister, mother was able to resolve her displacement of those feelings onto her child. Their relationship improved and Carol began to emerge from her depression.

Fraiberg's placement of the needs of the baby as a central focus of intervention led us to conceptualize problems of attachment faced by adoptive parents with later-placed infants and children, arbitrarily designated by us as after 5 months of age (Frank & Rowe, 2002). In thinking of ghosts as Fraiberg conceptualized them, we look at three sources: the ghosts of the parents (the experiences that shaped their need or desire to adopt), the adoption process itself, and the ghosts of the adopted babies and children emanating from their prenatal environment and pre-adoption experiences in orphanages or foster care. We examine the consequences of these ghosts and their effects on parent-child attachment.

Pre-Adoptive Parent Ghosts

The ghosts for the adoptive parents-to-be begin with their considering adoption as the road to parenthood, their fertility situation, and the first steps in the adoptive process, such as the home study. They will need to mourn the loss of the idealized biological baby they wished to conceive and bear. Women in particular have fantasies of the child they will have, often from earliest childhood. They imagine what their child would look like, their hair and eye color. They imagine their behavior, including personality, temperament, and intellect. The child they adopt likely will not match these fantasies. Grieving the fantasies allows parents to come to terms with their conflicts about parenting versus conceiving and bearing the child.

The Sadness of Infertility

This feeling may never be totally resolved, but for some adoptive parents, deciding that it is more important to parent than to pursue conception frees them to move forward. Those who cannot leave these ghosts behind are prone to difficulty later in feeling entitled to claim and parent the adoptee. Women and men who do not explore their feelings about the causes of their infertility, which partner may have the "problem," or who feels inadequate, may have difficulty functioning in mutually positive ways as parents. Situations in which one partner wants to adopt and the other does not but goes along anyway may present problems in their relationship after they become parents. Members of families with both birth and adopted children may experience conflicting feelings about one another.

Lack of pregnancy as a developmental stage is another ghost for adoptive parents. Because so much emotional energy is involved with the adoption process itself, it is easy for waiting parents to *not* think about the baby or child they hope to get or about parenting issues they might face. During pregnancy, birth parents have the opportunity to think about, discuss, and learn about delivery, infant care, changes in lifestyle, attitudes about child-rearing, and issues of family responsibility. Another reason why prospective adoptive parents avoid thinking about the baby is the stress created by the unknown outcome of the process, which prevents them from being able to mentally prepare for parenthood. Fear that the adoption will not succeed because the birth mother or father may decide not to relinquish the child can be debilitating (Frank & Rowe, 1990).

Often in private adoptions with a lawyer or intermediary, no counseling is provided. In agency adoptions, prospective parents must attend a certain number of hours of counseling and education. Some people choose to avoid the agency process while others may seek out an agency to engage in the counseling process. For people who are attuned to these issues, experiencing some of the above stressors may actually help them later to put themselves in their child's shoes when she or he grieves for the lost biological parents. Their ability to empathize with the adoptee's feelings as well as their respect for the uniqueness of their particular child's inner life may be enhanced.

Fantasies About Birth Parents and Relatives

During the waiting period, other ghosts arrive for new parents in the form of the child's birth relatives. These fantasies may encompass the birth family's history: physical and cognitive development, personality traits, temperament, and talents that will become the child's heritage. As soon as children are old enough to understand something about the meaning of adoption, they, too, have fantasies about their birth parents. For children who are foreign born, parents have fantasies about how they will relate to their child's birth country. In closed adoptions, where there is little information, adoptive parents' fantasies will influence their perceptions of their newly arrived child. One adoptive mother said, "She doesn't need to think about the country where she was born, she's an American now."

In open adoptions, the presence of more information may temper the fantasies. However, when adoptive parents have a relationship with the birth mother or father, or attend the birth, the emotional bond created especially between the two mothers may affect or inhibit attachment between adoptive mom and baby, if adoptive mother does not feel empowered to take up the role of caregiver. Similar situations occur when foster parents adopt a foster child who has been living with them.

Feeling Entitled to Be the Parent

When potential adoptive parents feel insecure about taking on the identity as *real* parents, their ability to relate to their child may be affected (Smith & Miroff, 1987). Some women feel that because they were unable to produce the child biologically, the child will not attach to them, or the older child will not love them as he or she would have loved the birth mother. Others may feel that the adopted child is so "special" they do not deserve him or her, or that the child will seek out and wish to live with the birth family. Some parents struggle with the feeling the adopted child will never be good enough for them. Conflicts involving entitlement may contribute to postadoption depression syndrome (Bond, 1995; see Chapter 4 for further discussion). In other situations, lack of a sense of entitlement can have a negative impact on a parent's comfort discussing adoption in or outside of the family.

Postadoption Ghosts

Once the child enters the home, experiences from the adoptive parent's childhood have the potential to impact the parents' ability and style of parenting. They include a person's early relationships with parents, siblings, and extended family, and memories of how they were parented (Main & Goldwyn, 1984). To the extent that parents are unaware of these early influences, their parenting may be controlled more by their past experiences than by what is specific to or good for their child.

Ghosts may be more noticeable (as in posttraumatic stress disorder [PTSD]) when there has been trauma, abuse, or neglect, but can also be seen in minor situations:

> Will was raised by a rigid father who had high expectations, and was able to live up to what his father expected. When, years later, he adopted a 4-year-old daughter with neglect and other physiological issues, the grandfather was unable to accept the child's academic difficulties. Grandfather continued trying to impose his child-rearing methods and standards, causing pain and discomfort for all involved, including the child as she entered adolescence.

Emotional compatibility is an important component of the parent-child relationship. For instance, the relationship between a spirited, strong-willed child and a temperamentally reserved parent may be filled with friction unless the adult understands and accepts the child as is. Positive, helpful, useful ghosts are those that can help a parent understand a current dilemma in family life:

> Natalie complained that her 4-year-old son would not go to sleep at night for his father, insisting that mother remain with him because he was "scared of the witches." She recalled that when she was 4, she would stay in her parents' bed until her father came home from work and "saved her from the snakes." The recollection allowed her to put herself in her son's shoes and be more understanding of his nighttime fears. In addition, her child was adopted from a rural orphanage, and had never been outside at night. Mom's understanding of her own childhood fears helped her be more empathic to her son.

Empathy coupled with emotional availability help adoptive (and all) parents to understand and accept their child as she or he is in the present moment and intervene in more growth-promoting ways. Many behaviors considered inappropriate for a particular child can be understood by reflecting on what the parent experienced and then reviewed in the present day adoption context. These reflected-on past experiences can lead to parental empathy that is useful to all family members.

Children's Ghosts

In infancy, ghosts arrive before (and after) birth in the form of genetic inheritance and prenatal experience. They include the baby's inherited characteristics, physiology, temperament, cognitive capacities, and in utero environment. Coming from the birth mother are her pregnancy experience, health and nutrition, life circumstances, inherited defects and talents, and drug or alcohol abuse, all of which influence the fetus. After birth, babies can be visited by prenatal ghosts, which can affect their relationships with adoptive parents (Fraiberg, 1987). Physiological ghosts can be seen in the crack baby who comes to a foster home appearing overstimulated, with an irritating cry and who does not like to look at the human face. The new parent worries about the baby and may not know how to elicit the baby's gaze or how to calm him or her, adding to attachment difficulties.

Adopted children who spent months or years in orphanages or children who were cared for by many people in early years are apt to have experiences that affect their ability to trust enough to make positive new connections in subsequent placements. The attachment process is affected by relationships previously made and/or broken, influencing the type and amount of emotional connectedness possible within the adoptive family.

Finally, there are the external ghosts. Continuing changes in adoption practice, legal risks, and degrees of openness in the relationship to the birth family create ghosts for adoptive parents and the child. In closed adoptions where there is no contact or information, ghosts are imaginary, but still have influence. In semi-open adoptions with letters and pictures, knowing about reality does not prevent child or parent from fantasizing about birth relatives. Helping the parents become aware of these ghosts before and after the child enters the home shifts their focus to connecting with the child, learning about the attachment process, and beginning a loving parent-child relationship.

INTERVENTION WITH ADOPTIVE FAMILIES: DEVELOPMENTAL GUIDANCE, PARENT-CHILD GROUPS, AND PARENT-CHILD THERAPY

In our 25 years of educational and clinical work with adoptive families, many theorists such as John Bowlby, Mary Ainsworth, Mary Main, Margaret Mahler, Vera Fahlberg, Holly van Gulden, Rene Spitz, Erik Erikson, Anna Freud, Donald Winnicott, Stanley Greenspan, and Sally Provence (many reviewed in Chapters 2 through 5) influenced our work. Chief among them, Henri Parens' Early Child Development Project at Eastern Pennsylvania Psychiatric Institute had a particularly salient role in our understanding and thinking. His main objective was to help parents understand early child development in order to improve their parenting skills. The educational content of the project was based on psychodynamic theories of early development and research, specifically Mahler's work.

With the recent research in attachment theory, much work has been done to understand the attachment process and describe the co-construction of the parent-child relationship in adoptive families. Our experience and their theories led us to develop a working schema that includes several kinds of intervention with adoptive families, both preventive and therapeutic. We describe and illustrate three modes of intervention: developmental (parent) guidance, parent-child groups, and parent-child therapy. From our training and experience with the work done since the 1970s on infant development and attachment, we felt that Margaret Mahler's developmental theory and Selma Fraiberg's treatment techniques were most practical for our work with families and young children. In our clinical practice, we were guided by Fraiberg's work with parents and child present. The goal is to facilitate and promote parent-child attachment from day one. We believe that with work and practice, parents with their ghosts and children with early attachment disruptions can begin to build a meaningful and satisfying relationship.

Developmental Guidance

Fraiberg and her colleagues Vivian Shapiro, Edna Adelson, and Alicia Lieberman created "Developmental Guidance" in the family's home (Fraiberg, 1987). The therapy was relationship-based counseling and education in child development coupled with emotional support for parents experiencing stress in their roles. Many of their parents were involved with child protective services. Our form of developmental guidance utilized Fraiberg's methods in an office-based practice with parents across the socioeconomic spectrum. Few had connections to child protective services or were mandated to receive parenting education. Usually they wanted to solve child behavior problems or improve their relationships with their children.

Parent and child attend sessions together. The clinician offers emotional support for the parental role and teaches parents and children to express and process negative emotions. The parents are helped to identify the child's emotional needs and to respect the motivation and meaning of their child's behavior. They learn to recognize and compare their own expectations with the actual abilities and temperament of their child. The emphasis is on *identifying and exploring parents' ghosts* so that they understand the connection between their own upbringing and their subsequent parenting style.

Developmental guidance can begin as crisis intervention initially, then weekly or monthly, depending on the situation. Sometimes the parent(s) is seen alone to obtain a more thorough or traumatic history, or later to discuss issues that might be inappropriate to the age or stage of the child. Some examples of situations in which developmental guidance is helpful are: a child from an orphanage who rocks on a chair when anxious or upset; a child who does not want to continue music lessons whose mother has been unable to allow the child to make decisions for herself; or a 9-year-old who has been distorting her family history, telling peers about her many birth siblings—and how she used to take long rides into the mountains of Peru with her birth parents. These situations provide opportunities for parents to communicate with their children in ways that reinforce their attachment, while helping children cope with the realities of belonging to two families and often, two countries.

Parent-Child Groups: Education for Adoptive Parenting

The adoptive family parent-child groups were modeled on the prevention-early-intervention groups created by Dr. Henri Parens. Few adoptive parents receive in-depth didactic information about child development, postadoptive relationships, and daily family life (Frank & Rowe, 1986). "After Adoption" parent-child groups were specifically for adoptive families and served as a medium through which they could describe their circumstances and experiences and express their feelings about adoption. The group provides an open forum to discuss their feelings about the adoption process and their roles as adoptive parents. In addition, they learn about normal cognitive and emotional development and possible variations in their particular children. Issues of infertility, birth parents, ethnicity and culture, lack of medical information, and talking to children about adoption are discussed in the group while the children are still small, and in the context of the stages of early development. Parents want to know how to respond to and educate extended family members, friends, and the community about adoption.

Adoption groups meet weekly, attended by parent and child. Two leaders assist parents in observing the children, comment on the children's behavior and its correspondence to the normal developmental stages of separation-individuation, and anticipate the next steps. The attachment process in the late-adopted child may look different; however, that child will need the same amount of time to complete the developmental tasks that result in a secure relationship with the adoptive parent. Adding adoption topics to discussions of development encourages parents to explore their feelings and consider solutions to some of the parental dilemmas inherent in being an adoptive family. Children under 4 can actually communicate their feelings about situations discussed (for example, "tell group leaders about how hard it is to sleep in my bed").

Participation in the adoption groups enables a range of benefits to be realized: (a) it provides a safe environment to process feelings and behavior; (b) encourages development of realistic age-appropriate expectations of their young child and adoption; (c) improves tolerance for normal aggression, fosters independent activity, with the child's need for comforting, dependency, and attachment (d) helps parents understand overlapping stages in the adoption of an older child; (e) provides mutual support of other parents; (f) alleviates anxieties parents have about diagnoses such as reactive attachment disorder; (g) provides support to navigate early intervention systems; and (h) enables parents to value child development over adoptive status.

Parent-Child Psychotherapy

When things are not going well and people feel the need for therapy or counseling, most children under 7 are seen with their parents. Parent-infant therapy emphasizes the parent-child relationship as the client. As Parens stated, "Look for the problem in the child, or in the parent, or in the space between them" (personal communication, 1989). At the center of treatment is the support of the adults and children in their efforts to connect and understand one another, listen to one another, and prevent the visitation of one generation of ghosts as permanent residents affecting the lives of the family.

When children whose pre-adoptive life experiences occurred in a dysfunctional family environment, foster, or orphanage care, the adoptive family needs more intensive intervention. Parent-child therapy can help parents explore the impact of the past and work through conflicts that prevent them from parenting their children adequately. Understanding the child who hoards food or takes other kids' things, or identifying with a child's traumatic experiences can strengthen the parent-child relationship. Feeling too much pity can prevent parents from setting appropriate limits or cause overindulgent reactions to misbehavior and tantrums that are not growth-promoting for the child.

Therapeutic Format

The importance of having parents and their child together is for the therapist to observe emotions and be able to hear and interpret both sides . . . parent and child. The therapist acts as a real object to both parent and child, considering conflicts both within the parents and between parents and the child. Psychodynamic theories and precepts, including the therapeutic alliance, transference, how past experiences affect present parenting behavior, conscious and unconscious, and the intergenerational transmission of trauma, are part of the therapist's arsenal used to facilitate the child's adjustment:

> Three-year-old Annie was adopted by a single parent when she was 11 months old. She cried in daycare for her mommy. A caregiver called to say she was immature, and nothing they did could prevent her from crying for mommy. Mother and therapist took a different tack and talked with Annie and the teachers to help understand why Annie was so worried, and help her to express her fears so that she could better tolerate the separation until she could manage better by herself. As she became more attached and understood that mommy would come back for her, she became less upset during the day.

Flow of Sessions

Because the parent-child relationship is primary to our work, all three forms of intervention involve having parent and child attending together for the majority of the sessions. The initial evaluation includes a session with parents alone to get history of the adoption and the child, then a session with parent and child to observe the parent-child interactions and child's developmental status. A third session is to discuss recommendations and plans for intervention with the parents. The number of sessions is based on individual needs. Sometimes parents who are in a group come for individual sessions to tackle a nongroup problem; sometimes referrals are made for more specific resources.

While working with parents and their birth children and adoptive parents and their children in different settings, we became aware that the parents' understanding of physical, cognitive, and emotional development of early childhood was crucial to their ability to empathize and remain emotionally available. This education enabled them to have more appropriate expectations of their toddlers' and preschoolers' puzzling and often erratic behavior, resulting in more patience and less angry and punitive reactions to their children.

PARENTING CORNERSTONES FOR ADOPTIVE FAMILIES

Greater understanding of child development and parenting than is possessed by many new parents (biological or adoptive) is necessary to ensure a healthy attachment and subsequent parent-child relationship. Children adopted after 5 months of age are likely to show variations in both the timing and quality of their initial attachment to new adoptive parents. It may be helpful to consider special parenting behaviors that will facilitate a mutually empathic emotional connection. Developing these special parenting techniques is what the authors refer to as *remedial parenting*.

Attachment and Emotional Connection

The journey from infant to individual, symbiosis to object constancy, takes place in about three and a half years, usually in a predictable and chronological order (Mahler et al., 1975). In adoption, the moment of the child's arrival in the family heralds the beginning of this process. Each child is an individual who develops on his or her own timetable, according to genetic and constitutional givens and interaction with the physical and emotional environment. Children who do not arrive soon after birth will have experienced the loss of familiar people and environments, which influences their ability to build this new relationship. Adults, although emotionally prepared to welcome their new addition, will also be experiencing the start of a new relationship—akin to falling in love after the first meeting.

Attachment begins with the symbiosis (Mahler et al., 1975), a time-dependent process. When the infant or child joins the family, parent and child begin to get to know one another, spend time together, and develop an emotional bond. Babies who arrive soon after birth are helped to achieve this connection because the parents attend to their care and nurturing needs. Over the first 6 months the baby begins to experience basic trust and the feeling of being loved.

Vera Fahlberg, pediatrician and foster care consultant, in her book *A Child's Journey Through Placement* (1991), discusses how attachment difficulties may manifest themselves as behavioral, psychological, or cognitive problems, or developmental delays. Fahlberg explains how infants who have developed a first attachment in another family, birth or foster, before placement must have time to grieve that loss and then adjust to a new family.

For the child who comes a year later, the process begins then and is affected by his or her experiences before placement. Some children may cry and be clingy, holding on to the parent tightly. Rather than a sign of attachment, this behavior often illustrates panic and stress over the loss of a familiar environment. It is important for parents to allow the older child the clinging and the closeness usually provided to a younger infant to foster attachment and facilitate the new relationship. Attaching cannot be rushed and if the baby from birth needs 6 months, the child who comes later (despite advanced cognitive ability) is still emotionally navigating a process that is time-dependent. Spending time together allows a parent to learn about his or her child while permitting the child to experience the nuances of early infancy: holding, cuddling, and comforting as much as possible while verbalizing affection and empathy:

> Lily was adopted from China at 13 months, not yet walking, but raring to go and able to express her opinions, needs, and desires without words. She appeared to attach immediately when her new parents removed her from the orphanage. She clung to them during the long trip home and showed anxiety and fear on separating at bedtime. During the first 6 weeks with her parents, because she was not yet walking, they were able to create the closeness necessary for attachment to begin. She slept in a crib in their room and they carried her about in a cloth baby sling. The sling eventually became Lily's "transitional object" and her parents encouraged her to use it when they were not able to be with her, or when she was distressed.

After the initial attachment stage and establishment of the symbiosis, Mahler's separation-individuation phases become the focus of the parent-child relationship (Mahler et al., 1975). When parents understand the antagonistic emotions and the intrinsic fears of the child in relation to separation, and in the adopted child's case, experiences of loss, they can be more empathic with a child's fears of abandonment. The child who has established basic trust in the first 8 months, either of life or time in the new home, begins to move away from the secure base to explore the physical environment beyond the parent-child dyad. He or she starts a "love affair with the world," known as the *practicing phase* when the toddler seems not to need contact with a parent, and is often oblivious of parental whereabouts. Despite the exhilaration with these explorations, sudden pangs cause the child to fall apart and want to be held and comforted, in a phrase, to return to the parent's orbit for emotional refueling (Mahler et al., 1975).

As the child's conflict between staying close versus wanting to explore the world escalates, he or she enters the *rapprochement phase*. Parents are often confused after the apparent independence of the practicing stage child because rapprochement behavior often looks like regression. Even parents who know this phase is normal have a hard time accepting their child's clingy, seemingly irrational, fearful, and negative, sometimes aggressive behavior toward them—at first, usually the mother and then others, including peers.

Children who are adopted during this phase suffer the contradictory pulls of wanting to explore but also need the security of proximity. Because they are not yet attached to their new parents, they are less likely to seek comfort or refueling from their parents and may indiscriminately seek anyone. Many adopted children are experiencing behavior in two developmental stages simultaneously. The more empathic and patient adoptive parents can be during this time, remaining emotionally available to seemingly contradictory behaviors in their children, the better able the child is to maintain forward movement through the attachment process.

Some toddlers act out these conflicts, and adults who are unaware of heightened ambivalence during this time focus on stopping or changing the behavior (tantrums, hitting parent, refusal to stay in room, etc.) or worry about it as signs of problems to come. Other children, in contrast, cease to respond, put up walls, withdraw, or ignore the attempts of peers or adults to interact with them. This passivity may be seen as "good behavior," a sign of adjustment; yet it masks anxiety and inability to connect emotionally. *All child behavior is communicating something about a child's emotional life*. It is important for parents to understand the normal emotional conflicts of the young child to the best of their ability, and respond in growth-promoting ways that will preserve the newly developing relationship. Although anyone living with a 2-year-old will often feel perplexed, adoptive parents may have more uncertainty about how to respond to the child's progress toward separation and their own ambivalence about giving in to the child's need for contact or encouraging independence too early. The developmental task for the adopted child in this stage is to discover how to manage both kinds of behavior within a family setting at a time when he or she may still be reacting to the loss of his past life and its people, places, and activities.

A child in the rapprochement stage joining the family after 18 months, who has not had a primary attachment relationship, is at risk for failing to form a strong-enough attachment with his or her new parent(s). Without the opportunity to have a symbiosis (which may look really out of place in an almost 2-year-old), he or she will be handicapped in undergoing the separation-individuation stages as well. Experiencing a *remedial symbiosis* while simultaneously engaging in the behaviors of the more typical 2-year-old allows the child to establish roots in the new attachment relationship. This means that parent and child need to engage in the attachment behaviors of early infancy such as lap-time and getting acquainted with security (transitional) objects:

Boris, who arrived from a Romanian orphanage at 24 months, was large for his age and not yet speaking English. He was a handsome toddler with a pleasant demeanor and seemed naturally inclined to cuddle. Shortly after arrival, he became interested in his mother's parka with a furry hood. He carried it with him and although it was summer, continued to hold it close and stroke the fur. His mom was ambivalent about encouraging this closeness and they spent much time with him hanging over her lap, legs dangling. This awkward but engaging portrait of mother-son attachment brought criticism from relatives and observers. This behavior mimicked the mother-child dyad of early infancy that leads to the establishment of the symbiosis. Mother was encouraged to provide these experiences when she asked if he was "too old" to be permitted to spend time on her lap "acting like a baby." A few months passed and Boris began to show the more conflicted behaviors of the rapprochement. He was easily frustrated and dissolved into tantrums, wanted to do things by himself, and directed his aggression toward mother when she inevitably disappointed him. He hit and kicked mother and she worried about his male aggression, a ghost from her own past, and the unknown details of his family history.

Mother, a new adoptive parent, had no experience to rely on. Because she didn't know about the progression of the phases, it was hard for her to understand his, or her own, ambivalence and she didn't know how to respond to his behavior. As mother learned about the normal sequence of the attachment process with its expectable ebb and flow of aggression, she became comfortable employing parenting behaviors that allowed him the closeness to navigate both the symbiosis and the rapprochement phases.

The fur hood became Boris's security object. He slept with it and wanted to take it with him when they went out. This assisted him in his emerging individuation as it does with infants who get accustomed to an object and use it to bridge their early separations from parents. Because Boris was nearing 3, he was to start nursery school shortly and thanks to a sympathetic staff, was able to bring the parka hood with him.

Object Constancy: Consolidating New Relationships

Mahler's (Mahler et al., 1975) last phase of the separation-individuation process is called *on the road to object constancy*. The phrase reflects the continuity of a process through which the child can differentiate and acknowledge the interconnectedness of self and mother. He understands that she will return to him when she leaves and he has internalized a mental image of the parent in his mind. Language development (including learning English for foreign-born children), identification with the parent, and growth of imagination and symbolic play all contribute to the emerging personality of the young child at this time. The beginning achievement of object constancy enables the child to be ready for nursery school and other activities in the world separate from the parent, which is a lifelong cycling and integration of dependency-independency needs. Many return visits will occur to separation-individuation, most markedly in adolescence, but many researchers in infancy and attachment believe that by this time, a child's patterns of attachment are laid down and will determine both his approach to and the quality of his adult relationships (Main & Goldwyn, 1984).

Two Stages at One Time

Our goal as we work with all families is teaching the attachment process, its significance to emotional, cognitive, and physical development of children and how it enhances the parent-child relationship. Usually infants progress through the stages of attachment, symbiosis and separation-individuation, in a somewhat predictable and chronological order. When the baby arrives in early infancy, attachment from the baby's side and parents' side begin simultaneously, reaching symbiosis when the baby is about 6 months old (Mahler et al, 1975) and proceeds through the separation-individuation stages until object constancy is achieved at about 3½ years.

Children who enter the family after 5 or 6 months are experiencing several of these stages at the same time. Their need to be close to mother to form the attachment is at odds with the drive to be independent and explore the world. These children need to experience with their new parents the stage(s) they missed in infancy. It is important for parents to understand emotional development as it takes place in their particular child and to respond in ways that facilitate the new parent-child relationship. To create an environment for attachment, we want parents to focus on what is called a "holding environment" (Winnicott, 1958), as parents of an infant do by holding the baby close to feed, nurture, and care for him. This closeness is the foundation for beginning the relationship. Emotional availability is thereby shown by the parents and learned by the child.

Navigating two stages at the same time (simultaneously) can be conflict-ridden for parents as well as the child. For parents, it means living through "infancy" with an older child who is saying good-bye to past experiences while beginning to negotiate the new attachment. Conflicts regarding closeness and separateness abound. Clingy, cranky behavior in young, recently adopted children does not usually indicate emotional connection to the new parent; most often, it is anxiety rooted in feelings of abandonment or grieving for previous caregivers or familiar environments. It should not be interpreted as negative behavior (to be disciplined) as these behaviors are probably innate survival mechanisms. When a child cries inconsolably at times and cannot accept comforting, parents should be supportive in remaining nearby and allowing the child to sense a closeness, rather than leaving a child alone to cry it out. Despite the counsel of well-meaning friends or relatives, an adopted child will not be spoiled but will benefit by having free access to parent's nurturing activities in the first months in a new home. Understanding this behavior allows parents to provide emotional and physical closeness and empathy for the child's feelings and needs for comfort and attachment.

Parents' knowledge of normal physical, cognitive, and language development in early childhood will help them to understand the child they have as unique. Too frequently, the child's medical or family history has gaps and raises uncertainties. Biological endowment may be unknown or distorted in the record and the actual environment may have been a source of developmental delays in many areas. Specifically, language development can be affected by neglect, lack of stimulation, or beginning life in a different culture or language. Later adopted children may start school well before they have achieved the same level of object constancy as their peers. They may look like kindergarteners, but have many holes in their development. Sometimes evaluations are needed and parents should advocate with schools and other institutions so that the areas of concern identified by these assessments are addressed (see Chapter 11).

Attachment Disorder

Children who come with a history of disrupted attachments will demonstrate gradations in both the nature and quality of their past interactions and in their potential to build a new relationship. These children can be helped to reach their potential if new adoptive parents are encouraged to learn parenting techniques that will bind them together in a loving relationship. Attachment proceeds over time, nurtured by proximity and innumerable positive interactions between parents and child. Separation-individuation continues throughout life, along with the tension between dependence and independence, and is reworked in the context of one's present experiences, influenced by the past and subject to change in the future (Frank & Rowe, 2002). Brodzinsky and Schechter in their book, *The Psychology of Adoption* (1990), reviewed studies relating attachment issues to psychological and academic problems of middle childhood and adolescence. They concluded that the earlier a child was placed in a permanent home, and the fewer placements the child had, the less the risk to the child. In studying older children, Brodzinsky found that when they begin to understand the meaning of adoption, that is, being relinquished by the birth parents, they often began to experience feelings of loss, grief, and confusion about their relationship with their adoptive parents.

For many adoptive families, the idea that love is all it takes to ensure attachment is still prevalent, despite research that shows how complex the attachment process can be for children in their families from birth. Van Gulden and Bartels-Rabb (1993) said, "however much love enhances bonding and attachment, it cannot cure psychological problems." With professional guidance parents can identify the problems, which ones can be solved, which ones cannot, and work to build the best possible relationship with their child given the realities of the child they have" (p. 29).

Many adopted children are currently being diagnosed with reactive attachment disorder or RAD. This diagnosis made too early can lead families to more intensive therapies than may be warranted because these children may have some form of what Ainsworth described as "disorganized attachment"[1] or attachment delays related to their experiences before joining the adoptive family (Ainsworth et al., 1978).[2] Attachment disorder can be thought of as the pathological end of the spectrum of normal connectedness of child to parent. This diagnosis may be a disservice, leading to intrusive treatments in some children who are showing signs of delayed connection to their new families. Rather than diagnosing a "disorder," except in the most severe situations, we think in terms of *broken* or *insufficient* attachments. Adopted older children with traumatic past experiences who appear to have disorganized attachment benefit most if remedial attachment work begins as early as possible. With time, effort, and some specific parent education or therapy, many of these children will form the essential emotional ties that will bind them to their parents in loving relationships.

Temperament and Personality

Although understanding the cognitive and physical aspects of a child's development is necessary, *accepting and empathizing with the child's emotional status is paramount* to building a secure relationship. Temperament and personality are inborn with each child and then modified by emotional experiences, nurturing or lack of it, and these ghosts are brought with the smallest child into the new family. Chess and Thomas (1987) listed three types of temperament, categorizing young children as easy (calm, relaxed, easily satisfied); difficult (moody, sensitive, and hard to calm); and slow to warm up (shy, cautious, and inhibited).

The challenge for parents is to begin to identify the child's temperament, and accept the *inevitable* effects on the parent-child relationship and family life. For example, some people are risk takers and will always approach new things; others are more cautious and not willing to dive right in. Later, when thinking of children who search for their birth relatives, some are risk takers, and others uninterested or uncurious. Likewise, some classify themselves as introverts or extroverts, and see "the world through rose-colored glasses" or experience life as a "half-empty glass." This point applies to parents and therapists as well as to children. Often in genetically related families, parents expect their children to have temperaments that are similar to their own or to other relatives. "He is stubborn just like Uncle Harry; she is shy in new situations just like me." Or "He didn't get that from me!" "He has to learn not to cry when he can't have me right away," said the mother of a 2-month-old. Although it is so difficult for a parent to love the baby and hate the behavior, the good-enough parent realizes that the child is not capable of changing himself at his age, and learns to *respond* rather than *react*. If the parent of the 2-month-old could say to herself, "He can't help it: he's only been here 2 months. I am the adult and should model calmness and comfort him until he is able to settle down," she could then empathize with the baby's fears and longing, allowing her to calm him and comfort him through his inevitable upsets.

A shy, slow-to-warm-up 3-year-old at music class won't leave Mom's lap to join the dancing children despite mother and the teacher's persuasive efforts. The mother, out-going and always a joiner, urges her not to be scared and to move into the group, telling her it will be fun. For adopted children who joined their family at a later age, it is important to allow time for the child to remain close, until she feels ready to separate from Mom.

Any parent deciding when to push and when to allow independence to come from the child walks a fine line. If a child feels insecure, she needs closeness until she feels inwardly safe enough to separate. This behavior corresponds to the rapprochement stage of separation-individuation and although it usually occurs between 18 months and 2½, the adopted child would probably need extra time to get to that stage despite her chronological age. Pausing, being mindful, and empathizing with the child's needs allows the parent to respond with attachment-enhancing behaviors. This may feel wrong at the moment because a parent thinks education about appropriate behavior should be offered rather than comfort for a child's opposing feelings. This is what is meant by being *emotionally available*:

Katie, who initially lived with her birth family and then in an orphanage, arrived at age 3 from overseas. She was accepted in a high-powered kindergarten. Within the first semester, teachers recognized her inability to attend to academic activities. Although she spoke English, it was evident that this child, learning a second language at 4, did not understand the meaning of the abstract ideas or the concepts commonly used in American kindergartens. She exhibited learning differences in attention as well as mild hyperactivity. She also misinterpreted social cues in various settings and reacted aggressively to other children. Katie was tested by a school psychologist with expertise in international adoption, and recommendations for placement in a special school setting ameliorated the social situation. When parents were helped through developmental guidance to review her background and present capabilities and to look realistically at where she was academically, they changed their initial expectations to match her current abilities. Respecting her temperament, they became less critical and more supportive of her actual social-emotional-cognitive level of functioning, which elevated her self-esteem, resulting also in improvement in her social skills.

Roadblocks to Object Constancy

For children who spent several years in an environment lacking adequate love and nurturing, even the most sophisticated and caring parents will experience difficulty providing the necessary conditions to make up for deprivations and allow for the establishment of a normal attachment and separation-individuation process. These children did not develop basic trust, have never felt real love, and may not have an adequate sense of self. In addition, all they have lost confuses them. Some are concerned about the peers they left behind, and beg to bring them along. Internationally adopted children have been told that they are coming to America, to join a family in this rich land where they will be lucky to get a mother and father who will LOVE them. In this condition, they must begin at "ground zero"! They have no understanding of these concepts: family, love, mother, father, or what is required to be a partner in a two-way attachment process with a parent figure. The adoptive parent, on the other hand, has already developed patterns of attachment, experienced all the above abstract concepts, and is exceedingly motivated to become involved in a parent-child relationship with their adored adopted child. They have waited and longed for this experience and have more than enough love to outweigh whatever difficulties relating to the child may bring.

This is why adoptive parents need to be aware of and come to terms with the need for more understanding of what the adoptive situation adds to parenting. As adoptive parents increase their knowledge of child development in general and the particulars of their child's body, mind, emotions, and past experiences (in other words their children's adoption ghosts, as well as their own ghosts), they are better able to foster emotional connectedness and feel more successful as parents.

Our experience at After Adoption has taught us that most parents can learn new parenting techniques and gain better understanding of the concepts that enhance relationships. In addition, the parent-child relationship grows as the parents develop a verbal and nonverbal emotional dialogue with their children. Interactions based on empathy, mutual respect, love and affection, and sensitivity to the child's viewpoint are the pillars of emotional connection.

ENHANCING THE PARENT-CHILD RELATIONSHIP IN ADOPTIVE FAMILIES: DEVELOPING AN ADOPTION DIALOGUE

Families need to develop a *dialogue* about adoption that is not limited to the parents telling the child a story about his origins and how he became a member of his family. There is no one right way because each family and story will be different. Discussions of adoption take place throughout childhood and will change as a child's understanding matures (Brodzinsky & Schechter, 1990). Discussions should happen in stages that relate to the child's ability to assimilate the information. Curiosity is an important prerequisite to learning and parents can respond with discussion appropriate to the child's cognitive stage from toddlerhood to adolescence. Although children may have a rudimentary grasp of abstract concepts, until age 7 fantasies and imagination rule their thinking.

Timing depends on the readiness and interest of the child. Starting off with just the word, *adoption*, used in a warm loving way is sufficient for the very young child. As the child gets old enough to question where babies come from, parents can discuss pregnancy and birth in a basic way, only giving as much information as the child seems to want at that moment. As the dialogue evolves, connecting the stories of birth, "all children are born and grow in a woman's tummy," and adopting a baby or child who grew in a "birth mother" or birth lady's tummy can be connected.

The first conversations about adoption are usually easier on the child than the parents. Often, the initial conversations bring more anxieties to the parents who are worrying about the effects of this information. For the child under 7, the story of adoption is probably equal to other abstract, not related personally stories about death, parenting, divorce, sex, and marriage. Children adopted from an orphanage or foster care will need to master many more challenging concepts as they gain experience living in their family. When explaining the reasons for the birth parents decision to relinquish them, children will dispute and fantasize about why they were "given away." They will also fantasize "solutions": The birth parent could buy a house, or go to the ATM machine for money. One helpful explanation is that the birth parent, sometimes the age of the child's teen babysitter, just was not ready to be a parent yet. One 10-year-old, told that her birth mother had been 15 when she was born, said, "Well, now she is 26 and she could take care of me now." That idea was both frightening and consoling at the same time.

Each family creates a dialogue specific to their family, and the more open the conversation, the easier it is for the child to adjust (Hoopes, 1982; Witmer et al., 1963). The ease with which a child fully accepts his adoptedness is directly related to the degree of the adopted parents' success in accepting and feeling entitled to their own status as adoptive parents. It is helpful when parents realize that children pick up and respond to the feelings and nuances more than they do to what is being said (Smith & Miroff, 1987).

Limit Setting and Discipline

Educating parents about discipline and setting limits is an integral part of all of our parenting work because of the impact on the parent-child relationship. Parental behaviors that promote attachment and build the relationship are more important in the long run than the immediate disciplinary issue. The goal of parental limit setting should be to teach children the boundaries of their behavior, which will allow them to develop self-discipline and take responsibility for their actions. When limits are set in firm but reasonable ways in an environment of warmth and empathy, parents are likely to be successful in reaching this goal. If one considers "discipline" according to its root, meaning "to teach or educate," and also understands the need to use empathy and comfort in the process, the job becomes more satisfying. Sometimes, parents are ambivalent about comforting and empathizing with the child when he or she misbehaves, but children are better able to comply when they feel they are still loved even though they disobeyed (Parens, Scattergood, Singletary, & Duff, 1987).

Empathy and communication are the cornerstones of positive limit setting. It takes more time and effort to teach children appropriate behaviors and/or language. Explaining why the behavior is not allowed and permitting discussion by the child is important. Many children naturally exhibit orneriness and temper tantrums when anxious and/or angry. When parents accept this as normal for the situation and age of the child, the child feels understood. He begins to regulate his behaviors in response to that empathy (Bowlby, 1951). Knowledge of normal child development, as well as of the behaviors that are rooted in neglect, abuse, broken attachments, and/or orphanage life, is essential when parenting adopted children.

Learning limits is made more effective through the establishment of logical connections between events and ideas. As children mature and their own reasoning and cognitive understanding replaces magical thinking (approximately 7 or 8 years), they begin to understand the consequences of their actions. Parents have the responsibility to ensure that the consequences they choose for a particular behavior are appropriate, by taking into consideration the incident, the age of the child, the child's feelings at the moment, and empathizing with the child's ability to comply with the parents' wishes. Consequences that are too severe, too strung out, or too far removed from the situation promote fear in the child, which does not allow him to develop self-control. The child's anger will limit his ability to internalize the reason the behavior was not acceptable.

When using "time out" as a consequence, parents must consider both the risks and benefits to the child. The concept of time out was initiated to remove the child from the situation and allow everyone involved time to settle down. Parents think that the child will "learn the lesson" and behave more appropriately. For certain ages and stages of development, this intervention may be effective. But for young children who do not have a fully developed conscience, and still have imaginary thinking, the risks may be greater than not learning the lesson. Many times a misbehaving child is frustrated and when put in time out becomes angry and fearful. At this point, the child needs comfort and support in order to learn the lesson. For children who are adopted, especially those adopted later in life, time outs may not be appropriate. Holly van Gulden (van Gulden & Bartels-Rabb, 1993) suggests that parents should stay within sight of the child or within talking range to minimize the child's feelings of abandonment.

Time-in together is probably a better way to respond to a child who is upset or misbehaving. Then, the parent has a better chance of talking with a child and teaching within the parent-child relationship the lessons of self-control and civil behavior. T. Berry Brazelton in *Touchpoints* (1992) talks about how parents must help the young child to control his behavior until the child is of an age and stage of development where he or she has internalized limits that constitute good behavior. The more time parents spend helping their child learn in a respectful, empathic way, the more quickly the child will understand the parents' limit setting.

Dealing With Loss and Grief in Adoption

A common and often difficult issue facing adoptive parents is whether, when, how, and to whom they communicate their child's history and adoptive circumstances. This is especially pertinent to discussing adoption with one's child who did not ask to be adopted and may be conflicted by the reasons, for example, "Why did you take me from my birth parents and relatives, or my country?" These questions bring up the parental ghosts such as entitlement to parent, fantasies about stealing someone else's baby, and rescue conflicts.

Feelings of loss, regret, and grief in children who were adopted are expressed differently at many stages of life. How adoption is discussed in the family can affect whether a child feels a strong sense of inclusion, or feels devalued and uncertain about belonging to their family. Conscious awareness of loss usually surfaces sometime after age 7. Children begin to live more outside of their families and are more tuned in to their inner worlds. They are taking steps away from parents' omnipotent answers to all questions to musing about the questions themselves, leaving parents to wonder about the quantity and content of adoption information that should be shared, if the child wants information, and what to say to the child who asks no questions at all.

The less defensive parent who anticipates these questions and is sensitive to how much a child wants to talk can be helpful to a questioning child. For those children who do not ask, a parent might say, "You haven't asked much about adoption since you were 6, and I thought now that you are older, you may be thinking about it in a more grown-up way." If there is grieving to be done, parental willingness to bring up the subject, and not avoid the differences between being adopted and being born into a family, may encourage questions (Kirk, 1964a).

Once they have understood the biological facts of reproduction, and something about the social and cultural aspects of family life in their community, children of elementary school age begin to construct a picture of their birth parents. One 7-year-old asked if her birth mother looked like her 14-year-old babysitter. An 8-year-old boy asked if his birth father was an old family friend. A 9-year-old told her mother that she looked in the mall for a woman who had a nose like hers.

Although preschoolers may wish to hear how they were adopted and entered their homes, older children discover the reality that their birth mother relinquished them for adoption and ask why. Just as preschoolers try to make sense of reproduction by developing their own theories and mixing them with their parents' explanations, older children try to reconcile their theories with the available facts, confronting emotions including incredulity, sadness, disappointment, anger, and guilt. These feelings have to be experienced and digested for the child to come to a more mature understanding of adoption. Children may believe they were relinquished because there was something wrong with them or they were bad babies. Some fear they will hurt their adoptive parents' feelings or anger them if they ask questions about birth parents. Although preschoolers are often open about expressing feelings, older children worry more about their parents' ability to tolerate their questions or feelings and may keep much more to themselves.

Usually, the elementary school child has internalized the idea that love and hate, anger and affection, can be felt toward their parents without ruining the relationship completely (i.e., the preschooler's "I won't be your best friend any more" changes to the 8-year-old's "I'm so mad at Jenny that I won't sit with her at music today"). Once they accept that ambivalence is part of love, they can identify with the adoptive family's characteristics, activities, and values. At the same time, urges toward individuation compel children to understand more about the reality of having a mixed heritage and the need to integrate various parts of their backgrounds. Parents and therapists can help by encouraging thoughtful consideration of who the child is becoming.

Grieving about losses may manifest itself differently for the child who has experienced multiple placements before being adopted. When a child enters a new home, he or she has no real idea that this is a "forever" home. Often a honeymoon period occurs, with the child on good behavior to ensure acceptance takes place. But soon the ghosts of loss, hurt, and anger surface. The child without trust in new attachment figures may break rules, steal, lie, or act out physically or sexually. The child's frightened message is "I'm going to leave here anyway, so I'd better make sure I don't get too close" or "Families don't last, and this one won't last either." Parents who can keep in mind how long trust takes to reestablish after it has been broken multiple times realize that this testing behavior will go on for a long time. Testing is what we do when we are doubtful or convinced that we are not worthy of the task.

How many times must the adult swear unconditional love before even a temperamentally optimistic child can feel safe enough? Optimistic parents, whose own positive experiences have mitigated their traumatic ones, will be more confident of their ability to win over an untrusting child.

The older the child, the longer it takes to build trust and gain confidence that abandonment will not occur. Part of the task is helping children to develop the psychological identification that distinguishes them as individuals. Knowing yourself, having empathy and respect for a child's narrative, and allowing for age-appropriate decision making helps children grow and gain self-confidence. What is this identification process that is so critical to success and confidence in later life? It takes us back to the initial attachment process, when it is important for babies to make the emotional connections that shape their personalities and make them into someone who is a unique individual as well as a member of a particular family.

A common experience for elementary school children is the family tree assignment. Teachers ask children to make a portrait of their geographical, ethnic, and historical roots, which again offers challenge and opportunity for family members to help with identity issues in adoption. If there has been sensitivity to not insisting on discussing adoption when a child is not receptive, parents will be able to listen to their child to discover what she is ready for and wants to include. A 10-year-old who moved to a new school said she would like to be the one to decide whether to tell classmates that she was adopted, because now she was the boss of that information. Is it farfetched to think that a 10-year-old is old enough to be boss of her adoptive information? At this age, the child's self-esteem will flourish if she feels her parents trust her as she masters new facts about herself and the world. When children learn about heredity, genes, and blood relationships, the adopted child has a better understanding of the differences between biological and adoptive relationships. Reactions are as varied as children and include feelings of relief, a sense of enlightenment, heightened interest in learning more about birth parents, denial of any interest, or feelings of loss and grief.

Adopted children will have feelings about their adoption, and many times in their development will struggle with whether their birth parents made an adoption plan. Adoptive parents can help their children to express their feelings and get explanations for what puzzles or troubles them. The more open the family discussions have been from the beginning of verbal communication, the more likely it is that communication will continue no matter how intense or complex the subject becomes. In domestic, open, or kinship adoptions, situations are more complicated and getting guidance to maneuver relationships may be indicated.

Therapists should help family members to explore before acting. Some families have not spoken much with their children about their feelings about searching for birth relatives. Learning about adoption is an ongoing adventure that parents hope to share with children, but some of this learning has to be pursued alone by the child. However, parents can still guide, instruct, and set limits. A 9-year-old who wants suddenly to look for her birth mother the day after a fight about bedtime can have her anger respected without rushing into action before she is ready. Because these are the years when youngsters appear to seriously confront the "sad side" of relinquishment and adoption, opportunities to meet with and talk to other adopted people their age, as well as with adolescent and adult adoptees, are beneficial. It helps children see into their own futures. The more experience parents have in listening to children and discussing feelings together, the more consoling and comforting they can be to one another during periods of self-discovery and grieving.

PRACTICAL POINTS

- It is important for adoptive parents and their therapists to understand that there are discrepancies between the child's psychological and chronological age. Parenting interventions should be geared to the former.
- It is helpful if parents can recognize that children can occupy multiple developmental stages simultaneously.
- Adoptive parents who are cognizant of their own ghosts as well as those of their children are better able to understand parent-child interactions contributing to a more positive parent-child relationship.

CONCLUSION

Our experience in the past three decades providing parenting programs through Parenting Services for Families and After Adoption has shown us that all parents can learn parenting techniques and gain understanding of the concepts that enhance relationships. Developmental guidance, parent-child groups, and parent-child therapy can assist parents in observing their child's behavior and communication. As parents learn to respond empathically and appropriately to their children's emotional needs, the children gain a sense of closeness and of feeling understood. In addition, the parent-child relationship grows as the parents develop a verbal and nonverbal emotional dialogue with their children. Even though adoptions vary widely in their details as do child characteristics and situations, the differences among parents in all families have more to do with their own past histories, temperament, how they were parented, the effects of trauma, and other life experiences. Family relationships in adoption are a work in progress, a lifelong journey of building closeness, parents learning when to let go, and children becoming independent while experiencing the emotional security of belonging to their family. We have covered parenting the young child. In this next chapter, parenting in adolescence and throughout the lifetime is examined.

NOTES

1. This term refers to the relational pattern of individuals who had abusive childhoods or early losses that they were unable to mourn (often the case with postinstitutionalized children).
2. Some children who arrive with ADHD or other neurological or sensory problems may be more emotionally labile and difficult to handle, thus eliciting negative responses from parents. These are children who do not make eye contact or sleep well. They push away from affectionate advances or show indiscriminate affection toward strangers and may appear to have an attachment disorder. Treatment of these other issues as well as consideration of attachment issues may be necessary.

Chapter 9

ADOPTIVE PARENTING OF TEENAGERS AND YOUNG ADULTS

Joseph White

Parenting of adolescents and young adults can present challenges for any parent—either adoptive or birth—due to the developmental characteristics of youth at this age. These typical characteristics can interact with the difficult history of some adopted children, resulting in further challenges to the parent-child relationship.

DEVELOPMENTAL THEMES OF ADOLESCENCE AND EARLY ADULTHOOD

The Development of Identity

One particularly salient developmental theme in adolescence and young adulthood is that of *identity development*. The 20th-century psychosocial theorist Erik Erikson (1956), who was integral to modern thinking on adolescent social development, discussed identity formation in the adolescent years as follows:

> Adolescence is the last and the concluding stage of childhood. The adolescent process, however, is conclusively complete only when the individual has subordinated his childhood identifications to a new kind of identification, achieved in absorbing sociability and in competitive apprenticeship with and among his agemates. (p. 66)

Erikson expands on this idea, discussing how identity is both about inner consistency and identification with a group:

> The term identity expresses such a mutual relation in that it connotes both a persistent sameness within oneself (self-sameness) and a persistent sharing of some kind of essential character with others. I can attempt to make the subject matter of identity more explicit only by approaching it from a variety of angles—biographic, pathographic, and theoretical—and by letting the term identity speak for itself in a number of connotations. At one time, then, it will appear to refer to a conscious *sense* of *individual identity*; at another to an unconscious striving for a *continuity of personal character*; at a third, as a criterion for the silent doings of ego *synthesis*; and, finally, as a maintenance of an inner *solidarity* with a group's ideals and identity. (p. 57)

As teens begin in earnest the process of identity formation, they often try out various roles and identities (Pruitt, 1999). Parents might observe that the teen's interests and tastes change rapidly as he or she looks for a good fit. Many interests, such as fashion and music preferences, are influenced in part from the peer group to which the teen is most interested in belonging.

Individuation and Independence

A separate, but related developmental task in the teen and young adult years is *individuation,* defined by Jung (1971), who states, "In general, it is the process by which individual beings are formed and differentiated [from other human beings]; in particular, it is the development of the psychological individual as a being distinct from the general, collective psychology" (par. 757).

As the teen or young adult approaches the time when he or she will live as an adult, there is a natural and necessary desire to be more independent—to make one's own decisions and complete more tasks without assistance. This drive for autonomy helps to prepare the teen to engage in critical thinking about everyday life events and to function more independently in the early adult years. Parents who do too much for their older teens and young adults might face the backlash of rebellion if their children have the ego strength to assert their need for independence. These teens may generalize their efforts to assert themselves such that they engage in impulsive actions or try to act independently in situations in which the parent's assistance or supervision truly is needed.

On the other hand, youth who have anxieties about growing up or who have less confidence in their own ability may avoid independent decision making. In these cases, by doing too much for their older children, parents might be inadvertently saying with their actions, "You needed me to do this for you. You are not capable of being independent." In both cases, parents might foster an unnecessary dependency by failing to give their children room to grow in autonomy.

Some parents may go to the other extreme, reacting to the teen or young adult's push for independence by cutting off support altogether. Here the message is, "Unless you are utterly dependent on me, you are on your own." This creates an unnecessary rift in the parent-child relationship and leaves the teen without support that he or she might still need.

The search for identity and the drive for independence create some natural conflict in most parent-child relationships. Research suggests that the most common arguments between parents and teens center on grades, household chores, money, and peers Allen, Chango, Szwedo, Schad, & Marston, 2012). When teens come from families who are warm and supportive, with rules that are clearly defined and parent-child communication that is open, youth are better able to accept increasing levels of responsibility. Overcritical, restrictive parenting may make it more difficult for adolescents to live independently when the time comes (Pruitt, 1999). When parent-child disagreements are met with active listening on the part of the parents, children are better able to develop the autonomy necessary to assert themselves in the world outside the home (Allen et al., 2012).

A search for identity in the adolescent may activate insecurities a parent has about his or her own identity. This is true for both adopted and nonadopted children. For example, the parent might see in his or her child the potential to revisit unrealized dreams, and in doing so, attempt to live vicariously through the child. It is important for all teens and young adults to have the autonomy to pursue their own goals with healthy support from their parents.

Identity Development and Individuation in Adopted Adolescents and Young Adults

For adopted teens and young adults, the tasks of identity development and individuation can be particularly complex. Studies indicate that being adopted is a significant part of the identity of adopted adolescents and adults, and continues to be so throughout the lifespan (e.g., McGinnis et al., 2009). Many variables affect the degree of impact that being adopted has on development during this period, including when the child was adopted (whether in infancy, early or middle childhood, or in adolescence), the quality of attachment to the adoptive parents, and the child's history prior to placement. For example, a child who was adopted at infancy might feel less identification with his or her birth parents than a child who was adopted at age 9 or 10 and has clear memories of the birth family.

Family Memories and Adoption Stories

Fiese and colleagues (1999) highlight the importance of family narratives in the development of both collective and individual identity. The stories that families tell about their experiences shape the meanings of those experiences and provide insight into the relationships between family members. As family members create together their narratives, children begin, from early in life, to internalize the meanings contained therein, and this assigned meaning can have a powerful effect on the individual's sense of identity into adulthood.

The family narrative in general, and the adoption story in particular, is critical in the development of identity in the adopted child (Brodzinsky, Schechter, & Marantz, 1992), with the emphasis being not only on the facts of the child's history, but on meaning he or she constructs from them. This story is first constructed in the context of the adoptive family, and includes information on how the child came to be adopted and perhaps subtle positive or negative messages about the birth family (Grotevant & Von Korff, 2011). The basic questions of adolescence and young adulthood are potentially answered in part through this story and its meaning for the individual—questions such as "Who am I?" and "What will I become as I grow into adulthood?" The former can be fully answered only by means of a coherent adoption narrative that makes connections to both the adoptive family and the birth family (Hartman & Laird, 1990). Lifton (1994) describes this "search for the adopted self . . . in which one sifts through the pieces of the psyche in an attempt to understand who one was so that one can have some sense of who one is and who one can become. It is the quest for all the missing pieces of the self so that one can become whole" (p. 12). It can be difficult, however, to construct a coherent narrative when information about the birth family is limited due to sealed or incomplete records, posing a serious dilemma for the adopted child (Lifton, 2010; Pivinck, 2010).

Sense of Belonging

A related issue is that of a "sense of belonging." As they begin to try new roles, tastes, experiences, and ideas that are divergent from those of their parents, many adolescents feel like strangers in their own homes. For the adopted child, however, these differences may be assigned additional meaning. Adopted youth and young adults might feel that some of these natural differences between youth and parents come from being from another place and family. As they try on various identities, youth may ask themselves, "Am I more like my adoptive parents, or more like my birth family?" The desire to answer this question can sometimes culminate in a search for the birth family.

Case Study—"Aaron"

Aaron was adopted at age 2 after being born to a mother who was addicted to cocaine. As Aaron got older, he became more and more curious about his birth parents. At 13 years of age, Aaron stated that he felt he "could never really know himself" because he "didn't know where he came from." There were sparse records about his birth mother and her history, but the birth father was not known.

Aaron's therapist encouraged him to discover his gifts and talents and helped him articulate the personality traits that made him unique in his family. She then encouraged Aaron to speculate on where each of those traits came from. For example, Aaron was a talented athlete. His adoptive parents, one an accountant and the other a teacher, had never been very involved in sports. Aaron speculated that perhaps his birth father shared his athletic gifts and had played football when he was in school. In making this connection, Aaron started the process of writing a narrative that included the birth parents he knew so little about.

INDIVIDUATION, INDEPENDENCE, AND THE ADOPTIVE PARENT-CHILD RELATIONSHIP

Because individuation is related to both the ties and the boundaries between persons, it would follow that healthy individuation would depend at least in part on the quality of that individual's attachments. One measure of quality of attachment is the security and stability of the parent-child relationship through adulthood.

Howe (2001) examined the childhood experiences of adult adopted people and their current levels of contact with their adoptive mothers. In cases where people had searched for and found a birth relative, current levels of contact with their birth mother were also measured. Age at placement was used as a proxy measure to examine whether older placed children reported different adoption experiences and what their current levels of contact were with their adoptive and birth mothers. Results indicated that age at placement was correlated with adopted people's reported experiences of being adopted and current rates of contact with their adoptive and birth mothers. Those placed at older ages were most likely to report that they did not feel they belonged in their adoptive families while growing up and did not feel loved by their adoptive mother. These individuals were least likely to remain in high-frequency contact with their adoptive mother and were least likely to remain in high-frequency contact with their birth mother. The author concluded that children adopted at older ages were more likely to have experienced an insecure attachment relationship with their adoptive mother.

Teens who are adopted have more internalizing and externalizing behavior problems than children living with their biological parents, even when one controls for differences between adoption groups (Weinberg, Waldman, van Dulmen, & Scarr,

2004). These adjustment issues take into account differences in school performance and learning disabilities (Brodzinsky, Schecter, Braff, & Singer, 1984; Miller et al., 2000) and delinquency (Miller et al., 2000). Weinberg and colleagues point out that there has historically been disagreement among researchers as to why adolescents who are adopted are perceived as having more adjustment problems and point to Wierzbicki's (1993) meta-analysis of 66 published studies comparing the psychological adjustment of adoptees and nonadoptees. Although the mean effect size across studies was .72, indicating significantly higher levels of maladjustment for adoptees versus nonadoptees, Wiezbicki noted that the effect size might have been skewed by studies reporting the percentage of adoptees in clinical populations, in which adoptees are significantly overrepresented. Weinberg and colleagues further cite studies suggesting that adopted children are overrepresented in clinical treatment settings because adoptive parents are more acquainted with navigating systems of care and assistance, and they point out that with their above average incomes and education, adoptive families have the resources to seek help even for developmentally normal children.

   Much of the data on differential adjustment, including the study by Weinberg and colleagues (2004), relies on parental report of child behavior problems. However, even the perception by adoptive parents that their adopted children have more behavior problems than nonadopted peers may be disruptive to the parent-child relationship, resulting in a less secure base from which to complete the developmental task of individuation. As previously stated, the healthiest process of individuation comes about in families in which attachment is secure and communication is healthy. The following scenario illustrates the potential dangers of an adoptive parent's belief that her child has more behavior problems and that these problems result from being adopted.

Case Study—"Rosa"

Rosa was adopted at age 4 by a couple who had already raised two birth children. Rosa's birth mother initially expressed anxiety that a child Rosa's age "might not be able to bond" with her adoptive mother. In her first few years of elementary school (a time when most children are growing in autonomy), Rosa insisted on doing more things for herself, and often wanted to play alone in her room when the family was at home. Rosa's adoptive mother concluded that Rosa had never really attached to her, and their relationship deteriorated as the adoptive mother alternated between overcontrolling behaviors (e.g., making choices for Rosa that would be appropriate for her to choose, such as what outfit to wear, which play activities to engage in) and withdrawal when power struggles with Rosa became too overwhelming. This escalated into increased mother-daughter conflict in the preteen and early adolescent years.

The Unique Perspective of Adoptive Parents of Adolescents

The meaning assigned by adoptive parents to child behavior problems (even developmentally typical ones) can be critical to the impact of these issues on the parent-child relationship. If, for example, parents assume that a child's natural efforts toward independence result instead from never having been sufficiently bonded with the parents, they might react in more extreme ways that frustrate the child's efforts toward autonomy and provoke further disruption. Empirical data have been sparse and inconsistent regarding insecurities and doubts of adoptive parents, leading some researchers (e.g., Borders, Black, & Pasley, 1998) to question the assumption that adoptive parents have any more anxiety or self-doubt than birth parents. Still, it should be noted that the adolescent years can be a challenging time for any parents, and even the typical parent-child conflict during this period can lead to doubts in one's parenting abilities and anxieties about the child's future. This is particularly true for parents who are experiencing this developmental stage for the first time. Because of the uniqueness of the family narrative for children who are adopted, the challenges of this period will be interpreted by the parents within the context of their larger family history, including the adoption story.

The basic questions around individual identity (Who am I? Where did I come from? What will I be?) also have a different context for adopted children, and this comes with a host of unique challenges for adoptive parents. For example, how should the adoptive parent react when the child wants more information about his or her birth family? Should parents help to facilitate this process? What if they feel their child might be emotionally harmed by the answers they seek? In some cases, adoptive parents might also find it hard not to take personally, at least on a subconscious level, this desire on the part of their child to connect with the birth family. The impact of these variables and the answers to the associated questions will be different for each child and family.

Another unique task for adoptive parents with regard to identity formation is how to assist their child in integrating a complex and diverse history, some of which may be incomplete, in order to answer questions such as "Where do I come from?" and "What experiences have helped to shape who I am?" In addition, how do parents approach these tasks if the history includes abandonment (or perceived abandonment), trauma, and loss?

INSIGHTS FOR PARENTS AND THERAPISTS

Although empirical data on approaching the above challenges is still somewhat limited, theoretical insights, anecdotal information, and key research studies can provide guidance for parents, therapists, and others who work with adopted youth. First, it is critical that adoptive parents understand what is typical adolescent and young adult development. Most agencies and organizations that facilitate adoption provide (and even require) parenting education for adoptive parents. However, if the child is young and parent education is provided only at the beginning of the adoption process, even the education that is provided regarding the adolescent and young adult years will not be well-remembered or integrated when it is needed much later. Additionally, even though the challenges of the adolescent and young adult years may be similar for adoptive and birth parents (especially for children who were adopted early in life), as noted above, some issues regarding identity and autonomy will be unique to the adopted child. For this reason, adoptive parents should be connected with knowledgeable professionals and quality resources for educating themselves about this stage in their family's life cycle and ensuring that they are aware of any potential pitfalls or unique issues that may exist for their child.

Need for Information About Birth Families

Adoptive parents also require support regarding the child's need for information about birth families, beginning with the insight that this desire for information is normal for many adopted children and does not represent a failure on the adoptive parent's part, nor does it signify a desire to disengage from the adoptive family. When parents feel more comfortable about their child's need for information about the birth family, they can serve as effective "identity agents" for their children (Von Korff et al., 2010). The concept of *identity agents* was introduced in Chapter 4, The Adoptive Mother.

Von Korff and colleagues adapt the work of Schachter and Ventura (2008) in their discussion of adoptive mothers as identity agents. Schachter and Ventura use the theoretical notion that the process of identity formation is a collaborative task of children and the identity agents in their lives, rather than being accomplished individually by the child. In other words, adoptive children form their identities in collaboration with significant persons in their lives who are actively working to encourage and influence identity development. Von Korff and colleagues point out that this framework is particularly relevant to discussions of identity development in adopted children "because it focuses analysis on links between adoptive parents' efforts to (a) address connections between the adoptive and birth family, and (b) foster adoptees' identity development" (p. 122). In their study, Von Korff and colleagues test this framework by means of a longitudinal study of four adoptive families and comparison of data gleaned from interviews with adoptive mothers when the children were ages 6, 13, and 23 and measurement of identity formation in children at ages 13 and 23. Their analysis of the data showed that adoptive mothers purposefully employ strategies to influence adoptive identity during their children's childhood and adolescence. They found that adoptive mothers who acted as identity agents for their children created opportunities to talk with their children about adoption. The individual theories these mothers had about adoptive identity formation had an impact on the way in which they employed these strategies.

Research suggests that when the child's desire for information about the birth family is supported, the result is generally positive for both adoptive parents and their adopted children. In a study by Grotevant et al. (2008), adoptive parents and their teens were interviewed about their postadoption contact arrangements. The sample included families with no contact, stopped contact, contact without meetings, and contact with face-to-face meetings between the adopted child and birth mother. Researchers examined the relationship between different openness arrangements and the experiences and feelings of adopted children and adoptive mothers. Adoptive families that had contact with birth mothers reported higher levels of satisfaction about their openness arrangements, more positive feelings about the birth mother, and more factual and personal knowledge about the birth mother than did families without contact. The highest levels of satisfaction were seen in adolescents and adoptive mothers who had contact and meetings with birth mothers; those with no contact and those who had stopped contact reported the least satisfaction with their arrangements. Participants having no contact were more likely to want increased contact in the future. A large portion of those who already had contact said they would like that contact to increase, less than 1% of all participants wanted to see the level of contact with birth mothers decrease.

Navigating the Search

When a child who has not previously been in contact with a birth family wishes to search for them, there are several important considerations. They include:

- Is the adopted child's search for information truly motivated by a search for identity, or is it a form of rebellion against the adoptive family? If there is current conflict with the adoptive family, it may be advisable to spend some time resolving this conflict first.
- Has the adopted child idealized the birth family? Is he or she prepared for the possibility that some of the information uncovered might be negative or uncomfortable? If not, it may be advisable to spend some time in therapy preparing for various outcomes, including the possibility that there will be some things the child does not like about his or her birth family.
- Based on what is known about the birth family and the current functioning of the adopted child, is it physically and emotionally safe for the child to pursue information about them and/or make contact? It might not be advisable to pursue further information or contact if the adopted child is currently emotionally fragile or if the birth family situation is volatile. In addition, an ongoing assessment should be made regarding the psychological impact of information and/or contact. If the adopted child begins to appear emotionally overwhelmed, it might be time to take a break from this pursuit.

Grotevant et al. (2008) conclude that when adoptive parents agree to have contact with their child's birth family, "they need to move from thinking of themselves as a nuclear family that has added a child to an adoptive kinship network in which their child permanently connects families of birth and rearing" (p. 100).

Open Access to Birth and Adoption Records

Freundlich (2007) analyzed adoption records law in light of current research on the outcomes of access to information on birth families. Her principal findings include:

- Civil rights concerns are raised by the fact that the only individuals in the United States not routinely given access to their original birth certificates are adopted persons.
- Lack of access to birth and adoption records can cause serious physical and mental health problems for adopted persons due to missing medical information.
- In the states that have passed laws to allow more access to records, the dire consequences predicted by those opposed to more open access have not materialized.
- The claim that birth mothers do not want their children to have information about their birth and adoptions is unfounded.
- The claim that abortion rates will rise as a result of more open access to adoption records is also unsupported by the research. In fact, in states that have passed laws for more open access, there is evidence that abortion rates have declined and adoption rates have increased as a result.
- Adopted children are interested in information about their birth and adoption histories because they are seeking knowledge of their histories, not necessarily because they wish to search for their birth families. And in situations in which

they do seek their birth families, this is not a rejection of their adoptive families but rather another path to learning more about themselves and their histories.

- It can benefit birth mothers as well to know what happened to children placed for adoption, as there is evidence to suggest that this information helps assuage grief that birth mothers may face as a result of their decision to place their children for adoption.
- Contrary to arguments made by open records opponents, most state relinquishment documents do not guarantee birth mothers anonymity from the children they placed for adoption, and in the few situations where they do, the language may not be legally binding.

In light of these findings, Freundlich recommends that state laws be changed to offer unrestricted access for adult adopted persons to their original birth certificates, and that in states where this has already occurred, to build on this by offering further access to information in adoption agency and court records. She further recommends that continued research be conducted on the impact of access to records on adopted persons, birth families, and adoptive parents and that educational programs be developed to help dispel myths surrounding access to records.

IDENTITY FORMATION IN INTERNATIONAL, TRANSCULTURAL, AND TRANSRACIAL ADOPTEES

In their groundbreaking study on transracial, transcultural, and international adoption, McGinnis et al. (2009) found that race and ethnicity were significant factors in the identity of transracial and transcultural adoptees and that the importance of these variables in identity development increases in adolescence and adulthood. Most transracial adoptees either considered themselves white or wanted to be white as children, but as adults were able to successfully integrate an acceptance of their race and/or ethnicity. The authors cite "lived experiences" such as travel to their native countries, attending racially diverse schools, and role models of the child's own race/ethnicity as factors that facilitated healthy racial/ethnic identity development in the sample studied. Even so, contact with birth relatives was rated most important by adoptees in promoting healthy identity development.

McGinnis et al. (2009) recommend: expanding preparation and postplacement support for parents who adopt across race and culture; developing empirically based practices and resources to prepare children in transracial and transcultural adoptions to cope with racial bias; and increasing research on risk and protective factors related to adopted children in general, and those adopted transracially or transculturally in particular.

The Adoption Narrative

As previously mentioned, the adoption narrative itself is critical to the identity development of many adopted teens and young adults. For this reason, it is important that adoptive parents and therapists who work with adoptees assist the adopted child in constructing a coherent narrative that assists the young person in feeling confident about his or her identity and future. This can be a challenge for children with very difficult histories or in cases where little information is available. For example, Zoppi (2010) points out that most adoption stories do not include information about birth fathers. She argues that, even in the absence of information about the birth father, adoptive parents and therapists can assist adoptees in creating stories that include information about him by encouraging the child to integrate his or her own fantasies about the birth father. This process may begin with imagining what the birth father might be like as a father and as a man and integrating images of the birth father with images of other men. Doing this, Zoppi argues, will help the child develop more secure attachment and identity, develop stronger attachments to adoptive parents, maintain better connections to the past, and construct a more coherent life narrative. She recommends that adoptive parents and professionals create a safe environment for talking about birth father fantasies and initiate the discussion through open-ended questions, gradually helping adoptees integrate their birth father fantasies into a more coherent image of self and other.

Effective Teatment of Trauma in the Lives of Adopted Children

A large proportion of children adopted in the United States are adopted from the child welfare system, meaning that presumably a high number of these children have had traumatic early experiences. Serious pathological reactions to abuse, such as reactive attachment disorder (RAD), are quite rare, and fears about RAD are perhaps exaggerated among the general public, including potential adoptive parents. However, even in cases in which early abuse and neglect does not cause RAD, attachment is an important issue. Trust is essential to healthy attachment, and in cases of neglect and abuse, the child's trust has been violated by a primary caregiver. In addition, Busch (2005) points out that even in the ideal circumstances, it takes an infant some time (up to a year or two) to securely attach to a primary caregiver. We should expect no less from an older child (and in many cases, more time and work are required).

As understanding grows about the impact of trauma on development, we are also better appreciating the need to address traumatic experiences at multiple points in the lifespan. One example would be in the case of children who are survivors of sexual abuse. There is an immediate need for treatment once the abuse is discovered and the child is placed in a safe environment. However, even if symptoms of trauma are successfully addressed in childhood, there may be a need to revisit these issues as the child goes through puberty and begins to come to terms with himself or herself as a sexual being. Likewise, survivors of sexual abuse might benefit from further therapeutic work when they become sexually active, and when they have children of their own, as each of these important milestones also adds a potential new perspective to their own memories of abuse. Similar connections could be made for survivors of physical abuse or neglect.

For all of these reasons, it is essential that both adoptive parents and therapists who work with adopted children be educated regarding the impact of trauma and well-versed in trauma-informed treatment approaches. In 2010, the American Psychological Association launched the Effective Providers for Child Victims of Violence Program to help inform clinicians and other professionals who work with child survivors of abuse, neglect, and violent crime about evidence-based treatments for victimized children (de Arellano et al., 2011). The advisory group for this initiative recommends that therapists working with child victims of trauma be trained in the following trauma-focused interventions: Trauma-Focused

Cognitive-Behavioral Therapy (TF-CBT), Child-Parent Psychotherapy (CPP), Alternatives for Families: A Cognitive-Behavioral Therapy (AF-CBT), and Cognitive Behavioral Interventions for Trauma in Schools (CBITS). They also recommend Parent-Child Interaction Therapy (PCIT). While not specifically a trauma-focused approach, PCIT can be an effective tool for changing negative parent-child interactions that may persist after a child has been abused or neglected.

Effective treatment of trauma in the lives of children can help children construct a narrative that integrates the trauma history in ways that frame the child as a survivor, rather than a victim, and can address cognitive distortion regarding the self that could otherwise impair the development of healthy identity. This is especially true of cognitive-behavioral approaches, which have at their core the child's thoughts, attitudes, and interpretations of the trauma.

Supporting Adolescents' Natural Desire for Autonomy

Adoptive parents and professionals who are well-versed in adolescent development will recognize the need for greater autonomy in the lives of teens. Therapists can help to support adoptive parents in realizing that this need for autonomy is natural in most children and does not signify a rejection of the adoptive parents. As young people request more independence and freedoms, giving them a way to earn this freedom by showing responsibility can teach important lessons and skills that will benefit them throughout life. As teens gradually show they are more capable of accepting responsibility, parents may wish to take carefully considered "calculated risks" that allow teens some measure of freedom while still preserving the necessary safety and supervision that adolescents need. This sometimes occurs in deliberate negotiation between parent and adolescent in which the child wants a particular freedom that the parent is not comfortable giving without condition, and then caveats are articulated that provide the parent reassurance that their child will be safe, but allow the teen some measure of the freedom he or she is requesting (Allen et al., 2012). For example, the teen might request to stay out past his or her curfew. The parent might say that this is acceptable provided that the teen call every hour and check in.

Creating a Sense of Belonging and Purpose

Adoptive parents and professionals can assist adopted children, youth, and young adults in creating a sense of purpose and belonging by watching for and encouraging the child's gifts and talents. Careful attention should be paid to noting the particular talents in which the child is most interested in investing.

Beginning in the middle school years, discussing goals and dreams for the future and steps toward those goals can be helpful. This strategy has also been identified as an effective way to help youth avoid risky behaviors such as drug and alcohol use and early sexual behavior (see Jemmott, Jemmott, & Fong, 2010).

It should be noted that it is extremely important, especially in the older teenage and young adult years, that parents make it clear they accept the child for who he or she is, rather than making acceptance conditional on the child's fulfilling the parents' own dreams for him or her. All parents (including parents of children who are not adopted) have hopes and dreams for their children, some of which never come to fruition. An important factor in maintaining a healthy parent-child relationship into the son's or daughter's adulthood is the parents' ability to let go of unrealized dreams for their children. Healthy individuation and identity development requires that adult sons or daughters pursue their own life's goals.

PRACTICAL POINTS

- The adoptive parent's understanding of typical adolescent development is critical. Therapists can assist parents by providing information about typical development and, where appropriate, framing anecdotes from the parents within this context.
- Therapists and adoptive parents play key roles in supporting the child's need for a healthy identity and a coherent adoption narrative, which includes information about birth families.
- Adopted children who experienced traumatic abuse or neglect prior to placement need therapeutic support that addresses this issue in the form of trauma-informed treatment approaches. Therapists and adoptive parents should be prepared for the possibility that trauma-related issues will need to be revisited at various points in the course of development.

CONCLUSIONS

Parenting adolescents and young adults, whether adopted or nonadopted, presents inherent challenges associated with the major tasks of this developmental period, including the development of identity and the drive for independence and autonomy. The difficult (or missing) history of some adopted children can result in further challenges to the parent-child relationship. Both the facts of the adoption history and their perceived meaning play a critical role in the development of identity in the adopted child. Healthy individuation can be affected by both the quality of attachment and the degree to which birth families normalize or pathologize behaviors associated with the drive for autonomy and independence.

Chapter 10

THERAPEUTIC INTERVENTIONS WITH ADOPTED CHILDREN AND ADOPTIVE PARENTS
A Psychoanalytic Developmental Approach

Theodore Fallon Jr.

INTRODUCTION

The previous two chapters examined the tasks that adoptive parents face in raising an adopted child—in the early years (Chapter 8) and in adolescence (Chapter 9). The focus of those chapters is on the dance between parent and child. The interventions offered involve attention to the dance. These chapters consider normative trends and offer wonderful interventions when the developing adopted child falls outside of those norms. These interventions usually work well, resulting in improvement in the situation. What happens when these interventions are not enough? This present chapter offers one approach to that problem.

In this chapter, I offer a *psychoanalytic developmental approach*. In the tradition of psychoanalysis, the approach focuses on what is happening inside the individual. By *psychoanalytic*, I am not subscribing to any particular set of procedures, any particular structure of the mind,[1] or even to a frequency or length of treatment, although to do work from this perspective does require getting to know the child and the parent intimately. I only mean to point to a deep psychology that focuses on the interior of the mind.

DEVELOPMENT OF THE HUMAN MIND

The approach I propose is developmental because it considers a fine-grained under-standing of the dynamic interplay of forces at work in the process of the maturing individual (Fonagy & Target, 2002; Lane & Garfield, 2005). This developmental process occurs inside the child. Just as the physical body of the child develops from an infant with particular capabilities, and matures to an adult functioning body, so the infant mind, beginning from its limited capacities, develops into a psychologically independently functioning adult.

A *separate, autonomous* developmental process also takes place inside the parent (Blum, 1983). Consider the young adult, more or less accomplished in the tasks of taking care of him- or herself, must become an individual who now cares for another. With each new phase of the maturing child, parents face new challenges within themselves, finding and cultivating the emotional resources to nurture their child as well as themselves. These new accomplishments of becoming a parent are no less of a transformation than the transition that occurs in adolescence, although much less has been written about them. Maturation to parenthood is separate from the child's development, although the hurdles faced by the parent are linked to what the child presents to the parent. Whatever the challenges presented to the parent by the child, however, the parent must make choices and complete tasks of their own; in a reciprocal manner, the parents' maturation to parenthood has strong influences on the child's development—hence my use of the words *separate* and *autonomous* (Desmarais, 2006; Hushion, Sherman, & Siskind, 2006; Landerholm, 2001).

THERAPEUTIC INTERVENTION IN A PSYCHOANALYTIC DEVELOPMENTAL APPROACH

The underlying assumption in the psychoanalytic developmental approach is that the individual is capable of determining his or her own course in development. Not infrequently in development, however, problems arise, leading to distress and emotional and/or behavioral symptoms. From this perspective, then, behavioral and emotional symptoms are manifestations of underlying developmental problems. This approach's goal is for the individual to understand, at both a cognitive and an emotional level, what is interfering with progressive development. Once understood by the individual, then that person can decide for him- or herself how and in what ways he or she wants to move forward. It is in this manner that presenting problems resolve.

The psychoanalytic developmental approach is not prescriptive; rather, it is a collaborative process in which the practitioner brings a fine-grained understanding of development while the individual(s), in this case the adoptive parent and the adopted child, bring their experience of themselves. Together, the analyst and the individual(s) survey the landscape of the individuals' perception(s) and inner world(s). If the collaboration works well, the individual(s) comes to recognize new perspectives and reorganize their understanding of the world. The individual(s) are then capable of seeing their way forward in development and can make decisions accordingly. Progressive development then resumes. In this way, the practitioner can be respectful of the individual's autonomous development.

Notice in the above two paragraphs, I have attached an ambiguous (s) to the word *individual*. In psychoanalytic work with children, it is essential to include the parent in the process. At the same time, I want to reiterate that this work is with the interior of the mind. In work with children, it is a given that although the interior of the child's mind and the parent's mind are separate, they are inexorably linked. In my discussion up to now this connection is an important missing link. I will say more about this missing link below.

PARENT PROBLEMS AND CHILD PROBLEMS IN THE CONTEXT OF A PSYCHOANALYTIC DEVELOPMENTAL APPROACH

From this psychoanalytic developmental perspective, a review of the literature reveals that those difficulties that occur in the adoptive situation are the same developmental forces occurring as in the nonadoption situation (e.g., Barnes, Katan, & Spitz, 1953; Tubero, 2002; Vorus, 2004). Although it is true that the adoption situation puts particular additional burdens on the child, the parent, the relationship between parent and child, and on the environment around the parent and child, both inside and outside the family, the underlying problems in maturing are the same as seen in other cases. Although the incidence of problems in the adoption situation in some contexts is higher than in the nonadoption situation, the vast majority of adoptive parents and adopted children manage. I make this statement here, however, for a different reason than the implied ones made in other chapters.

Consider the growing of a tree as you might consider the growing of a child. There is a constant pressure for the tree to grow, to become what it has the potential to become, be that a small beautiful dogwood or a tall pine. Depending on what conditions the tree thrives in best and the nutrients available and nurturing provided, the growing tree will be stronger or weaker, taller or shorter. There may also be damage along the way in the form of strains such as rocky soil or shading from other trees, or traumas as in lightning strike or branches lost in a storm. The tree will make efforts to adapt to the strain such as growing deeper roots, producing a higher chlorophyll concentration in the leaves to adapt to the low light conditions, or grow around the damage and make structural repairs. If the tree is growing in a windy area, say a coastal region or in a drier climate, the tree will attempt to grow in a manner that is optimal to the weather of the environment, producing shorter branches, deeper roots, and so on, growing into the environment. Notice in this description there is no reference to pathology. There is also an implication that no matter how the tree is growing, one can always think of new and creative ways to optimize the resources and the environment so that the tree grows stronger, taller, straighter, more full, more flowers, more fruits.

So it is with a child. There is a constant pressure from within the child to grow. Each child has constitutional potentials. These potentials do change, depending on what has come before, but they also have limitations in their mutability. As part of that potential, each child has particular strengths and weaknesses in the ways it perceives the world and takes in nurturing. For the child to realize his or her growth potential, the levels of challenge and nurturance must be optimal. With levels of challenge too low and levels of nurturing too high, the child reacts complacently and growth can be slowed. With levels of challenge too high and levels of nurturing too low, the child feels deprived and becomes frustrated, overwhelmed, and disorganized. Optimal levels of nurturing and challenge are different for each child, different for the same child at different points in development, and even different from day to day, depending on sleep, nutrition, challenges faced, and so on (Parens, 2010).

Just as with our tree analogy, for any adopted child and adoptive parent, strains and traumas occur along the way, some particular to the adoption situation. With these strains and traumas, efforts at adaptation and repair—all aimed to help the child grow into the environment—are mustered. In the adoption situation, what is experienced as strain and trauma depends on the internal makeup of the individuals involved. These are the burdens of adoption. In the developing adopted child and in the adoptive parent, these burdens become challenges. When the challenges are met at each developmental stage, new meaning is made, the personality reorganizes, and we say the individual has matured.

In my work with children, I do not think of pathology, but rather of the ways through which growth is promoted and/or interfered. In most situations there are aspects of both. In terms of the nurturing and providing of resources, always present are opportunities to improve to create the optimal growth environment for any particular child and to assist the parents in their own growth into parenthood. An understanding of the developmental process is vital to assisting in the creation of a optimal environment for growth and easing the developmental discomfort that is inevitable along the way for both parent and child.

The Missing Link—Between Parent and Child

So far in this chapter, I have introduced an approach to parents and children that focuses on the interior of the mind and those processes that spur its development. In that context, there is a body of knowledge about the development of the mind/ personality across the lifespan. We know a great deal about the psychological capacities of a new born infant (Basch, 1988; Emde, 1983a/1983b) and are even discovering its capacities as a fetus in the womb (Sherkow, 2004); these capacities are complex and yet rudimentary, just as the physical body of a newborn is highly capable physiologically, but lacks locomotion and ability to manipulate the world. Just as with the physical body, the human mind begins its maturation through life in infancy with complex yet rudimentary capacities. With the assistance of a parent, this maturing mind goes through a series of developments that, if all is successful, will result in an autonomous well-functioning adult. This adult will then complete the cycle by passing its mind onto the next generation.

I have also introduced the concept of parental development. Parenthood is an important stage in human development: It is the child's way of producing another child. If we understand that development in parenthood is a separate process, although certainly connected with the development of the child, then we can conceptualize that difficulty in one arena (either the child or the parent) does not necessitate difficulty in the other (the parent or the child).

This bidirectional focus is particularly important if we consider special-needs children. If it is the child's constitutional disposition that is creating difficulty, the focus of intervention needs to be on how to support the child's development and get the child back on track. This can be done by fortifying the parent's already present capacities and possibly by providing services directly to the child. Similarly, there may be a difficulty in the parent's development.

Thus, we have an autonomously developing child and an autonomously developing adult. The questions come to mind: Where and how do these two autonomously developing orbs meet? What is the link between the parent and child?

INTERGENERATIONAL TRANSMISSION OF THE HUMAN MIND—THE MISSING LINK

The concept that is missing in my description so far is the normative process of *intergenerational transmission* (Blos, 1985; Shabad, 1993; Silverman & Lieberman, 1999). I refer here to the process by which the human mind is passed from one generation onto the next. This key concept is essential in guiding assessment, particularly when unmet developmental challenges are present and particularly when irregularities exist in the context of the developing child and the developing parent, such as the situation of adoption. The intergenerational transmission of the mind/personality connects the developmental process of the parent with the developmental process of the child. Nonetheless, it is an underlying principle that is essential in guiding therapeutic interventions with parents, families, and children and has significant and far-reaching implications in thinking about adoption.

Many clinicians who work with families and children at a deep psychological level see this process demonstrated repeatedly. However, the way it penetrates the very fabric of human existence is not always fully appreciated. In this regard, I mention two bodies of work that point to these far-reaching implications, one by George Engel and the second by Greenspan and Shankar.

George Engel and colleagues (Engel, Reichsman, Harway, & Hess, 1985; Engel, Reichsman, & Viderman, 1979) followed for 47 years the development of an infant who was born with a tracheal esophageal fistula. The condition of this infant necessitated the placement of a gastric feeding tube at birth. Because the mother of this infant was not psychologically prepared to handle a child with a gastric feeding tube, and because of her own emotional response, this infant was handled in a very particular and emotionally insensitive way during feeding. Prior to Monica's verbal development, the fistula was repaired and the gastric tube removed. Thereafter, Monica went on to have a normal development with good enough parents.

What occurred next was quite remarkable. Although the abnormality in her early development occurred preverbally, and although Monica herself had no conscious memory of the abnormal handling that she received, she persisted in handling first her dolls and then, as a mother, her own infants just as she had been handled preverbally during her gastric tube feeding by her mother. Even as Monica's husband provided Monica's children with normal empathic handling during feeding, Monica tried to correct her own children's handling of their dolls to repeat the particular way she, Monica, had been handled as a preverbal infant.

The important message here is that parents will handle their children the way they were handled in childhood: A code is passed on from one generation to the next. Although the case of Monica calls attention to one tiny aspect of that process, this intergenerational transmission involves the entire re-creation of the mind and has been going on for eons. In fact, Greenspan and Shankar (2004) link this intergenerational transmission of the human personality even to nonhuman primate parenting. Their work has convincingly demonstrated that this intergenerational transmission process reproduces the human mind generation after generation and is as conservative and at the same time evolving as reliably as chromosomes, genes, and molecular genetics itself.

EVALUATING THE PARENT-CHILD DYAD

What does this mean for our present discussion of adoptive parents and adopted children? When considering irregularities in the context in which the developing mind of the child is forming, such as with adoption, it is crucial to recognize that parents will be using and attempting to pass on to the next generation the code that will perpetuate the human mind. This code is given by parents to their children who then as parents pass it on to their children. This process continues unless there is a conscious and concerted effort by a parent to behave differently, and even that is difficult. Hence, the code that parents of adopted children are using is the one that they were given as children. For certain aspects of the parenting process, however, the code may not apply, for example in the circumstance of adoption in which the adopted child faces different circumstances than the parent's own childhood.

In the normative nonadoption process, the code is not flawless, just as the human genome is not flawlessly transmitted from one generation to the next. In fact, we know that even the best parents can be assisted to do even better if we bring to their awareness these two concepts of the developing mind and intergenerational transmission. In addition, it is not just the code that determines the parent's ability to carry out what they need to do as parents. It is also the parent's internal resources that determine their ability to do what heavy lifting there is to be done. Many parents' own mind conditioning (or lack thereof) and their own constitutional capacities and limitations determine whether or not they can carry through with the code that they were given.

For example, many parents will frequently recognize that their own anger or anxiety interfere with their parenting ability, but will still not be able to act differently. Many times, the parent's capacities will interfere with even the recognition of a problem until it affects some major portion of his or her life or the lives of their children. So when difficulties arise within a parent-child dyad, it is for the practitioner to determine:

- Whether it is a problem with the child's constitutional predisposition (such as with a special-needs child) or whether it is a difficulty with the parenting.
- If it is a problem with parenting, is it with the code that was given to the parent by their own parents or is it the parents' capacity to carry out that code?
- If it is a problem with the parent's code, is that because that code, constructed for a biological parenting situation (reflecting the parent's own background), does not encompass the situations that arise in adoption?

Most clinical situations involve some combination of these problems. The practitioner's knowledge and experience will assist in sorting out these elements. Once assessed, the possible admixture of therapeutic interventions becomes obvious to the experienced practitioner. Just to review, these interventions include (from least intensive to most intensive) parent education, parent guidance, work with the system including dyadic, triadic, quadratic, and "poly-atic" (family therapy is one of many examples here), intensive individual work with the child, and finally intensive individual work with the child and the parent separately. You note that I did not list intensive individual work with the parent alone. Such treatment usually does not bring relief to the problem in time to assist in the child's development—the parent may be helped, but not before the child has grown and left the family.

At this point in our discussion, it should be acknowledged that problems might arise in the adoption situation having little to do with adoption. In other words, adoptive parents and adopted children are vulnerable to the same problems as any other parent and child. In the next section, however, I focus on problems particular to the adoptive parent and adopted child.

Adoption: Irregularities in the Context of Development

In the context of development, what is special about the adoption situation? When compared with the nonadoption situation, the adoption situation presents at least four irregularities.

1. For the child, adoption means loss. These losses come in various forms. Even if the child is adopted at birth, there is a loss that comes in the form of the lost life that the child would have had with his or her birth parents (Fallon & Brabender, 2012). This loss includes loss of an actual relationship/attachment with a biological parent that developed if the child had spent any time with a biological parent, including moments at birth and delivery when significant bonding has been shown to occur.

With each loss, these children lose momentum in their development; with each loss of attachment, the children lose potential. These potentials include cognitive ability, ability to attach, flexibility and resilience, and faculties that are used to address life, including organizational capacities, identifications, and capacities for autonomy. Each of these losses has left an indelible mark on the child's development (i.e., you cannot change the child's history), and each of these losses must be worked through again and again at each developmental stage.

2. For the parent, adoption means parenting a child who is genetically dissimilar, and the parents may not be prepared to address the genetic peculiarities. As an example of this, Steve Soumi's research (Suomi et al., 1981) with anxiety in rhesus monkeys has examined what happens when you take a combination of mothers and babies who are genetically dissimilar. Soumi examined mothers genetically prone to anxiety. When these mothers were raised by their well-adjusted biological parents, they were every bit as capable of raising their own offspring who were also genetically prone to anxiety. However, when their biological mothers did not raise these mothers, the latter did poorly with their anxiety-prone infants. The tentative conclusion here is that genetic and behavioral evolution have likely evolved together and when biology is split from parenting, there may be challenges.

Practically speaking, we do not have the ability to look at an individual's genetic predisposition for various behavioral components. And we do not want to overestimate the importance of genetics (for example, language is nearly 100% transmitted from parent to child, but is almost 0% genetic). In this regard, we can take a lesson from schizophrenia, considered one of the most genetically determined psychiatric disorders. Through twin studies, we understand that the genetic contribution to the disease is somewhere between 25% and 50%, while the environmental contribution is somewhere between 50% and 75%. Nonetheless, we can use Soumi's work to understand that these challenges may be contributing to problems that present in adoption situations.

3. Children who are adopted sometime after birth will have made their way along the path toward self-identification and identity formation. With the event of adoption, there will be the challenge for the child of what to do with these aspects of their own personality that they have already developed. Consider the tension of second-generation immigrants stuck between their parents' old country traditions and those they face in their new country. For the adopted child, this tension between the old and the new is much more intense because it all occurs within the child's singular developing personality.

4. The adoption situation involves at least three parties rather than two. At minimum, there is the birth parent(s), the adopted parent(s), and the child. All of the parties must deal with this aberration in their own development. As we are not talking about the birth parents' development, we will not mention their development challenge further. However, for both the adopted child and the adoptive parents, places must be found in their identities for all three parties. That is, the adopted child and adoptive parent's narrative histories (the answer to the questions: Who am I? Where do I come from? What am I doing with this life?) must include a coherent explanation of the role played by the birth parents, the adoptive parents, and the adopted child. In other words, the adopted children (on their own and together with the adoptive parent) must come to understand their place in the world in which there are two sets of parents (regardless of their degree of contact with the birth parents). Similarly for the adoptive parents, their development must accommodate the reality that the child has an origin that is not of themselves.

Adoption: Challenges to the Developing Child

Let us consider some examples of problems that present themselves in the adoption situation, how to understand these problems, and consider how to address them therapeutically. As we have identified earlier, psychological development of the child and the parent is a key part of that understanding. So, let's begin our examples early in the child's life and in parenthood and move chronologically through development. We begin by taking as examples the stages identified by René Spitz (1965) and named for what he called the *organizers* of these stages.

Example 1—The Social Smile

The first organizer that appears in the child at approximately 4 months of age is the social smile, when the child perceives a human face and smiles in response (Polak, Emde, & Spitz, 1964). When this does not happen, other than the obvious deficit of blindness, we can imagine two possibilities for its cause: either the child is suffering an anaclitic depression (Spitz, 1946) or the child has constitutional challenges such as autism. With either of these possibilities, there may be other associated signs and symptoms, including feeding, sleeping, and other regulatory difficulties, failure to thrive, fussiness, and irritability.

The parent developmental counterpart to the child's development at this stage is the emotional task of taking an intense interest in the child. Daniel Stern (1985) referred to this intense interest as *primary maternal preoccupation*. The parent must attend to the child physically or the child will die, or at least fail to thrive. In addition to this physical caring, the infant requires sustained emotional attention as well (Spitz & Wolf, 1946). This kind of sustained intense emotional attention from the parent, although it may have been practiced with other infants for short periods of time, is demanded for the first time in most new parents' development.

Normatively, there is a positive feedback loop between parent and infant. The infant smiles, the parent smiles back, the infant responds with a smile, and the parent reciprocates with a bigger smile. This is usually accompanied with verbal cooing from both parent and child. At a certain point, the infant will begin to get overstimulated and the parent will back off in response. This is the dance between the parent and infant (Stern, 1985). Even under normative circumstances, the dance does not always go well. Either the infant or the parent may not respond. Or the infant is overstimulated or the parent is overstimulating. When such lapses in responsiveness happen repeatedly, however, a breakdown can ensue. The presenting symptom may be a depressed mother, a failure-to-thrive infant, or both. At such a juncture, a psychoanalytic investigation into development is worth the time and effort. Because the process between infant and parent is reciprocal, either the parent or the child may exhibit the presenting symptom. The possible primary cause(s) of the breakdown might be in the infant (anaclitic depression or constitutional) or in the parent and may or may not be manifested by the member of the dyad who presents the problem or symptom.

In the adoption situation, the child has experienced a loss that puts the child at increased risk of an anaclitic depression. Also, infants with constitutional problems such as autism who do not respond to their birth parents are at increased risk of being rejected and abandoned by their parent. On the adoptive parent side, the potential problems are many, including a reduced self-esteem, mourning the loss of the possibility of a biological child, or an identity crisis in coming to terms with seeing oneself as a person who is infertile.

These challenges may be on the surface of the adoptive parent's mind or they may be unconscious. For example, many women are not aware of their identification with their own mothers, but this identification is key in being able to take on motherhood. One question for each woman is how important the component of fertility is in the identification with her mother. If fertility is important, then a significant reorganization of that identification must occur to permit a woman to take on the role of motherhood. If that does not occur, then it will be difficult for the mother to emotionally invest in her new child.

On the other hand, a parent will become depressed, withdrawn, and usually unconsciously rageful if the child does not respond to her social bids. This rage occurs in the face of the normative hardship for the parent in taking on the mammoth task of caring for an infant. But in this case, the source of the depressed parent is in the child, not the parent. The parent is responding normatively to a nonresponsive child.

Example 2—Stranger Anxiety/Separation Anxiety

At age 7 months, in normative development, the child is able to differentiate between strangers and those who are familiar (Spitz, 1965; Tennes & Lampl, 1964). With exposure to a stranger, the child will reference those familiar to the child, gauge their response, and respond synchronously. Without a familiar face around, regardless of whether a stranger is present, children will respond with separation anxiety. Under normative circumstances, much can go awry.

In the adoption situation, significant additional challenges exist. During this developmental period, children can become excessively clingy, demanding, and irritable. Even when parents respond normatively, the child's resistance to accepting the support may challenge the parent's sense that this child belongs to them. The parent's ability to reassure and soothe the child may be compromised for parental reasons that are minor and would not affect a normative situation, but because of the child's sensitivity, a parent-child bond is significantly stressed.

Adoptive parents face additional challenges with a child at this stage. The necessity of adoption frequently leads the adoptive parents to struggle with feelings of failure at not being able to produce their own child. This may put adoptive parents at risk for feeling inadequate, overly confronted by the child, or crowded by the child's excessive clingy behavior. Any residual issues of separation anxiety in parents will be reignited as the child moves into this developmental stage. If there are fears in the adoptive parents regarding the child's safety or of being able to protect the child from the harsh world or their own anger or anxiety in response to the child, they will exacerbate the child's anxiety and interfere with the child's development.

Example 3—The Everlasting No

Normatively, between 18 and 24 months, most children begin to experience separateness from their own parents. As a first step in developing and exercising their autonomy, children use a primitive way of drawing a line between them and others— whatever you say, I am not that. This translates to the word no. In this context, it becomes understandable that sometimes you can ask children at this developmental level if they want a cookie and the answer will be no, followed by taking the cookie. Just like the first physical steps a child takes in walking, there is much faltering in the beginning. If this developmental process is not understood, it is easy to see how parents might misinterpret the child's use of no as disrespect or a challenge to the parent's authority, or as the child rejecting the parent, rather than a bid for independence.

Over and above the normative challenges of parenting a 2-year-old, adoptive parents may be particularly anxious about their role as parents to the adopted child and particularly sensitive to rejection, feeling disrespected, or having their authority challenged, especially if the parent is struggling with seeing him or herself as a good parent. For the adopted child, frustration with this autonomy by the parent (that is, the parent saying, "It is not okay to say no to me as parent") will usually be understood as the parent's rejection of the child. The adopted child already has experience with rejection in the form of loss of the birth parent, which can awaken painful memories. These memories might, in turn, elicit feelings of hopelessness, hostility, rage, and reduced self-esteem, leading the child to either withdraw or respond aggressively toward himself, the parent, or another such as a sibling or daycare worker.

The developmental challenge for the parent is to figure out how to support the child's growing autonomy while at the same time set appropriate limits. If the child responds in a hypersensitive way to the adoptive parent's limit-setting, in order to help the child move along in his or her development, the parent will need to tolerate the child's hate and at the same time create a loving, supportive, and yet firm environment. Many times the child's response may provoke the adoptive parents into feeling rejected and challenged, and thereby lead them to respond more aggressively toward the child, exacerbating the situation further.

Another problem that can occur in the adoptive child's struggle for autonomy is that the child may begin to notice differences between themselves and the parents. This burgeoning awareness may lead the child to call attention to these differences. For the adopted parent anxious about rejection, again, this may be taken as a further affront to the parent role. Anxious parents may respond with aggression or withdrawal or both. Aggression can be subtle and even out of the parent's conscious awareness. For example, it may be in the form of the parent telling the child more than he or she can handle regarding the adoption, or telling the child nothing at all. In the optimal situation, the parent is able to accept the child's bid for independence and work with the child to explore the separation, differences, and his or her origins. It is particularly important to recognize what the child is capable of understanding at this age and what may be overwhelming regarding information about the adoption. It is in this stage that the child can begin to create a world and a sense of self that includes the birth parent in a realistic way, whatever that is.

Example 4—Theory of Mind/Mentalization/The Oedipal Period

Between the ages of 3 and 7 years, normative development brings the child to the capacity to imagine his or her own mind and the mind of another (Fonagy et al., 2002; Fonagy & Target, 2002). When this challenge is met, this capacity allows the child important psychological independence from parents and others. With this function in place, the child can hold a realistic view of a parent in mind even in the parent's absence (Mahler et al., 1975), can imagine a relationship between two other people,[2] is now for the first time capable of deception, and can consider his own thoughts and feelings (Mayes & Cohen, 1996). With this independence, the child normatively is capable of being on his own for short periods of time, for instance, to school. This development is the culmination and consolidation of previous accomplishments.

However, during this period between the ages of 3 and 7 years, the child is developing these capacities, and just as with walking, the child is very shaky, lurching this way and that at the beginning. If previous developmental challenges have not adequately been met, then the process will be even shakier. For example, the child may not have learned to soothe him- or herself. During this period, if the child is struggling to keep the mother in mind and not able to do so, separation anxiety again appears, and may lead to more intense and purposive challenges of authority than seen earlier. This circumstance sets up a hostile dependence within the child, who vacillates between clinging to the parent and disrespectfully devaluing the parent.

The normative developmental challenges for the parent of an Oedipal child include the challenge of realistically assessing the child's ability to set boundaries, care for himself, and negotiate a place within the family among siblings and in relation to the parents. If the parents did not do well in this stage of their own development and have not been able to remediate this for themselves, then the parents may overestimate or underestimate (or both) the child's ability to carry out these tasks. The child at this age is not capable of doing these tasks autonomously.

In the adoption situation in the child's mind, with three parties involved (birth parent, adoptive parent, self), there are additional challenges. The child is now capable of imagining a birth parent who is not present but who has an existence. The child is capable of hypothesizing and constructing narratives independently. If a trusting relationship has been established with the parent, the parent may be able to hear some of these narratives and help the child establish ones that are more reality-based and that will provide his scaffolding for a realistic worldview.

If the child is given too much information about his origins and the reality of his relationships (between himself and his birth and adoptive parents), he will become affectively overwhelmed and may either withdraw or have motoric outbursts. If given too little information, the child will develop his own fantasies that cater to his own internal psychological needs. In either case, the developing ability to form realistic relationships with others will be compromised.

For the adoptive parent, the challenge is not only to assess the child's capacity for understanding his situation and provide him the support he needs to create a realistic narrative, but also to create a psychological as well as physical space in which the child has sufficient support and also sufficient opportunity to exercise appropriate independence. For this, parents need to feel secure in their role and identity as the child's psychological parents. In the child's new capacity for independence, new expressions of individuality will appear. If these manifestations are threatening, adoptive parents may see their efforts thus far as failures. If these failures evoke hopelessness, the parents may abdicate their responsibility of assisting the child in achieving a balance between individual expressions and social awareness.

Another difficulty that may arise for the adoptive parent is in his or her ability to realistically assess the child's abilities. For example, sometimes, because of anxieties about separation, parents may not draw appropriate boundaries and you find the parents allowing or even encouraging the child to sleep in the parental bed. This not only interferes with the parent-child bond, but also the bond between the parents.

Example 5—School Age

Once the challenges in the Oedipal period have been met, the children are ready to manage themselves for periods of time and are in a position to begin to learn about the world. Difficulties in this developmental phase might show themselves when the child is without a parent (for instance, when the child is in school). Here the child may suffer separation anxiety because of the inability to adequately keep the mother in mind.

For the adoption situation, the child may have already had much experience feeling abandoned and these fears are reawakened. Or, if the child has not been able to develop a clear sense of self, internalize the process of boundary setting, and differentiate this from hostility and challenging of authority, the school-age child may become oppositional. These problems—seen in adopted as well as nonadopted children—are routine. However because adopted children and adoptive parents have entered development with additional burdens and challenges, these problems are also cumulative.

Example 6—The Family Romance

Originally a Scottish tale that was highlighted by Freud and later elaborated by Bruno Bettelheim, the Family Romance is a common normative fantasy of children between the ages of 6 and 11 (Freud, 1906–1908; Watters, 1956). In this fantasy, children imagine that they have been adopted and that their real parents are nobler, kinder, and more loving. These fantasies arise out of their increased capacity to imagine and as defense against unpleasant, sometimes overwhelming feelings of frustration, sadness, disappointment, and the like.

In the case of an adopted child, the image of the birth parent may be constructed as a nobler, kinder, more loving parent. Although normative among all children, adoptive parents may misconstrue this fantasy as a rejection of their parenthood by the adopted child. At this point in the adoption situation, with the adopted child's increased capacity to imagine, there may be an increased demand to fill in the details. It then becomes a challenge for the adopted child, adoptive parents, and sometimes the birth parents to help continue to construct a realistic narrative for the child that will ultimately be incorporated into the child's identity (Sherick, 1983; Wieder, 1977). Many adopted children will drop hints about their wonderings, although may be quick to disavow them. For the adopted children who keep their imaginings under wraps, it becomes a challenge for the adoptive parents to determine the line between keeping the children in the dark and overwhelming them with information that the children are not ready to hear. Although this developmental period is usually a quiescent time in terms of presenting problems, much is happening behind the scenes, particularly with the child developing a narrative of his or her life, origins, purposes, roles, positions in the world, and ultimately meaning. This narrative plays a critical role in adolescence, leading to identity formation (Farber, 2006).

Example 6—Adolescents

In normative development, adolescence is a time when the child begins to establish him- or herself as independent from his parents. Parents' role is to stay present so that the adolescent can leave them behind. Parents who doubt whether they have adequately carried out their parental functions may have difficulty being left. At this time, a significant developmental challenge for parents is to support the adolescent's independence and at the same time not abandon him or her. Adolescents' newfound independence and identity can be fragile and regression to younger child states is not uncommon. For parents, however, it can be quite jarring when an adult-looking person behaves as an adult one moment and as a latency-age child the next (Tubero, 2002). In addition, adult-level judgment is not usually present until the end of adolescence or the beginning of young adulthood. The parent of an adolescent needs to continue to provide adequate supervision while at the same time not usurping his or her tenuous, newfound independence.

In this newfound independence, adopted adolescents will begin to live into their narrative (Wilkinson & Hough, 1996). If this narrative is unrealistic, these adolescents will behave in an unreasonable manner with regard to the world. Likewise, adoptive parents may find themselves anxious for their adolescent if they have not been able to develop their own realistic narrative of themselves and their child. The challenge here for the parent is to know when to hold and know when to fold.

With their new autonomy, many adopted adolescents will want to seek out their birth parents, and many of them will do so with or without their adoptive parents' support. Adoptive parents may feel betrayed and left behind. However, if both the adopted child and the adoptive parents have developed a realistic narrative, the incorporation of birth parents into the identity of the adolescent will be a natural one that the adoptive parents can support and in which the adopted child will feel secure.

Example 7—Young Adulthood

As adolescents transition to young adulthood, they head toward an autonomous life, albeit usually with emotional and many times financial support, at least initially. Fruits of all their parents' labor and all their successes in meeting the previous developmental challenges allow these young adults to step into the world with a realistic sense of themselves, their autonomy and confidence rooted in their actual abilities. However, unmet developmental challenges leave the young adult compromised in his or her ability to function autonomously.

With the increased burdens of development, seeing adopted children and their parents lag in this development is not uncommon. If expectations are that the child moves on in life when the young adult is not ready, then the young adult is at risk. If, however, expectations are that it may take more time, development usually continues. In this context, it is important to foster as much autonomy as the young adult can manage, keeping in mind the optimal environment to promote growth. In the adoptive situation, the tasks of separation, individuation, and identity formation are more complex than in the nonadoptive situation. Accordingly, it is not uncommon to see the developmental work (maturation) of adolescence extend beyond the teenage years, into young adulthood, and even beyond.

Example 8—Parenthood

The penultimate challenge for adopted children is to become parents themselves. As was laid out at the beginning of this chapter, the challenge of parenthood is to make another parent. Whatever unmet challenges linger, these will likely be faced again as this parent now helps his or her own child through development. The adopted adult, just as any parent, faces the entire developmental process again in helping their child through the process, this time in the role of parent. Adoption introduces many twists and turns in that process, compared with the nonadoptive situation, many of them unexpected.

For example, as the adopted woman becomes pregnant, she naturally turns to her mother for information and support. However, the adoptive parent (now a grandparent) may never have lived through a pregnancy and delivery. So it should not be surprising that the adopted child (now parent) may seek support from the birth parent if available, or harbor the wish/fantasy of doing so but not do so for fear of hurting her adoptive parents. One such example can be found on the Internet.[3]

PRACTICAL POINTS

- When the family or child presents for treatment, even if one party is not physically present, therapists should consider the impact the triad (birth and adoptive parents and child) has on the underlying developmental challenges that both the child and adoptive parents are facing in this moment.
- Work to help both the child and the parent understand the developmental challenges they are facing in this moment and how each affects the other.
- Respect for the autonomy of both the parent and the child in relation to developmental decisions is essential.

CONCLUSION

I have laid out a schematic of development for parents and children, although much more should be understood regarding this development. For those interested, I recommend Henri Parens' DVD *Parenting for Emotional Growth* (2010). In addition, I have outlined some of the additional challenges that are faced by adopted children and adoptive parents in their development. When there are difficulties in facing these developmental hurdles, emotional and behavioral symptoms begin to appear—anxiety, depression, withdrawal, attention problems, oppositional, provocative and acting out behaviors in children, and abuse, neglect, withdrawal, depression, and anxiety in parents.

These symptoms are the presenting complaints as the parents and children come through the door to your office. The developmental problems are usually well hidden beneath the symptoms. The clinician, with knowledge of the deep psychological development, can begin to work collaboratively with these parents and children to sort out the source of these symptoms. I have provided guidelines to begin this process. It is the collaboration and the sorting out of the thoughts, feelings, and symptoms that will open up the interior of the minds of these children and parents. This process is both diagnostic and therapeutic, and if successful, transforms the lives of these parents and children.

In this chapter, I have focused inward on processes within the adopted child—developmental processes. Once seen, these developmental processes show the way for the adoptive parent to support the adopted child. In the next chapter, the authors look outward, thinking about how the adoptive parents, for themselves and as an example for the child, face and address a world in which others, because of their ignorance, are wearying at best and destructive at worst for the adoptive parent and adopted child.

NOTES

1. It is useful to remember that all of the manualized therapies (e.g., CBT, DBT) have their origins in and are contained in the psychoanalytic canon (Target, 1993; Wright, 1924).
2. This period is described extensively in the psychoanalytic literature as the Oedipal period, in which the child struggles with what to do with the new found realization that he has two parents that are in a relationship from which he is excluded.
3. This story can be found at http://library.adoption.com/articles/when-adoptees-become-parents.html

Chapter 11

ADOPTIVE PARENT AS CONSULTANT, EDUCATOR, AND ADVOCATOR

Virginia M. Brabender and Toni Whitmore

The adoptive parent or parent-to-be embarks on a path that is well traveled and yet unique to each family situation. Mothers and fathers who choose to have children, whether through adoption or through giving birth, will find a staggering number of books, articles, guides, and manuals meant to educate, prepare, and show the difficulties and rewards of parenthood. Yet the adoptive parents face an added layer of complex issues when they embark on this choice to enlarge their family to include adopted children. Even at the outset of the parenting process, the contemplative stage, they will find that most of the verbal and written references concerning child rearing are framed for birth parents. Why is this? Parenting biological children is the norm— it guides the societal notions of what it means to be a parent, a child, and a family. This chapter explores those extra responsibilities of the adoptive parent given this societal bias and the particular needs of his or her adopted child.

When adoptive parents contemplate raising a child, a variety of activities may come to mind with any one activity being predicated on the developmental stage of the child. Soothing the newborn, exploring with the toddler, assisting the 7-year-old with homework, and setting limits with the teenager are all accessible images. Rarely would any parent be surprised to be called on to perform any one of them. Yet, some activities associated with adoptive parenting may not be ones that are anticipated. Many of these activities have to do with the adopted child's relationship to the world outside of the nuclear family. The better the adoptive parent can anticipate the need to take on the important roles of consultant, educator, and advocate, and prepare for them, the more likely he or she is to discharge them more effectively.

The adoptive parent serves as a consultant when he or she provides assistance to other parties in understanding the dynamics of adoption as they apply to his or her child. The parent serves as educator when he or she provides knowledge based on personal experience, reading, and other modes of discovery to individuals or groups of individuals interesting in learning about adoption. For example, an adoptive parent may be called on to talk to prospective parents about the experience of adopting within a particular country. Advocacy occurs when the adoptive parent engages in activities to advance the well-being of adoptive children and families, their own and others. These roles overlap. For example, when a parent helps a teacher to understand the behavior of his or her child that may be related to adoption, that parent is also educating by increasing knowledge and advocating, advancing not only that child but potentially other adopted children. Whether the intervention is considered knowledge or advocacy is merely a matter of the emphasis of the intervention.

The following situations reveal why it is that the adoptive parent is inevitably and frequently called on to provide advice, consultation, and education.

Situation 1

Shelley and Ed adopted Roberto when he was 6 months and took him to a family reunion when he was 1 year old. Although Roberto's aunts, uncles, and first cousins had already met him, his more distant relatives were introduced to him during this event. Shelley was sitting at a table holding and entertaining Roberto when her great aunt, who had already praised Roberto's adorableness, asked Shelley about the adoption. Initially, she inquired whether they had done everything they could do to have a child of their own. Shelley responded, "Well, we consider Roberto our own." The aunt responded, "Well, of course you do. That's not what I meant." Shelley vaguely told the group that Ed and she had indeed been through some fertility treatment, but they were very happy with Roberto. A cousin asked about their trip to Ecuador and Shelley narrated many of the details, some of which involved hardships such as Roberto coming down with a fever while they were staying at a hotel in Ecuador and completing the legal process there. The same cousin said, "That sounds really hard. . . . I suppose Roberto's family was very poor. I just wonder why you didn't adopt in this country—there are many children who need a good home here." By this time, Ed had ambled over and joined the conversation. He explained that the couple felt they had more control in an international adoption—they were uncomfortable with the advertising that was required by agencies and they wondered if their being in their mid-40s would make them unattractive. Another cousin then asked if other people stare at them because Roberto is darker than they are. At this time, Ed said in a clipped tone, "Not really," and abruptly changed the conversation. On the way home, they agreed that they would forego future reunions.

Situation 2

Sandra, the mother of a 5-year-old adopted daughter (Martha), received a call from the kindergarten teacher. Sandra's was a kinship adoption from a cousin who was in and out of drug facilities. Martha was formally adopted when she was 4 but had lived with Sandra since she was 3. Martha's teacher was disturbed because of two behaviors Martha exhibited. Martha was found storing candy wrappers in her cubby, and when the teacher directed her to throw the wrappers away, Martha became distraught. On another occasion, the teacher was reading a story involving the birth of a baby duck. Again, Martha sobbed, and could not be consoled. On still another occasion, Martha felt that her printing was too sloppy, even though it was well on par with her classmates, and she became sullen and withdrawn. The teacher indicated she was perplexed by these behaviors.

Situation 3

Sarah, an adopted daughter in the seventh grade, returned home from school in a state of dejection. Upon exploration, her parents learned that in science class, the teacher in conjunction with an introductory lesson on genetics had students construct genograms. The students were asked to link their physical characteristics based on characteristics of their parents. Sarah was paralyzed because she didn't know the characteristics of her biological parents; she knew the characteristics of her adoptive parents were irrelevant to the exercise and was embarrassed to ask the teacher for further direction. The teacher asked her if she were feeling sick. Sarah said yes and she spent the rest of the afternoon in the nurse's office. Sarah was worried that this assignment would be continued the next day.

These are situations that we have derived from our research and our personal experiences. All of them are likely to create a discomfort in the adoptive parent that may be a signal that a problem exists, a problem that requires assessment and most likely intervention. We will return to our three situations; but before we do, it is important for the adoptive parent, or practitioner treating the adoptive parent, to recognize that such situations are regular occurrences in families, adoptive and those that depart from the traditional structure of a married, heterosexual couple with biological children. Several factors account for why these situations that evoke tension, hurt, and confusion often occur in the lives of adoptive parents.

THE ROOTS OF PROBLEMS FACING ADOPTIVE PARENTS

The types of situations facing adoptive parents are not driven by a solitary factor, but rather by a set of forces. In any one situation, factors relatively idiosyncratic to that situation may operate. However, some factors exert their influence on a broader level because they emerge from the larger societal system in which adoptions take place. They relate to how a particular society regards not simply adoption, but more generally, the status of being different—out of the mainstream. Although in the introduction of this book, the point was made that adoption in some fashion touches everyone's lives, it nonetheless is the case that most nuclear families do not have an adopted child as a member. Therefore, the manner in which a society contends with those bearing a minority status shapes attitudes toward adoption and behaviors that derive from those attitudes. Among the factors creating these circumstances, we discuss two in particular: (1) lack of knowledge and the mechanisms that perpetuate it; and (2) micro-aggressions. The complexion of these attitudes and related behaviors will also be affected by adoption-specific schemas, largely unconscious, which are also important for the adoptive parent to recognize.

Lack of Knowledge and Overgeneralization

Although everyone knows someone who is adopted or has adopted, the knowledge derived from these experiences is passing rather than intimate. A more fine-grained understanding of the realities and dynamics of adoption is wrought through an immersion in the adoption literature, the direct experience of being a member of the adoption triad, close association with a member of the triad, or some combination of these factors. In the absence of these critical exposures, individuals tend to be influenced by sources of information that may provide a skewed picture of adoption.

Stories in the media are one source of information. What qualifies a story as news is that it is in some way remarkable. Ordinary examples of adoptive families flourishing do not constitute news. Adoption disruptions and adversarial relationships between adoptive and birth parents are seen as far more worthy of attention (Pavao, 2007).[1] Even in those accounts that are given, the particular details are frequently chosen to entertain or shock rather than to provide a full picture of the family's situation. Often, the strengths of adoptive parents are ignored. For example, foster-to-adoption parents distinguish themselves for the level of preparation they have for the tasks of parenting (Gailey, 2010). Their education is extensive before and after the adoption. Yet these facts, and the overall effectiveness with which these parents function, is passed over in favor of a story about a child who has a strikingly negative outcome in such a family.

Another source of information is the set of disproven or oversimplified scientific findings that have become ensconced in the public consciousness. The findings of early studies pointed to the conclusion that adopted children have greater psychopathology than nonadopted children because of their overrepresentation in mental health setting (Mech, 1973; Wierzbicki, 1993). However, subsequent research demonstrated that adoptive parents have a lower threshold for using mental health resources (Ingersoll, 1997; Miller et al., 2000). Furthermore, differences in the severity of psychological problems are not primarily attributable to adoptive status but rather, the negative life events (for example, sexual abuse) that preceded the adoption (Brodzinsky, 2011). Adopted children manifest more frequent internalizing and externalizing behaviors, learning disabilities, and lower levels of adjustment, but the effect sizes between them and nonadoptees is low to moderate (Juffer & Van IJzendoorn, 2005; Miller et al., 2000). Moreover, they do not show greater vulnerability to severe psychopathology, and their levels of self-esteem are comparable to those of their nonadopted counterparts through childhood into adulthood (Borders et al., 1998; Borders, Penny, & Portnoy, 2000; Irhammer & Bengstsson, 2004). In some studies, adopted children evidenced fewer psychological problems than their nonadoptive counterparts. For example, Sharma and colleagues (1998) observed that adopted adolescent boys and girls showed a lower incidence of certain social problems than nonadopted teens. Studies comparing adopted and nonadopted adults reveal levels of functioning that are minor or absent altogether (e.g., Borders et al., 2000; Smyer, Gatz, Simi, & Pederson, 1998).

Micro-Aggressions

When adoptive parents are the targets of insults and hurts, often the individuals inflicting these harms are unaware that they are doing so. Donald Wing Sue (2010) has termed such acts *micro-aggressions*, which he defines as "the everyday verbal, non-verbal, and environmental slights, snubs, or insults, whether intentional or unintentional, that communicate hostile, derogatory, or negative messages to target persons based solely upon their marginalized group membership" (Sue, 2010, p. 3). As Sue points out, micro-aggressions occur to enable individuals to deny their biases while preserving the social inequities that these biases beget.

Sue notes that micro-aggressions can take three forms. The first form, micro-assaults, involves the direct expression of consciously held attitudes toward a marginalized group. For example, middle-school children who on the playground brand one another as "gay" as if this designation is inherently negative are committing a micro-assault. Relative to the micro-assault, the micro-insult is far subtler and generally involves the expression of an unconscious attitude. For example, when an elderly person is told, "You don't look your age at all," the implication is that something is wrong with being elderly. As is true in this example, micro-insults frequently present themselves as compliments (Sue, 2010). Yet, the receiver either does not enjoy the compliment at all or feels a more complex affective reaction in relation to it. Also unconscious is the micro-invalidation, which denies the negative experiences of a marginalized group. For example, when a law enforcement officer claims to treat all individuals equally under the law but responds with greater alacrity and vigor to offenses of one race over others, he or she commits a micro-invalidation.

The members of adoptive families constitute a marginalized group within many societies. In the United States, for example, a strong pronatalist and patriarchal culture exists in which the optimal family is seen as composed of a mother, father, and biological children (Wegar, 1997, 2000). Implicit in this societal paradigm is a privileging of biological/genetic ties over other types of relations (Brakman & Scholz, 2006). Families with alternate structures depart from the societal ideal, and adoption as a way of building a family is such an alternate structure, as is the stepfamily, the gay or lesbian family, or the foster family. All of these types of nontraditional families are the targets of micro-aggressions and, as others have noted (e.g., Leinaweaver, 2008), the adoptive family is no exception. For the most part, adoptive parents will face micro-insults and micro-invalidations. Situations 1 and 2 are characterized primarily by a combination of these. In the example of the family reunion, the relatives' use of the common phrase "a child of your own" is an example of a micro-insult that is commonly inflicted on adoptive parents and rooted in the pronatalist sentiments described earlier. When Shelley confronts her great aunt on her communication, the great aunt disavows ("That's not what I meant") the pejorative element of her statement. In so doing, she inflicts, most likely unwittingly, a micro-invalidation. Shelley has been hurt and yet that reality has not been affirmed. In the face of this invalidation, she might easily regard herself as being excessively sensitive. However, the situation deteriorates further as Shelley and Ed are questioned on why they are adopting internationally, a query possibly rooted in xenophobia. This micro-insult was joined by a comment about differences in skin color suggesting racial prejudice. Adoptive families present to others complex stimuli and elicit reactions that blend a variety of prejudices.

Adoptism

These various forms of discrimination, whether simple or complex, constitute *adoptism*, a term coined by Steinberg and Hall (2000) to describe deprecatory, devaluing, stereotyping attitudes, and related behaviors toward adopted individuals and their families, adoptive and birth. They write, "Adoptism is a cultural belief that families formed by adoption are less truly connected than are birth families; that birth families should be preserved at all costs and under all circumstances except the most severely harmful; that people who were adopted were first rejected, maybe for a reason" (p. 108). Adoptism may be combined with any number of the other isms such as racism and sexism. Expectant or new gay parents are confronted by family and friends with doubts about the appropriateness of two men or two women adopting (Savage, 2000). The adoptive parent is called on both to intervene with those who influence his or her child, but also to help the child cope with manifestations of adoptism, given that many will occur with the parent's knowledge. For example, Miles (2000) points out that around the age of 3 or 4, the child is likely to hear comments from others about why he or she doesn't look like his or her parents.

Common sense would dictate that being on the receiving end of micro-aggressions is damaging to a child's well-being. Joining common sense in support of this conclusion are empirical studies. For example, Lee (2010) studies 1,834 couples, all of whom had adopted children. When parents saw their child as having been the object of racially discriminatory comments, that child was more prone to internalizing and externalizing behaviors than the child whose parents did not perceive him or her as being treated in a discriminatory fashion. Furthermore, Asian and Latin American children were perceived to receive these comments more frequently than Eastern European children.

Implications for Therapists

For therapists, recognizing that adoptive parents and children can be subject to micro-aggressions is important for how the therapist thinks about and responds to the adoptive parent. In the absence of this awareness, the therapist could easily mistake the client's hurt as hypersensitivity. After all, micro-aggressions are subtle and without a broader perspective, it could seem to the therapist as if the client is making "something out of nothing." Consider the following situation:

> Blythe, an adoptive gay father, recently adopted a 3-year-old child through the child welfare system. He found that so many colleagues at work made comments expressing essentially the same sentiment: "Your child is so lucky—will he ever realize it?" Blythe felt that the underlying message was that the child was unworthy. Blythe expressed that this message is fundamentally hostile. Yet, he found it difficult to respond because on a surface level, the communication seemed supportive.

In such a circumstance, the therapist might be inclined to concentrate his or her therapeutic efforts on changing Blythe's view of the interpersonal event. For example, the therapist might question whether the current circumstance reminded Blythe of some event that occurred in the past. In taking such a stance, the therapist is failing to convey empathy for the parent's distress in the here and now and in essence, committing another micro-aggression by invalidating the parent's reaction. On the other hand, by recognizing the micro-aggression as such, the therapist can work with the parent to recognize that an array of responses are possible and that a consideration of context can guide the parent in selecting one that will be consonant with the parent's goals. In some circumstances, the parent may want to educate the other party about the effects of his or her attitude. In other circumstances, the parent may wish to minimize or terminate the relationship altogether. Whatever deliberate response the parent selects, it is likely to be an antidote to the helplessness that is engendered by being a passive recipient of a micro-aggression.

ACTION IMPLICATIONS

We now look at different venues in which parental advocacy can be crucial to the well-being of the child.

Family, Friends, and Members of the Community

Often, important acts of advocacy occur even before the child enters the family. Grandparents and other family members can benefit greatly from being included in a psychoeducation that occurs before or after the adoption. Therefore, an important act of advocacy for the child is to encourage their participation. It is also important for family members to realize that family members other than those in the immediate family have their own ongoing reactions to a family's abandonment of the effort to have a biological child and embrace of the plan to adopt. Pavao (2005) provided a stunning example of a hurtful comment made by a grandparent on seeing a room that had been decorated for her 8-year-old granddaughter. According to Pavao, the grandmother said, "What a beautiful room for someone else's child" (p. 23). The feelings of loss that we describe in Chapter 4 in relation to adoptive mothers can be acute for grandparents who are facing mortality, and have a particularly keen desire to see their own genetic lines sustained. When no forum exists for the expression of loss, these feelings are at greater risk to be acted out, often in ways that are not productive. Adoptive parents do themselves and their children a service by creating appropriate opportunities for grandparents and other family members to express their reactions to such painful realities as the discontinuation of their genetic lines or the absence of a grandchild who might resemble them.

School

According to Smith and Riley's (2006, p. 30) report, "School is where adopted children face the most challenges and parents express the most concerns." It is also the place where children spend much of their waking time. Consequently, what happens during the school day is crucial in shaping how the child feels about him- or herself, the identity the child forms, and how others are perceived. Given the power of the child's school experiences, a core responsibility of adoptive parenting is engaging with the school to ensure that the child's experience is constructive and healthy. This involvement includes a variety of activities.

Parental Attunement

Adoptive parents must be attuned to direct and indirect manifestations of the child's school experiences:

> Margaret moved to Baltimore with her 5-year-old adopted daughter Alexandra just in time to enroll her in kindergarten. The private school had many multiethnic children as students and Alexa was quickly accepted and welcomed. Margaret had explained to the teacher and administrators that Alexa was adopted at an early age and seemed to adjust to school well, having spent three years in a Montessori preschool.
>
> One evening in the bathtub, Alexa covered herself with soapsuds and wouldn't let Margaret wash her off. Margaret asked Alexa why she liked having the suds all over her skin. "I want to be white, mom," pleaded Alexa. "My skin is too dark." Margaret thought about how to deal with this double-edged issue—white is often considered superior in our American society and Alexa was Asian, not African American.
>
> Margaret asked Alexa to look at her and tell her what she saw. "I see freckles, mom, brown eyes, red hair, white skin—you're white, mom, and I am not." She asked Alexa what did she see when she looked at her friend Shana, an adopted child from Mexico. Did she think any less of Shana because she had darker skin? Margaret explained that in her family, people weren't judged by the color of their skin—that was why she could make Alexa a part of her family and no one would notice the color of her skin. But that wasn't true in all families, or in all schools. But Alexa could show that she was in a different kind of family—one with different shades and colors and that family was proud of its family rainbow.

Margaret responded in a helpful way to her daughter by realizing that Alexa might be communicating a reaction through the soapsuds. A less-attuned parent might have simply insisted that the child remove the soapsuds. Margaret's exploratory attitude unearthed material that might otherwise have been inaccessible. Often, it is through indirect clues that children communicate. By decoding Alexa's emotional language, Margaret was able to have a conversation with Alexa about the important topic of racial differences.

Parental Intervention

While the issue still stayed with Alexa, Margaret also knew that she needed to speak with all the kindergarten educators and the principal. Most likely, a 5-year-old did not on her own come up with this white-dark metaphor; some child said something. While precisely what was said was not known, the parental emphasis on pursuing the issue was critical. Initial attempts to address racist incidents may not be successful. For example, a teacher who enjoys white privilege may exhibit incredulity on receiving reports that her Asian student was the recipient of racial slurs and insults (Gidluck & Dwyer, 2006). Tenacity in such a circumstance and, if possible, the help of other similarly situated parents may be essential commodities.

Although in our discussion of Alexa's experience we surmised that a child was the source of some discriminatory comment, sometimes teachers make these comments. When teachers make discriminatory or stereotyping comments, they can be especially influential given that for the young child, the teacher stands in the parent's stead. Sometimes the communications in the classroom are not specific to the individual student but rather to his or her family structure. The early school years are when the child begins to realize that his or her family structure is nontraditional (Brodzinsky, 2011; Evan B. Donaldson Institute, 2006) and may also recognize that his or her particular family structure may not be accepted and appreciated by all (Steinberg & Hall, 2000). Teachers can play a crucial role in whether an adopted child comes to see his family as on a par with all others, or something less than the traditional family (Dwyer & Gidluck, 2009). As illustrated in Situation 3, how the teacher transmits her assumptions about traditional and nontraditional families may come in the form of lessons and assignments. When he or she is presenting material, if the examples are entirely from traditional, racially homogeneous, nonadoptive families, then the child may ascribe diminished value to his or her own family and conclude that families such as his or hers are not even worth mentioning. Adoptive parents play a useful role in sharing their views on how teachers might alter assignments to make them more inclusive. For children of all ages, the kinds of reading resources present in the classroom and the library provide a perspective on nontraditional resources. Adoptive parents serve not only their own children's needs but also those of their classmates by providing suggestions on material offering a positive view of the life of the nontraditional families.[2]

The suggestions thus far provided assume that the communication of the child's adoptive status to various parties within the school system may serve the child's adjustment and the capacity of the school district to meet the child's needs. However, research on the implications of adoption-related disclosures could yield valuable information to guide parents on this sensitive decision (Biafora, Javier, Baden, & Camacho-Gingerich, 2007). Who should receive this information? How detailed should the information be concerning the child's background? In what context is the material best shared? These are all questions worthy of exploration.

Beyond monitoring and interventions based on monitoring, adoptive parents are called on to provide consultation to teachers about adoption and about the racial and

ethnic issues that often accompany adoption.[3] Were Alexa's teacher to express perplexity as to how she might instigate a constructive conversation about families of
different structures, including adoptive families, Margaret may provide her with
assistance. One emphasis of pre-adoption preparation is often the handling of questions that frequently are posed by friends, family, neighbors, and even passersby. This
background can qualify the adoptive parents to offer some assistance in how to frame
issues that emerge in the classroom or on the playground. The adoptive parent must
also serve as consultant to the teacher in helping him or her to understand the child. In
the beginning of this chapter, a vignette (Situation 2) was shared in which a kindergarten teacher was concerned about certain behaviors of an adoptive child—hiding
wrappers, perfectionism in writing, and the reaction to the birth of the baby duck.
These seemingly mysterious behaviors may well be comprehensible to the adoptive
parent. Hoarding behaviors—not unusual in adoptive children—often represent a
symbolic attempt at undoing the loss of the birth parents and ensuring the continued
presence of the adoptive parent. The perfectionism might be a fear of any self-
perceived inadequacies that invite loss, and the reaction to the duck story could be a
grieving over a lost past. The loss is quite fresh because it is during this period that the
child begins to grasp its enormity. Aiding the teacher in understanding these reactions
will stimulate that teacher's empathy for, and capacity to respond sensitively to, the
child. Parents might also recommend that a unit on adoptive and other types of
nontraditional families be included in relevant courses such as health (Fishman &
Harrington, 2007).

At times, teachers may inappropriately attribute a child's behavior to his or her
reaction to the adoption:

> Two first-grade girls got separated from their class at the zoo and were not found for 45
> minutes. Both girls were distraught. When a parent angrily confronted the teacher, she
> said that the daughter responded with such intensity because she was adopted.

In this case, both first-graders, only one of whom was adopted, were responding
reasonably to a frightening situation. The teacher, to abdicate responsibility for an
untoward event, used this facet of the child's identity—being adopted—defensively.
Adoption, summoned as an explanation of various aspects of the child's behavior
to the neglect of other possible factors, is another manifestation of adoptism
(Steinberg & Hall, 2000). It also entailed the commission of micro-aggressions against
both the child and her parents. One could see why the teacher might be eager to
externalize responsibility for the event. To prevent the child from inappropriately
receiving blame, the parent must assist the teacher in recognizing those realities
outside of the adoption—such as both children's vulnerability in being in a group of
strangers—that could give rise to the behavior in question.

Resources exist to help the parent perform an advocacy role within the schools.
For example, *Families Adoption in Response (FAIR)* has created a book *Adoption
and the Schools: A Resource Guide for Parents and Teachers* (Wood & Ng, 2001),
which outlines dilemmas commonly experienced by adopted school children and
possibilities for expanding them in order to lessen discomfort and foster a more
inclusive environment.

Therapists working with adoptive parents should recognize when the difficulties that
the parent is encountering with a school system are so great as to require additional
professional assistance. If the therapist is not an adoption specialist, then he or she

might refer the parent to one. The adoption specialist can inform the parent of his or her rights and help the parent to services that the child needs. The adoption specialist can also coach the parent to work with the school to successfully address climate issues.

The Workplace

Over time, the changes that have been seen in the workplace stance toward parents have been dramatic. The effects on adoptive families have been enormous.

The Workplace in the Past

Historically the work environment, particularly within the financially competitive private sector, has not been worker-friendly about parental leave and benefits for parents expecting children either through pregnancy or through adoption. Following World War II, when American troops returned, many women who had replaced men in the workplace returned to their homes and the rise of the baby boom generation officially began in January 1946. While mothers remained home, there was not the pressure on employers to provide maternity-related benefits, and adoption benefits were virtually nonexistent. The labor participation rate of women had to increase dramatically for there to be pressure for systemic reform from within to improve parental benefits for both men and women.

As referenced in Chapter 1, the United States experienced a dramatic rise in the adoption rate following the Korean War in the mid-1950s. Children, often abandoned because of and during the U.S. occupation, became eligible for adoption in the United States. The struggling South Korean economy, the strict norms of a traditional Asian society, and the absence of an established middle class did not provide an environment that could culturally and financially absorb and adopt children who were abandoned during the war. Many of these children were of mixed race and not culturally or racially accepted into traditional South Korean families.

Following the 1960s, the number of American women going to college, pursuing nontraditional careers and advanced graduate degrees, and entering the labor market dramatically increased. The emergence of the women's movement as a civil rights issue during this time propelled many women to break the gender glass ceiling in college admissions. This led them to compete for places in graduate, medical, and law schools, and eventually for jobs traditionally thought of as male employment. Now families with two working parents would require adequate child care, parental leave, and a myriad of services for their families. Yet, a gap existed:

> Charlotte and Andrew initiated their international adoption process for a Korean infant in the 1970s. Andrew was a professor at a prominent academic institution and Charlotte worked for a leading children's rights social service agency. Neither employer, while seemingly open to diversity and social justice as part of their community responsibility, offered adoption benefits and each provided only minimal maternity leave for their personnel. Four weeks' leave without pay was the maximum maternity leave and vacation time could be added to the 4 weeks. There was no paternity leave for fathers and Charlotte decided to resign from her position and be a stay-at-home mother, a requirement of the adoption agreement they were asked to sign. Charlotte agreed to remain at home and this contract was in effect until the adoption was finalized in court.

Although neither Charlotte nor Andrew worked for a for-profit employer, they lacked benefits that were enlightened or family-friendly, or that even remotely reflected the stated mission and vision of their employers. The employer did not view parental rights and parental leave as part of employee benefits nor was adoption a part of the cultural norm of society.

The Workplace Today

In our current society, it is the cultural norm to expect parental leave benefits and almost everyone believes that all parents should have family-friendly choices provided within the workplace. A parent may decide that it would be in the best interest of the child, especially the adopted child, to be in the home full time while the child is adjusting to the new family environment. A family should be able to have options and resources to assess the parenting, economic, and family needs that best suit the family.

In the late 1990s, it became not just a cultural norm, but also a legislative mandate. One of the historic changes in legislation was the passage of the Family and Medical Leave Act of 1993 under President Clinton. With this sweeping legislation, most parents became eligible for up to 12 weeks of unpaid parental leave when expecting a child. One of the goals of this legislation was to bring parity to adoption benefits with benefits provided to biological parents in the workplace

But there are some hidden differences and biases in the workplace, affecting female workers who are adopting. Adopting mothers do not qualify for the sick leave that most pregnant women employees can include in their maternity leave time. Although adopting parents may encounter a broad spectrum of specific issues that require personal leave (e.g., time off for the case study interviews; possible travel out of state or to another country; and court appearances for the adoption proceedings), these absences are often not covered under parental leave benefits and do not strictly qualify for sick leave time.

The Dave Thomas Foundation for Adoption

One outstanding corporate model has become the gold standard for employers to follow in providing parental benefits for adoption parents—the example set by Dave Thomas, the founder of Wendy's restaurants and the Dave Thomas Foundation for Adoption (Pertman, 2011). His business plan within his own corporate empire, Wendy's International Inc., set the bar high and he and the foundation have provided the template for other corporations through the Adoption Friendly Workplace Program. Through the Thomas Foundation, created more than 18 years ago, the employer can receive an employer tool kit to incorporate and implement adoption benefits policy as part of their business policy for all employees who are eligible (see http://www.adoptionfriendlyworkplace.org).

The foundation has created an annual awards program to promote, publicize, and reward the top 100 best adoption-friendly workplaces (Dave Thomas Foundation for Adoption, 2011, The *Adoption-Friendly Workplace, A Guide to Implementing an Adoption Benefits Policy, Employer Tool Kit*) provides a step-by-step guide along with the business analysis of why this is good social and economic policy for a company. Companies submit their applications to the foundation to be included on the annual 100 Best Adoption Friendly Workplaces list; the basic criteria are based on financial assistance and paid leave that is offered to employees who are adopting. The top 100 companies are honored each fall and the list is published in *Employee Benefit News*, a leading publication for human resource managers.

The corporate employer must sell the benefits policy to the company's board of directors, and an economic argument must go hand in hand with the social good will argument. The employer is urged to see it as a recruiting tool for hiring top-level employees and a template for their work-life employee benefits. The economic incentive for the company, besides the general public relations benefit, is that productivity is improved and the employees have a heightened sense of goodwill and loyalty toward their employers. The actual utilization of the benefits is less than 1% of eligible employees, according to the Thomas Foundation.

The spectrum of companies on the list represents a broad range of industries including financial institutions, food services, energy corporations, pharmaceuticals, and several leading universities. The awards list is just one way to publicize and secure an employer's attention. The web page and resources available to both parents and employers provide a step-by-step plan and advocacy outline for changing the culture within the workplace and society at large.

The foundation urges parents to be advocates of change for their children and for themselves as adoptive parents. It provides guidelines for parents to propose adoption benefits to their employer. When the employer has implemented such benefits, there are guidelines for the employer to apply for the Foundation's Best Workplace list through the online survey on the foundation's website. Parents are encouraged to become leaders within their workplace and build community with other workers and parents.

The golden benchmark set by Wendy's International is up to $24,300 (maximum financial assistance) and up to 6 weeks' paid leave. The range within the 100 best list went from the maximum to a minimum of $5,000 with 4 weeks' paid leave. There were variables also as to size of company and number of employees.

The foundation's employee advocacy guidelines also provide a framework for addressing the issues facing parents as they interact with other organizations, such as schools, religious institutions, social service agencies, and community organizations. It outlines a communication strategy that addresses cultural, educational, training, and support groups within the workplace and society at large. The impact of the program and the corporate leadership shown by Thomas have resulted in a measureable increase in U.S. companies offering benefits for adopting parents. During the 1990s, the participation increased from 11% to 30% and reached close to 50% until the country's economic recession began to take its toll in 2008. Major corporations vie to make the Dave Thomas Foundation's Annual Best Adoption-Friendly Workplaces list, as well as the *Working Mother* magazine's "100 Best Companies" list. One of the criteria for inclusion is an adoption benefits program.

Employers, too, often have the philosophy that parental leave, and specifically adoption benefits, are not in the company's economic best interest, will lead to a decrease in productivity, and are an expensive perk best left out of incentives. What the Thomas Foundation and research have shown is that the benefits provide equity for all families at a minimal cost. Unfortunately with the economic downturn, adoption-related benefits were often one of the first to be curtailed as human resources looked to trim expenses (Dave Thomas Foundation for Adoption, 2010; Pertman, 2011).

Although the foundation's adoption-friendly workplace is a visionary program, it is not the standard, even among larger corporations. Smaller businesses, including family-owned enterprises, which are a large percentage of the U.S. economy, believe that increasing health care premiums and flexible employee benefits impair their competitiveness and are an unfair burden on their bottom line. During difficult economic times, such as the U.S. marketplace has been facing for several years, it is difficult to make the argument for expanded, voluntary services for employees.

It is only through education and advocacy, on the part of the productive employees within the company, that the attitude and practices will change in favor of adoptive parental leave and benefits.

The Broader Society

In thinking about adoptive parents' responses to the ways in which society broadly views adoption, we can identify two major requirements. The first requirement is to learn to maintain a healthy parental self-regard despite the shifting societal currents in regard to adoption. At one moment, adoption is seen as an act of altruism, a posture that ignores, in many cases, the extreme longing prospective parents have to be caregivers, a yearning that motivates the wish to bring a child into their home. At other times, adoption is viewed with extreme suspicion, as an act of predation upon what is rightfully another's. Although adoption is a common phenomenon, the fact that most families are not adoptive makes adoption, along with any other nontraditional structure, vulnerable to others' projections and distortions. Adoptive parents at times will find that whatever parenting behaviors they exhibit will be found to be controversial by some subgroup.[4] Hardiness is needed for maintaining one's balance as an adoptive parent, particularly when the adoption creates a transracial/transcultural family. Transracial adoptive families differ from most others on not only one dimension but at least two, making them especially prone to others' biases and misperceptions. Moreover, race is a stimulus for intense reactions, connected to conflicts that often lie outside of awareness. Throughout various chapters of this book (for example, Chapters 5 and 6), the resources adoptive parents can use to maintain equilibrium in the midst of impinging forces were identified. These include, but are not limited to, psychotherapy, consultation with adoption specialists, affiliation with other adoptive parents, support and self-help groups, teamwork with one's partner in parenting (whether a spouse or other party), and access to the adoption literature.

At the same time, adoptive parents benefit all members of the kinship network when they are participants in society's conversation about adoption and activists on behalf of social justice. Although the issues are many, a small collection has particular import:[5]

1. The occurrence of child trafficking is well documented and has continued to occur despite the reforms of the Hague Convention. Individuals who have adopted children or especially those who seek to adopt may feel that they are working against their own self-interests by calling for stricter regulations. Ultimately, however, adoption is best protected when it is regulated and when strong safeguards are in place against abusive practices, which are often motivated by financial interests. Never should an adoptive family have to experience the agonizing doubt as to whether the child who enters its home did so by means that were wholly ethical and legal. Prospective adoptive parents, in order to ensure the soundness of the adoption, will want to carefully investigate whatever means they choose to pursue the adoption before making a commitment.

2. Adoptive parents can also make a contribution by participating in efforts to open adoption records. As Pavao (2005, p. 117) wrote, "Adopted people are the only citizens of the United States who do not have access to their original—and only true—birth certificates. This is a civil right." Access to birth certificates—whether an adoptee chooses to see it—is for many an essential element of their identity formation.

Furthermore, many of the fears about openness in general and open records specifically have been dispelled by research. For example, Carp (2007) describes a study of the effects of opening adoption records in the United States, Great Britain, and Australia from 1953 to 2007. He found that actual privacy violations were either exceedingly rare or nonexistent. He suggests the use of contact preference forms or contact vetoes to balance access to information with privacy rights. Currently, an effort is underway in many states to unseal adoption records. However, success is by no means assured. For example, in New Jersey, Governor Christie conditionally vetoed a bill to unseal adoption records so that birth mothers who were promised anonymity would have it preserved (Livio, 2011).

3. Related to the issue of sealed records is that of gathering and maintaining national statistics on adoption. Although statistics are required to be maintained on foster care and international adoptions, no similar mandate exists on other types of adoption (Haslanger & Witt, 2005). According to Biafora and Esposito (2007), "Very little progress has been made by federal authorities in capturing consistent and reliable data on the extent of formal adoptions processed privately or independently through adoption mediators" (p. 33). The absence of comprehensive statistics information about adoption renders difficult policy making and planning of resources for adoptive families. A recent achievement in the area of adoption is the development and administration of the National Survey of Adoptive Parents, which is "the first-ever large-scale, population-based survey regarding adopted children under age 18 that includes all adoption types in the United States in which neither of child's biological parents lives in the household: international adoptions, adoptions from the foster care system, and other domestic adoptions" (p. 293). This survey has yielded a treasure trove of data that continues to be mined.

4. The research is clear that the satisfactions of adoption for adoptive parents are enormous, but the challenges, real. The chapters of this book document many of these challenges, such as helping young children to form healthy attachments, assisting school-age children in coping with discrimination based on their status as minority group members, aiding older adopted children to overcome the effects of trauma, or supporting adolescents in identity development. Adoptive families benefit from access to resources in meeting these challenges. As has been said repeatedly in this book, funding for both pre-adoption education and postadoption services falls far short of meeting the needs of adoptive families. Research has shown that adoptive parent participation in both pre-adoption and postadoption educational and therapeutic experiences has a positive effect on outcome, and the reciprocal is also true. For example, Palacios, Sanchez-Sandoval, and Leon found that in 90% of intercountry cases of adoption disruption, pre-adoption education was absent. Adoptive parents may vary in terms of the specific resources needed. For example, a survey of gay and lesbian adoptive parents revealed a need for pre-adoptive counseling groups for those children about to be placed in a family (Brooks et al., 2012). These children would benefit from a forum in which to explore their reactions not only to the adoption itself but also their adoption by gay or lesbian parents. Collaboration is needed between adoption professionals and members of the kinship network in forging advocacy efforts to ensure that private and public funders recognize the criticalness of these resources.

5. Many children, especially those in the public system, need parents. Limiting parenthood based on variables such as the candidate's sexual orientation, marital status, and race reduces the potential for this need to be met and goes against an accumulating body of research on parenting effectiveness of particular groups subject historically to discrimination in the adoption process. For example, although gay and lesbian prospective parents continue to be the targets of discrimination, the research overwhelmingly shows that homosexual adoptive parents do not differ in their parenting behaviors from homosexual biological parents or heterosexual biological or adoptive parents, and that the adjustment levels of their children do not differ (Brodzinsky, Green, & Katuzny, 2012). Every adoptive parent has a stake in ensuring that those criteria that are used to screen applications for adoptive parenthood are relevant to parental effectiveness. Pertinent criteria support adoption success, which benefits all adoptive families. In some cases, the limiting factor in adoptions is money. Some foster parents who want to adopt do not do so because of lack of adequate state subsidies to enable this transition (Smith, 2010); necessary resources to make adoption possible.

Challenges to Parents' Assumption of Advocacy, Consultative, and Educational Roles

Assuming the roles of advocate, consultant, and educator, in addition to all of the other functions parents might perform, may be difficult. Among the obstacles to these activities are those residing within the parents, the parents' perceptions of their children, and the system in which these meta-parenting activities occur. First, for some parents, the demands of this role are at odds with their own personality styles. It requires a level of courage and willingness to buck what is normative. The other parties may well respond negatively to requests for some resources, sensitivity, or considerations. The challenge for the adoptive parent is to be tenacious despite initial negative responses. The parent also must often take on a different perspective from those offered by others. Sometimes the other people who are offering a given view are figures of authority—teachers, physicians, mental health workers, and so on. Not only does the advocacy role require a willingness to challenge these figures, but also to construct one's own truth about the situation, based on knowledge of one's own child and adoption phenomena. For some parents, having this intellectual independence may not come easily, depending on the stance a parent has taken toward authority figures in the past. Parents may also recoil from performing these functions because they are consumed with dealing with their own stress in relation to their child's engagement with are different systems. The Evan B. Donaldson Adoption Institute (2006) reports that adoptive parents experience considerable stress in dealing with their children's school lives. The institute's report documents the comment of one mother who had adopted several children from foster care, "It's a rare week when I don't get several calls from school complaining about at least one of my kids." Energy devoted to anxiety management can be diverted away from making an intervention in the school.

Sometimes advocacy is difficult because of the personality makeup or the developmental stage of the child. Parental assertiveness and advocacy can be an awkward and difficult role for a parent of a shy child. Such a child may resist parental intervention, and may see such effort as drawing unwanted attention to her differences and difficulties:

> While walking her dog as her mother watched nearby, 8-year-old Pamela, who was adopted when she was 8 months old, was stopped by a Caucasian woman. The woman asked, in a rather belligerent tone, if she were Japanese. Pamela diffidently responded,

"No, I am from Korea." The woman's retort was, "Doesn't matter: Asians are all the same." Pamela's mother could sense that Pamela did not want her to engage in a verbal confrontation. The mother chose to note quietly to the woman that no one should accost a young child on the street in that way and certainly not deliver an insulting and ethnically insensitive verbal comment. Following the interaction, the mother explained to Pamela how not everyone is as open to cultural and ethnic differences as her family is. She offered a forum to gently discuss views on adoption and prejudices and explain that it may happen again, but as a family, they would try to help people understand who they are.

In this vignette, the mother took into account the child's personality style while also offering her the protection she needed.

In adolescence, advocacy becomes a matter of particular sensitivity because this activity may be experienced as an affront to the young person's independence. Once again, parents need to inform their responses with an awareness of this developmentally expected stance. Parents at this point often do well to coach their child into becoming his or her own advocate. If the child has role models outside the family, this achievement may be facilitated as the child is exposed to a greater range of advocacy styles and behaviors. Such role models are likely to be especially effective if they, too, have been subjected to discrimination and have found ways to address it.

A third obstacle to special parenting roles adoption typically demands are provided by social institutions themselves. As noted previously, initial efforts to effect change may be unsuccessful, and when change bears some cost to institutions, the resistance to it is likely to be great. For example, employers realize that when maternity or paternity leave is expanded to include the provision of paid leave to adoptive parents to enable them to spend time with a newly adopted child, the organization will need to find alternate means to cover this employee's responsibilities. School districts seeking to address the cognitive needs of those adopted children who experienced trauma, deprivation, and poor nutrition must bear the expense for early screenings and assessments. As the Smith and Riley (2006) observes, often, these evaluations are done too late to be optimally useful. However, like individuals, institutions and organizations have emotional resistances to responsiveness to adoption issues. For example, parents seeking to have school districts respond with greater sensitivity to the emotional issues associated with adoption may need to have administrators and faculty members address their own attitudes toward a range of topics related to diversity.

PRACTICAL POINTS

- Therapists and adoptive parents must recognize that micro-aggressions are part of everyday interactions. Adoptive parents for their own well-being should develop strategies to handle these manifestations of bias toward adoptive children and families.
- Therapists should demonstrate empathy toward parents who are on the receiving end of these acts.
- To assist their children, adoptive parents should acquire the skills of being an advocate and an educator, and these skills should be deployed in a wide range of settings but primarily those in which the adoptive child and parents function.

CONCLUSIONS

Adoptive parents must continually attend to the broader environment in which their adopted child and their family reside. The reality of discrimination and prejudice that takes the form of micro-aggressions and stereotyping necessitates that the adoptive parent embrace the roles of educator, consultant, and advocate. We see in this chapter that parents' enactment of these roles must depend on context, that is, whether the venue for advocacy activity is the home, the school, the neighborhood, or the broader sociocultural environment. However, it is not sufficient for parents to perform tasks associated with these roles; Adopted children are often the targets of adoptism and ultimately will need to manage their own environments. Accordingly, parents must assist their children in learning self-advocacy through modeling, family discussion about prejudice and stereotyping, and, particularly when the child differs from the parents in race and cultural background, providing role models outside the family who share these identity features with the child.

The last chapter of this book develops further on what therapists and parents need to do to educate themselves fully on adoption. For therapists, this education is necessary to treat the adoptive parent successfully; for parents, it is needed to fully embrace the role of being an adoption advocate/educator. The authors also provide an extended study of an adoptive family to see in a more integrated way the role of intervention. Finally, the authors stand back and consider what research directions might be pursued that will benefit adoptive parents and the therapists who treat them.

NOTES

1. Occasionally positive stories do occur, such as the narrative by mother/author Kristin Gunst (2005). She describes her journey as a single mom adopting her second child from China. Yet, these stories, often authored by adoptive parents themselves, are rare even though the outcomes of most adoptions are positive for both adoptive parents and children.
2. Some children's literature makes an important contribution by correcting common but incorrect assumptions about adoptive families. For example, Valerie Westfall (author) and Richard Cowdrey's (illustrator) (2011) book for young children playfully and engagingly addresses the misconception that adoptive parents love their children less than biological parents. Other good suggestions for books for children of different ages can be found in Fishman and Harrington's (2007) chapter.
3. Dwyer and Gidluck (2009) make the interesting point that the Canadian teachers whom they encountered had a racially homogeneous peer group at work and therefore lacked the experiential basis to understand the plight of a child who is in a racial/ethnic group very different from his or her birth culture.
4. During the *Wendy Williams Show* on January 3, 2012, it was pointed out that Hollywood star Angelina Jolie, a mother parenting within a transracial family, had come under fire for her daughter's hair extensions. The show host, Wendy Williams, astutely observed that the criticism that the process of installing the extensions is too painful for young children had rarely been leveled against black parents. Williams's implication seemed to be that the criticism was at least in part a response to the transracial aspect of the adoption.
5. To keep abreast of new advocacy-related issues in adoption, the reader should consult the web page of the Adoption Institute at http://www.adoptioninstitute.org/index.php

Chapter 12

MEETING THE NEEDS OF ADOPTIVE PARENTS
Practice, Training, and Research

Patricia G. Ramsey, Virginia M. Brabender, and April E. Fallon

In this last chapter, we pull together much of what has been discussed in prior chapters by introducing the reader to an adoptive family, Danielle, Mark, and Ayana, and show them proceeding through various stages of adoptive parenthood. These three individuals represent compilations of various individuals we have treated, and their names are invented. We discuss the implications of their life circumstances for practice, training, and research.

PRACTICE

Throughout this text, we have offered brief vignettes, but thought for this last chapter, the reader might benefit from getting to know one particular family in greater depth. We illustrate some of the characteristic issues adoptive families experience over their lifetimes and the array of mental health resources that might be mobilized to help them successfully negotiate the challenges of different developmental periods. Four principles guide our analyses. First, adoptive parents are continually faced with the challenge of addressing differences, the difference between their child and themselves, their child and nonadopted children, and their family and nonadoptive families. Second, when adoptive families address the usual conflicts of a given developmental stage, adoption provides a unique twist. Third, mental health professionals cannot competently treat adoptive families without knowing a great deal about the dynamics of adoption. When uninformed therapists treat adoptive parents, they are likely to fall back on common misconceptions about adoption such as the common fallacy that children by virtue of adoption have greater psychopathology than biological children. Friedlander (2003, p. 751) wrote, "As professionals, we should at least be knowledgeable enough to do no harm." She went on to say that with knowledge, therapists could contribute significantly to the well-being of all members of the triad. Fourth, individuals treating adoptive parents must be ready to collaborate with other professionals. Rarely does a single type of assessment or intervention suffice.

Vignette 1

Danielle, a 33-year-old dentist, had been seeing her therapist for 2 years in psychodynamically oriented psychotherapy when she adopted a child from Ethiopia. At the time she began in individual treatment, she and her husband had gone through several years of unsuccessful fertility treatment. During her first year of treatment, she focused intensively on her experiences of loss in relation to the infertility. She explored how this loss re-evoked her feelings of loss in relation to the death of a sibling and her mother's miscarriage. Both events had occurred in the first 5 years of her life.

Throughout this period, Danielle considered the possibility of adopting a child. By the end of the first year of therapy, she and her husband had begun the adoption process. During her second year of therapy, she discussed her anxiety about whether she could love this child as much as a biological child. She also talked a great deal about her fears that her efforts to adopt would be no more successful than her efforts to conceive. She was terrified that her destiny was to be childless. She expressed worry about her mother's reaction to the adoption—she saw her mother's rather indifferent attitude toward the adoption as an expression of her continuing grief over her two deceased children. This supposition also angered Danielle in that it meant that her existence was insufficient to satisfy her mother.

Early into her third year of treatment, Danielle and her husband traveled to Ethiopia and brought home a 15-month-old baby girl whom they named Ayana. Initially, Danielle was excited and happy, but as the weeks wore on, she became unusually reticent and flat in treatment. When the therapist commented on this change, Danielle explained that she was extremely tired. She indicated that her baby was up for many hours of the night and couldn't get on a schedule. She felt that her exhaustion prevented her from fully enjoying her child. She also wondered whether her child was capable of forming an attachment to her. When Ayana became distressed, Danielle's efforts to soothe her seemed to intensify her crying and thrashing. After 3 months in the home, Ayana did not seem to prefer Danielle to other caregivers. She found herself being annoyed when Ayana appeared eager to go from her arms to those of another relative such as her mother-in-law. Sometimes she felt herself drawing back from Ayana when this occurred.

Danielle's fatigue was affecting her marriage: Her interest in having sexual relations with her husband had diminished considerably. She and her husband were bickering more than usual. Each night she was desperate to have him return from work, and, when he was late, she angrily confronted him.

Danielle reported that she was intensely aware of the reactions of others in the community to her child. She noticed people staring at her and the baby and believed it was because she was White and the child was Black. These reactions were even more pronounced when she and her also-White husband were with Ayana. She felt angry toward these people because she imagined they were thinking she was not entitled to have this child. Her associations led her and the therapist to see this suspiciousness as a punishment for bringing pleasure into her own life when her mother was many years later still suffering from the loss of two children.

Although the sessions seemed to be somewhat productive, Danielle's emotional flatness, so uncharacteristic of her, made the therapist wonder if she was missing something. She arranged to have a supervision session with a therapist whose practice included many individuals who were members of the adoptive triad. This supervisor also had written articles on adoption and was active within the adoptive community. The supervisor began the meeting by noting that adoptive parents are highly diverse in their reaction to infertility, adoption, and the unfolding events of parenting, and that it would be important to think about Danielle's unique responses. His initial observation was that Ayana seemed to be in a physiologically dysregulated state. In addition to the assistance Danielle was obtaining from psychotherapy, she also needed professional help in facilitating Ayana's adjustment to her new home. The supervisor recommended that the therapist help Danielle to identify postadoption services beyond the individual therapy to help her and her husband as different challenges arise. Also, the supervisor felt that an adoption specialist could coach Danielle to interact with Ayana in such a way that she would provide an optimal caregiving environment for an attachment to occur. The supervisor wondered if Ayana's early experiences with caregivers had undermined her ability to form a secure attachment. He suggested that Ayana's reactions to Danielle might be self-protective. If so, then Danielle needed to learn how to read Ayana's subtle cues of her longing for care even though they were masked by her apparent avoidance of it.

The supervisor also carefully reviewed with the therapist the material from the sessions. It was evident that, although Danielle's incapacity to have a biological child was a stunning disappointment, she had ceased to talk about this loss. He wondered if she felt that now that she had an adopted daughter, she was "prohibited" from feeling sad about her infertility. He noted that this denial might prevent her from fully embracing her maternal role with Ayana and contribute to her emotional flatness. The supervisor also wondered whether Danielle's inability to conceive a child with her husband had affected her construction of their relationship as defective or lacking in vitality.

The supervisor also reflected on Danielle's preoccupations with community members' reactions to the multiracial aspect of their family. He asked a number of questions, many of which the therapist had not considered. What were Danielle's thoughts and feelings about having a child of a different race? What had been Danielle and her husband's previous experience with Black individuals and the Black community? What thoughts did Danielle have about the integration of that child's heritage into the family's life? He gave the therapist of number of reading resources on this topic. He also suggested that she encourage Danielle to connect with other parents who had adopted children from Ethiopia and to learn about and perhaps contact Ethiopian communities in her area. He also explained that, although he could not with any confidence elucidate the meaning of Danielle's preoccupation that others were looking at the baby and her, he wondered if it were in part a projection of both her own attention to this aspect and to any attached feelings that are unacceptable to her. He wondered if Danielle was feeling guilty because she subconsciously believed that adoption was a kind of kidnapping.

Analysis of Vignette 1

The therapist in this vignette demonstrated an ethical attitude toward her own clinical work in that she recognized the limitations of her competence. As Porch (2007) described, this limitation is common among generalist mental health professionals. When the therapist recognized that the therapy was floundering, she sought the assistance of someone who could enable her to be more effective with Danielle. Yet, this therapist is like many others in not recognizing how both infertility and adoption affect parents over their lifetimes. Had she been aware of her limitations, she would have been more likely to obtain this supervision at an earlier point and possibly helped Danielle to circumvent some of the problems she encountered. In particular, during the pre-adoptive period, she could have helped Danielle to explore her feelings about race and the prospect of raising a black child and becoming a multiracial and conspicuous adoptive family.

The supervisor helped the therapist see that the sting of infertility or the pain of losing a biological child does not end with an adoption. In fact, even the birth of a biological child may not eradicate that conception of the inadequate self constructed after a period of infertility. Furthermore, as the supervisor wisely noted, infertility also can alter the internalized representation of the couple as a vital unit. At times, one partner may perceive him- or herself as inadequate and this self-scheme may camouflage a view of the couple as defective.

A particularly important contribution of the supervisor was to point out that Danielle and Mark had been insufficiently prepared for the responsibilities attached to transracial adoption, if they were prepared at all. He noted that although the therapist might be able to help Danielle address some transracial adoption issues, specific postadoption counseling for Danielle, Mark, and probably other family members would be critical in order for all of them to respond constructively to the multiracial identity of their family, and Ayana's complex identity. Furthermore, these concerns should be addressed as early as possible because they might influence major decisions in regard to where the family lives, where the child goes to school, and so on. Given that it is critical that children have healthy role models of their own race, it is vital that families live, work, and play in diverse settings where this is possible (Pavao, 2005).

In discussing Danielle's guilt, the supervisor was able to "normalize" these feelings by citing research that has found that many adoptive parents feel that they have done something illicit (Bonovitz, 2004). As Brabender, Swartz, Winzinger, and Fallon discuss in Chapter 4, adoptive mothers report that a component of this guilt in international adoptions is uprooting a child from his or her culture. However, as Bonovitz found, very often the guilt and shame attached to this perception are well sealed off from consciousness and emerge in other forms such as depression.

The supervisor noted that the kinds of issues Danielle was presenting in treatment could evoke a variety of reactions in the therapist. For example, the therapist herself was newly married and in the supervision sessions realized that Danielle's experiences with infertility aroused her own anxiety. The supervisor wondered whether the therapist's de-emphasis of infertility following the adoption was in part an effort to manage her own apprehensions. The supervisor pointed out that the therapist's reflections on her own ongoing reactions to the array of concerns that may be stimulated by adoption would enable her to serve her client most effectively (Grotevant, 2003).

The supervisor recommended to the therapist that Danielle and Mark take advantage of an array of resources, but in some areas, particularly rural, such resources are absent. Furthermore, obtaining more help with parenting typically requires spending additional money, which may be in limited supply especially after a family has borne the expenses of an adoption. Parents adopting from foster care, in contrast, often have access to subsidized postadoption counseling. It is at this juncture that good practice requires a commitment to advocacy. Clinicians can help adoptive parents and their child by lobbying third-party payers for coverage of postadoption counseling and related interventions.

Vignette 2

When Ayana was ready to enter grade school, her parents placed her in a private elementary school whose core values were acceptance and celebration of the diversities among human beings and maintaining a diverse student body. Ayana thrived in this setting, and did well academically. However, many of the parents, including Danielle and Mark, worried at times whether the curriculum was insufficiently challenging in math and the sciences. One day, Danielle was visiting her friend Harriet, a parent of another child in Danielle's class. The two girls were playing in the next room. The mothers were talking about the curriculum issue. Danielle said that although she had significant concerns about the curriculum, she was going to find her own means of supplementing Ayana's education. The other mother inferred that Danielle simply did not want to make the financial sacrifice to send her daughter to another school in the area, which was known to be both more rigorous and more expensive. She muttered, "I do understand. Blood is thicker than water." At first Danielle was perplexed by Harriet's statement. She explained that her reason for keeping her in the school was the large presence of many nontraditional families and many students of color, as well as the values of the institution. However, when she left, the impact of Harriet's comment hit her. She realized that Harriet had made other comments suggesting a negative attitude toward adoption such as repeatedly mentioned a news story she had heard about an adoption disruption. Danielle questioned whether she wanted to remain friends with a person harboring this attitude toward adoption.

Danielle was no longer in individual therapy. However, she did attend a support group for parents of adopted children. Many of the adoptions were international, and the several families were multiracial. At the meeting that occurred several days after the incident with Harriet, Danielle talked about how she had been upset and had been avoiding any interaction with Harriet. The other members of the group said that they had had many similar experiences and reflected that they were always more painful with someone who had appeared to have attitudes and values more aligned with their own. It was especially difficult when the person expressing such a sentiment was a friend. For all of the members it raised question about whether such friendships were worth maintaining.

Different members had a variety of responses to Danielle's story. However, three points of agreement were struck. First, members believed that the protection of Ayana was a fundamental responsibility. The fact that the parent of a friend exhibited a prejudicial attitude raised a red flag—would Ayana be subjected to an environment in which her esteem for herself was undermined rather than nourished? Second, members saw it as of utmost importance that Danielle protect her own parental self-regard. They noted that having one's parental commitment and generosity questioned over time would erode Danielle's positive view of herself as a parent. Third, members of the group observed that without corrective input, Harriet would express her attitudes to others and engage in behaviors consistent with those attitudes. Group members felt that in situations such as this one, parents have a responsibility to the broader community of parents and children who are affected by prejudicial views such as Harriet's. Members recommended that although Danielle had been quiet in the moment, she should create another opportunity to convey to Harriet her own view of adoption and the hurtfulness of Harriet's attitude. Danielle left the session feeling less alone and bolstered by the group support. She also was clearer about her options to address her conflict with Harriet.

Analysis of Vignette 2

For many adoptive parents, access to a group of individuals who are experiencing the same challenges is invaluable. Even had Danielle still been in individual treatment, she might not have found the solace that the parent group could provide. We have discussed elsewhere (Brabender, Fallon, & Smolar, 2004) that self-help groups and support groups are useful for treating an array of psychological problems. A self-help group is "a routinized meeting of people who are brought together by a common problem, heritage, or situation and who talk and learn from one another new perspectives on that identified problem" (p. 257). Because professionals are only minimally involved—if at all—this resource is often available at no or low cost. This factor can be particularly important for adoptive families who may, along the way, have had considerable expenses associated with the adoption itself or other health and educational services. Online self-help groups are also useful for families that live in geographically remote areas. However, online groups can involve some hazards (for example, having a member's personal information accessed by individuals outside the group; see Brabender, 2002, Chapter 8) that must be recognized prior to participation.

In the vignette, Danielle participated in a support group, which like a self-help group is composed of members who share a problem or situation—in Danielle's case, being parents within an adoptive family. However, support groups are different from self-help groups in that they typically have a professional leader. This arrangement carries the advantage that the professional can actively screen members. For example, the leader may compose a group of parents whose children are within a particular age range and present a common set of issues. In a support group, the professional leader can provide psychoeducational information concerning the challenges families typically face. For example, the leader could include a module on how to deal with racist, adoptist, or other discriminatory comments. Above all, though, support groups provide exactly that—support. Unlike traditional group psychotherapy in which clients' defenses may be challenged to enable them to achieve a new level of awareness, both support and self-help groups bolster members' existing resources (Kalodner & Hanus, 2010).

Although parents generally give their experiences in such groups positive ratings (Smith, 2010), one of the biggest problems with self-help and support groups is their lack of availability, especially in some geographic areas (Gailey, 2010). In one study, 33% of adoptive parents complained about the inaccessibility of an appropriate group (McDonald et al., 2001). Often, adoptive parents themselves must organize these and other supports such as respite care. Doing so has certain advantages such as the assurance that the group's structural features (e.g., time, meeting place) will be convenient for the organizers. The process of organizing a group may contribute to a sense of parental self-efficacy in that the parents are taking initiative in solving their own problems. Still, the lag time between when problems arise and the actual beginning of the group can create a gap during which adoptive parents are left to fend for themselves.

Vignette 3

When Ayana was 15, Danielle received a call from the school because a teacher had discovered that Ayana was carrying a drink that was both alcoholic and a soft drink in her backpack. This behavior was clearly in violation of school policy. Ayana was suspended from school and her parents were directed to pick her up immediately. Up until the present, Ayana had not shown any behaviors that brought her negative attention at school. However, her angry outbursts at home had prompted Danielle and Mark 3 months prior to this event to arrange for Ayana to have sessions with an adolescent psychotherapist with considerable experience in the area of adoption. Ayana valued her sessions with the therapist greatly.

After hanging up the phone, Danielle said to herself, "And now it begins." She saw a span of years extending before her in which such calls from the school would be routine. In fact, when she was contemplating adoption, many of her family members warned her that this kind of thing would occur. She imagined particular relatives assuming a self-satisfied, "I told you so" attitude. However, when she called Mark, he immediately recollected engaging in similar behaviors when he was Ayana's age and was less concerned. At the same time, he did feel that, in addition to discussing the incident with Ayana, they should apprise her therapist of its occurrence.

When Ayana was retrieved, she was initially hostile. Danielle became tearful, and Ayana also began to sob. She said she was just trying to fit in. Mark gently probed to find out whose acceptance she was seeking. Her first response of "everyone" narrowed eventually to a very specific group of teenage girls who were known to Danielle and Mark as troublemakers—girls who had been suspended from school before and who were reputed to have had some brushes with the law. By virtue of the geographic area in which they resided, Danielle and Mark also knew that they came from a lower socioeconomic stratum than most of the families in the community including Danielle and Mark's. The girls were of varied races but all members of minority groups, in contrast to Ayana's typically more heterogeneous group of friends.

A family meeting was held with Ayana's therapist. Ayana talked about how when she was with her friends that her parents knew and liked, a part of herself remained hidden. She spoke of her admiration of the more daring group who appreciated those hidden parts of herself. She talked about how these girls did not completely accept her although they affectionately teased her for being a wholesome athlete. She said she wanted to shed this image and be more herself. She had wanted to ask her parents if she could have body piercings but she knew that they would respond negatively.

As part of Ayana's treatment, the therapist at times met with Ayana's parents separately, and she did so on this occasion. Whereas Danielle expressed great alarm at this recent development, Mark was dismissive, still connecting the events to his own youthful indiscretions. Some tension was present within this couple because of the disparity in their reactions. The therapist took a position that was different from each of their stances. She talked about Ayana's process of identity formation, which was well underway during this developmental period. It seemed that Ayana had internalized many of her adoptive parents' values, interests, and moral principles. The therapist wondered whether a part of Ayana that she saw as hidden was that part connected to her birth family, a question that the therapist would keep in mind during her sessions with Ayana. At this point in the conversation, Danielle recalled a reality TV show that fascinated Ayana. It was about unmarried teen mothers who attempted to raise their babies but struggled with various problems such as drug addiction, minor theft, and tumultuous relationships with boyfriends. Ayana remarked to Danielle, "So that's what my birth mother was like." Danielle tried to engage Ayana in a conversation about that connection, but Ayana told her mother to "lighten up" and said, "I was only kidding." Danielle said she did not pursue the topic further but wondered if she should have and was glad that the therapist would explore this subject with Ayana.

Analysis of Vignette 3

Although virtually all parents would be unhappy at receiving this call from the school, for adoptive parents, such an event can be especially anxiety-arousing because a pronatalist society primes them to expect that their children will have behavioral difficulties. The theoretical perspective from which the Adoptive Child Syndrome (Kirschner, 1990) derives—the view that adopted children are doomed to develop severe psychological difficulties—may be seductive to parents in its simplicity, but ultimately handicaps them in recognizing and implementing sensitive and constructive interventions. Ayana's situation requires that parents grapple with complexity. In seeing Ayana's behavior as a manifestation of adolescent phenomena, Mark is correct. However, if that view leads to a dismissal of her actions as mere youthful restiveness, then, Ayana's parents might miss the possible struggles underlying her behaviors. Danielle's fatalistic stance—her sense that her worst fears were finally being realized—might promote hopelessness rather than a commitment to problem solving. It is at this juncture that a therapist knowledgeable about adoption issues can help to foster calm as parents, child, and therapist work together to understand the meaning of the behaviors at issue. Certainly were the therapist to take on a merely problem-solving, behavioral, or psychoeducational approach without helping the family to understand the meaning of Ayana's behavior, that therapist would be unlikely to meet the family's psychological needs. Fortunately, the therapist understood the complexity of possible underlying motivations and was able to help the parents understand and respond more effectively.

Because of her expertise on adoption, the therapist could also educate school personnel about the relationship between Ayana's behaviors and the psychological issues with which she is grappling. At times, part of the therapist's role is to help school personnel to be more empathic of the adoptive adolescent's experiences, even amidst any of their misdeeds. If the school officials, including the counseling staff, merely take a punitive orientation toward behaviors such as those Ayana manifested, she could point out that suspension and expulsion often trigger adoptees' deep fears of abandonment and rejection. Furthermore, in interpreting these explorations as simply bad behavior, the school personnel might be undermining Ayana's efforts to form a more complete identity. The therapist might work with school staff to think beyond the usual punitive approaches to these infractions and come up with a restitution model to foster rather than disrupt connections. For example, Ayana might "give back to the school" and connect with a wider range of peers by participating in community service.

Vignette 4

Now Ayana is 16 and she is beginning to be increasingly curious about her country of origin and her birth family. She tells Mark that she is yearning to go to Ethiopia and see if she can find her birth mother. She tells him that she has not told Danielle because she believes it will hurt her too much. Mark gently tells her that he believes Danielle is prepared for this possibility. After Ayana agrees to have a conversation with her mother with Mark present, he wonders if Danielle is as fully prepared as he said she was, and how this next phase of their family life will unfold. He also wonders if this might not be a good time to contact an adoption specialist not simply to work with Ayana but also them. Ayana proceeds to tell Danielle about her interest and Danielle responds with such enthusiasm that Mark perceives it as a false response. He notes that since Ayana made this communication, he has been beset by many worries about possible negative outcomes. When Mark presents Danielle with the possibility of seeing the adoption specialist, Danielle expresses relief. Several days later, they meet with the specialist, who sees the family together, Ayana separately, and Mark and Danielle separately. During the couple meeting, the adoption specialist helps Danielle and Mark realize that the feelings they are having are normal and expected. She helps the family to get a realistic view of what is involved and the roles that they might play. She talks about the writings of Pavao (2005) on this topic, who counsels parents to serve not as the director of the search but rather as an administrative assistant to the child who can thereby take ownership of this initiative.

Analysis of Vignette 4

Ayana's interest in searching for her birth mother is common among adoptees. Muller and Perry (2001a,b) wrote that at least half of all adopted children engage in a search. However, according to the Child Welfare Information Gateway (2004), this number appears to be on the rise. Given the attention the media has given to the search process, many more adoptees may be interested in searching. Searches may also be spurred by the positive outcomes that researchers have found in connection with adopted children's contact with birth parents. For example, Mendenhall, Berge, Wrobel, Grotevant, and McRoy (2004) found that adolescents who had contact with their birth mothers and birth fathers expressed a higher level of satisfaction with the degree of contact than those who did not.

If Danielle took advantage of the different types of resources offered to her by her therapist, she probably was in a favorable position to receive Ayana's news of her interest in a search. One very positive effect of getting postadoption counseling in the early years following the adoption is that adoptive parents can recognize its helpfulness and make use of it again as new issues arise during childhood, pre-adolescence, and adolescence. For many reasons, counseling by an adoption specialist is highly desirable at this time, not only for the adoptive parent but also for the family. Many fine sources are available to help the adoptive parents work with their child and to take care of themselves during the search process.

Even as Danielle and Mark assist Ayana in searching, they will have their own feelings with which to reckon, and these feelings may be strong and volatile and differ across individuals and situations. At times, the parents may feel curiosity and excitement as they anticipate meeting individuals who are their kin via their child. Yet, they may be anxious that the search will not consummate in a reunion and concerned about how that outcome might affect their child. If the search does lead to a reunion, they may also be afraid that they will have to compete with the birth parents for their child's attachment and affection and may resent having to share their child.[1] One large-scale study in Great Britain (Triseliotis, Feast, & Kyle, 2005) obtained findings that would be reassuring to Danielle and Mark: The vast majority of adoptive parents did not feel that their relationship with their child was undermined by the child's contact with birth parents. The adoption specialist aware of such findings can share them with the parents.

Vignette 5

Mark, now 85, was predeceased by Danielle. Two years following Danielle's death, Ayana was concerned about the fact that her dad had not returned to his "usual self." He seemed withdrawn and listless. In his interactions with his grandchildren, this normally effervescent grandfather seemed to be going through the motions. Although Mark put up some resistance, Ayana was eventually successful in getting him to speak to a therapist. The therapist learned that Mark had had a good deal of career success and had a rich and loving relationship with Danielle. He missed her greatly. However, with time he admitted that he continually dwelt on events associated with their efforts to conceive a child. He lamented the fact that he had never had testing at the time that he and Danielle were trying to conceive. The results of her fertility testing were inconclusive; she had wanted him to be tested but he refused for reasons that he himself could not identify. Now he realized that he had been afraid to learn that he was sterile, a fact he would have found intolerably emasculating. He felt that he allowed his wife to bear all of the pain associated with their inability to conceive.

An additional source of pain was even more difficult for Mark to contemplate. He felt a kind of despair in confronting his mortality in the context of not having a child who would take his family lineage into the future. He experienced this failure as a betrayal of his own father. At the same time, he regarded these feelings as contemptible. His relationships with Ayana, her husband, and his two grandchildren were precious to him. In longing for a biological child, he saw himself also betraying them. Ayana's tenderness during his struggles after Danielle's death merely intensified his guilt and remorse. He could only imagine Danielle's reaction had she known what he was feeling at this time.

Mark's treatment lasted 6 months. His work largely entailed becoming more fully cognizant of the feelings he was attempting to suppress and realizing that rather than making him a morally deficient person, they simply represented aspects of his humanity. He was able to go on enjoying fully his relationships with Ayana, his son-in-law, and their children, knowing that everyone experiences disappointments in life, and he was no different.

Analysis of Vignette 5

This vignette makes the important point that infertility and adoption can influence one's entire life. As Pavao wrote, "Adoption is not a snapshot in time. It is a moving picture that goes on through life and into the ones that follow" (2005, p. xi). This observation is no less true for adoptive parents than adopted children. Abundant research (see Chapter 1) shows the satisfactions of being an adoptive parent are great. However, the losses attached to infertility do not end with adoption but can remain throughout an individual's life. Although the nature of the loss may distinguish adoptive parents from nonadoptive parents, most parents experience some feelings of regret or loss. As Erikson (1950/1995) stated, in a person's later years a reflection on one's life is quite natural. Some elderly parents may feel disappointed that they had a son not a daughter or vice versa; they may regret that they were too busy or lived too far from their children to be close to their grandchildren; they may have concerns about their children's lifestyle choices. Therapists who are well versed in adoption issues can help adoptive parents identify and make peace with lingering or resurgent feelings of loss.

In the next section, we offer some counsel to deepen the therapist's training in this area and reiterate some of the major themes in the book.

TRAINING

The vignettes in this chapter and many others in this book illustrate that therapists working with adoptive parents and any other members of the adoption triad must have an in-depth understanding of the dynamics of adoption. Unfortunately, this aspect of family work and counseling is often overlooked in training programs. Recently one of my students and I (PR) went to the websites of 154 graduate programs, including those offering PhDs and PsyDs in counseling and clinical psychology, masters in social work, and degrees in marriage and family counseling. We included major public and private universities and made sure to have at least two programs from each state. We explored each website, looking at course offerings and at areas of concentration to see if the word *adoption* came up. To our surprise, only one university (University of Massachusetts in Amherst, home of the Rudd Adoption Research Center) had a course on adoption or mentioned adoption as a concentration. Other institutions may have incorporated adoption issues into their curricula, but although they often mentioned other specialties, adoption was not among them.

In contrast, many institutions and community organizations offer in-service adoption training programs for professionals in the field. These typically range from a few sessions to a semester-long course (Porch, 2007). In a 2003 report, the Casey Family Services listed several adoption training options for practitioners. However, few of these programs are affiliated with preservice graduate programs. Thus, practicing therapists who may have already solidified their clinical worldview and strategies can add some new information about adoption issues, but students are not learning these perspectives as part of their basic understanding of development and families.

All of the aforementioned studies support the premise on which this book is based: Training in adoption is extremely inadequate for the generalist practitioner. We hope that this book has made a start in addressing the need for the generalist mental health practitioner. Yet no one book can suffice, and, for the reader who would like to delve further, we would like to offer some direction. Our other purpose in this section rests on a point that we made in Chapter 1: Ultimately, the practitioner needs to take into account the perspectives of all members of the triad, even if he or she is working only with one member. Therefore, at this time, we broaden our scope to include the triad. We present the following material with the hope that practitioners will advocate for this type of training and that academicians will develop courses along the lines that we describe. The reader should note that although the following suggestions are specific to adoptive families, they also are relevant to working with clients dealing with an array of complex family situations (see Lamb's [1999] discussion of a range of such nontraditional family constellations).

Becoming Knowledgeable Adoption Practitioners

What does the general practitioner need to know to work competently with adoptive parents and potentially other members of the triad? First, all practitioners should have a comprehensive understanding of child, adolescent, and adult development. These courses should include in-depth discussions about how adoption-related losses and identity issues are manifested at different stages so that mental health professionals can help parents interpret and understand their children's behaviors from that perspective. Not only will this information help parents to respond more effectively, it will also provide information to use for advocating for their children if they encounter conflicts at schools and other institutions. Furthermore, this comprehensive background will enable therapists to provide guidelines and suggestions to parents about how to talk with their children about their adoptions at different life stages as described by Brodzinsky (2011). As seen in the vignettes in this chapter and others, adoption issues shift as children go through different developmental stages, and parents and practitioners need to understand how to interpret and respond to them. For example, Ayana's interest in searching for her birth family as a young adult is different from a 5-year-old child who wants to return to her or his birth family "because they would let me get that video game."

To respond to the particular needs of adoptive parents, courses on adult development should include a strong focus on parenting in complex families, and the impact of adoption on parents. For example, many older persons whose children cannot parent their offspring may suddenly find themselves raising their grandchildren. In many cases, they have to rapidly reorient their lives and, at a point when they may have been looking forward to retirement, assume the responsibilities of one or more young children. In a contrasting example, highly educated people accustomed to controlling their worlds are confounded when things "go off track" and are beyond their abilities to organize and manage. While many families face disruptions (e.g., divorce, job loss, illness of a child), almost all adoptive parents, like Danielle and Mark, have to deal with infertility, the pre-adoptive "hoops" that parents have to go through, and the lack of control about when and how the adoption will occur. In some cases they also have to adjust to their children's psychological or physical problems that are either obvious at the time of adoption or emerge during childhood and adolescence. As with grandparent adoptions, these challenges often require a basic reorientation of parents' expectations.

In one study (Bergen & Ramsey, 2010b), many parents talked about their dismay when the gap between their educational aspirations for their children and their children's academic abilities and interests widened over the years. They described how they had struggled to adjust their expectations and to support their children finding and following paths, often different from those taken by their parents and other family members. Likewise some parents struggle to come to terms with emotional and behavioral issues that are far more extreme than those they had expected, based on their own lives. For example, in Chapter 4 the adoptive mother Camilla found it to be unimaginable that her teenage daughter would steal her jewelry. One of the authors of this chapter (PR) is a member of an adoptive parent group that has been meeting for 10 years. We are a self-selected group, and most of our children (adopted from foster care and through private international and domestic agencies) have faced significant challenges. All of us are highly educated professionals, and, as our children have grown up, we have gone down paths that have taken us far from the worlds where we grew up and expected to raise our children. We were not prepared to deal with the juvenile and adult justice systems, school failure and expulsion, and, most recently, raising or helping to raise the offspring of our adolescent and young adult adopted sons and daughters. We are grateful to have each other because our extended family members, friends, colleagues, and even therapists often cannot see beyond their own shock and dismay, and their advice and condolences seem naive and patronizing.

Thus, when learning about adult development, future clinicians need to understand how adoption, even before it occurs, can undermine adoptive parents' confidence and sense of control. They need to have well-honed strategies to prepare parents to face unexpected and sometimes frightening situations and to provide realistic advice and support to help parents to gain confidence and skills in the face of many challenges.

Many of the problems that adoptive families face reflect the racial, cultural, and economic inequities of our society (Baden, 2007; Gailey, 2010). Therapists should have courses or workshops that involve in-depth analyses of how those divisions and inequities are perpetuated and how they influence all members of the adoptive kinship network. In terms of race, they need to be able to help parents understand white privilege and how that makes it difficult for white people, including adoptive parents, to understand the experiences of people of color and transracial adoptees in particular (see Chapter 6). Danielle's surprise about how the members of the community reacted to the fact that her child was a different race than her adoptive parents illustrates how white privilege can limit parents' awareness of the struggles their children may face. In Chapter 11, a situation was described in which Shelley and Ed's relatives questioned why they adopted Roberto, a Hispanic child. In another vignette in that chapter, a neighbor woman told 8-year-old Pamela that being Korean as opposed to Japanese is a meaningless distinction. Such micro-aggressions are common occurrences in the lives of adoptive families and adoptive parents need help in coping with them. In a recent study of adult transracial adoptees (Green & Ramsey, 2010), several participants noted that their parents had good intentions but did not understand their experiences as people of color. One reported that she was very close with her parents but also felt a distance from them because they were not aware of the hardships she faced as a racial minority in her school. "White people in general are not aware of the kind of racism and prejudices that exist in the world because they . . . never feel it, but I think my parents grew to understand . . . there was a lot more to it than a lot of other people think." Had her parents been better prepared to recognize and talk about racism, they would have been able to provide more timely and meaningful support and validation.

In terms of culture, parents who adopt internationally or from different domestic cultural groups often rely on a few short-term cultural exposures (e.g., culture camps, adoption agency "Latino Days," a few films and books) that acknowledge children's birth culture but do not provide the skills to support developing an integrated adoptive-birth identity (McGinness et al., 2009). One Korean adoptee in the Green and Ramsey (2010) study described learning about traditional Korean crafts as "just kind of . . . fake. Because . . . none of the modern Asian people I had met actually did any of that stuff." Therapists can help parents recognize the depth and pervasiveness of cultural differences and to accept their own limitations to impart authentic cultural values and day-to-day cultural information and skills. They can encourage parents to support their children's identity by providing access to skills and knowledge that may facilitate connections (e.g., taking classes in the language of their birth country, joining local groups from their birth country, and, when feasible, traveling to their homeland) (McGinness et al., 2009).

Therapists also need to understand how economic disparities shape experiences and decisions of birth and adoptive families and how they cast a long shadow on adoptees and their families (Gailey, 2010). Many adolescent adoptees distress their parents by befriending the wrong crowd, who are often from low-income families (Pavao, 2005, p. 69). As young adults, they may pursue lifestyles that replicate the experiences of their birth parents (e.g., poverty, abusive relationships, early pregnancies, illegal activities). These choices often represent an intersection of economics, race, and culture. For example, an adoptee from Latin American may be drawn to a Latino gang in a poor neighborhood. Ayana's desire to be part of a more daring crowd and to drink with them suggests this attraction. Rather than just wringing their hands about their children's bad decisions or assuming that their children are inherently pathological, adoptive parents need to understand how their children may experience the contradictions and tensions between the relative affluence of their adoptive families and the poverty of most of their birth families. Therapists can help parents see these behaviors in the context of economic inequities and as responses to guilt and/or the need to belong and feel affirmed.

In addition to understanding the developmental and societal contexts of adoption, therapists need to be aware of the particular clinical issues related to adoption. Porch (2007) lists the following clinical issues that affect all members of the adoptive triad: *loss, identity, variability of experience, acknowledgment of difference between adoptive and biological families*, and *stigmatization of adoption.* We briefly discuss each of these issues below in terms of adoptive parents but want to emphasize that each has multiple dimensions and affects all members of the adoption triad. In terms of optimal training, these issues need to be woven into both developmental and clinical courses and workshops so that practitioners understand them as "normative" adoption challenges and learn effective strategies to support adoptees and their families to move through crises and to emerge with more resilience and better coping skills. The reader will note that this list echoes many of the themes that have emerged in this book.

Loss is a basic reality for all members of the adoptive triad. Furthermore, as Brodzinsky (2011) points out, it is a unique loss because "it is not a permanent form of loss, such as death" (p. 204) and as a result it "too often goes unrecognized by society" (p. 204). As a result, adoptees may fantasize about what life might have been like with their birth families and may not resolve the loss or attach fully to their adoptive parents. Moreover, they may hear from teachers, friends, and family members that they should feel grateful for being adopted, rather than being supported to acknowledge and express their grief at losing their birth family. As we saw in the case of Danielle, adoptive parents too have significant losses, including infertility, disappointment at not raising their "own" children, and adjusting their expectations to accommodate the needs and interests of their adopted children (as mentioned earlier). They also may find it challenging to respond effectively to some of the destructive ways that their sons and daughters express their own losses (e.g., for example, in Chapter 4, one set of parents struggled with their child lying to her teacher, another with bullying behavior on the playground). Therapists can help parents reinterpret their children's behavior and depersonalize it as well as gain confidence and skills to raise difficult children (Casey Family Services, 2003). As an example of how this work may be done, practitioners at the Center for Adoption Support and Education (CASE) in Maryland work intensively with children to help them "understand and manage their feelings of grief and loss" (Casey Family Services, 2003, p. 41) and with their parents "to work through their own struggles of lost dreams and feelings of shame and guilt" (p. 41).

Forming a coherent and integrated *identity* is a challenge for many adoptees who may feel torn between their birth and adoptive families and, in some cases, between their birth and adoptive race, culture, and social class allegiances. As one transracial adoptee said, "If you're adopted . . . your whole life is like a jigsaw puzzle . . . you're always trying to put the pieces together and . . . there are always pieces missing" (Green & Ramsey, 2010). As noted in Chapters 4 and 9, adoptive parents need to understand this process so that they can facilitate the many steps that their sons and daughters may go through during this complex journey and not personalize what may seem to be rejection (e.g., searching for their birth families, temporarily living with other families, joining unfamiliar peer groups). In addition to responding to these challenges, adoptive parents also need to develop their identities that may take them in new directions. Parents who adopt transracially, internationally, or both need to see themselves as members of multiracial and multicultural families. Many parents go on to express these identities and solidarity with their children by becoming activists in social justice movements. Those whose children are struggling emotionally or academically need to redefine themselves as parents of children with special needs and learn to be strong advocates for their children. Henderson (2007) notes that the mental health and academic communities have neglected adoption issues in part to deny the racial, cultural, and social class divisions in our society. However, doing so has left practitioners ill equipped to address the psychological needs of all members of the triad.

Variability of experience and *acknowledgment of difference between adoptive and biological families* are really two sides of the same coin and so are discussed together. All individuals have unique histories and needs, and this is true of adoptees and their parents. At the same time, therapists need to be aware that there are specific challenges that adoptive families face, as described earlier. Moreover, evidence suggests that parents should be open about discussing these differences with their children but not to overemphasize them (Porch, 2007). Training for mental health professionals should include case studies and other experiences that will help them learn how to tease out which behaviors or psychological issues are related to adoption and which ones are not. They should also gain skills in helping parents see these distinctions and find effective ways to respond and, when appropriate, discuss them with their children (see Brodzinsky, 2011).

Stigmatization of adoption shows up in many forms in the popular media—from fairy tales about abandonment and evil stepparents to current television shows that glorify birth family reunions. Interestingly, rosy images of adoption as the perfect happy ending are also featured in stories and media. Both of these portrayals obscure the complexities of adoption and potentially create problems for adoptees and their parents. As discussed in Chapter 11, in our society that values blood ties, adoption is often seen as second best (Fisher, 2003; Palacios, 2009). Adoptees are viewed with suspicion because of their unknown and possibly shameful past, and adoptive parents are pitied for their infertility and failure to be "real" parents (Porch, 2007). Transracial adoptees may suffer from double stigmatization if they are also facing racist attitudes in their schools and communities. At the other extreme, overly positive portrayals may pressure adoptive families and engender feelings of failure if their experiences do not live up to these romanticized images. Therapists need to be able to help adoptive parents understand how they may have internalized negative stereotypes or unrealistic expectations and how those may be affecting their abilities to parent and their relationships with their children.

Training Processes

In terms of specific training experiences, these developmental, societal, and clinical perspectives need to be woven into all courses and internships in social work and clinical and counseling psychology programs. Moreover, students should have the opportunity to learn first-hand about the experiences and perspectives of all members of the adoption triad in class discussions and in their clinical internships. Reading some of the excellent books written by adoptees and more recently adoptive and birth parents is another way of learning about how individuals experience adoption different ways. Visiting blogs, chat rooms, and websites that are sponsored by different adoption groups is another strategy. Although not "scientific evidence," these sources provide insights into how adoption has affected and continues to influence the lives of all members of the adoption triad. To understand the adoption experience, students should also observe and then participate in counseling sessions with different members of the triad at all stages of the relinquishment and pre- and postadoption process and do clinical work with a wide range of adoptive families.

In addition to learning about adoption and related issues, trainees also need to understand that adoption services go well beyond individual therapy and a specific period of time. First, any work with adoptive parents will probably involve other family members at some point, so therapists should be skilled at providing family therapy or able to work closely with colleagues who can. Second, as illustrated in the vignettes in this chapter and others, adoption issues are lifelong and clients may need extended services or may frequently return for a few sessions as issues arise. Pavao describes this pattern as a "brief long-term therapy model" (2007, p. 284). For these reasons, practitioners should assist parents in obtaining ongoing assistance through parent support groups. As described earlier, these groups, whether they are online or in person, are cost-effective and many parents report that they are a "life-savers" because they help to normalize adoptive experiences and provide genuine support and useful advice (Casey, 2003). Third, therapists need to be able to work with a range of practitioners because families in crisis may need intensive, comprehensive, "wrap-around" services in order to avoid adoption disruptions (e.g., respite care and intervention or coordination with schools, foster care and juvenile justice systems, treatment centers, hospitals, and other agencies) (Casey, 2003). Fourth, to get needed services, practitioners may need to become advocates or to encourage parents to play that role (see Chapter 11). Finally, they need to be prepared to provide consultation or training to other professionals such as teachers and school counselors to help create adoption-sensitive environments for adoptees and their families.

RESEARCH

The very human struggles of adoptive families should be the impetus to the research that is done in this area. The story of Danielle and Mark has significance for what problems adoption researchers might address to serve the well-being of the adoptive families these characters represent. Knowledge of such looming questions also helps practitioners because it enables them to identify what might be understandable gaps in their ability to grasp the family's dynamics. We recognize that our vignette cannot possibly represent adoptive families in their great variety. Yet, two questions we might extract from Danielle and Mark's story would seem to have applicability to a great range of adoptive families.

First, we might observe that although Danielle was in therapy, she did not access postadoptive services until she was prompted by her therapist to do so. Questions arise as to whether some of the difficulties that Danielle experienced might have been anticipated before Ayana entered the home so that she might have had the necessary assistance in dealing with the issues Ayana presented. Presumably, Danielle and Mark proceeded through an evaluation to establish their adequacy to be adoptive parents. Future research might investigate the potential of assessment data not only to establish parental fitness to adopt but also to identify potential challenges parents may face, and strengths on which they may capitalize. A comprehensive personality assessment yields a wealth of information relevant to parenting. A prime example of such a feature is attachment style (see Chapter 3). We know from the literature that many children such as Ayana who are adopted when they are older than 1 year have not achieved a secure attachment style, one possible consequence of which may be a lack of the usual attachment behaviors more securely attached infants manifest. Indeed, Ayana initially rejected, at least apparently, Danielle's attempts to nurture her. In addition to her other psychological burdens such as her sadness over her infertility, Danielle may have had attachment issues that made it especially difficult to cope with Ayana's apparent preference for other figures. If these had been identified in advance, Danielle might have received very specific psychological coaching that might have lessened the stress placed on all family members.[2] However, additional information beyond attachment style can be useful in assisting parents, such the adoptive parent's capacity to engage in self-reflection[3] and his capacity for affect management.

Such information obtained prior to adoption placements might help to develop a more detailed picture of adoptive bonding and attachment. Bowlby and Ainsworth and their followers have provided us with a wealth of information about the ontogeny of the normal attachment process. We have little information about how the bond occurs when adoption occurs after the first year. Thus, we do not know how this process proceeds, if it follows a "normal" course but is simply delayed, or if it follows a somewhat different route. In this book, we have described research efforts (Suwalsky, Hendricks, & Bornstein, 2008; Swartz et al., 2012) that explores bonding and attachment processes in adoptive families, but these are fledgling efforts. With the late-placed adoptees (5 years and above) and kinship adoption, which often occurs even later, what can we expect? Research can guide our work with adoptive parents from these latter groups and can help them adjust their assumptions and expectations about what and how attachment might evolve as well as activities that might enhance the process. With later adoptions, the child is likely to have developed an attachment style in relationship with a prior parental figure. If adoptive parents have a different style, how will this disparity affect the transition and bonding process?

Second, the question of how professionals can most effectively support adoptive parents through the vicissitudes of contemplating an adoption, preparing for it, and raising their adoptive child through all of the developmental phases of childhood, adolescence, and young adulthood, demands further exploration. We saw in this vignette that Danielle and Mark made use of a variety of supports and services from differently credentialed professionals. During different phases of Ayana's childhood and adolescence, the resources they tapped changed. Other adoptive families may have made different choices based on their views of what is helpful, but their access to resources may be limited by geography, income, and other factors. For example, some adoptive parents meet their psychological needs by obtaining help from an adoption specialist, a person who has training in all core adoption-related areas. Others are treated by individuals who are generalist practitioners but with some training in adoption. Still others pursue help through work with professionals with little or no background in adoption. Evidence is needed on the outcomes associated with each of these choices so that parents can make informed choices and graduate programs can provide optimal training for professionals.

Likewise, like Danielle, some adoptive parents take advantage of support groups or self-help groups. A comparison of the relative merits of group versus individual interventions would also be useful. Also it would be helpful to compare groups with and without professional leaders and online versus face-to-face groups. In addition, do interventions informed by different theoretical models (for example, psycho-dynamic versus cognitive-behavioral) lead to varied outcomes? A recent report of the Evan B. Donaldson Institute (Smith, 2010) strongly advocated for rigorous evaluation of postadoption interventions.

In considering treatment effectiveness, researchers would do well to recognize the multiple facets of adoptive parents' identities. Adoptive parents differ from one another in terms of race, ethnicity, sexual orientation, marriage status, religion and spirituality, education, political views, immigration status, and age at the time of the adoption, to name a few. The families of adoptive parents also vary on types of adoptions: transracial versus same-race, intercountry versus domestic, foster care versus private, kinship versus out of family, and open versus closed. Moreover, some have biological children whereas others do not. These variations affect the services that parents need. For example, what works well for a white upper middle-class gay couple who adopted a child through the foster care system may not be useful for a middle class straight African American woman who adopted a relative. When studying outcomes of different resources, researchers should take care not to extrapolate beyond the groups studied. However, ideally, research designs should aim to capture possible interactions between various approaches and adoptive parent characteristics.

Third, transracial/transcultural families such as Danielle and Mark's could benefit from further empirical study of the ways in which adoptive parents can assist their children in integrating all aspects of their multiple and complex identities. Within the literature, many different means are suggested. They differ in type and intensity. Adoptive parents need to know whether some efforts are broadly more beneficial than others, and to what extent the usefulness of any particular type of exposure or immersion is dependent on the characteristics of the parents, the child (for example, personality features and developmental stage), and the natal culture itself.

Fourth, adoption is a lifelong process, and its meaning changes for all members of the triad and the entire adoptive kinship network over time. For Mark, the resurgence of feelings of loss in relation to biological offspring evoked guilt in relation to Ayana. Although the literature contains some anecdotal evidence such as that which we have provided, the organized empirical study of common challenges and issues that may exist for adoptive parents beyond the years of active child rearing has yet to take place. With greater knowledge, human service professionals could help adoptive parents to anticipate possible reactions, an anticipation that can lessen the capacity of such feelings to undermine the adoptive parent's well-being. When problems do arise, greater knowledge of their scope and character could aid professionals in being responsive to the needs of adoptive parents as they advance in age and proceed through the later stages of human development.

PRACTICAL POINTS

- Therapists working with adoptive parents must recognize that each stage of childhood is likely to evoke a special set of reactions and concerns, which may be beneficially explored in treatment.
- Likewise, therapists should appreciate that within each stage of the adoptive parent's adult life, infertility and adoption have changing meanings.
- Therapists are best able to treat adoptive parents successfully when they know the limits of their own competence and have a readiness to refer parents to modalities and specialists who are best equipped to address different aspects of the parents' problems and dilemmas.
- Therapists perform a service to adoptive parents when they advocate for a greater coverage of adoption-related topics in graduate curricula.

CONCLUSIONS

Overwhelmingly, adoptive parents express satisfaction with their lives and with their relationships with their adoptive children (Gailey, 2010; Smith, 2010). Most adoptive parents say that they would make the decision to adopt, and to adopt the same child, even when they were faced with significant challenges over the course of that child's development. Part of the reason that adoptive parents fare well is because of the prodigious resources they bring to the parenting endeavor (see Chapter 1). Still, their journey could be eased and the frequency of negative outcomes such as adoption disruptions could be lowered through advances in training, practice, and research. As assessment models include personality information such as the adoptive parents' attachment style, capacity for mentalization, and affect regulation, we might be able to customize pre-adoption and postadoption services based on the unique needs of each parent. Within this framework, the goal of assessment then becomes not merely identifying individuals who would not make good adoptive parents but in effectively preparing those who are approved to take this important step. With advances in research and professional training, adoptive parents will have greater access to providers who are knowledgeable about adoption. Practitioners, in turn, will have access to counseling and treatment strategies that are based on sound research. Furthermore, they will be able to adapt them to work effectively with a wide range of adoptive parents who, along with their sons and daughters, are developing complex identities.

NOTES

1. In the poignantly instructive DVD *First Person Plural*, written, produced, and directed by Deann Borshay Liem (2002), Deann's adoptive mother talks about the fear of losing Deann on anticipating the contact between the two families. At this point, Deann is well-established in her adulthood. The mother's expression of her feelings illustrates that at any age that the topics of search and reunion emerge, the adoptive parent can feel a sense of threat.

2. A 2011 issue of the *Journal of Personality Assessment* contains a special series that focuses on the assessment of adult attachment and interventions that proceed from this attachment (for example, see George & West, 2011).
3. Priel, Melamed-Hass, Besser, and Kantor (2000) found that the greater Israeli adoptive mothers' ability to self-reflect, the fewer the externalizing symptoms they perceived in their school-age children. These investigators looked at self-reflection as part of the Parental Awareness semi-structured interview (Newberger, 1980). Fonagy, Bateman, and Bateman (2011) discuss how this function can be measured through strategic additions to, and special coding of, the Adult Attachment Interview (Hesse, 2008).

References ────────────────────────────

Abel, S. (2000). Becoming fathers. Parenting, 14 (8), 132.

Adamec, C. A., & Miller, L. C. (2007). *The encyclopedia of adoption*. New York, NY: Infobase.

Adamec, C., & Pierce, W. (2000). *The encyclopedia of adoption* (2nd ed.). New York, NY: Infobase.

Agrawal, R. (n.d.). Adoption: Under Hindu, Muslim, Christian and Parsi Laws. Retrieved from http://www.legalserviceindia.com/articles/hmcp_adopt.htm

Ahmad, I. (1999). Islamic view of adoption. In C. Marshner & W. Pierce (Eds.), *Adoption Factbook III* (pp. 245–249). Washington, DC: National Council for Adoption.

Ainsworth, M. D. (1954). Patterns of attachment behavior shown by the infant in interaction with his mother. *Merrill-Palmer Quarterly, 10*(1), 51–58.

Ainsworth, M. D. (1985). Patterns of attachment. *Clinical Psychologist, 38*(2), 27–29.

Ainsworth, M.D. (1989). Attachments beyond infancy. *American Psychologist, 44*, 709–716.

Ainsworth, M. D. S. (1963). The development of infant-mother interaction among the Ganda. In B. M. Foss (Ed.), *Determinants of infant behavior* (pp. 67–104). New York, NY: Wiley.

Ainsworth, M. D. S., Blehar, M. C., Waters, E., & Wall, S. (1978). *Patterns of attachment: A psychological study of the strange situation*. Hillsdale, NJ: Erlbaum.

Aktar, S. & Abdullah, A. (2007). A comparative study on Hindu law between Bangladesh and India. *Asian Affairs, 29*(4), 61–69.

Alderfer, M. A., Cnaan, A., Annunziato, R. A., & Kazak, A. E. (2005). Patterns of post-traumatic stress symptoms in parents of childhood cancer survivors. *Journal of Family Psychology, 19*(3), 430–440. doi:10.1037/0893–3200.19.3.430

Alexander, R., & Curtis, C. M. (1996). A review of empirical research involving the transracial adoption of African American children. *Journal of Black Psychology, 22*(2), 223–235. doi:10.1177/00957984960222007

Allen, J.P., Chango, J., Szwedo, D., Schad, M., & Marston, E. (2012). Predictors of susceptibility to peer influence regarding substance use in adolescence. *Child Development, 83*, 337–350.

Allen, J., Fonagy, P., & Bateman, A. (2008). *Mentalizing in clinical practice*. Washington, DC: American Psychiatric.

American Academy of Child and Adolescent Psychiatry. (2011). The adopted child. Retrieved from http://www.aacap.org/cs/root/facts_for_families/the_adopted_child

American Psychiatric Association. (2000). *Diagnostic and statistical manual of mental disorders* (4th ed.). Washington, DC: Author.

American Psychological Association. (2003). Guidelines on multicultural education, training, research, practice, and organizational change for psychologists. *American Psychologist, 58*(5), 377–402. doi:10.1037/0003–066X.58.5.377.

Anderson, J., Farr, S., Jamieson, D., Warner, L., & Macaluso, M. (2009). Infertility services reported by men in the United States: National survey data. *Fertility and Sterility, 6*, 2466–2470.

Andresen, I. L. (1992). Behavioural and school adjustment of 12–13-year old internationally adopted children in Norway: A research note. *Journal of Child Psychology and Psychiatry, and Allied Disciplines, 33*(2), 427–439. doi:10.1111/j.1469–7610.1992.tb00877.x

Appell, A. R. (2012). Legal issues in lesbian and gay adoption. In D. M. Bordzinsky & A. Pertman (Eds.), *Adoption by lesbians and gay men: A new dimension in family diversity* (pp. 36–61). New York, NY: Oxford University Press.

Aquinas, T. (1274). *Summa theologica.* New York, NY: Benzinger Brothers.

Arnold, K. D. (2011, February 20). Older parenting: A modern day fountain of youth. *The older dad.* Blogsite. Retrieved from http://www.psychologytoday.com/blog/the-older-dad/201102/older-parenting-modern-day-fountain-of-youth

Asbury, E.T., Cross, D., & Waggenspack, B. (2003) Biological, adoptive, and mixed families: Special needs and the impact of the international adoption. *Adoption Quarterly,7*(1), 53–72.

Asbury, E. T., Cross, D. R., & Waggenspack, B. (2004). Biological, adoptive, and mixed families. *Adoption Quarterly, 7*(1), 53–72. doi:10.1300/J145v07n01_05

Ashe, N. S. (2011). Older parent adoption. *Older parent adoption.* Retrieved from http://www.adopting.org/adoptions/oder-parent-adoption-2.html

Askeland, L. (Ed.). (2006). *Children and youth in adoption, orphanage, and foster care: A historical handbook and guide.* Westport, CT: Greenwood Press.

Averett, P., Nalavany, B., & Ryan, S. (2009). An evaluation of gay/lesbian and heterosexual adoption. *Adoption Quarterly, 12*(3–4), 129–151. doi:10.1080/10926750903313278

Baden, A. L. (2007). Identity, psychological adjustment, culture, and race: Issues for transracial adoptees and the cultural-racial identity model. In R. A. Javier, A. L., Baden, F. A. Biafora, & A. Camacho-Gingerich (Eds.), *Handbook of adoption: Implications for researchers, practitioners, and families* (pp. 359–378). Thousand Oaks, CA: Sage.

Baden, A. L. (2008). Contextualizing race, culture and identity for transracially and internally adopted persons: Lessons from a personal and professional journey. *Journal of Social Distress and the Homeless, 17*(1 & 2), 106–125.

Baden, A. L., & Steward, R. J. (2000). A framework for use with racial and culturally integrated families: The Cultural-Racial Identity Model as applied to transracial adoption. *Journal of Social Distress & the Homeless, 9*(4), 309–337.

Baden, A. L., & Steward, R. J. (2007). The cultural-racial identity model: A theoretical framework for studying transracial adoptees. In R. A. Javier, A. L., Baden, F. A. Biafora, & A. Camacho-Gingerich (Eds.), *Handbook of adoption: Implications for researchers, practitioners, and families* (pp. 90–112). Thousand Oaks, CA: Sage.

Baden, A., Treweeke, L. M., & Ahlewalia, M. K. (2012). Reclaiming culture: Reculturation of transracial and international adoptees. *Journal of Counseling Psychology, 90*(4), 387–509.

Bailey, D. B., Hebbeler, K., Spiker, D., Scarborough, A., Mallik, S., & Nelson, L. (2005). Thirty-six-month outcomes for families of children who have disabilities and participated in early intervention. *Pediatrics, 116*(6), 1346–1352. doi:10.1542/peds.2004–1239

Baker, J. K., Seltzer, M. M., & Greenberg, J. S. (2011). Longitudinal effects of adaptability on behavior problems and maternal depression in families of adolescents with autism. *Journal of Family Psychology, 25*(4), 601–609. doi: http://dx.doi.org.ezproxy.fielding.edu/10.1037/a0024409

Bakermans-Kranenburg, M. J., van IJzendoorn, M. H., & Juffer, F. (2003). Less is more: Meta-analyses of sensitivity and attachment interventions in early childhood. *Psychological Bulletin, 129*(2), 195–215. doi:10.1037/0033–2909.129.2.195

Barkley, R. A. (2003). Attention-deficit/hyperactivity disorder. In E.J. Mash & R.A. Barkley (Eds.), *Child psychopathology* (2nd ed., pp. 75–143). New York, NY: Guilford Press.

Barnes, M. J., Katan, A., & Spitz, R. (1953). The working-through process in dealing with anxiety around adoption. *American Journal of Orthopsychiatry, 23*(3), 605–620. doi:10.1111/j.1939–0025.1953.tb00087.x

Barnett, B., Blignault, I., Holmes, S., Payne, A., & Parker, G. (1987). Quality of attachment in a sample of 1 year old Australian children. *Journal of the American Academy of Child & Adolescent Psychiatry, 26*(3), 303–307. doi:10.1097/00004583–198705000–00003

Barnhill, C. (2010). Churches adopt adoption: Churches are getting real about adoption's challenges—and helping families after the child arrives. *Christianity Today*, 1–3.

Barth, R. P., & Berry, M. (1991). Preventing adoption disruption. *Prevention in Human Services, 9*(1), 205–222. doi:10.1300/J293v09n01_13

Barth, R. P., Berry, M., Yoshikami, R., Goodfield, R. K., & Carlson, M. L. (1988). Predicting adoption disruption. *Social Work, 33*(3), 227–233.

Barth, R. P., & Brooks, D. (1997). A longitudinal study of family structure and size and adoption outcomes. *Adoption Quarterly, 1*(1), 29–56. doi:10.1300/J145v01n01_03

Barth, R. P., Gibbs, D. A., & Siebenaler, K. (2001). *Assessing the field of post-adoption services: Family needs, program models and evaluation issues*. Chapel Hill and Research Triangle Park: University of North Caroline School of Social Work, Jordan Institute for Families, and Research Triangle Institute. Retrieved from http://aspe.hhs.gov/hsp/PASS/lit-rev-01.htm

Basch, M. F. (1988). Reflections on development: The self-object experience of the newborn. *Progress in Self Psychology, 4*, 101–104.

Baumann, C. (1999). Adoptive fathers and birthfathers: A study of attitudes. *Child & Adolescent Social Work Journal, 16*(5), 373–391. doi:10.1023/A:1022347729368

Becker, G. (1997). *Healing the infertile family: Strengthening your relationship in the search for parenthood*. Berkeley, CA: University of California Press.

Becker-Weidman, A. (2006). Treatment for children with trauma-attachment disorders: Dyadic developmental psychotherapy. *Child and Adolescent Social Work Journal, 23*(2), 147–171. doi:10.1007/s10560–005–0039–0

Belanger, K. (2009). A Rural Miracle of adoption. *Child Welfare League of America: Childrens Voice*. Jan–Feb, Retrieved from http://www.cwla.org/voice/0901adoption.htm

Belanger, K., Copeland, S., & Cheung, M. (2008). The role of faith in achieving positive adoption outcomes for African American children. *Child Welfare, 87*(2), 123.

Bennett, S. (2003). Is there a primary mom? Parental perceptions of attachment bond hierarchies with lesbian adoptive families. *Child and Adolescent Social Work Journal, 20*(3), 159–173. doi: 10.1023/A:1023653727818

Benoiton, S. H. (2007, April 2). Parental age limits in international adoption. *Older parent adoption*. Blogsite. Retrieved from http://older-parent.adoptionblogs.com/weblogs/parental-age-limits-in-international-adoption

Benson, P. R. (2010). Coping, distress, and well-being in mothers of children with autism. *Research in Autism Spectrum Disorders, 4*(2), 217–228. doi:10.1016/j.rasd.2009.09.008

Bergel, V., & Crymes, J. T. (1990). *An exploratory study of the impact of older child adoption on large adoptive families with biological children*. Baltimore, MD: University of Maryland. Retrieved from http://search.proquest.com/docview/303873887?accountid=10559

Bergen, D., & Ramsey, P.G. (2010a, April). Complex ethnic-cultural ecologies influencing identity development of adolescent adoptees: Views of parents and adolescents. Paper presented at the American Educational Research Association, Denver, CO.

Bergen, D., & Ramsey, P. G. (2010b, July). *Successes and challenges of adoptive teens and young adults and their families* (with Doris Bergen). Paper presented at the Third International Adoption Research Conference (ICAR3), Leiden, The Netherlands.

Bergin, A. (1983). Religiousity and mental health: A critical reevaluation and meta-analysis, *Professional Psychology Research and Practice, 14*(2), 170–184.

Bergin, A., Masters, K., & Richards, P. (1987). Religiousness and mental health reconsidered: A study of an intrinsically religious sample. *Journal of Counseling Psychology, 34*(2), 197–204. doi: 10.1037/0022-0167.34.2.197

Bergman, A. S., & Fahey, M. F. (2011). *Ours, yours, mine: Mutuality and the emergence of a separate self.* Northvale, NJ: Aronson.

Berkowitz, D., & Marsiglio, W. (2007). Gay men: Negotiating procreative, father, and family identities. *Journal of Marriage and Family, 69*, 366–381. doi: 10.1111/j.1741-3737.2007.00371.x

Berry, M., & Barth, R. P. (1989). Behavior problems of children adopted when older. *Children and Youth Services Review, 11*(3), 221–238. doi:10.1016/0190-7409(89)90022-4

Berry, M., & Barth, R. P. (1990). A study of disrupted adoptive placements of adolescents. *Child Welfare: Journal of Policy, Practice, and Program, 69*(3), 209–225.

Berry, M., Barth, R. P., & Needell, B. (1996). Preparation, support, and satisfaction of adoptive families in agency and independent adoptions. *Child & Adolescent Social Work Journal, 13*(2), 157–183. doi:10.1007/BF01876644

Beschle, D. L. (1989). God bless the child?: The use of religion as a factor in child custody and adoption proceedings. *Fordham Law Review, 58*(3), 383–426.

Besser, A., & Blatt, S. J. (2007). Identity consolidation and internalizing and externalizing problem behaviors in early adolescence. *Psychoanalytic Psychology, 24*, 126–149.

Biafora, F. A., & Esposito, D. (2007). Adoption data and statistical trends. In F. Biafora, D. Esposito, R. A. Javier, & A. L. Baden (Eds.), *Handbook of adoption: Implications for researchers, practitioners, and families* (pp. 32–43). Thousand Oaks, CA: Sage.

Biafora, F. A., Javier, R. A., Baden, A. L., & Camacho-Gingerich, A. (2007). The future of adoption. In R. A. Javier, A. L. Baden, F. A. Biafora, & A. Camacho-Gingerich (Eds.), *Handbook of adoption: Implications for researchers, practitioners, and families* (pp. 527–537). Thousand Oaks, CA: Sage.

Bibring, G. L., Dwyer, T. F., Huntington, D. S., & Valenstein, A. F. (1961). A study of the psychological processes in pregnancy and of the earliest mother-child relationship: I. Some propositions and comments. *The Psychoanalytic Study of the Child*, 16, 9–24.

Biller, H. B., & Kimpton, J. L. (1997). The father and the school-aged child. In M. E. Lamb (Ed.). *The role of the father in child development* (3rd ed., pp. 143–161). New York, NY: Wiley.

Birenbaum-Carmeli, D. (2009). The politics of "The Natural Family" in Israel: State policy and kinship ideologies. *Social Science & Medicine, 69*(7), 1018–1024. doi:10.1016/j.socscimed.2009.07.044

Black, M. M., & Teti, L. O. (1997). Promoting mealtime communication between adolescent mothers and their infants through videotape. *Pediatrics, 99*(3), 432–437. doi: 10.1542/peds.99.3.432

Block, J. H. (1976). Debatable conclusions about sex differences. *Contemporary Psychology, 21*, 517–522.

Blos, P. Jr. (1985). Intergenerational separation-individuation: Treating the mother-infant pair. *Psychoanalytic Study of the Child, 40*, 41–56.

Blum, H. P. (1983). Adoptive parents: Generative conflict and generational continuity. *Psychoanalytic Study of the Child, 38*, 141–163.

Blum, H. P. (2004). Separation-individuation theory and attachment theory. *Journal of the American Psychoanalytic Association, 52*(2), 535–553.

Boer, F., Versluis-den Bieman, H. J. M., & Verhulst, F. C. (1994). International adoption of children with siblings: Behavioral outcomes. *American Journal of Orthopsychiatry, 64*(2), 252–262. doi:10.1037/h0079528

Boivin, J., Rice, F., Hay, D., Harold, G., Lewis, A., van den Bree, M. M. B., & Thapar, A. (2009). Associations between maternal older age, family environment and parent and child wellbeing in families using assisted reproductive techniques to conceive. *Social Science & Medicine, 68*(11), 1948–1955. doi:10.1016/j.socscimed.2009.02.036

Bond, J. (1995). Post adoption depression syndrome. *Roots and Wings* (Spring). Retrieved from http://www.adopting.org/pads.html

Bonovitz, C. (2004). Unconscious communication and the transmission of loss. *Journal of infant, child, and adolescent psychotherapy, 3*(1), 1–27.

Bonovitz, C. (2006). Unconscious communication and the transmission of loss. In K. Hushion, S.B. Sherman, D. Siskind, & C. Bonovitz (Eds.), *Understanding adoption: Clinical work with adults, children, and parents.* (pp. 11–33). Northvale, NJ: Aronson.

Bonovitz, J. (2000). From foreign born to feeling at home. In S. Akhtar & S. Kramer (Eds.), *Thicker than blood: Bonds of fantasy and reality in adoption* (pp. 121–138). Northvale, NJ: Aronson.

Borders, L. D., Black, L. K., & Pasley, B. K. (1998). Are adopted children and their parents at greater risk for negative outcomes? *Family Relations, 47*, 237–241.

Borders, L. D., Penny, J. M., & Portnoy, F. (2000). Adult adoptees and their friends: Current functioning and psychosocial well-being. *Family Relations, 49*, 407–418.

Bornstein, M. H., Putnick, D. L., Suwalsky, J. T. D., & Gini, M. (2006). Maternal chronological age, prenatal and perinatal history, social support, and parenting of infants. *Child Development, 77*(4), 875–892. doi:10.1111/j.1467–8624.2006.00908.x

Bos, H. (2010). Planned gay father families in kinship arrangements. *The Australian and New Zealand Journal of Family Therapy, 31*(4), 356–371.

Bos, H. M. W., van Balen, F., & van den Boom, D. C. (2005). Lesbian families and family functioning: An overview. *Patient Education and Counseling, 59*, 263–275. doi: 10.1016/j.pec.2004.10.006

Bowlby, J. (1944). Forty-four juvenile thieves: Their characters and home-life. *International Journal of Psychoanalysis, 25*, 107–128.

Bowlby, J. (1951). Maternal care and mental health, Monograph. *Bulletin of the World Health Organization*, 3, 355–534.

Bowlby, J. (1956). The growth of independence in the young child. *Royal Society of Health Journal, 76*, 587–591. doi:10.1177/146642405507600912

Bowlby, J. (1958). The nature of the child's tied to his mother. *International Journal of Psych-Analysis, 39*, 350–373.

Bowlby, J. (1973). *Separation: Anxiety and anger* (Vol. 2). New York, NY: Basic Books.

Bowlby, J. (1980). *Loss: Sadness and depression* (Vol. 3). New York, NY: Basic Books.

Bowlby, J. (1988a). *A secure base: Parent-child attachment and healthy human development.* New York, NY: Basic Books.

Bowlby, J. (1988b). Developmental psychiatry comes of age. *American Journal of Psychiatry, 145*(1), 1–10.

Bowlby, J. (1991). *Attachment and loss: Volume 1 attachment* (Vol. 1). New York, NY: Basic Books. (Original work published 1969)

Boyer, B. A. (2008). Theoretical models in health psychology, and the model for integrating medicine and psychology. In B.A. Boyer & M.I. Paharia (Eds.), *Comprehensive handbook of clinical health psychology* (pp. 3–30). Hoboken, NJ: Wiley.

Boyer, B. A., Knolls, M. L., Kafkalas, C. M., Tollen, L. G., & Swartz, M. (2000). Prevalence and relationships of posttraumatic stress in families experiencing pediatric spinal cord injury. *Rehabilitation Psychology, 45*(4), 339–355. doi:http://dx.doi.org.ezproxy.fielding.edu/10.1037/0090–5550.45.4.339

Boyer, B. A., Tollen, L. G., & Kafkalas, C. M. (1998). A pilot study of posttraumatic stress disorder in children and adolescents with spinal cord injury. *SCI Psychosocial Process, 11*, 75–81.

Boyer, B. A., Ware, W., Knolls, M. L., & Kafkalas, C. M. (2003). Posttraumatic stress in families with pediatric spinal cord injury. *SCI Psychosocial Process, 16*, 85–94.

Brabender, V. (2002). *Introduction to group therapy*. New York, NY: Wiley.

Brabender, V., Fallon, A., & Smolar, A. (2004). *Essentials of group therapy*. New York, NY: Wiley.

Brakman, S.-V., & Scholz, S. J. (2006). Adoption, ART, and a re-conception of the maternal body: Toward embodied maternity. *Hypatia, 21*(1), 54–73.

Bramlett, M. D. (2010). When stepparents adopt: Demographic, health and health care characteristics of adopted children, stepchildren, and adopted stepchildren. *Adoption Quarterly, 13*(3–4), 248–267. doi:10.1080/10926755.2010.537954

Bramlett, M. D., & Radel, L. F. (2008). *Adopted children with special health care needs: Characteristics, health, and health care by adoption type. ASPE research brief*. Washington, DC: U.S. Department of Health and Human Services, Office of the Assistant Secretary for Planning and Evaluation. Retrieved from http://www.cdc.gov/nchs/slaits/nsapsn.htm

Bramlett, M. D., & Radel, L. F. (2010). The national survey of adoptive parents: An introduction to the special issue of adoption quarterly. *Adoption Quarterly, 13*(3–4), 147–156. doi:10.1080/10926755.2010.524870

Brand, A. E., & Brinich, P. M. (1999). Behavior problems and mental health contacts in adopted, foster, and nonadopted children. *Journal of Child Psychology and Psychiatry, and Allied Disciplines, 40*(8), 1221–1229. doi:10.1111/1469–7610.00538

Brazelton, T. B. (1992). *Touchpoints: The essential reference*. New York, NY: Addison-Wesley.

Bretherton, I. (1992). The origins of attachment theory: John Bowlby and Mary Ainsworth. *Developmental Psychology, 28*(5), 759–75. doi:10.1037/0012–

Briggs, L., & Marre, D. (2009). Introduction: The circulation of children. In D. Marre & L. Briggs (Eds.), *International adoption: Global inequalities and the circulation of children* (pp. 1–28). New York, NY: New York University Press.

Brodsky, K., & Rosenfeld, D. (2005). Meeting the needs of adoptive Jewish families. *Contact: The Journal of the Jewish Life Network, 73*(3), 5–8.

Brodzinsky, D. M. (1987). Adjustment to adoption: A psychosocial perspective. *Clinical Psychology Review, 71*, 25–47. doi:10.1016/0272–7358(87)90003–1

Brodzinsky, D. M. (2005). Reconceptualizing openness in adoption: Outcomes for adolescents within their adoption kinship networks. *Psychological issues in adoption: Research and practice* (pp. 145–166). Westport, CT: Praeger.

Brodzinsky, D. M. (2006). Family structural openness and communication openness as predictors in the adjustment of adopted children. *Adoption Quarterly, 9*(4), 1–18. doi:10.1300/J145v09n04_01

Brodzinsky, D. M. (2011). Children's understanding of adoption: Developmental and clinical implications. *Professional Psychology: Research and Practice, 42*(2), 200–207.

Brodzinsky, D.M., Green, R. J., & Katuzny, K. (2012). Adoption by lesbians and gay men: What we know, need to know, and ought to do. In D. M. Brodzinsky & A. Pertman (Eds.), *Adoption by lesbians and gay men: A new dimension in family diversity* (pp. 233–253). New York, NY: Oxford University Press.

Bordzinsky, D. M., & Pertman, A. (2011). *Adoption by Lesbians and Gay Men: A New Dimension in Family Diversity*. New York: Oxford University Press.

Brodzinsky, D. M., & Pertman, A. (Eds.). (2012). *Adoption by lesbians and gay men: A new dimension in family diversity*. New York, NY: Oxford University Press.

Brodzinsky, D. M., & Schechter, M. D. (1990). *The psychology of adoption.* New York, NY: Oxford University Press.

Brodzinsky, D. M., Schecter, D.E., Braff, A. M., & Singer, L. M. (1984). Psychological and academic adjustment in adopted children. *Journal of Consulting and Clinical Psychology, 52,* 582–590.

Brodzinksy, D.M., Schechter, M.D., & Marantz, R. (1992). *Being adopted: The lifelong search for self.* New York, NY: Doubleday.

Brodzinsky, D. M., Smith, D. W., & Brodzinsky, A. B. (1998). *Children's adjustment to adoption: Developmental and clinical issues.* Thousand Oaks, CA: Sage.

Brooks, D., Allen, J., & Barth, R. P. (2002). Adoption services use, helpfulness, and need: A comparison of public and private agency and independent adoptive families. *Children and Youth Services Review, 24*(4), 213–238. doi:10.1016/S0190–7409(02)00174–3

Brooks, D., & Barth, R. P. (1999). Adult transracial and inracial adoptees: Effects of race, gender, adoptive family structure, and placement history on adjustment outcomes. *American Journal of Orthopsychiatry, 69*(1), 87–99. doi:10.1037/h0080384

Brooks, D., Kim, H., & Wind, L. (2012). Supporting gay and lesbian adoptive families before and after adoption. In D. Brodzinsky & A. Pertman (Eds.), *Adoption by lesbians and gay men: A new dimension in family diversity* (pp. 150–183). New York, NY: Oxford.

Brooks, D., Simmel, C., Wind, L., & Barth, R.P. (2005). Contemporary adoptive families and implications for the next wave of adoption research. In D. Brodzinsky & J. Palacios (Eds.), *Psychological issues in adoption: Linking theory, research, and practice* (pp. 1–25). Westport, CT: Greenwood Press.

Bunch, S., Eastman, B., & Griffin, L. (2007). Examining the perceptions of grandparents who parent in formal and informal kinship care. *Journal of Human Behavior in the Social Environment, 15*(4), 93–105.

Burgess, K. B., Marshall, P. J., Rubin, K. H., & Fox, N. A. (2003). Infant attachment and temperament as predictors of subsequent externalizing problems and cardiac physiology. *Journal of Child Psychology and Psychiatry, 44*(6), 819–831. doi:10.1111/1469–7610.00167

Burgner, M. (1985). The Oedipal experience: Effects on development of an absent father. *International Journal of Psychoanalysis, 66,* 311–320.

Burke, W. T., & Abidin, R. R. (1980). Parenting stress index (PSI): A family systems assessment approach. In R. R. Abidin (Ed.), *Parent education and intervention handbook* (pp. 516–527). Springfield, IL: Thomas.

Burlingham, D., & Freud, A. (1944). *Infants without families.* Oxford, UK: Allen & Unwin.

Busch, L. (2005). Older child adoption: A psychologist's story of love and attachment. *International Adoption Articles Directory.* Post-Adoption Learning Center (Pal Center, Inc.; www.adoptionarticlesdirectory.com).

Butler-Sweet, J. (2011). 'Race isn't what defines me': Exploring identity choices in multiracial, biracial, and monoracial families. *Social Identities: Journal for the Study of Race, Nation, and Culture, 17*(6), 747–769.

Carlson, E. A. (1998). A prospective longitudinal study of attachment disorganization/disorientation. *Child Development, 69*(4), 1107–1128. doi:10.1111/j.1467–8624.1998.tb06163.x

Carp, E. W. (Ed.). (2002). *Adoption in America: Historical perspectives.* Ann Arbor, MI: University of Michigan Press.

Carp, E. W. (2007). Does opening adoption records have an adverse social impact? Some lessons from the U.S., Great Britain, and Australia, 1953–2007. *Adoption Quarterly, 10*(3–4), 29–52.

Casey Family Services. (2003). *Strengthening families & communities: Promising practices in adoption-competent mental health services.* Retrieved from http://www.caseyfamilyservices.org/userfiles/pdf/pub-2003-promising-practices-report.pdf

Cassidy, J. (2008). The nature of the child's ties. In J. Cassidy & P. R. Shaver (Eds.), *Handbook of attachment: Theory, research, and clinical applications* (2nd ed., pp. 3–22). New York, NY: Guilford Press.

Castle, J., Groothues, C., Colvert, E., Hawkins, A., Kreppner, J., Sonuga-Barke, E., Beckett, C., Kumsta, R., Schlotz, W., Stevens, S., & Rutter, M. (2009). Parents' evaluation of adoption success. *American Journal of Orthopsychiatry, 79*(4), 552–531.

Ceballo, R., Lansford, J. E., Abbey, A., & Stewart, A. J. (2004). Gaining a child: Comparing the experiences of biological parents, adoptive parents, and stepparents. *Family Relations, 53*(1), 38–48. doi:10.1111/j.1741–3729.2004.00007.x

Center for Children With Special Needs. (2012). *Talking with parents for childcare professionals.* Retrieved from http://www.cshcn.org/childcare-schools-community/talking-parents-child care-professionals

Centers for Disease Control and Prevention. (2011). *National diabetes fact sheet: National estimates and general information on diabetes and prediabetes in the United States, 2011.* Atlanta, GA: U.S. Department of Health and Human Services, Centers for Disease Control and Prevention. Retrieved from http://www.cdc.gov/diabetes/pubs/pdf/ndfs_2011.pdf

Chan, R. W., Raboy, B., & Patterson, C. J. (1998). Psychosocial adjustment among children conceived via donor insemination by lesbian and heterosexual mothers. *Child Development, 69*(2), 443–457. doi: 10.2307/1132177

Chess, S., & Thomas, A. (1987). *Know your child: An authoritative guide for today's parents.* New York, NY: Basic Books.

Child Welfare Information Gateway. (2004). *Searching for birth relatives.* Retrieved from http://www.childwelfare.gov/pubs/f_search.cfm

Child Welfare Information Gateway (2005). Funding adoption programs and services. Retrieved from https://www.childwelfare.gov/adoption/adopt_managers/funding_programs.cfm.

Child Welfare Information Gateway. (2006). *Adoption.* Retrieved from http://www.childwelfare .gov/adoption/index.cfm

Child Welfare Information Gateway. (2012a). *Foster parents considering adoption.* U.S. Department of Health & Human Services. Retrieved from http://www.childwelfare.gov/ pubs/f_fospar.cfm

Child Welfare Information Gateway. (2012b). *Selecting and working with an adoption therapist.* Accessed at https://www.childwelfare.gov/pubs/f_therapist.cfm

Child Welfare League of America (CWLA). (2000). *Standards of excellence for child welfare services: Adoption services.* Retrieved from http://www.cwla.org/programs/standards/ cwsstandardsadoption.htm

Child Welfare League of America (2005). State fact sheets. Retrieved from http://www.cwla .org/advocacy/statefactsheets/statefactsheets05.htm

Child Welfare League of America (CWLA). (2007). *Kinship care.* Retrieved from http://www. cwla.org/programs/kinship/adoption.htm

Cicchetti, D., Toth, S. L., & Rogosch, F. A. (1999). The efficacy of toddler-parent psychotherapy to increase attachment security in offspring of depressed mothers. *Attachment & Human Development, 1*(1), 34–66. doi:10.1080/14616739900134021

Clark, P., Thigpen, S., & Yates, A. M. (2006). Integrating the older/special needs adoptive child into the family. *Journal of Marital and Family Therapy, 32*(2), 181–194. doi:10.1111/ j.1752–0606.2006.tb01599.x

Clements, Fr. George | The HistoryMakers. (2003). *Interview.* Retrieved from http://www .thehistorymakers.com/biography/fr-george-clements-39

CNN. (2012, November 30). Tonight on AC360: Parents appeal to U.S. Supreme Court for Baby Veronica. Accessed at http://ac360.blogs.cnn.com/2012/11/30/tonight-on-ac360-parents-appeal-to-u-s-supreme-court-for-baby-veronica/

Coakley, J. F., & Berrick, J. D. (2008). Research review: In a rush to permanency: Preventing adoption disruption. *Child & Family Social Work, 13*(1), 101–112. doi:10.1111/j.1365–2206.2006.00468.x

Coates, S. W. (2004). John Bowlby and Margaret S. Mahler: Their lives and theories. *Journal of the American Psychoanalytic Association, 52*(2), 571–601.

Cohen, N. J., Coyne, J. C., & Duvall, J. D. (1996). Parents' sense of "entitlement" in adoptive and nonadoptive families. *Family Process, 35*(4), 441–456.

Cohen, N. J., & Farnia, F. (2011). Children adopted from China: Attachment security two years later. *Children and Youth Services Review, 33*(11), 2342–2346. doi:10.1016/j.childyouth.2011.08.006

Cohen, N. J., Lojkasek, M., Zadeh, Z. Y., Pugliese, M., & Kiefer, H. (2008). Children adopted from China: A prospective study of their growth and development. *Journal of Child Psychology and Psychiatry, 49*(4), 458–468. doi:10.1111/j.1469–7610.2007.01853.x

Cole, S. A. (2005). Foster caregiver motivation and infant attachment: How do reasons for fostering affect relationships? *Child and Adolescent Social Work Journal, 22*(5–6), 441–457. doi:10.1007/s10560–005–0021-x

Coley, R. L. (2001). (In)visible men: Emerging research on low income, unmarried, and minority fathers. *American Psychologist, 50*(9), 743–753.

Collard, C. (2009). The transnational adoption of a related child in Quebec, Canada. In D. Marre & L. Briggs (Eds.), *International adoption: Global inequalities and the circulation of children* (pp. 119–134). New York, NY: New York University Press.

Colón, A. R., & Colón, P. A. (2001). *A history of children: A socio-cultural survey across millennia*. Westport, CT: Greenwood Press.

Contrada, R., & Baum, A. (2010). *The handbook of stress science: Biology, psychology and health*. New York, NY: Springer.

Conway, P., & Valentine, D. (1988). Reproductive losses and grieving. In D. Valentine (Ed.), *Infertility and adoption: A guide for social work practice* (pp. 42–64). New York, NY: Haworth Press.

Cooper, M. L., Shaver, P. R., & Collins, N. L. (1998). Attachment styles, emotion regulation, and adjustment in adolescence. *Journal of Personality and Social Psychology, 74*(5), 1380–1397. doi:10.1037/0022–3514.74.5.1380

Cornell, D. (2005). Adoption and its progeny: Rethinking family law, gender, and sexual difference. In S. Haslanger & C. Witt (Eds.), *Adoption matters: Philosophical and feminist essays* (pp. 19–46). Ithaca, NY: Cornell University Press.

Cowling, V. (2003). *What are the special characteristics of families who provide long term care for children of parents with mental illness?* (Unpublished master's thesis). School of Behavioral Science, University of Melbourne, Australia.

Daly, K. (1988). Reshaped parenthood identity: The transition to adoptive parenthood. *Journal of Contemporary Ethnography, 17*(1), 40–66. doi:10.1177/0891241688171002

Dave Thomas Foundation or Adoption (2010). 2010 best adoption friendly workplaces list. Accessed at http://www.davethomasfoundation.org/what-we-do/adoption-friendly-workplace/2010-best-adoption-friendly-workplaces-list/

Dave Thomas Foundation for Adoption. (2011). *Adoption-friendly workplace—A guide to implementing an adoption benefits policy—Employer toolkit*. Columbus, OH: Dave Thomas Foundation for Adoption.

Davids, M. (2002). Fathers in the internal world: From boy to man to father. In J. Trowell & A. Etchengyoen (Eds.), *The importance of fathers: A psychoanalytic re-evaluation* (pp. 67–92). New York, NY: Brunner-Rutledge.

de Arellano, M., Briggs-King, E., Flores, L., Bigfoot, D., Mannarino, A., Rivera, S., . . . Solarz, A. (2011). *Effective providers for child victims of violence program: The EP program booklet*. Washington, DC: American Psychological Association.

DeBerry, K. M., Scarr, S., & Weinberg, R. (1996). Family racial socialization and ecological competence: Longitudinal assessments of African-American transracial adoptees. *Child Development, 67*(5), 2375–2399.

Deiner, P. L., Wilson, N. J., & Unger, D. G. (1988). Motivation and characteristics of families who adopt children with special needs an empirical study. *Topics in Early Childhood Special Education, 8*(2), 15–29. doi:10.1177/027112148800800203

DeSimone, M. (1996). Birth mother loss: Contributing factors to unresolved grief. *Clinical Social Work Journal, 24*(1), 65–76. doi:10.1007/BF02189942

Desmarais, S. (2006). "A space to float with someone": Recovering play as a field of repair in work with parents of late-adopted children. *Journal of Child Psychotherapy, 32*(3), 349–364. doi:10.1080/00754170600996879

De Verthelyi, R. F. (1996). Intercountry adoption of Latin American children: The importance of early bilingual/bicultural services. *Cultural Diversity & Mental Health, 2*(1), 53–63. doi:10.1037/1099–9809.2.1.53

Dickens, C. (1837). *Oliver Twist.* New York, NY: Bantam Dell. 055321101–1

Dickens, C. (1852–1853). *Bleak House.* New York, NY: Bantam Dell. 055321223–0

Dolan, J. (2012, January 1). *The intersectionality of race, adoption and parenting: How white adoptive parents of Asian born children talk about race within the family.* Amherst, MA: University of Massachusetts. Retrieved from http://scholarworks.umass.edu/rudd_diss_umass/3

Dolbin-MacNab, M. (2006). Just like raising your own? Grandmothers' perceptions of parenting a second time around. *Family Relations, 55,* 564–575.

Dozier, M., Higley, E., Albus, K. E., & Nutter, A. (2002). Intervening with foster infants' caregivers: Targeting three critical needs. *Infant Mental Health Journal, 23*(5), 541–554. doi:10.1002/imhj.10032

Dozier, M., & Rutter, M. (2008). Challenges to the development of attachment relationships faced by young children in foster and adoptive care. In J. Cassidy & P. Shaver (Eds.), *Handbook of attachment: Theory, research, and clinical applications* (2nd ed., pp. 698–717). New York, NY: Guilford Press.

Dozier, M., Stovall, K. C., Albus, K. E., & Bates, B. (2001). Attachment for infants in foster care: The role of caregiver state of mind. *Child Development, 72*(5), 1467–1477. doi:10.1111/1467–8624.00360

Draper, E. (2010, March 5). Adoption bid finds families: Churches and government team up and halve the number of kids awaiting placement. *Denver Post.* Retrieved http://www.denverpost.com/news/ci_14516591

Dwyer, S. C., & Gidluck, L. (2009). Building inclusive classrooms and communities: How teachers and parents can work together to support families created through transracial adoption and other nontraditional families. *Our Schools, Ourselves, 18,* 18–35.

Eldridge, S. (2009). *20 things adoptive parents need to succeed.* New York, NY: Random House.

Emanuel, R. (2002). On becoming a father: Reflections from infant observation. In S. Budd, J. Trowell, & A. Etchegoyer (Eds.), *The importance of fathers: A psychoanalytic re-evaluation* (pp. 131–146). New York, NY: Brunner-Routledge.

Emde, R. N. (1983a). The prerepresentational self and its affective core. *Psychoanalytic Study of the Child, 38,* 165–192.

Emde, R. N. (Ed.). (1983b). *René A. Spitz: Dialogues from infancy. Selected papers.* New York, NY: International Universities Press.

Engel, G. L., Reichsman, F., Harway, V. T., & Hess, D. W. (1985). Monica: Infant-feeding behavior of a mother gastric fistula–fed as an infant: A 30-year longitudinal study of enduring affects. In E. J. Anthony & G. H. Pollock (Eds.), *Parental influences in health and disease* (pp. 29–90). Boston, MA: Little, Brown.

Engel, G. L., Reichsman, F. K., & Viederman, M. (1979). Monica: A 25-year longitudinal study of the consequences of trauma in infancy. *Journal of the American Psychoanalytic Association, 27,* 107–126.

Erikson, E. H. (1950/1995). *Childhood and society*. New York: Norton.

Erikson, E. H. (1956). The problem of ego identity. *Journal of the American Psychoanalytic Association, 4*, 56–121.

Esposito, D., & Biafora, F. A. (2007). Toward a sociology of adoption: Historical deconstruction. In R. A. Javier, A. L. Baden, F. A. Biafra, & A. Camacho-Gengerich (Eds.), *Handbook of adoption: Implications for researchers, practitioners, and families* (pp. 17–31). Thousand Oaks, CA: Sage.

Evan B. Donaldson Adoption Institute. (2002). *National adoption attitudes survey. Harris Interactive*. Retrieved from http://www.adoptioninstitute.org/survey/Adoption_Attitudes_Survey.pdf

Evan B. Donaldson Adoption Institute. (2006). *Adoption in the schools: A lot to learn. Promoting equality and fairness for all children and their families*. Retrieved from http://www.adoptioninstitute.org/policy/2006_09_adoption_in_the_schools.php

Evan B. Donaldson Adoption Institute. (2010). *Keeping the promise: The critical need for post-adoptive services to enable children and families to succeed*. Retrieved from http://www.adoptioninstitute.org/publications/2010_10_20_KeepingThePromise.pdf

Fahlberg, V. (1991). *A child's journey through placement*. Indianapolis, IN: Perspectives Press.

Fallon, A., & Brabender, V. (2003). *Awaiting the therapist's baby: A guide for expectant parent-practitioners*. Hillsdale, NJ: Erlbaum.

Fallon, A., & Brabender, V. (2012). A secure connection: The tethering of attachment and good enough maternal care. In S. Akhtar (Ed.), *The mother and her child: Clinical aspects of attachment, separation, and loss* (pp. 15–43). New York, NY: Aronson.

Farber, S. K. (2006). Sometimes I feel like a motherless child, a long way from home: Complex adolescent identity formation in a transcultural adoption. *Journal of Infant, Child, and Adolescent Psychotherapy, 5*(1), 24–45. doi:10.2513/s15289168jicap0501_2

Farr, R. H., Forssell, S. L., & Patterson, C. J. (2010). Parenting and child development in adoptive families: Does parental sexual orientation matter? *Applied Developmental Science, 14*(3), 164–178.

Farr, R. H. & Patterson, C. J. (2011, April). Coparenting and child adjustment among lesbian, gay, and heterosexual adoptive parent families. Poster session presented at the meeting of the Rudd Adoption Institute, Amherst, MA.

Fassino S., Pierò A., Boggio S., Piccioni V., & Garzaro L. (2002). Anxiety, depression and anger suppression in infertile couples: A controlled study. *Human Reproduction, 17*(11), 2986–2994. 10.1093/humrep/17.11.2986

Feigelman, W. (1997). Adopted adults. *Marriage & Family Review, 25*(3–4), 199–223. doi:10.1300/J002v25n03_05

Ferketich, S. L., & Mercer, R. T. (1989). Men's health status during pregnancy and early fatherhood. *Research in Nursing & Health, 12*(3), 137–148.

Fiese, B.H., Sameroff, A.J., Grotevant, H.D., Wamboldt, F.S., Dickstein, S., & Fravel, D.L. (Eds.). (1999). *The stories that families tell: Narrative coherence, narrative interaction, and relationship beliefs*. Maldon: MA: Blackwell Publishers.

Finger, R., Qi, Y., Fabian, M., Kennan, J., & Stoddard, R. (2012). Experiences of families inquiring about donating or adoption embryos: Results of an online survey. *Adoption Quarterly, 15*, 57–66. doi: 10.1080/10926755.2012.661335

Finley, G. E. (1998). Parental age and parenting quality as perceived by late adolescents. *Journal of Genetic Psychology, 159*(4), 505–506. doi:10.1080/00221329809596167

Fisher, A. P. (2003). Still "not quite as good as having your own"? Toward a sociology of adoption. *Annual Review of Sociology*, 29, 335–361. doi:10.1146/annual.soc.29.010202.100209.

Fishman, F., & Harrington, E. S. (2007). School issues and adoption: Academic considerations and adaptation. In R. A. Javier, A. L. Baden, F. A. Biafora, & A. Camacho-Gingerich

(Eds.), *Handbook of adoption: Implications for researchers, practitioners, and families* (pp. 256–280). Thousand Oaks, CA: Sage.

Fiske, A., Kitayama, S., Markus, H.R., & Nisbett, R.E. (1998). The cultural matrix of social psychology. In D. Gilbert & S. Fiske & G. Lindzey (Eds.), The Handbook of Social Psychology (4th ed., pp. 915–81). San Francisco: McGraw-Hill.

Fitzgerald, B. (1999). Children of lesbian and gay parents: A review of the literature. *Marriage & Family Review, 29(1)*, 57–75. doi: 10.1300/J002v29n01_05

Flaks, D. K. (1995). Research issues. In A. Sullivan (Ed.), *Issues in Gay and Lesbian Adoption: Proceedings of the Fourth Annual Peirce-Warwick Adoption Symposium* (pp. 1–10). Washington, DC: Child Welfare League of America.

Flaks, D. K., Fisher, I., Masterpasqua, F., & Joseph, G. (1995). Lesbians choosing motherhood: A comparative study of lesbian and heterosexual parents and their children. *Developmental Psychology, 31*(1), 105–114. doi: 10.1037/0012-1649.31.1.105

Fleming, J., & Burry, K. (1988). Coping with infertility. In D. Valentine (Ed.), *Infertility and adoption: A guide for social work practice* (pp. 37–41). New York, NY: Haworth Press.

Flynn, D. (2002). The adoptive father. In S. Budd, J. Trowell, & A. Etchegoyer (Eds.), *The importance of fathers: A psychoanalytic re-evaluation* (pp. 203–221). New York, NY: Brunner-Routledge.

Foli, K. J. (2010). Depression in adoptive parents: A model of understanding through grounded theory. *Western Journal of Nursing Research, 32*(3), 379–400. doi:10.1177/0193945909351299

Foli, K. J., & Gibson, G. C. (2011). Sad adoptive dads: Paternal depression in the post-adoption period. *International Journal of Men's Health, 10*(2), 153–162. doi:10.3149/jmh.1002.153

Foli, K. J., & Thompson, J. R. (2004). *The post-adoption blues: Overcoming the unforeseen challenges of adoption.* Emmaus, PA: Rodale Books.

Follett, K. (1989). *Pillars of the earth.* New York, NY: Penguin Books.

Fonagy, P. (2001). *Attachment theory and psychoanalysis.* New York, NY: Other Press.

Fonagy, P., Bateman, A., & Bateman, A. (2011). The widening scope of mentalizing: A discussion. *Psychology and Psychotherapy: Theory, Research, & Practice, 84*(1), 98–110.

Fonagy, P., Gergely, G., Jurist, E., & Target, M. (2002). *Affect regulation, mentalization, and the development of the self.* New York, NY: Other Press.

Fonagy, P., Steele, M., Steele, H., Moran, G. S., & Higgitt, A. C. (1991). The capacity for understanding mental states: The reflective self in parent and child and its significance for security of attachment. *Infant Mental Health Journal, 12*(3), 201–218. doi:10.1002/1097–0355(199123)12:3<201::AID-IMHJ2280120307>3.0.CO;2-7

Fonagy, P., & Target, M. (2002). Early intervention and the development of self-regulation. *Psychoanalytic Inquiry, 22*(3), 307–335. doi:10.1080/07351692209348990

Fonseca, C. (2009). Transnational connections and dissenting views: The evolution of child placement policies in Brazil. In D. Marre & L. Briggs (Eds.), *International adoption: Global inequalities and the circulation of children* (pp. 154–173). New York, NY: New York University Press.

Fraiberg, S. H. (1987). Pathological defenses in infancy. In L. Fraiberg (Ed.), *Selected papers of Selma Fraiberg* (pp. 183–202). Columbus, OH: Ohio State University Press.

Fraiberg, S., Adelson, E., & Shapiro, V. (1975). Ghosts in the nursery: A psychoanalytic approach to the problems of impaired infant-mother relationships. *Journal of the American Academy of Child Psychiatry, 14*(3), 387–421. doi:10.1016/S0002–7138(09)61442-4

Frank, E., & Rowe, D. A. (1981). Primary prevention: Parent education, mother–infant groups in a general hospital setting. *Journal of Preventive Psychiatry, 1*(2), 169–178.

Frank, E., & Rowe, D. (1986). Clinical interventions in parent-infant groups around issues related to separation-individuation. *Infant Mental Health Journal, 7*(3), 214–224. doi:10.1002/1097–0355(198623)7:3<214::AID-IMHJ2280070305>3.0.CO;2-6

Frank, E., & Rowe, D. (1990). Preventive-intervention groups with adoptive parents and their babies in zero to three, *Bulletin of National Center for Clinical Infant Programs, 10*(5), 19–25.

Frank, E., & Rowe, D. (2000). Attachment and separation-individuation in foreign-born children adopted after the age of five months. In S. Akhtar & S. Kramer (Eds.), *Thicker than blood: Bonds of fantasy and reality in adoption* (pp. 91–120). Northvale, NJ: Aronson.

Frank, E., & Rowe, D. (2002). *Becoming a family, building relationships, belonging: The attachment process in children adopted after the age of five months.* Pamphlet for Parents.

Frankel, S. A., & Wise, M. J. (1982). A view of delayed parenting: Some implications of a new trend. *Psychiatry, 45*(3), 220–225.

Frasch, K. M., Brooks, D., & Barth, R. P. (2000). Openness and contact in foster care adoptions: An eight-year follow-up. *Family Relations, 49*(4), 435–446.

Freeark, K., Rosenblum, K. L., Hus, V. H., & Root, B. L. (2008). Fathers, mothers and marriages: What shapes adoption conversations in families with young adopted children? *Adoption Quarterly, 11*(1), 1–23. doi: 10.1080/10926750802291393

Freud, A. (1963). The concept of developmental lines. *Psychoanalytic Study of the Child, 18,* 245–265.

Freud, A., & Dann, S. (1951). An experiment in group upbringing. *Psychoanalytic Study of the Child, 6,* 127–168.

Freud, S. (1906–1908). "Family romances." In James Strachey (Ed.), *Standard edition* (Vol. IX, pp. 235–241). London, England: Hogarth Press.

Freud, S. (1953). *Three essays on sexuality.* In J. Strachey (Ed. & Trans.), *Standard edition and complete psychological works of Sigmund Freud* (Vol. 7, pp. 7–243). London, England: Hogarth. (Original work published in 1905)

Freundlich, M. (2002). Adoption research: An assessment of empirical contributions to the advancement of adoption practice. *Journal of Social Distress and the Homeless, 11*(2), 143–166. doi:10.1023/A:1014363901799.

Freundlich, M. (2007). A legal history of adoption and ongoing legal challenges. In R. A. Javier, A. L. Baden, F. A. Biafora, & A. Camacho-Gingerich (Eds.), *Handbook of adoption: Implications for researchers, practitioners, and families* (pp. 44–57). Thousand Oaks, CA: Sage.

Friedlander, M. (2003). Misunderstood, marginalized, mythologized. *Journal of counseling psychology, 31*(6), 745–752. doi:10.1177/0011000003258389

Gailey, C. W. (2010). *Blue-ribbon babies and labors of love: Race, class, and gender in U.S. adoption practice.* Austin, TX: University of Texas Press.

Gallese, V., Eagle, M. N., & Migone, P. (2007). Intentional attunement: Mirror neurons and the neural underpinnings of interpersonal relations. *Journal of the American Psychoanalytic Association, 55*(1), 131–176.

Garner, A. (2005). *Families like mine: Children of gay parents tell it like it is.* New York, NY: Perennial Currents.

Gartrell, N., & Bos, H. (2010). US national longitudinal lesbian family study: Psychological adjustment of 17-year-old adolescents. *Pediatrics, 126*(1), 28–36. doi:10.1542/peds.2009-3153

Gartrell, N., Rodas, C., Deck, A., Peyser, H., & Banks, A. (2006). The USA national lesbian family study: Interviews with mothers of 10-year-olds. *Feminism & Psychology, 16(2),* 175–192. doi: 10.1177/9059-353506062972

Geen, R. (2003). *Caring for children: Facts and perspectives* (Policy Brief No. 2). Washington, DC: The Urban Institute. Retrieved from http://www.urban.org/UploadedPDF/310809_caring_for_children_2.pdf

Geen, R., Malm, K., & Katz, J. (2004). A study to inform the recruitment and retention of general applicant adoptive parents. *Adoption Quarterly, 7*(4), 1–28. doi:10.1300/J145v07n04_01

Gendell, S. (2001) In search of permanency: a reflection on the first three years of the Adoption and Safe Families Act implementation. Family Court Review, 39, 25–36.

George, C., Kaplan, N., & Main, M. (1984). *Adult attachment interview*. (Unpublished manuscript). University of California, Berkeley, CA.

George, C., & Solomon, J. (2008). The caregiving system: A behavioral systems approach to parenting. In J. Cassidy & P. R. Shaver (Eds.), *Handbook of attachment: Theory, research, and clinical applications* (2nd ed., pp. 833–856). New York, NY: Guilford Press.

George, C., & West, M. (2011). The adult attachment projective picture system: Integrating attachment into clinical assessment. *Journal of Personality Assessment, 93*(5), 407–416. doi:10.1080/00223891.2011.594133

Gianino, M. (2008). Adaptation and transformation: The transition to adoptive parenthood for gay male couples. *Journal of GLBT Family Studies, 4*(2), 205–243.

Gibbons, C. & Jones, T. (2003). Kinship care: Health profiles of grandparents raising their grandchildren. *Journal of Family Social Work, 7*(1), 1–14. DOI: 10.1300/J039v07n01_01

Gidluck, L., & Dwyer, S. C. (2006). Families of Asian children adopted by white parents: Challenges of race, racism, and racial identity in Canada. *Our Diverse Cities, 2*, 78–82.

Gill, J. (2012). Where do our children fit in? White mothering of Asian children and the construction of racial and ethnic identities. *Journal of Social Distress and the Homeless, 21*(3 & 4), 222–256.

Gilmore, K. (2008). Birth mother, adoptive mother, dying mother, dead mother. In E. L. Jurist, A. Slade, & S. Bergner (Eds.), *Mind to mind: Infant research, neuroscience and psychoanalysis* (pp. 373–397). New York, NY: Other Press.

Gjerdingen, D. K., & Froberg, D. G. (1991). The fourth stage of labor: The health of birth mothers and adoptive mothers at six-weeks post-partum. *Family Medicine, 23*(1), 29–35.

Glidden, L. M. (1986). Families who adopt mentally retarded children: Who, why, and what happens. In J. J. Gallagher & P. M. Vietze (Eds.), *Families of handicapped persons: Research, programs, and policy issues* (pp. 129–142). Baltimore, MD: Brookes.

Glidden, L. M. (1990). The wanted ones: Families adopting children with mental retardation. In L. M. Glidden (Ed.), *Formed families: Adoption of children with handicaps* (pp. 177–205). Binghamton, NY: Haworth.

Glidden, L. M. (2000). Adopting children with developmental disabilities: A long-term perspective. *Family Relations, 49*(4), 397–405. doi:10.1111/j.1741–3729.2000.00397.x

Glidden, L. M., Billings, F. J., & Jobe, B. M. (2006). Personality, coping style and well-being of parents rearing children with developmental disabilities. *Journal of Intellectual Disability Research, 50*(12), 949–962. doi:10.1111/j.1365–2788.2006.00929.x

Glidden, L. M., Flaherty, E. M., & McGlone, A. P. (2000). Is more too many? Adjustment in families with adopted children with developmental disabilities. *Adoption Quarterly, 4*(1), 67–80. doi:10.1300/J145v04n01_05

Gold, R. M. (1999). Adoption: The Jewish view. *Adoption Quarterly, 3*(1), 3–13. doi:10.1300/J145v03n01_02

Goldberg, A. E. (2010). *Lesbian and gay parents and their children: Research on the family life cycle*. Washington, DC: American Psychological Association.

Goldberg, A. (2012). *Gay dads: Transitions to adoptive fatherhood*. New York, NY: NYU Press.

Goldberg, A., Downing., J. B., & Moyer, A. M. (2012). Why parenthood, and why now: Gay men's motivations for pursuing parenthood. *Family Relations, 61*(1), 157–174. doi: 10.1111/j.1741–3729.2011.00687.x

Goldberg, A. E., Downing, J. B., & Richardson, H.B. (2009). The transition from infertility to adoption: Perceptions of lesbian and heterosexual couples. *Journal of Social and Personal Relationships, 26*, 938–963.

Goldberg, A. E., & Gianino, M. (2011). Lesbian and gay adoptive parent families: Assessment, clinical issues, and intervention. In D. M. Brodzinsky & A. Pertman (Eds.), *Adoption by lesbians and gay men: A new dimension in family diversity* (pp. 204–232). New York, NY: Oxford University Press.

Goldberg, A. E., Moyer, A. M., Kinkler, L. A., & Richardson, H. B. (2012). "When you're sitting on the fence, hope's the hardest part": Challenges and experiences of heterosexual and same-sex couples adopting through the child welfare system. *Adoption Quarterly, 15*, 288–315.

Goldsmith, D. (1990). "Individual vs. Collective Rights: The Indian Child Welfare Act." *Harvard Women s Law Journal, 13*(Spring), 1–12.

Golombok, S., Cook, R., Bish, A., & Murray, C. (1995). Families created by the new reproductive technologies: Quality of parenting and social and emotional development of the children. *Child Development, 66*(2), 285–298.

Graber, J. A., & Brooks-Gunn, J. (1996). Expectations for and precursors of leaving home in young women. In W. Damon, J. A. Graber, & J. S. Dubas (Eds.), *New directions for child development*. San Francisco, CA: Jossey-Bass.

Graff, E. J. (2010). *Anatomy of an adoption crisis.* Retrieved from http://www.foreignpolicy .com/articles/2010/09/07/anatomy_of_an_adoption_crisis

Gray, D. (2002). *Attaching in adoption: Practical tools for today's parents.* Indianapolis, IN: Perspectives Press.

Green, J. (1999). *The velveteen father: An unexpected journey to parenthood.* New York, NY: Villard Books.

Green, W., & Ramsey, P. G. (2010, July). *Ethnic identities of transracial adoptees.* Paper presented at the Third International Adoption Research Conference (ICAR3), Leiden, The Netherlands.

Greenberg, M., & Morris, N. (1994). Engrossment: The newborn's impact upon the father. In S. H. Cath, A. R. Gurwitt, & J. M. Ross (Eds.), *Father and child: Developmental and clinical perspectives* (pp. 87–100). Hillsdale, NJ: Analytic Press.

Greenspan, S. I. (1994). "The second other": The role of the father in early personality formation and the dyadic-phallic phase of development. In S. H. Cath, A. R. Gurwitt, & J. M. Ross (Eds.), *Father and child: Developmental and clinical perspectives* (pp. 123 138). Hillsdale, NJ: Analytic Press.

Greenspan, S. I., & Shanker, S. (2004). *The first idea: How symbols, language and intelligence evolved in early primates and humans.* Cambridge, MA: Capo Press.

Grimm, B., & Hurtubise, I. (2003a). Part I: A background to the review process. Child and family services review: An ongoing series. *Youth Law News, 24*(1), 1–11.

Grimm, B., & Hurtubise, I. (2003b). Part II: An examination of placement and visitation. Child and family services review: An ongoing series. *Youth Law News, 24*(1), 12–26.

Groark, C. J., McCall, R. B., & Fish, L. (2011). Characteristics of environments, caregivers, and children in three central American orphanages. *Infant Mental Health Journal, 32*(2), 232–250. doi:10.1002/imhj.20292

Grossman, K., Grossman, K. E., Kindler, H., & Zimmerman, P. (2008). A wider view of attachment and exploration: The influence of mothers and fathers on the development of psychological security from infancy to young adulthood. In J. Cassidy & P. Shaver (Eds.), *Handbook of attachment: Theory, research, and clinical applications* (2nd ed., pp. 833–856). New York, NY: Guilford Press.

Grotevant, H. D. (2003). Counseling psychological meets the complex world of adoption. *Counseling Psychologist, 31*(6), 753–762. doi: 10.1177/0011000003258388

Grotevant, H. D., & McRoy, R. G. (1990). Adopted adolescents in residential treatment: The role of the family. In D. Brodzinsky & M. D. Schechter (Eds.), *The psychology of adoption* (pp. 167–186). New York, NY: Oxford University Press.

Grotevant, H. D., & McRoy, R. G. (1998). *Openness in adoption: Exploring family connections.* Thousand Oaks, CA: Sage.

Grotevant, H. D., Perry, Y. V., & McRoy, R. G. (2007). Openness in adoption: Outcomes for adolescents within their adoptive kinship networks. In *Adoption factbook IV* (pp. 439–452). Alexandria, VA: National Council for Adoption.

Grotevant, H. D., & Von Korff, L. (2011). Adoptive identity. In S. J. Schwartz, K. Luyckx and V. L. Vignoles (Eds.), *Handbook of identity theory and research* (Vol. 5, pp. 585–601). New York, NY: Springer.

Grotevant, H. D., Wrobel, G.M., Von Korff, L., Skinner, B., Newell, J., Friese, S., & McRoy, R.G. (2008). Many faces of openness in adoption: Perspectives of adopted adolescents and their parents. *Adoption Quarterly, 10*, 79–101.

Groza, V., Proctor, C., & Shenyang, G. (1998). The relationship of institutionalization to the development of Romanian children adopted internationally. *International Journal of Child & Family Welfare, 98*(3), 198–217.

Groza, V., & Rosenberg, K. F. (2001). *Clinical and practice issues in adoption: Bridging the gap in adoptees placed as infants and as older children.* Westport, CT: Greenwood Press.

Groze, V. (1991). Adoption and single parents: A review. *Child Welfare, 70*(3), 321–332.

Gunnar, M. R., & Kertes, D. A. (2005). Prenatal and postnatal risks to neurobiological development in internationally adopted children. In D. Brodzinsky & J. Palacios (Eds.), *Psychological issues in adoption: Research and practice* (pp. 47–65). Westport, CT: Praeger.

Gunsberg, L. (1994). Selected critical review of psychological investigations of the early father-infant relationship. In S. H. Cath, A. R. Gurwitt, & J. M. Ross (Eds.), *Father and child: Developmental and clinical perspectives* (pp. 65–86). Hillsdale, NJ: Analytic Press.

Gunst, K. (2005). *Adopting a waiting child, a single mom shares her journey to adopt her second child from China.* Retrieved from http://www.ranbowkids.com/ArticleDetails .aspx?id+78

Gurwitt, A. R. (1994). Aspects of prospective fatherhood. In S. H. Cath, A. R. Gurwitt, & J. M. Ross (Eds.), *Father and child: Developmental and clinical perspectives* (pp. 275–300). Hillsdale, NJ: Analytic Press.

Habersaat, S. A., Tessier, R., & Pierrehumbert, B. (2011). International adoption: Influence of attachment and maternal monitoring style in the emergence of behavioural problems in adolescence in relation to age at adoption. *Schweizer Archiv Für Neurologie Und Psychiatrie, 162*(1), 21–26.

Hackett, L. (1992). *Industrial revolution.* Website article. Retrieved from http://history-world .org/Industrial%20Intro.htm

Handford, J. (2012) *Daughters for a time.* Las Vegas, NV: Amazon Publishing.

Hardy, D. R. (1984). Adoption of children with special needs: A national perspective. *American Psychologist, 39*(8), 901–904. doi:10.1037/0003–066X.39.8.901

Hartmann, H. (1958). *Ego psychology and the problem of adaptation* (D. Rappaport, Trans.). New York, NY: International Universities Press.

Hartman, A., & Laird, J. (2009). Family treatment after adoption. In D. M. Brodzinsky & M. D. Schechter (Eds.), *The psychology of adoption*, (221–239). New York, NY: Oxford University Press.

Haslanger, S., & Witt, C. (2005). Introduction: Kith, kin, and family. In S. Haslanger & C. Witt (Eds.), *Adoption matters: Philosophical and feminine essays.* Ithaca, NY: Cornell University Press.

Hastings, R.P., & Taunt, H.M. (2002, March). Positive perceptions in families of children with developmental disabilities. *American Journal on Mental Retardation, 107*(2), 116–127. doi: 10.1352/0895-8017(2002)107<0116:PPIFOC>2.0.CO;2

Haugaard, Jeffrey J. (1998). Is adoption a risk factor for the development of adjustment problems? *Clinical Psychology Review, 18*(1), 47–69. doi:10.1016/S0272–7358(97)00055-X

Haugaard, J. J., Moed, A.M., & West, N.M. (2000). Adoption of children with developmental disabilities. *Adoption Quarterly, 3*(4), 81–92. doi:10.1300/J145v03n04_06

Haugaard, J. J., Wojslawowicz, J. C., & Palmer, M. (1999). Outcomes in adolescent and older-child adoptions. *Adoption Quarterly, 3*(1), 61–69. doi:10.1300/J145v03n01_05

Hays, P. A. (2008). *Addressing cultural complexities in practice assessment, diagnosis, and therapy* (2nd ed.). Washington, DC: American Psychological Association.

He, W., Sengupta, M., Velkoff, V.A., & DeBarros, K. A. (2005). *65+ in the United States: 2005.* Retrieved from https://www.census.gov/prod/2006pubs/p23-209.pdf

Hegar, R. L. (2005). Sibling placement in foster care and adoption: An overview of international research. *Children and Youth Services Review, 27*(7), 717–739. doi:10.1016/j.childyouth.2004.12.018

Henderson, D. B. (2007). Why has the mental health community been silent on adoption issues? In R. A. Javier, A. L. Baden, F. A. Biafora, & A. Camacho-Gingerich (Eds.), *Handbook of adoption: Implications for researchers, practitioners, and families* (pp. 403–417). Thousand Oaks, CA: Sage.

Herman, E. (2008). *Kinship by design: A history of adoption in the modern United States.* Chicago, IL: University of Chicago Press.

Hesse, E. (2008). The adult attachment interview: Protocol, method of analysis, and empirical studies. In J. Cassidy & P. R. Shaver (Eds.), *Handbook of attachment theory and research* (2nd ed., pp. 552–558). New York, NY: Guilford Press.

Hodapp, R. M., Ly, T. M., Fidler, D. J., & Ricci, L. A. (2001). Less stress, more rewarding: Parenting children with down syndrome. *Parenting: Science and Practice, 1*(4), 317–337. doi:10.1207/S15327922PAR0104_3

Hodges, J., Steele, M., Hillman, S., Henderson, H., & Kaniuk, J. (2005). Change and continuity in mental representations of attachment after adoption. In D. Brodzinsky & J. Palacios (Eds.), *Psychological issues in adoption: Research and practice* (pp. 93–116). Westport, CT: Praeger.

Hoffman, K. T., Marvin, R. S., Cooper, G., & Powell, B. (2006). Changing toddlers' and preschoolers' attachment classifications: The circle of security intervention. *Journal of consulting and clinical psychology, 74*(6), 1017–1026. doi:10.1037/0022-006X.74.6.1017

Holditch-Davis, D., Sandelowski, M., & Harris, B. G. (1999). Effect of infertility on mothers' and fathers' interactions with young infants. *Journal of Reproductive and Infant Psychology, 17*(2), 159–173. doi:10.1080/02646839908409095

Hood, D. (2005). The orphan myth. In P. Kruger & J. Smolowe (Eds.), *A love like no other: Stories from adoptive parents* (pp. 226–238). New York, NY: Riverhead Books.

Hoopes, Janet L. (1982). *Prediction in child development: A longitudinal study of adoptive and non-adoptive families. The Delaware family study.* New York, NY: Child Welfare Leagues of America.

Hosley, C. A., & Montemayor, R. (1997). Fathers and adolescents. In M. E. Lamb (Ed.), *The role of the father in child development* (3rd ed., pp. 162–178). New York, NY: Wiley.

Howard, J. A., Smith, S. L., & Ryan, S. D. (2004). A comparative study of child welfare adoptions with other types of adopted children and birth children. *Adoption Quarterly, 7,* 1–30. doi 10.1300/J145v07n03_01

Howe, D. (2001). Age at placement, adoption experience and adult adopted people's contact with their adoptive and birth mothers: An attachment perspective. *Attachment & Human Development, 3*(2), 222–237. doi:10.1080/14616730110058025

Howes, C., & Spieker, S. (2008). Attachment relationships in the context of multiple caregivers. *Handbook of attachment: Theory, research, and clinical applications* (2nd ed., pp. 317–332). New York, NY: Guilford Press.

Huda. (n.d.). Adopting a child in Islam: Islamic legal rulings about foster parenting and adoption. *Adoption in Islam.* Retrieved from http://islam.about.com/cs/parenting/a/adoption.htm

Hushion, K. (2006). International adoption: Projection and externalization in the treatment of a 4-year-old-child and her parents. In K. Hushion, S. B. Sherman, & D. Siskind (Eds.), (pp. 35–46) *Understanding adoption: Clinical work with adults, children, and parents.* Lanham, MD: Aronson.

Hushion, K., Sherman, S., & Siskind, D. (Eds.). (2006). *Understanding adoption: Clinical work with adults, children, and parents.* Lanham, MD: Aronson.

Ilicali, E. T., & Fisek, G. O. (2004). Maternal representations during pregnancy and early motherhood. *Infant Mental Health Journal, 25*(1), 16–27. doi:10.1002/imhj.10082

Ingersoll, B. D. (1997). Psychiatric disorders among adopted children: A review and commentary. *Adoption Quarterly, 1*(1), 57–73. doi: 10.1300/J145v01n01_04

Ingersoll, B., Meyer, K., & Becker, M. W. (2011). Increased rates of depressed mood in mothers of children with ASD associated with the presence of the broader autism phenotype. *Autism Research, 4*(2), 143–148. doi:10.1002/aur.170.

Irhammer, M., & Bengtsson, H. (2004). Attachment in a group of adult international adoptees. *Adoption Quarterly, 8*(2), 1–25. doi: 10.1300/J145v08n02_01

Jacobsen, T., Edelstein, W., & Hofmann, V. (1994). A longitudinal study of the relation between representations of attachment in childhood and cognitive functioning in childhood and adolescence. *Developmental Psychology, 30*(1), 112–124. doi:10.1037/0012-1649.30.1.112

Jaser, S. S., Whittemore, R., Ambrosino, J. M., Lindemann, E., & Grey, M. (2008). Mediators of depressive symptoms in children with type 1 diabetes and their mothers. *Journal of Pediatric Psychology, 33*(5), 509–519. doi:10.1093/jpepsy/jsm104

Jaser, S. S., Whittemore, R., Ambrosino, J. M., Lindemann, E., & Grey, M. (2009). Coping and psychosocial adjustment in mothers of young children with type 1 diabetes. *Children's Health Care, 38*(2), 91–106. doi:10.1080/02739610902813229

Jemmott, J.B., Jemmott, L.S., & Fong, G.T. (2010). Efficacy of a theory-based abstinence-only intervention over 24 months: A randomized controlled trial with young adolescents. *Archives of Pediatric Adolescent Medicine, 164*, 152–159.

Jerome, L. (1993). A comparison of the demography, clinical profile and treatment of adopted and non-adopted children at a children's mental health centre. *Canadian Journal of Psychiatry, 38*(4), 290–294.

Johns, M. (2002). Identification and dis-identification in the development of sexual identity. In J. Trowell & A. Etchegoyen (Eds.), *The importance of fathers: A psychoanalytic re-evaluation.* New York, NY: Brunner-Routledge.

Judge, S. (2003). Developmental recovery and deficit in children adopted from Eastern European orphanages. *Child Psychiatry and Human Development, 34*(1), 49–62. doi:10.1023/A:1025302025694

Juffer, F. (2006). Children's awareness of adoption and their problem behavior in families with 7-year-old internationally adopted children. *Adoption Quarterly, 9*(2–3), 1–22.

Juffer, F., & van IJzendoorn, M. (2005). Behavior problems and mental health referrals of international adoptees: A meta-analysis. *Journal of the American Medical Association, 293*, 2501–2514. doi: 10.1001/jama.293.20.2501

Juffer, F., & Van IJzendoorn, M. H. (2007). Adoptees do not lack self-esteem: A meta-analysis of studies on self-esteem of transracial, international and domestic adoptees. *Psychological Bulletin, 133*, 1067–1083.

Jung, C.G. ([1921] 1971). Psychological Types, Collected Works, Volume 6, Princeton, N.J.: Princeton University Press.

Kalodner, C. R., & Hanus, A. E. (2010). Groups across settings. In R. K. Conyne (Ed.), *The Oxford handbook of group counseling* (pp. 399–415). New York, NY: Oxford.

Kanter, J. (2000). The untold story of Clare and Donald Winnicott: How social work influenced modern psychoanalysis. *Clinical Social Work Journal, 28*(3), 245–261. doi:10.1023/A:1005179617180

Kaye, S., & Kuyalanka, K. (2006). *State gay adoption laws and permanency for foster youth.* Maryland Family Policy Impact Seminar. Retrieved from http://www.hhp.umd.edu/FMST/_docsContribute/GayadoptionbriefFINAL0806.pdf

Kazak, A. E., Alderfer, M., Rourke, M. T., Simms, S., Streisand, R., & Grossman, J. R. (2004). Posttraumatic stress disorder (PTSD) and posttraumatic stress symptoms (PTSS) in families of adolescent childhood cancer survivors. *Journal of Pediatric Psychology, 29*(3), 211–219. doi:10.1093/jpepsy/jsh022

Kennedy, H., & Moran, G. (1991). Reflections on the aim of child analysis. *Psychoanalytic Study of the Child, 46,* 181–198.

Kern, I. (1982). The joys of motherhood over 35. *Papers in the Social Science, 2,* 43–56.

Kim, W. J. (1995). International adoption: A case review of Korean children. *Child Psychiatry and Human Development, 25*(3), 141–154.

Kim, W. J., Davenport, C., Joseph, J., Zrull, J., & Woolford, E. (1988). Psychiatric disorder and juvenile delinquency in adopted children and adolescents. *Journal of the American Academy of Child & Adolescent Psychiatry, 27*(1), 111–115. doi:10.1097/00004583-198801000–00017

Kirk, H. D. (1964a). *Shared fate: A theory of adoption and mental health.* New York, NY: Free Press.

Kirk, H. D. (1964b). *Shared fate: A theory and method of adoptive relationships.* New York, NY: Free Press.

Kirk, H. D. (1984). Shared fate: A theory and method of adoptive relationships. New York, NY: Free Press.

Kirschner, D. (1990). The adopted child syndrome: Considerations for psychotherapy. *Psychotherapy in Private Practice, 8*(3), 93–100. doi:10.1300/J294v08n03_12

Kohut, H. (1971) *The analysis of the self.* New York, NY: International Universities Press.

Kohut, H. (1977). *The restoration of the self.* New York, NY: International Universities Press.

Kohut, H., & Wolf, E. S. (1978). The disorders of the self and their treatment: An outline. *International Journal of Psychoanalysis, 59,* 413–425.

Kosmin, B. A., & Keysar, S. P. (2009). *American Religious Identification Survey 2008.* Hartford, CT: Trinity College.

Kovacs, M., Finkelstein, R., Feinberg, T. L., Crouse-Novak, M., Paulauskas, S., & Pollock, M. (1985). Initial psychologic responses of parents to the diagnosis of insulin-dependent diabetes mellitus in their children. *Diabetes Care, 8*(6), 568–575. doi:10.2337/diacare.8.6.568

Krementz, J. (1982). *How it feels to be adopted.* New York, NY: Alfred A. Knopf.

Kriebel, D. K., & Wentzel, K. (2011). Parenting as a moderator of cumulative risk for behavioral competence in adopted children. *Adoption Quarterly, 14,* 37–60. 10.1080/10926755.2011.557945

Kupecky, R., & Anderson, K. (1998). Infertility and adoption. In V. Groza & K. F. Rosenberg (Eds.), *Clinical and practice issues in adoption: Bridging the gap between adoptees placed as infants and as older children, revised and updated* (pp. 21–36). Westport, CT: Greenwood.

Lam, D. S. Y., Leung, S. P., & So, K. T. (2007). Age of onset of asthma symptoms. *Hong Kong Journal of Paediatrics, 12,* 11 14. Retrieved from http://www.hkjpaed.org/pdf/2007;12;11-14.pdf

Lamb, M. E. (1986). The changing roles of fathers. In M. E. Lamb (Ed.), *The father's role: Applied perspectives* (pp. 3–27). New York, NY: Wiley.

Lamb, M. E. (1997a). Fathers and child development: An introductory overview and guide. In M. E. Lamb (Ed.), *The role of the father in child development* (3rd ed., pp. 1–18). New York, NY: Wiley.

Lamb, M. E. (1997b). The development of father-infant relationships. In M. E. Lamb (Ed.), *The role of the father in child development* (3rd ed., pp. 104–120). New York, NY: Wiley.

Lamb, M. E. (1999). Parental behavior, family processes, and child development in nontraditional and traditionally understudied families. In M. E. Lamb (Ed.), *Parenting and child development in "nontraditional" families* (pp. 1–14). Mahwah, NJ: Erlbaum.

Landerholm, L. (2001). The experience of abandonment and adoption, as a child and as a parent, in a psychological motivational perspective. *International Forum of Psychoanalysis, 10*(1), 12–25. doi:10.1080/08037060117049

Landolt, M. A., Ribi, K., Laimbacher, J., Vollrath, M., Gnehm, H. E., & Sennhauser, F. H. (2002). Brief report: Posttraumatic stress disorder in parents of children with newly diagnosed type 1 diabetes. *Journal of Pediatric Psychology, 27*(7), 647–652. doi:10.1093/jpepsy/27.7.647

Landolt, M. A., Vollrath, M., Laimbacher, J., Gnehm, H. E., & Sennhauser, F. H. (2005). Prospective study of posttraumatic stress disorder in parents of children with newly diagnosed type 1 diabetes. *Journal of the American Academy of Child and Adolescent Psychiatry, 44*(7), 682–689. doi:10.1097/01.chi.0000161645.98022.35

Lane, R. D., & Garfield, D. A. (2005). Becoming aware of feelings: Integration of cognitive-developmental, neuroscientific, and psychoanalytic perspectives. *Neuropsychoanalysis, 7*(1), 5–30.

Langridge, D., Sheeran, P., & Connolly, K. (2005). Understanding the reasons for parenthood. *Journal of Reproductive and Infant Psychology, 23*, 121–133. doi:10.1080/02646830500129438

Lansford, J. E., Ceball, R., Abbey, A., & Stewart, A. J. (2001). Does family structure matter? A comparison of adoptive, two-parent biological, single-mother, stepfather, and stepmother households. *Journal of Marriage and Family, 63*, 840–851.

Lapidus, C. (2006). Working with parents of internationally adopted infants and toddlers. In S. B. Sherman, K. Hushion, & D. Suskind (Eds.)., *Understanding adoption: Clinical work with adult, children, and parents* (pp. 47–60). Oxford, England: Jacob Aronson.

Leder, S., Grinstead, L. N., & Torres, E. (2007). Grandparents raising grandchildren: Stressors, social support, and health outcomes. *Journal of Family Nursing, 13*, 333–352.

Lee, R. M. (2010). Parental perceived discrimination as a post-adoption risk factor for internationally adopted children and adolescents. *Cultural Diversity and Ethnic Minority Psychology, 16*(4), 493–500. doi: 10.1037/a0020651

Leinaweaver, J. J. (2008). *The coordinated management of a culturally diffused identity: Internationally adopted people and the narrative burden of self.* (Doctoral dissertation). ProQuest. Retrieved from 3352402

Leishman, M. (n.d.). Age gaps: Mark Leishman share his thoughts on being an older parent. *Super dad column.* Retrieved from http://www.kiwifamilies.co.nz/Topics/Celebrity-Columns/Super+Dad+Column/Age+Gaps.html

Leung, P., & Erich, S. (2002). Family functioning of adoptive children with special needs: Implications of familial supports and children characteristics. *Children and Youth Services Review, 24*(11), 799–816. doi:10.1016/S0190–7409(02)00240–2

Leve, L. D., Scaramella, L. V., & Fagot, B. I. (2001). Infant temperament, pleasure in parenting, and marital happiness in adoptive families. *Infant Mental Health Journal, 22*, 545–558. doi: 1002/imhj.1017

Levy-Shiff, R. (2001). Psychological adjustment of adoptees in adulthood: Family environment and adoption-related correlates. *International Journal of Behavioral Development, 25*(2), 97–104. doi:10.1080/01650250042000131

Levy-Shiff, R., Goldshmidt, I., & Har-Even, D. (1991). Transition to parenthood in adoptive families. *Developmental Psychology, 27*(1), 131–140. doi:10.1037/0012–1649.27.1.131

Liem, D. B. (2000). *First person plural.* Berkeley, CA: Mu Films.

Lifton, B. J. (1976). The search. *New York Magazine, 25*(1), 15–19.

Lifton, B. J. (1994). *Journal of the adopted self: A question for wholeness.* New York, NY: Basic Books.

Lifton, B. J. (2010). Ghosts in the adopted family. *Psychoanalytic Inquiry, 30*, 71–79.

Lindsay, H. (2009). *Adoption in the Roman world.* New York, NY: Cambridge University Press. Retrieved from http://www.myilibrary.com?id=240247

Livio, S. K. (2011). *Gov. Christie conditionally vetoes adoptee birth certificate bill, insisting anonymity for mothers.* Accessed at http://www.nj.com/news/index.ssf/2011/06/gov_christie_conditionally_vet_3.html

Lohr, S. (1997, January 12). Creating Jobs. *New York Times*. Retrieved from file:///C:/Users/APRILF~1/AppData/Local/Temp/Steve%20Jobs%20-%20New%20York%20Times.htm

Lytton, H., & Romney, D. M. (1991). Parents' differential socialization of boys and girls: A meta-analysis. *Psychological Bulletin, 109*, 267–297. doi: 10.1037/0033–2909.109.2.267

Mabry, C. R., & Kelly, L. (2006). *Adoption law: Theory, policy, and practice*. Buffalo, NY: Hein.

MacCallum, F., Golombok, S., & Brinsden, P. (2007). Parenting and child development in families with a child conceived by embryo donation. *Journal of Family Psychology, 21*, 278–287. doi:10.1037/0893–3200.21.2.278

Mahler, M. S., & Stepansky, P. E. (1988). *The memoirs of Margaret S. Mahler*. New York, NY: Free Press.

Main, M. (1996). Introduction to the special section on attachment and psychopathology: 2. Overview of the field of attachment. *Journal of Consulting and Clinical Psychology, 64*, 237–243.

Main, M., & Goldwyn, R. (1984). *Adult attachment scoring & classification system*. (Unpublished manuscript). University of California.

Main, M., & Solomon, J. (1990). Procedures for identifying infants as disorganized/disoriented during the Ainsworth Strange Situation. In M. T. Greenberg, D. Cicchetti, & E. M. Cummings (Eds.), *Attachment in the preschool years* (pp. 121–160). Chicago: University of Chicago Press.

Mallon, G. P. (2000). Gay men and lesbians as adoptive parents. *Journal of Gay & Lesbian Social Services, 11*(4), 1–21.

Malm, K., & Welti, K. (2010). Exploring motivations to adopt. *Adoption Quarterly, 13*(3–4), 185–208. doi:10.1080/10926755.2010.524872

Mandell, D. S., Novak, M. M., & Zubritsky, C. D. (2005). Factors associated with age of diagnosis among children with autism spectrum disorders. *Pediatrics, 116*(6), 1480–1486. doi:10.1542/peds.2005–0185

Manuel, J., Naughton, M. J., Balkrishnan, R., Smith, B. P., & Koman, L. A. (2003). Stress and adaptation in mothers of children with cerebral palsy. *Journal of Pediatric Psychology, 28*(3), 197–201. doi:10.1093/jpepsy/jsg007

Marcovitch, S., Goldberg, S., Gold, A., Washington, J., Wasson, C., Krekewich, K., & Handley-Derry, M. (1997). Determinants of behavioural problems in Romanian children adopted in Ontario. *International Journal of Behavioral Development, 20*(1), 17–31. doi:10.1080/016502597385414

Marks, M. (2002). Letting fathers in. In S. Budd, J. Trowell, & A. Etchegoyer (Eds.), *The importance of fathers: A psychoanalytic re-evaluation* (pp. 93–106). New York, NY: Brunner-Routledge.

Marre, D., & Briggs, L. (Eds.). (2009). *International adoption: Global inequalities and the circulation of children*. New York, NY: New York University.

Marshner, W. H. (1999). Christian view of adoption. In C. Marshner & W. L. Pierce (Eds.), *Adoption factbook III* (pp. 243–244). Minnesota, MN: Park Press.

Marvin, R. S., & Britner, P. A. (2008). Normative development: The ontogeny of attachment. In J. Cassidy & P. R. Shaver (Eds.), *Handbook of attachment: Theory, research, and clinical applications* (2nd ed., pp. 269–294). New York, NY: Guilford Press.

Marx, J. (1990). Better me than somebody else: Families reflect on their adoption of children with developmental disabilities. In L.M. Glidden (Ed.), *Formed families: Adoption of children with handicaps* (pp. 141–174). Binghamton, NY: Haworth.

Matthews, J. D., & Cramer, E. P. (2006). Envisaging the adoption process to strengthen gay- and lesbian-headed families: Recommendations for adoption professionals. *Child Welfare, 85*(2), 317–340.

Mayes, L. C., & Cohen, D. J. (1996). Children's developing theory of mind. *Journal of the American Psychoanalytic Association, 44*(1), 117–142.

McCubbin, M. A., & McCubbin, H. I. (1993). Families coping with illness: The resiliency model of family stress, adjustment, and adaptation. In C. B. Danielson, B. Hamel-Bissell, & P. Winstead-Fry (Eds.), *Families, health, and illness: Perspectives on coping and intervention* (pp. 21–63). St. Louis, MO: Mosby.

McDonald, T. P., Propp, J. R., & Murphy, K. C. (2001). The postadoption experience: Child, parent, and family predictors of family adjustment to adoption. *Child Welfare, 80*(1), 71–94.

McGinn, M. F. (2007). Developmental challenges for adoptees across the life cycle. In R. A. Javier, A. L. Baden, F. A. Biafora, & A. Camacho-Gingerich (Eds.), *Handbook of adoption: Implications for researchers, practitioners, and families* (pp. 61–76). Thousand Oaks, CA: Sage.

McGinnis, H., Smith, S. L., Ryan, S., & Howard, J. A. (2009). *Beyond culture camp: Promoting healthy identity formation in adoption.* New York, NY: Evan B. Donaldson Adoption Institute. Available online at www.adoptioninstitute.org

McKay, K., Ross, L. E., & Goldberg, A. E. (2010). Adaptation to parenthood during the postadoption period: A review of the literature. *Adoption Quarterly, 13*(2), 125–144. doi:10.1080/10926755.2010.481040

McPherson, M., Arango, P., Fox, H., Lauver, C., McManus, M., Newacheck, P. W., . . . Strickland, B. (1998). A new definition of children with special health care needs. *Pediatrics, 102*(1), 137–139. doi:10.1542/peds.102.1.137

McRoy, R. L., Zurcher, M., Lauderdale, M. L., & Anderson, R. E. (1982). Self-esteem and racial identity in transracial and inracial adoptees. *Social Work, 27*, 522–526.

McRoy, R. G., Zurcher, L. A., Lauderdale, M. L., & Anderson, R. E. (1984). The identity of transracial adoptees. *Social Casework, 65*(1), 34–39.

Mech, E. V. (1973). Adoption: A policy perspective. In B. Caldwell & H. N. Ricciuti (Eds.), *Review of child development research* (Vol. 3, pp. 75–107). Chicago, IL: University of Chicago Press.

Melina, L. R. (1998). *Raising adopted children: Practical reassuring advice for every adoptive parent* (2nd ed.). New York, NY: HarperCollins.

Melosh, B. (2002). *Strangers and kin: The American way of adoption.* Cambridge, MA: Harvard University Press.

Mendenhall, T. J., Berge, J. M., Wrobel, G. M., Grotevant, H., & McRoy, R. G. (2004). Adolescents' satisfaction with contact in adoption. *Child and Adolescent Social Work Journal, 21*(2), 175–190.

Metcalfe, W. A. (2010). *The experience of older foster parents.* Fargo, ND: North Dakota State University of Agriculture and Applied Science.

Miall, C. (1987). The stigma of adoptive parent status: Perceptions of community attitudes towards adoption and the experience of informal social sanctioning. *Family Relations, 36*, 34–39.

Miall, C. E., & March, K. (2003). A comparison of biological and adoptive mothers and fathers: The relevance of biological kinship and gendered constructs of parenthood. *Adoption Quarterly, 6*(4), 7–39.

Mikulincer, M., & Shaver, P. R. (2003). The attachment behavioral system in adulthood: Activation, psychodynamics, and interpersonal processes. In M. P. Zanna (Ed.), *Advances in experimental social psychology* (Vol. 35, pp. 53–152). San Diego, CA: Academic Press.

Miles, C. G. (2000). Bonding across difference. In S. Akhtar & S. Kramer (Eds.), *Thicker than blood: Bonds of fantasy and reality in adoption* (pp. 21–59). New York, NY: Aronson.

Miller, B. C., Fan, X., Christensen, M., Grotevant, H. D., & van Dulmen, M. (2000). Comparison of adopted and non-adopted adolescents in a large nationally representative sample. *Child Development, 71*(5), 1458–1473. doi:10.1111/1467–8624.00239

Minkler, M., Roe, K., & Price, M. (1992). The physical and emotional health of grandmothers raising grandchildren in the crack cocaine epidemic. *The Gerontologist,* 32:752–760.

Modell, J., & Dambacher, N. (1997). Making a "Real" family: Matching and cultural biologism in American adoption. *Adoption Quarterly, 1*(2), 3–33.

Molinari, D.L., & Freeborn, D. (2006). Social support needs of families adopting special needs children. *Journal of Psychosocial Nursing and Mental Health Services, 44*(4), 28–34. Retrieved from http://search.proquest.com.ezproxy.fielding.edu/docview/225534307/13A4168E3C379F13931/18?accountid=10868

Momaya, M. L. (1999). *Motivation towards international adoption.* (Thesis). Retrieved from WorldCat. (443373282)

Morello, C. (2010, May 6). More children are being born to women over 35 than to teens, Pew study findings. *The Washington Post,* 1–2.

Moriarty, L. (2012) *The Chaperone.* New York, NY: Penguin Group.

Morris, M. B. (1988). *Last-chance children: Growing up with older parents.* New York, NY: Columbia University Press.

Muller, U., & Perry, B. (2001a). Adopted persons' search for and contact with their birth parents I: Who searches and why? *Adoption Quarterly, 4*(3), 5–37. doi: 10.1300/J145v04n03_02

Musil, C., Gordon, N., Warner, C., Zauszniewski, J., Standing, T., & Wykle, M. (2010). Grandmothers and caregiving to grandchildren: Continuity, change, and outcomes over 24 months. *The Gerontologist.* Retrieved http://gerontologist.oxfordjournals.org/content/early/2010/08/19/geront.gnq061.fulldoi:10.1093/geront/gnq061

Narad, C., & Mason, P. W. (2004). International adoptions: Myths and realities. *Pediatric Nursing, 30,* 483–487.

National Center for Health Statistics Division for Health Interview Statistics. (2009). *National survey of adopted parents.* Retrieved from http://www.cdc.gov/nchs/slaits/nsap.htm

Newberger, C. (1980). The cognitive structure of parenthood: Designing a descriptive measure. *New Directions for Child Development, 1,* 45 67.

Nickman, S. (2004). The holding environment in adoption. *Journal of Infant, Child & Adolescent Psychotherapy, 3,* 329–341. doi:10.1080/15289160309348469

Niemann, S., & Weiss, S. (2012). Factors affecting attachment in international adoptees at 6 months post adoption. *Children and Youth Services Review, 34*(1), 205–212. doi:10.1016/j.childyouth.2011.10.001

North American Council on Adoptable Children. (n.d.). *Adoption subsidy.* Retrieved from http://www.nacac.org/adoptionsubsidy/adoptionsubsidy.html

Novy, M. (2004). *Imagining adoption: Essays on literature and culture.* Ann Arbor, MI: University of Michigan Press.

O'Brien, M. (2007). Ambiguous loss in families of children with autism spectrum disorders. *Family Relations, 56*(2), 135–146. doi:10.1111/j.1741–3729.2007.00447.x

O'Connor, S. (2001). *Orphan trains: The story of Charles Loring Brace and the children he saved and failed.* Boston, MA: Houghton-Mifflin.

Office of the Assistant Secretary for Planning and Evaluation (ASPE). (2011). *Children adopted from foster care: Child and family characteristics, adoption motivation, and well being.* Retrieved from http://aspe.hhs.gov/hsp/09/NSAP/Brief1/rb.shtml

Onsker, G. (2011). Adoption Laws in India. *The Radical Humanist.* Retrived from http://www.theradicalhumanist.com/index.php?option=com_radical&controller=article&cid=62&Itemid=56

Olsen, T. (2010). Adoption is everywhere: Even God is into it. *Christianity Today*, 1–2.

Ones, K., Yilmaz, E., Cetinkaya, B., & Caglar, N. (2005). Assessment of the quality of life of mothers of children with cerebral palsy (primary caregivers). *Neurorehabilitation and Neural Repair, 19*(3), 232–237. doi:10.1177/1545968305278857

Osherson, S. (1999). *The hidden wisdom of parents: Real stories that can help you be a better parent.* Holbrook, MA: Adams Media.

Padovano, A. K. (2012). A strengths-based assessment of young adults raised as children of lesbian adoptive mothers: Identify development peer relationships, stigma and passing. (Unpublished doctoral dissertation). Widener University, Chester, PA.

Pakizegi, B. (2007). Single-parent adoptions and clinical implications. In R. A. Javier, A. L. Baden, F. A. Biafora, & A. Camacho-Gingerich (Eds.), *Handbook of adoption: Implications for researchers, practitioners, and families* (pp. 190–216). Thousand Oaks, CA: Sage.

Palacios J. (2009). The ecology of adoption. In G.Wrobel and E. Neil (Eds.). International advances in adoption research for practice. (pp. 71–94). New York, NY: Wiley.

Palacios, J., & Sanchez-Sandoval, Y. (2005). Beyond adopted/nonadopted comparisons. In D. Brodzinsky & J. Palacios (Eds.), *Psychological issues in adoption: Research and practice* (pp. 117–144). Westport, CT: Praeger.

Palacios, J., Sanchez-Sandoval, Y, & Leon, E. (2006). Inter-country adoption disruptions in Spain. *Adoption Quarterly, 9* (1), 35–55. DOI: 10.1300/J145v09n01_03

Panaccione, V. (2011, January 12). Advantages of being older parents. *Better parenting institute: Bringing joy and fulfillment to parent-child relationships.* Retrieved from http://www.betterparentinginstitute.com/Better-Parenting/parenting-child-raising-skills/advantages-of-being-older-parents/

Parens, H. (1980). An exploration of the relations of instinctual drives and the symbiosis/separation-individual process. *Journal of the American Psychoanalytic Association, 28*, 89–114.

Parens, H. (2010). *Parenting for emotional growth: A textbook, workshops, and curriculum for students in grades K–12.* Philadelphia, PA: Jefferson Medical College.

Parens, H., Scattergood, E., Singletary, W., & Duff, A. (1987). *Aggression in our children: Coping with it constructively.* Northvale, NJ: Aronson.

Patterson, C. J. (1992). Children of lesbian and gay parents. *Child Development, 63*, 1025–1042. doi: 10.2307/1131517

Patterson, C. J. (1994). Children of the lesbian baby boom: Behavioral adjustment, self-concepts, and sex role identity. In B. Greene & Herek (Eds.), *Lesbian and gay psychology: Theory, research, and clinical applications* (pp. 156–175). Thousand Oaks, CA: Sage.

Patterson, C. J. (1997). Children of lesbian and gay parents. In T. H. Ollendick & R. J. Prinz (Eds.), *Advances in clinical child psychology* (Vol. 19, pp. 235–282). New York, NY: Plenum Press.

Patterson, C. J. (2000). Family relationships of lesbians and gay men. *Journal of Marriage and the Family, 62*, 1052–1069. doi: 10.1111/j.1741-3737.2000.01052.x

Patterson, C. J. (2001). Families of the lesbian baby boom: Maternal mental health and child adjustment. *Journal of Gay & Lesbian Psychotherapy, 4*(3/4), 91–107.

Patterson, C. J. (2005). Lesbian and gay parents and their children: Summary of research findings. In *Lesbian & Gay Parenting* (pp. 5–22), Washington, DC: American Psychological Association.

Patterson, C. J. (2006). Children of lesbian and gay parents. *Current Directions in Psychological Science, 15*, 241–244. doi:10.1111/j.1467-8721.2006.00444.x

Pavao, J. M. (2005). *The family of adoption* (2nd ed.). Boston, MA: Beacon Press.

Pavao, J. M. (2007). Variations in clinical issues for children adopted as infants and those adopted as older children. In R. A. Javier, A. L. Baden, F. A. Biafora, & A. Camacho-Gingerich (Eds.), *Handbook of adoption: Implications for researchers, practitioners, and families* (pp. 283–292). Thousand Oaks, CA: Sage.

Pawelski, J. G., Perrin, E. C., Foy, J. M., Allen, C. E., Crawford, J. E., Del Monte, M., . . . Vickers, D. L. (2006). The effects of marriage, civil union, and domestic partnership laws on the health and well-being of children. *Pediatrics, 118*(1), 349–364. doi:10.1542/peds.2006-1279

Payne, J. L., Fields, E. S., Meuchel, J. M., Jaffe, C. J., & Jha, M. (2010). Post adoption depression. *Archives of Women's Mental Health, 13*(2), 147–151. doi:10.1007/s00737-009-0137-7

Pederson, F., Anderson, B., & Kain, R. (1980). Parent-infant and husband-wife interactions observed at five months. In F. Pederson (Ed.), *The father-infant relationship* (pp. 65–91). New York, NY: Praeger.

Perry, C. L., & Henry, M. J. (2009). Family and professional considerations for adoptive parents of children with special needs. *Marriage & Family Review, 45*(5), 538–565. doi:10.1080/01494920903050938

Pertman, A. (2005). And then everything changed. In P. Kruger & J. Smolowe (Eds.), *A love like no other: Stories from adoptive parents* (pp. 206–216). New York, NY: Riverhead Books.

Pertman, A. (2011). *Adoption nation: How the adoption revolution is transforming our families—And America*. Boston, MA: Harvard Common Press.

Pertman, A., & Howard, J. (2012). Emerging diversity in family life: Adoption by gay and lesbian parents. In D. M. Brodzinsky & A. Pertman (Eds.), *Adoption by lesbians and gay men: A new dimension in family diversity* (pp. 20–35). New York, NY: Oxford University Press.

Peterson, L., & Freundlich, M. (2000). Wrongful adoption. *Children's Voice, 1*, 20–23.

Pew Research Center. (2010). The decine of marriage and rise of new families. Retrieved from http://www.pewsocialtrends.org/files/2010/11/pew-social-trends-2010-families.pdf

Petta, G. A., & Steed, L. G. (2005). The experience of adoptive parents in adoption reunion relationships: A qualitative study. *American Journal of Orthopsychiatry, 75*(2), 230–241. doi:10.1037/0002-9432.75.2.230

Pierce, W. L. (1999a). Half-siblings, siblings, and search. In C. Marshner & W. L. Pierce (Eds.), *Adoption factbook III* (pp. 229–232). Waite Park, MN: Park Press Quality Printing.

Pierce, W. L. (1999b). Religious perspectives on adoption. In C. Marshner & W. L. Pierce (Eds.), *Adoption factbook III* (pp. 239–240). Waite Park, MN: Park Press Quality Printing.

Pierce, W. L. (1999c). Kinship care. In C. Marshner & W. L. Pierce (Eds.), *Adoption factbook III* (pp. 104–116). Waite Park, MN: Park Press Quality Printing.

Pine, F. (2004). Mahler's concepts of "symbiosis" and separation-individuation: Revisited, reevaluated, refined. *Journal of the American Psychoanalytic Association, 52*(2), 511–533.

Pivinck, B. A. (2010). Left without a word. Learning rhythms, rhymes, and reasons in adoption. *Psychoanalytic inquiry, 30*, 3–24.

Pleck, E. G., & Pleck, J. H. (1997). Fatherhood ideals in the United States: Historical dimensions. In M. E. Lamb (Ed.), *The role of the father in child development* (3rd ed., pp. 33–48). New York, NY: Wiley.

Polak, P. R., Emde, R. N., & Spitz, R. A. (1964). The smiling response. I. Methodology, quantification and natural history. *Journal of Nervous and Mental Disease, 139*, 103–109. doi:10.1097/00005053-196408000-00002

Pollack, D., Bleich, M., Reid, C. J., & Fadel, M. (2004). Classical religious perspectives of adoption law. *Notre Dame Law Review, 79*(693). Retrieved from http://papers.ssrn.com/sol3/papers.cfm?abstract_id=1105091

Pomerleau, A., Malcuit, G., Chicoine, J.-F., Séguin, R., Belhumeur, C., Germain, P., . . . Jéliu, G. (2005). Health status, cognitive and motor development of young children adopted from China, East Asia, and Russia across the first 6 months after adoption. *International Journal of Behavioral Development, 29*(5), 445–457. doi:10.1177/01650250500206257

Population Reference Bureau. (2011, December). The health and well-being of grandparents caring for grandchildren. *Today's Research on Aging, 2*, 1–6 http://www.prb.org/pdf11/TodaysResearchAging23.pdf

Porch, T. K. (2007). Counseling adoption triad members. In R. A. Javier, A. L. Baden, F. A. Biafora, & A. Camacho-Gingerich (Eds.), *Handbook of adoption: Implications for researchers, practitioners, and families* (pp. 293–311). Thousand Oaks, CA: Sage.

Prager, D. (1999a). Judaic view of adoption. In C. Marshner & W. L. Pierce (Eds.), *Adoption factbook III* (pp. 241–242). Minneapolis, MN: Park Press.

Prager, D. (1999b). Men and adoption. In C. Marshner & W. L. Pierce (Eds.), *Adoption factbook III* (pp. 362–364). Minneapolis, MN: Park Press.

Priel, B., Melamed-Hass, S., Besser, A., & Kantor, B. (2000). Adjustment among adopted children: The role of maternal self-reflectiveness. *Family Relations, 49*(4), 389–396. 10.1111/j.1741–3729.2000.00389.x.

Pruett, K. D. (1987). *The nurturing father: Journey toward the complete man.* New York, NY: Warner Books.

Pruitt, D. (1999). *Your adolescent: Emotional, behavioral, and cognitive development from early adolescence through the teen years.* New York, NY: Harper Collins.

Ragozin, A. S., Basham, R. B., Crnic, K. A., Greenberg, M. T., & Robinson, N. M. (1982). Effects of maternal age on parenting role. *Developmental Psychology, 18*(4), 627–634. 10.1037/0012–1649.18.4.627

Rawson, B. (1986). The Roman family. In B. Rawson (Ed.), *The family in ancient Rome: New perspectives* (pp. 1–57). New York, NY: Cornell University Press.

Recker, N. (2007). *In praise of older parents* (fact sheet No. HYG-5306–98). Family and Consumer Sciences. Columbus, OH: Ohio State University Extension. Retrieved from http://ohioline.osu.edu/hyg-fact/5000/pdf/Older_Parents.pdf

Reid, B. M. (1983). *Characteristics of families who adopt children with special needs* (Unpublished doctoral dissertation). University of Texas, Austin, TX.

Reilly, T., & Platz, L. (2003). Characteristics and challenges of families who adopt children with special needs: An empirical study. *Children and Youth Services Review, 25*(10), 781–803. doi:10.1016/S0190–7409(03)00079–3

Reitz, M., & Watson, K. W. (1992). *Adoption and the family system.* New York, NY: Guilford Press.

Rijk, C. H. A. M., Hoksbergen, R. A. C., & ter Laak, J. (2010). Development of behavioural problems in children adopted from Romania to the Netherlands, after a period of deprivation. *European Journal of Developmental Psychology, 7*(2), 233–248. doi:10.1080/17405620802063339

Rijk, C. H. A. M., Hoksbergen, R. A. C., ter Laak, J. J. F., van Dijkum, C., & Robbroeckx, L. H. M. (2006). Parents who adopt deprived children have a difficult task. *Adoption Quarterly, 9*(2–3), 37–61. doi:10.1300/J145v09n02_03

Roberts, J. E., Gotlib, I. H., & Kassel, J. D. (1996). Adult attachment security and symptoms of depression: The mediating roles of dysfunctional attitudes and low self-esteem. *Journal of Personality and Social Psychology, 70*(2), 310–320. doi:10.1037/0022–3514.70.2.310

Robinson, M., & Wilks, S. (2006). "Older but not wiser": What custodial grandparents want to tell social workers about raising grandchildren. *Social Work and Christianity, 33(2)*, 164–177.

Rolland, J. S. (1987). Family illness paradigms: Evolution and significance. *Family Systems Medicine, 5*(4), 482–503. doi:http://dx.doi.org.cardinal.fielding.edu/10.1037/h0089735

Roorda, R. M. (2007). Moving beyond the controversy of the transracial adoption of black and biracial children. *Handbook of adoption: Implications for researchers, practitioners, and families* (pp. 133–148). Thousand Oaks, CA: Sage.

Rosenberg, E. B. (2010). *The adoption life cycle: The children and their families through the years* (2nd ed.). New York, NY: Free Press.

Rosenthal, J. A., Groze, V., & Morgan, J. (1996). Services for families adopting children via public child welfare agencies: Use, helpfulness, and need. *Children and Youth Services Review, 18*(1–2), 163–182. doi:10.1016/0190–7409(95)00059–3

Rosenthal, J. A., Schmidt, D., & Conner, J. (1988). Predictors of special needs adoption disruption: An exploratory study. *Children and Youth Services Review, 10*(2), 101–117. doi:10.1016/0190–7409(88)90031-X

Rosnati, R., Iafrate, R., & Scabini, E. (2007). Parent-adolescent communication in foster, intercountry adoptive, and biological Italian families: Gender and generational differences. *International Journal of Psychology, 42*(1), 36–45. doi:10.1080/00207590500412128

Rosnati, R., & Marta, E. (1997). Parent-child relationships as a protective factor in preventing adolescents' psychosocial risk in inter-racial adoptive and non-adoptive families. *Journal of Adolescence, 20*, 617–631. doi:10.1006/jado.1997.0115

Ross, J. M. (1994a). In search of fathering: A review. In S. H. Cath, A. R. Gurwitt, & J. M. Ross (Eds.), *Father and child: Developmental and clinical perspectives* (pp. 21–32). Hillsdale, NJ: Analytic Press.

Ross, J. M. (1994b). From mother to father: The boy's search for a generative identity and the oedipal era. In S. H. Cath, A. R. Gurwitt, & J. M. Ross (Eds.), *Father and child: Developmental and clinical perspectives* (pp. 189–204). Hillsdale, NJ: Analytic Press.

Ross, L., Epstein, R., Goldfinger, C., Steele, L., Anderson, S., & Strike, C. (2008). Lesbian and queer mothers navigating the adoption system: The impacts on mental health. *Health Sociology Review, 17*(3), 254–266.

Row, S. (2005). *Surviving the special educational needs system: How to be a "velvet bulldozer."* London, UK: Kingsley.

Russell, G. (1999). Primary caregiving fathers. In M. E. Lamb (Ed.), *Parenting and child development in "nontraditional" families* (pp. 57–81). Mahwah, NJ: Erlbaum.

Russell, M. (2000). *Adoption wisdom: A guide to the issues and feelings of adoption* (2nd ed.). Santa Monica, CA: Broken Branch.

Sadler, L., Slade, A., & Mayes, L. (2006). Minding the baby: A mentalization-based parenting program. In J. G. Allen & P. Fonagy (Eds.) *Handbook of mentalization-based treatment* (pp. 271–288). New York, NY: Wiley.

Samuels, E. J. (2001). The idea of adoption: An inquiry into the history of adult adoptee access to birth records. *Rutgers Law Review, 53*(367), 1–49.

Sarnoff, C. A. (1994). The father's role in latency. In S. H. Cath, A. R. Gurwitt, & J. M. Ross (Eds.), *Father and child: Developmental and clinical perspectives* (pp. 253–264). Hillsdale, NJ: Analytic Press.

Sass, D. A, & Henderson, D. B (1999). Adoption issues: Preparation of psychologists and an evaluation of the need for continuing education. Paper presented at the 1999 meeting of the American Adoption Congress, McLean, VA.

Sass, D. A., & Henderson, D. B. (2007). In R. A. Javier, A. L. Baden, F. A. Biafora, & A. Camacho-Gingerich (Eds.), *Handbook of adoption: Implications for researchers, practitioners, and families* (pp. 312–325). Thousand Oaks, CA: Sage.

Savage, D. (2000). *The kid: What happened after my boyfriend and I decided to go get pregnant: An adoption story*. New York, NY: Penguin Putnam.

Savage, P. (2011, June 18). Odd girl in. *Psychology Today*, 1–3.

Sawyer, M. G., Bittman, M., La Greca, A. M., Crettenden, A. D., Borojevic, N., Raghavendra, P., & Russo, R. (2011). Time demands of caring for children with cerebral palsy: What are the implications for maternal mental health? *Developmental Medicine & Child Neurology, 53*(4), 338–343. doi:10.1111/j.1469–8749.2010.03848.x

Schachter, E. P., & Ventura, J. J. (2008). Identity agents: Parents as active and reflective participants in their children's identity formation. *Journal of Research on Adolescence, 18* (3), 449–476. doi:10.1111/j.1532–7795.2008.00567.x

Schachter, J. (2009). International adoption: Lessons from Hawai'i. In D. Marre & L. Briggs (Eds.), *International adoption: Global inequalities and the circulation of children* (pp. 52–68). New York, NY: New York University.

Schalesky, M. (2001). Marriage and infertility: Nothing I do helps. *Come Unity*. Retrieved from http://www.comeunity.com/adoption/infertility/nothingIdo.html

Schwartz, S. J., & Finley, G. E. (2006). Father involvement, nurturant fathering, and young adult psychosocial functioning: Differences among adoptive, adoptive stepfather, and nonadoptive stepfamilies. *Journal of Family Issues, 27*(5), 712–731. doi:10.1177/0192513X05284003

Selman, P. (2009). The movement of children for international adoption: Developments and trends in receiving states and states of origin, 1998–2004. In D. Marre & L. Briggs (Eds.), *International adoption: Global inequalities and the circulation of children* (pp. 32–51). New York, NY: New York University Press.

Senecky, Y., Agassi, H., Inbar, D., Horesh, N., Diamond, G., Bergman, Y. S., & Apter, A. (2009). Post-adoption depression among adoptive mothers. *Journal of Affective Disorders, 115*(1–2), 62–68. doi:10.1016/j.jad.2008.09.002

Severson, R. (1994). *Adoption: Philosophy and experience.* Dallas, TX: House of Tomorrow Productions.

Shabad, P. (1993). Repetition and incomplete mourning: The intergenerational transmission of traumatic themes. *Psychoanalytic Psychology, 10*(1), 61–75. doi:10.1037/h0079419

Shacochis, B. (2005). Keeping it all in the family. In P. Kruger & J. Smolowe (Eds.), *A love like no other: Stories from adoptive parents* (pp. 176–192). New York, NY: Riverhead Books.

Shapiro, V. B., & Shapiro, J. R. (2006). The adoption of foster children who suffered early trauma and object loss: Implications for practice. In K. Hushion, S. B. Sherman, & D. Siskind (Eds.), *Understanding adoption: Clinical work with adults, children, and parents* (pp. 91–114). Lanham, MD: Aronson.

Sharma, A. R., McGue, M. K., & Benson, P. L. (1996a). The emotional and behavioral adjustment of United States adopted adolescents: Part I. An overview. *Children and Youth Services Review, 18*(1–2), 83–100. doi:10.1016/0190–7409(95)00055–0

Sharma, A. R., McGue, M. K., & Benson, P. L. (1996b). The emotional and behavioral adjustment of United States adopted adolescents: Part II. Age at adoption. *Children and Youth Services Review, 18*(1–2), 101–114. doi:10.1016/0190–7409(95)00056–9

Sharma, A. R., McGue, M. K., & Benson, P. L. (1998). The psychological adjustment of United States adopted adolescents and their nonadopted siblings. *Child development, 69*(3), 791–802. doi:10.1111/j.1467–8624.1998.tb06243.x

Sharp, C., & Fonagy, P. (2008). The parent's capacity to treat the child as a psychological agent: Constructs, measures and implications for developmental psychopathology. *Social Development, 17*(3), 737–754. doi: 10.1111/j.1467–9507.2007.00457.x

Shaw, B. D., & Saller, R. P. (1984). Close-kin marriage in Roman society? *Man, New Series, 19*(3), 432–444. doi:10.2307/2802181

Shelley-Sireci, L. M., & Ciano-Boyce, C. (2002). Becoming lesbian adoptive parents: An exploratory study of lesbian adoptive, lesbian birth, and heterosexual adoptive parents. *Adoption Quarterly, 6*(1), 33–43.

Sherick, I. (1983). Adoption and disturbed narcissism: A case illustration of a latency boy. *Journal of the American Psychoanalytic Association, 31*(2), 487–513.

Sherkow, S. P. (2004). Child development: Twins: From fetus to child. By A. Piontelli. London: Routledge 2002, *Journal of the American Psychoanalytic Association, 52*(2), 619–625.

Shorey, H. S. (2010). Attachment theory as a social-developmental psychopathology framework for psychotherapy practice. In J. E. Maddux & J. P. Tangney (Eds.), *Social psychological foundations of clinical psychology* (pp. 157–176). New York, NY: Guilford Press.

Shorey, H. S., & Snyder, C. R. (2006). The role of adult attachment styles in psychopathology and psychotherapy outcomes. *Review of General Psychology, 10*(1), 1–20. doi:10.1037/1089–2680.10.1.1

Shorey, H. S., Snyder, C. R., Yang, X., & Lewin, M. R. (2003). The role of hope as a mediator in recollected parenting, adult attachment, and mental health. *Journal of Social and Clinical Psychology, 22*(6), 685–715. doi:10.1521/jscp.22.6.685.22938

Silverman, A. R., & Feigelman, W. (1981, August). *The adjustment of black children adopted by white families.* Paper presented at the Annual Meeting of the American Sociological Association, Toronto, Ontario, Canada.

Silverman, R. C., & Lieberman, A. F. (1999). Negative maternal attributions, projective identification, and the intergenerational transmission of violent relational patterns. *Psychoanalytic Dialogues, 9*(2), 161–186. doi:10.1080/10481889909539312

Silverstein, L. B., & Auerbach, C. F. (1999). Deconstructing the essential father. *American Psychologist, 54*(6), 397–407. doi: 10.1037/0003–066X.54.6.397

Simmel, C. (2007). Risk and protective factors contributing to the longitudinal psychosocial well-being of adopted foster children. *Journal of Emotional and Behavioral Disorders, 15*(4), 237–249. doi:10.1177/10634266070150040501

Simon, R.J., & Altstein, H. (2000). *Adoption across borders: Serving the children in transracial and intercountry adoptions.* New York, NY: Rowman & Littlefield.

Simon, S. (2010). *Baby, we were meant for each other: In praise of adoption.* New York, NY: Random House.

Skinner-Drawz, B. A., Wrobel, G. M., Grotevant, H. D., & Von Korff, L. (2011). The role of adoption communicative openness in information seeking among adoptees from adolescence to emerging adulthood. *Journal of Family Communication, 11*(3), 181–197. doi:10.1080/15267431003656587

Slade, A. (2008). Mentalization as a frame for working with parents in child psychotherapy. In E. L. Jurist, A. Slade, & S. Bergner (Eds.), *Mind to mind. Infant research, neuroscience and psychoanalysis* (pp. 307–334). New York, NY: Other Press.

Smith, D. W., & Sherwen, L. N. (1988). *Mothers and their adopted children: The bonding process.* New York, NY: Teresias Press.

Smith, J., & Miroff, F. (1987). *You're our child: The adoption experience.* New York, NY: Madison Books.

Smith, S., & Howard, J. A. (1991). A comparative study of successful and disrupted adoptions. *Social Service Review, 65*(2), 248–265. doi:10.1086/603836

Smith, S., & Riley, D. (2006). Adoption in the Schools: A Lot to Learn. New York: Evan B. Donaldson Adoption Institute. Policy Perspective. http://www.adoptioninstitute.org/publications/

Smith, S. L. (2010). *Keeping the promise: The critical need for post-adoption services to enable children and families to succeed.* New York, NY: Evan B. Donaldson Adoption Institute.

Smith, S. L., Howard, J. A., & Monroe, A. D. (2000). Issues underlying behavior problems in at-risk adopted children. *Children and Youth Services Review, 22*(7), 539–562. doi:10.1016/S0190–7409(00)00102-X

Smith-McKeever, T. C. (2005). Child behavioral outcomes in African American adoptive families. *Adoption Quarterly, 7*(4), 29–56. doi:10.1300/J145v07n04_02

Smock, P. J., & Greenland, F. R. (2010). Diversity in pathways to parenthood: Patterns, implications, and emerging research directions. *Journal of Marriage and the Family, 72*(3), 576–593. doi:10.1111/j.1741–3737.2010.00719.x

Smolowe, J. (1998). *An empty lap*. New York, NY: Simon & Shuster.

Smolowe, J. (2012). The reluctant family. *Adoptive families magazine*. Retrieved from http://www.adoptivefamilies.com/articles.php?aid=1658

Smyer, M. A., Gatz, M., Simi, N. L., & Pederson, N. L. (1998). Childhood adoption: Long-term effects in adulthood. *Psychiatry, 61*, 191–205.

Sobol, M. P., Delaney, S., & Earn, B. M. (1994). Adoptees' portrayal of the development of family structure. *Journal of Youth and Adolescence, 23*(3), 385–400. doi: 10.1007/BF01536726

Sperling, M. B., Foelsch, P., & Grace, C. (1996). Measuring adult attachment: Are self-report instruments congruent? *Journal of Personality Assessment, 67*(1), 37–51. doi:10.1207/s15327752jpa6701_3

Spitz, R. A. (1946). Hospitalism—A follow-up report on investigation described in volume 1, 1945. *Psychoanalytic. Studies of the Child, 2*, 113–117.

Spitz, R. (1965). *The first year of life: A psychoanalytic study of normal and deviant development of object relations*. New York, NY: International Universities Press.

Spitz, R. A., & Cobliner, W. G. (1965). *The first year of life: A psychoanalytic study of normal and deviant development of object relations*. New York, NY: International Universities Press.

Spitz, R. A., & Wolf, K. M. (1946). Anaclitic depression—An inquiry into the genesis of psychiatric conditions in early childhood. *Psychoanalytic Study of the Child, 2*, 313–342.

Sroufe, L. A. (1983). Infant-caregiver attachment and patterns of adaptation in preschool: The roots of maladaptation and competence. In M. Perlmutter (Ed.), *Minnesota Symposia on Child Psychology* (Vol. 16, pp. 41–81). Hillsdale, NJ: Erlbaum.

Sroufe, L., & Waters, E. (1977). Attachment as an organizational construct. *Child Development, 67*, 541–555.

Stacey, J., & Biblarz, T. J. (2001). (How) does the sexual orientation of parents matter? *American Sociological Review, 66*(2), 159–183. doi:10.2307/2657413

Steele, H. (2005). Editorial. *Attachment & Human Development, 7*(3), 205. doi:10.1080/14616730500317432

Steele, H., & Steele, M. (2008). *Clinical applications of the adult attachment interview*. New York, NY: Guilford Press.

Steele, H., Steele, M., & Fonagy, P. (1996). Associations among attachment classifications of mothers, fathers, and their infants. *Child Development, 67*(2), 541–555. doi:10.1111/j.1467-8624.1996.tb01750.x

Steele, M., Hodges, J., Kaniuk, J., Hillman, S., & Henderson, K. (2003). Attachment representations and adoption: Associations between maternal states of mind and emotion narratives in previously maltreated children. *Journal of Child Psychotherapy, 29*(2), 187–205. doi:10.1080/0075417031000138442

Steele, M., Hodges, J., Kaniuk, J., & Steele, H. (2010). Mental representation and change: Developing attachment relationships in an adoption context. *Psychoanalytic Inquiry, 30*(1), 25–40. doi:10.1080/07351690903200135

Steinberg, G., & Hall, B. (2000). *Inside transracial adoption: Strength-based, culture-sensitizing parenting for inter-country or domestic adoptive families that don't "match."* Indianapolis, IN: 2000.

Stern, D. B. (2009). Partners in thought: A clinical process theory of narrative. *Psychoanalytic Quarterly, 78*, 701–731.

Stern, D. N. (1985). *The interpersonal world of the infant: A view from psychoanalysis and developmental psychology*. New York, NY: Basic Books.

Stern, D. N. (1995). *The motherhood constellation: A unified view of parent-infant psychotherapy*. New York, NY: Basic Books.

Stewart, S. D. (2010). The characteristics and well-being of adopted stepchildren. *Family Relations, 59*(5), 558–571. doi: 10.1111/j.1741–3729.2010.00623.xe

Stritof, S., & Stritof, B. (2012). Raising grandkids: A growing trend. *Marriage.* Retrieved from http://marriage.about.com/cs/grandparenting/a/raisinggrandkid.htm?p=1

Strong, P. (2005). What is an Indian family? The Indian Child Welfare Act and the renascence of tribal sovereignty. *American Studies, 46*(3/4), 205–231.

Stuber, M. L. (2006). Posttraumatic stress and posttraumatic growth in childhood cancer survivors and their parents. In R. T. Brown (Ed.), *Comprehensive handbook of childhood cancer and sickle cell disease: A biopsychosocial approach* (pp. 279–296). New York, NY: Oxford University Press.

Sue, D. W. (2010). Microaggressions, marginality, and oppression: An introduction. In D. W. Sue (Ed.), *Microaggressions and marginality: Manifestation, dynamics and impact* (pp. 3–22). New York, NY: Wiley.

Suess, G., Grossman, K., & Sroufe, L. (1992). Effects of infant attachment to mother and father on quality of adaptation in preschool: From dyadic to individuation organisation of self. *International Journal of Behavioral Development, 15*, 43–65.

Sullivan, P. F., Wells, J. E., & Bushnell, J. A. (1995). Adoption as a risk factor for mental disorders. *Acta Psychiatrica Scandinavica, 92*(2), 119–124. doi:10.1111/j.1600–0447.1995.tb09554.x

Sullivan-Bolyai, S., Deatrick, J., Gruppuso, P., Tamborlane, W., & Grey, M. (2003). Constant vigilance: Mothers' work parenting young children with type 1 diabetes. *Journal of Pediatric Nursing, 18*(1), 21–29. doi:10.1053/jpdn.2003.4

Suomi, S. J., Kraemer, G. W., Baysinger, C. M., & Delizio, R. D. (1981). Inherited and experiential factors associated with individual differences in anxious behavior displayed by rhesus monkeys. In D. G. Klein & J. Rabkin (Eds.), *Anxiety: New research and changing concepts.* (pp. 179–200). New York, NY: Raven Press.

Sutfin, E. L., Fulcher, M., Bowles, R. P., & Patterson, C. J. (2008). How lesbian and hetero-sexual parents convey attitudes about gender to their children: The role of gendered environments. *Sex Roles, 58*, 501–513. doi 10.1007/s11199-007-9368-0

Suwalsky, J. T. D., Hendricks, C., & Bornstein, M. H. (2008). Families by adoption and birth: I. Mother-infant socioemotional interactions. *Adoption Quarterly, 11*(2), 101–125. doi:10.1080/10926750802374942

Swartz, A. (2010). The maternal-bonding process for mothers who adopt young, international children: A qualitative analysis. (Unpublished doctoral dissertation). Widener University, Chester, PA.

Swartz, A., Brabender, V., Fallon, A., & Shorey, H. (2012). The maternal-bonding trajectory for mothers who adopt young, international children: A qualitative analysis. *Journal of Social Distress and the Homeless*, 138–167.

Tan, T. X. (2008). Impact of biological children's adjustment on their siblings who were adopted from China. *Adoption Quarterly, 11*(4), 278–295. doi:10.1080/10926750802569814

Tan, T. X. (2011). Two-year follow-up of girl adopted from China: Continuity and change in behavioural adjustment. *Child and Adolescent Mental Health, 16*(1), 14–21. doi:10.1111/j.1475–3588.2010.00560.x

Tan, T. X., Marfo, K., & Dedrick, R. F. (2010). Early developmental and psychosocial risks and longitudinal behavioral adjustment outcomes for preschool-age girls adopted from China. *Journal of Applied Developmental Psychology, 31*(4), 306–314. doi:10.1016/j.appdev.2010.04.002

Target, M. (1993). Workshop on the outcome research and manual of technique. *Bulletin Anna Freud Centre, 16*(4), 294.

Target, M., & Fonagy, P. (2002). Fathers in modern psychoanalysis and in society: The role of the father and child development. In S. Budd, J. Trowell, & A. Etchegoyen (Eds.),

The importance of fathers: A psychoanalytic re-evaluation (pp. 45–66). New York, NY: Brunner-Routledge.

Tasker, F., & Golombok, S. (1995). Adults raised as children in lesbian families. *American Journal of Orthopsychiatry 65*, 203–15. doi 10.1037/h0079615

Teachman, J., & Tedrow, L. (2008). The demography of stepfamilies in the United States. *International handbook of stepfamilies: Policy and practice in legal, research, and clinical spheres*. New York, NY: Wiley.

Tedeschi, R. G., & Calhoun, L. G. (2004). Posttraumatic growth: Conceptual foundations and empirical evidence. *Psychological Inquiry, 15*(1), 1–18. doi: 10.1207/s15327965 pli1501_01

Telingator, C. J., & Patterson, C. (2008). Children and adolescents of lesbian and gay parents. *Journal of the American Academy of Child & Adolescent Psychiatry, 47*, 1364–1368.

Tennes, K. H., & Lampl, E. (1964). Stranger and separation anxiety in infancy. *Journal of Nervous and Mental Disease, 139*(3), 247–254. doi:10.1097/00005053–196409000–00005

Ternay, M. R., Wilborn, B., & Day, H. D. (1985). Perceived child-parent relationships and child adjustment in families with both adopted and natural children. *Journal of Genetic Psychology, 146*(2), 261–272. doi: 10.1080/00221325.1985.9914453

Terpstra, N. (2005). *Abandoned children of the Italian renaissance: Orphan care in Florence and Bologna*. Baltimore, MD: Johns Hopkins University Press.

Thompson, G. (2011, September 20). Parenting as an older adult. *Fifty is the new fifty*. Retrieved from http://www.fiftyisthenewfifty.com/lifestyle/parenting-as-an-older-adult .html

Thompson, R. J., Gustafson, K. E., Hamlett, K. W., & Spock, A. (1992). Stress, coping, and family functioning in the psychological adjustment of mothers of children and adolescents with cystic fibrosis. *Journal of Pediatric Psychology, 17*(5), 573–585. doi:10.1093/jpepsy/ 17.5.573

Tizard, B. (1991). Intercountry adoption: A review of the evidence. *Journal of Child Psychology and Psychiatry, 32*(5), 743–756. doi:10.1111/j.1469–7610.1991.tb01899.x

Tornello, S. L., Farr, R. H., & Patterson, C. J. (2011). Predictors of parenting stress among gay adoptive fathers in the United States. *Journal of Family Psychology, 25*(4), 591–600. doi:10.1037/a0024480

Toth, S. L., Rogosch, F. A., Manly, J. T., & Cicchetti, D. (2006). The efficacy of toddler-parent psychotherapy to reorganize attachment in the young offspring of mothers with major depressive disorder: A randomized preventive trial. *Journal of Consulting and Clinical Psychology, 74*(6), 1006–1016. doi:10.1037/0022–006X.74.6.1006

Treen, J. (2005). Reluctant no more (not that I ever was). In P. Kruger & J. Smolowe (Eds.), *A love like no other: Stories from adoptive parents* (pp. 195–205). New York, NY: Riverhead Books.

Triseliotis, J. (2002). Long-term foster care or adoption? The evidence examined. *Child & Family Social Work, 7*(1), 23–33. doi:10.1046/j.1365–2206.2002.00224.x

Triseliotis, J., Feast, J., & Kyle, F. (2005). *The adoption triangle revisited: A study of adoption, search and reunion experiences*. London, UK: British Association for Adoption and Fostering (BAAF).

Trowell, J., & Etchegoyen, A. (2002). *The Importance of fathers: A psychoanalytic re-evaluation*. New York, NY: Brunner-Routledge.

Tubero, A. (2002). Adoption, attachment, and reenactment in the therapeutic setting: A case study of an adolescent girl. *Journal of Infant, Child, and Adolescent Psychotherapy, 2*(1), 39–65. doi:10.1080/15289168.2002.10486385

Tyson, P. (1994). The role of the father in gender identity, urethral eroticism, and phallic narcissism. In S. H. Cath, A. R. Gurwitt, & J. M. Ross (Eds.), *Father and child: Developmental and clinical perspectives* (pp. 175–188). Hillsdale, NJ: Analytic Press.

United Nations. (2009). *Child adoption: Trends and policies.* Retrieved from http://www.un .org/esa/population/publications/adoption2010/child_adoption.pdf

U.S. Department of Health and human Services (2009). The AFCARS report. Accessed at http://www.acf.hhs.gov/programs/cb/resource/afcars-report-16.

U.S. Department of Health and Human Services. (2010). *Adoption statistics.* Accessed at http://www.childwelfare.gov/systemwide/statistics/adoption.cfm

U.S. Department of Health and Human Services. (2011). The National Survey of Adoptive Parents (NSAP). Retrieved from http://aspe.hhs.gov/hsp/09/nsap/index.shtml

U.S. Department of State. (2011). *Intercountry adoption.* Retrived from http://adoption .state.gov

U.S. National Library of Medicine. (2012, September 9). Male infertility. *MedlinePlus.* Text. Retrieved from http://www.nlm.nih.gov/medlineplus/maleinfertility.html

van den Dries, L. (201). Development after international adoption. (Doctoral dissertation). Leiden University, Leiden, Netherlands.

van den Dries, L., Juffer, F., van IJzendoorn, M. H., & Bakermans-Kranenburg, M. J. (2009). Fostering security? A meta-analysis of attachment in adopted children. *Children and Youth Services Review, 31*(3), 410–421. doi:10.1016/j.childyouth.2008.09.008

van den Dries, L., Juffer, F., van IJzendoorn, M. H., & Bakermans-Kranenburg, M. J. (2010). Infants' physical and cognitive development after international adoption from foster care or institutions in China. *Journal of Developmental and Behavioral Pediatrics, 31*(2), 144–150. doi:10.1097/DBP.0b013e3181cdaa3a

van der Kolk, B. A. (2005). Developmental trauma disorder: Toward a rational diagnosis for childen with complex trauma histories. *Psychiatric Annals, 35*(5), 401–408. Retrieved from http://search.proquest.com.cardinal.fielding.edu/docview/217061643/13935E36D661BEC1 D29/13?accountid=10868

Vandivere, S., Malm, K., & Radel, L.F. (2009). *Adoption USA: A chartbook based on the 2007 national survey of adoptive parents.* The U.S. Department of Health and Human Services, Office of the Assistant Secretary for Planning and Evaluation. Retrieved from http://aspe .hhs.gov/hsp/09/NSAP/chartbook/index.cfm

Vandivere, S., & McKlindon, A. (2010). The well-being of U.S. children adopted from foster care, privately from the United States and internationally. *Adoption Quarterly, 13*(3–4), 157–184. doi:10.1080/10926755.2010.524871

van Gulden, H., & Bartels-Rabb, H. (1993). *Real parents, real children: Parenting the adopted child.* New York, NY: Crossroad Publishing.

van IJzendoorn, M. (1995). Adult attachment representations, parental responsiveness, and infant attachment: A meta-analysis on the predictive validity of the adult attachment interview. *Psychological Bulletin, 117*(3), 387–403. doi:10.1037/0033–2909.117 .3.387

van Ijzendoorn, M. H., Bakermans-Kranenburg, M. J., & Juffer, F. (2007). Plasticity of growth in height, weight, and head circumference: Meta-analytic evidence of massive catch-up after international adoption. *Journal of Developmental and Behavioral Pediatrics, 28*(4), 334–343. doi:10.1097/DBP.0b013e31811320aa

van IJzendoorn, M. H., & Juffer, F. (2005). Adoption is a successful natural intervention enhancing adopted children's IQ and school performance. *Current Directions in Psychological Science, 14*(6), 326–330. doi:10.1111/j.0963–7214.2005.00391.x van IJzendoorn, M. H., & Juffer, F. (2006). The Emanuel Miller memorial lecture 2006: Adoption as intervention. Meta-analytic evidence for massive catch-up and plasticity in physical, socio-emotional, and cognitive development. *Journal of Child Psychology and Psychiatry, and Allied Disciplines, 47*(12), 1228–1245. doi:10.1111/j.1469–7610.2006.01675.x

Vashchenko, M., Easterbrooks, M. A., & Miller, L. C. (2010). Becoming their mother: Knowledge, attitudes, and practices of orphanage personnel in Ukraine. *Infant Mental Health Journal, 31*(5), 570–590. doi:10.1002/imhj.20272

Verhulst, F. C., Althaus, M., & Versluis-den Bieman, H. J. M. (1990a). Problem behavior in international adoptees: I. An epidemiological study. *Journal of the American Academy of Child & Adolescent Psychiatry, 29*(1), 94–103. doi:10.1097/00004583–199001000–00015

Verhulst, F. C., Althaus, M., & Versluis-den Bieman, H. J. M. (1990b). Problem behavior in international adoptees: II. Age at placement. *Journal of the American Academy of Child & Adolescent Psychiatry, 29*(1), 104–111. doi:10.1097/00004583–199001000–00016

Veríssimo, M., & Salvaterra, F. (2006). Maternal secure-base scripts and children's attachment security in an adopted sample. *Attachment & Human Development, 8*(3), 261–273. doi:10.1080/14616730600856149

Viana, A. G., & Welsh, J. A. (2010). Correlates and predictors of parenting stress among internationally adopting mothers: A longitudinal investigation. *International Journal of Behavioral Development, 34*(4), 363–373. doi:10.1177/0165025409339403

Volling, B. L., & Belsky, J. (1991). Multiple determinants of father involvement during infancy in dual- and single-earner families. *Journal of Marriage and the Family, 53*, 461–474.

Vonk, M. E., Lee, J., & Crolley-Simic, J. (2010). Cultural socialization practices in domestic and international transracial adoption. *Adoption Quarterly, 13*(3–4), 227–247. doi:10.1080/10926755.2010.524875

Von Korff, L., Grotevant, H. D., Koh, B. D., & Samek, D. R. (2010). Adoptive mothers: Identity agents on the pathway to adoptive identity formation. *Identity, 10*(2), 122–137. doi:10.1080/15283481003711767

Vorus, N. (2004). Treatment of an adopted child: The case of Roger. *Journal of Infant, Child, and Adolescent Psychotherapy, 3*, 391–397. doi:10.1080/15289160309348474

Wainright, J. L., Russell, S. T., Patterson, C. J. (2004). Psychosocial adjustment, school outcomes, and romantic relationships of adolescents with same-sex parents. *Child Development, 75*, 1886–1898. doi: 10.1111/j.1467-8624.2004.00823.x

Wallander, J. L., & Varni, J. W. (1992). Adjustment in children with chronic physical disorders: Programmatic research on a disability-stress-coping model. In A. M. LaGreca, L. Siegel, J. L. Wallander, & C. E. Walker (Eds.), *Stress and coping in child health* (pp. 279–298). New York, NY: Guilford Press.

Wallin, D. J. (2007). *Attachment in psychotherapy.* New York, NY: Guilford Press.

Walsh, F. (2012). The new normal: Diversity and complexity in 21st-century families. In F. Walsh (Ed.), *Normal family processes: Growing diversity and complexity* (4th ed). (pp. 3–27). New York, NY: Guilford.

Ward, M. (1997). Family paradigms and older-child adoption: A proposal for matching parents' strengths to children's needs. *Family Relations, 46*(3), 257–262. doi: 10.2307/585231

Warshaw, S. C. (2006). Losing each other in the wake of loss: Failed dialogues in adoptive families. In K. Hushion, S. B. Sherman, & D. Siskind (Eds.), *Understanding adoption: Clinical work with adults, children, and parents* (pp. 77–89). Lanham, MD: Aronson.

Watkins, M., & Fisher, S. (1993). *Talking with young children about adoption.* New Haven, CT: Yale University Press.

Watters, T. A. (1956). Forms of the family romance. *Psychoanalytic Review, 43*(2), 204–213.

Weathers, H. (2007, February). *We adopted four children—Then discovered they were autistic. Mail Online.* Retrieved from http://www.dailymail.co.uk/health/article-436039/We-adopted-children--discovered-autistic.html

Webb, R. (1999). *Men and infertility: The pain of not being a biological father.* Retrieved from http://www.comeunity.com/adoption/infertility/men.html

Webb, R. (2000). *Discussing adoption and infertility with your partner.* Retrieved from http://www.comeunity.com/adoption/infertility/discussing.html

Wegar, K. (1997). *Adoption, identity, and kinship: The debate over sealed birth records.* New Haven, CT: Yale University Press.

Wegar, K. (2000). Adoption, family ideology, and social stigma: Bias in community attitudes, adoption research, and practice. *Family Relations, 49*(4), 363–369. doi:10.1111/j.1741-3729.2000.00363.x

Weinberg, R. A., Waldman, I., van Dulmen, M., & Scarr, J. (2004). The Minnesota transracial adoption study: Parent reports of psychosocial adjustment at late adolescence. *Adoption Quarterly, 8*, 27–44.

Welsh, J. A., Viana, A. G., Petrill, S. A., & Mathias, M. D. (2008). Ready to adopt: Characteristics and expectations of preadoptive families pursuing international adoptions. *Adoption Quarterly, 11*, 176–203. doi: 10.1080/10926750802421982

Westfall, V., & Cowdrey, R. (2011). *Searching for . . . the you we adore.* Plano, TX: Swan River Publishing.

Westhues, A., & Cohen, J. S. (1990). *Well-functioning families for adoptive and foster children.* Toronto, Canada: University of Toronto Press.

Whitten, K. L., & Weaver, S. R. (2010). Adoptive family relationships and healthy adolescent development: A risk and resilience analysis. *Adoption Quarterly, 13*(3–4), 209–226. doi:10.1080/10926755.2010.524873

Wideman, M. V., & Singer, J. E. (1984). The role of psychological mechanisms in preparation for childbirth. *American Psychologist, 39*(12), 1357–1371. doi:10.1037/0003-066X.39.12.1357

Wiebe, D. J., Gelfand, D., Butler, J. M., Korbel, C., Fortenberry, K. T., McCabe, J. E., & Berg, C. A. (2011). Longitudinal associations of maternal depressive symptoms, maternal involvement, and diabetes management across adolescence. *Journal of Pediatric Psychology, 36*(7), 837–846. doi:10.1093/jpepsy/jsr002

Wieder, H. (1977). The family romance fantasies of adopted children. *Psychoanalytic Quarterly, 46*(2), 185–200.

Wierzbicki, M. (1993). Psychological adjustment of adoptees: A meta-analysis. *Journal of Clinical Child Psychology, 22*(4), 447–454. doi:10.1207/s15374424jccp2204_5

Wilkinson, S., & Hough, G. (1996). Lie as narrative truth in abused adopted adolescents. *Psychoanalytic Study of the Child, 51*, 580–596.

Wilson, S. L., & Weaver, T. L. (2009). Brief note: Follow-up of developmental attainment and behavioral adjustment for toddlers adopted internationally into the USA. *International Social Work, 52*(5), 679–684. doi:10.1177/0020872809337684

Wind, L. H., Brooks, D., & Barth, R. P. (2006). Adoption preparation: Differences between adoptive families of children with and without special needs. *Adoption Quarterly, 8*(4), 45–74. doi:10.1300/J145v08n04_03

Winnicott, D. W. (1949). Hate in the countertransference. *International Journal of Psychoanalysis, 30*, 69–75.

Winnicott, D. W. (1953). Transitional objects and transitional phenomena. *International Journal of Psychoanalysis, 34*, 89–97.

Winnicott, D. W. (1954a). Pitfalls in adoption. *The child and the outside world* (pp. 45–51). London, England: Tavistock.

Winnicott, D. W. (1954b). Two adopted children. *The child and the outside world* (pp. 52–65). London, England: Tavistock.

Winnicott, D. (1956). Primary maternal preoccupation. In Winnicott, D. (Ed.), *D.H. Winnicott: Collected Papers* (pp. 300–305). London, England: Tavistock

Winnicott, D. W. (1958). The capacity to be alone. *International Journal of Psychoanalysis, 39*, 416–420.

Winnicott, D. W. (1960a). The theory of the parent-infant relationship. *International Journal of Psychoanalysis, 41*, 585–595.

Winnicott, D. W. (1960b). The theory of the parent-infant relationship. *The maturational processes and the facilitating environment: Studies in the theory of emotional development* (pp. 37–55). New York, NY: International Universities Press.

Winnicott, D. W. (1964). *The child, the family, and the outside world.* Baltimore, MD: Penguin Books.

Winnicott, D. W. (1971). Mirror-role of mother and family in child development. In D. W. Winnicott (Ed.), *Playing and reality* (pp. 111–118). Middlesex, NJ: Penguin.

Winnicott, D. W. (1992). Primary maternal preoccupation. In D. W. Winnicott (Ed.), *Through paediatrics to psycho-analysis* (pp. 300–305). New York, NY: Basic Books. (Original work published in 1956)

Winzinger, M. (2010). Mothers' descriptions of creating emotional connections with their internationally adopted children. (Unpublished doctoral dissertation). Fielding Graduate University, Santa Barbara, CA.

Witmer, H., Herzog, E., Weinstein, E., & Sullivan, M. E. (1963). *Independent adoptions: A follow-up study.* New York, NY: Sage Foundation.

Wood, L., & Ng, N. (Eds.). (2001). *Adoption in the schools: Resources for parents and teachers.* Palo Alto, CA: Families Adoption in Response.

Wright, M. B. (1924). A manual of psychotherapy for practitioners and students: By Henry Yellowlees, O.B.E., F.R.P.S. (Glas.), M.R.C.P. (Edin.), D.P.M. (Lond.). (published by a. C. Black, Ltd., London, 1923. pp. 247). *International Journal of Psychoanalysis, 5*, 243.

Wrobel, G. M., Grotevant, H. D., & McRoy, R. G. (2004). Adolescent search for birthparents: Who moves forward? *Journal of Adolescent Research, 19*, 132–151.

Yarrow, A. (1987, January 26). Older parents' child: Growing up special. *New York Times.* Retrieved from http://www.nytimes.com/1987/01/26/style/older-parents-child-growing-up-special.html

Yogman, M. W. (1994). Observations on the father-infant relationship. *Father and child: Developmental and clinical perspectives* (pp. 101–122). Hillsdale, NJ: Analytic Press.

Yoon, D. P. (2001). Causal modeling predicting psychological adjustment of Korean-born adolescent adoptees. *Journal of Human Behavior in the Social Environment, 3(3)*, 65–82.

Yu, Y. C. (2000). *Intercountry adoption: Attitudes, needs, and beliefs of American parents who have adopted Chinese children.* Dissertation abstracts). Tallahassee, FL: Florida State University.

Yunginger, J. W., Reed, C. E., O'Connell, E. J., Melton, L. J., O'Fallon, W. M., & Silverstein, M. D. (1992). A community-based study of the epidemiology of asthma. Incidence rates, 1964–1983. *American Review of Respiratory Disease, 146*(4), 888–894.

Zhang, Y., & Lee, G. R. (2010). Intercountry versus transracial adoption: Analysis of adoptive parents' motivations and preferences in adoption. *Journal of Family Issues, 32*(1), 75–98. doi:10.1177/0192513X10375410

Zhang, Y., & Lee, G. R. (2011). Intercountry versus transracial adoption: Analysis of adoptive parents' motivations and preferences in adoption. *Journal of Family Issues, 32*(1), 75–98. doi:10.1177/0192513X10375410

Zoppi, J. (2010). *Creating space for birth fathers in adoption stories: The significance of the fantasized birth father on attachment and identity development of adoptees.* Paper presented at the Adoption Initiative's Sixth Biennial Adoption Conference, New York, NY.

Author Index

Abbey, A., 3, 98, 101, 125
Abdullah, A., 112
Abel, S., 121
Abidin, R. R., 140
Adamec, C., 106
Adamec, C. A., 11
Adelson, E., 24
Agrawal, R., 112
Ahlewalia, M. K., 84
Ahmad, I., 111–112
Ainsworth, M. D., 29
Ainsworth, M. D. S., 47–48, 50, 161
Aktar, S., 112
Albus, K. E., 58, 72
Alderfer, M. A., 143
Alexander, R., 54
Allen, J., 39–40, 137
Allen, J. P., 170, 179
Althaus, M., 52, 53
Altstein, H., 114
Ambrosino, J. M., 141
Anderson, B., 89
Anderson, J., 93
Anderson, K., 94
Anderson, R. E., 13, 114
Anderson, S., 121
Andresen, I. L., 51
Annunziato, R. A., 143
Appell, A., 20
Appell, A. R., 122
Aquinas, T., 9
Arnold, K. D., 107
Asbury, E. T., 145
Ashe, N. S., 107
Askeland, L., 8
Auerbach, C. F., 87
Averett, P., 20, 54
Ayers-Lopez, S., 18

Baden, A., 84
Baden, A. L., 106, 115–116, 202, 225

Bailey, D. B., 140, 141
Baker, J. K., 141
Bakermans-Kranenburg, M. J., 52, 53, 57, 74, 79
Balkrishnan, R., 141
Banks, A., 123
Barkley, R. A., 133
Barnes, M. J., 182
Barnett, B., 57
Barnhill, C., 110
Bartels-Rabb, H., 149, 161, 165
Barth, R. P., 13, 18, 54, 127, 134, 137, 138
Basch, M. F., 184
Basham, R. B., 107
Bateman, A., 39, 232
Bates, B., 58
Baum, A., 140
Baumann, C., 87, 93, 98
Becker, G., 93, 94, 95
Becker, M. W., 141
Becker-Weidman, A., 58–59
Belanger, K., 110
Belsky, J., 124
Bengtsson, H., 198
Bennett, S., 110
Benoiton, S. II., 106
Benson, P. L., 52, 53, 127, 198
Benson, P. R., 141
Berge, J. M., 221
Bergel, V., 127
Bergen, D., 224
Bergin, A., 128
Bergman, A., 41, 90, 157, 190
Bergman, A. S., 41, 42–43
Berkowitz, D., 93
Berrick, J. D., 134
Berry, M., 134, 137, 138
Beschle, D. L., 113, 128
Besser, A., 81, 232
Biafora, F. A., 8, 11, 12, 202, 208

271

Subject Index